R. CRUMB

R. CRUMB

Literature, Autobiography, and the Quest for Self

DAVID STEPHEN CALONNE

University Press of Mississippi • Jackson

The University Press of Mississippi is the scholarly publishing agency of
the Mississippi Institutions of Higher Learning: Alcorn State University,
Delta State University, Jackson State University, Mississippi State University,
Mississippi University for Women, Mississippi Valley State University,
University of Mississippi, and University of Southern Mississippi.

www.upress.state.ms.us

Designed by Peter D. Halverson

The University Press of Mississippi is a member of the
Association of University Presses.

First printing 2021

∞

Library of Congress Control Number available
Hardback ISBN 978–1-4968–3185–9
Trade paperback ISBN 978–1-4968–3186–6
Epub single ISBN 978–1-4968–3187–3
Epub institutional ISBN 978–1-4968–3188–0
PDF single ISBN 978–1-4968–3189–7
PDF institutional ISBN 978–1-4968–3190–3

British Library Cataloging-in-Publication Data available

CONTENTS

ACKNOWLEDGMENTS

R. Crumb: Literature, Autobiography, and the Quest for Self is the third book of a trilogy I have written exploring the American counterculture. In each of my preceding books—*The Spiritual Imagination of the Beats* (New York: Cambridge University Press, 2017) and *Diane di Prima: Visionary Poetics and the Hidden Religions* (New York: Bloomsbury, 2019)—I traced the ways American writers have pursued philosophical "enlightenment" in a culture that they found to be devoid of deeper values and meanings. It became increasingly clear to me that Crumb—whose work had fascinated me from my young adulthood—was depicting throughout his prolific and brilliant art many of the same spiritual and psychological topics that had confronted his literary contemporaries. Like other members of the Californian baby boom generation, I grew up during the early sixties with *Mad* magazine and became aware of Crumb's work when *Keep on Truckin'* and *Fritz the Cat* were ubiquitous. I recall seeing truck drivers barreling down California's old Highway 99 with "Keep on Truckin'" insignia emblazoned on their tire flaps. At that time—and still today—Crumb's genius has unfortunately been little understood by those who mistakenly see his work as little more than light and clever entertainment. In *R. Crumb: Literature, Autobiography, and the Quest for Self* I have sought to take Crumb seriously as well as humorously, and several people have helped me during its genesis and composition.

I thank Roni, who organized the Bukowski Gesellschaft Conference held in Andernach, Germany, in August 2012, where I delivered a lecture and had the pleasure of hearing Rolf Gran's presentation "Über die Bukowski Illustrationen von Robert Crumb," which insightfully explored Crumb's drawings to accompany Charles Bukowski's *The Captain Is Out to Lunch and the Sailors Have Taken Over the Ship*. I also thank Alan Golding and the conveners of the Louisville Conference on Literature and Culture since 1900, held at the University of Louisville in February 2020, where I spoke on "R. Crumb and the Beats." Jeffrey Weinberg, publisher of Water Row Press;

Everett Rand, editor of *Mineshaft* magazine; and Crumb's bibliographer Carl Richter all patiently answered my queries. At the University Press of Mississippi, I would like to thank Jordan Nettles, marketing assistant and digital publishing coordinator; Courtney McCreary, marketing assistant; Victoria Washington, marketing aide; Katie Keene, senior acquisitions editor; and Mary Heath, editorial associate, all of whom have worked with me tirelessly—and with the justly famous unfailing Mississippi gentility and kindness—from the outset preparing my manuscript for publication. Pete Halverson, senior book designer, created a lovely cover, and many thanks to Norman Ware for his superb copyediting. I would also like to express my gratitude the two anonymous reviewers, who made helpful comments on the manuscript. The interlibrary loan staff at Eastern Michigan University and the Hatcher Graduate Library at the University of Michigan have been generous in supplying me with articles and books. As always, I thank Maria Beye for everything. I have been sustained again during the composition of this book by playing as often as I can on my piano the keyboard music of William Byrd.

R. CRUMB

INTRODUCTION

Robert Crumb (1943–) is an artist who from adolescence has been intensely engaged with literature. He compulsively reads several genres—not only novels, stories, and poetry but also a wide range of historical, musical, biographical, psychological, and spiritual texts, which he has enjoyed for their philosophical and aesthetic power and from which he has often drawn ideas for his inventive art. Because Crumb is also an intensely autobiographical artist—he pours onto the page every conceivable detail concerning his inner life—his reading and creativity have evolved into a mutually enriching network of influences. As one studies Crumb from the outset of his career to the present, it becomes evident that he has embarked on a massive autobiographical enterprise in which personal, secret "confessions"—in a mode reminiscent of figures as diverse as Saint Augustine, Jean-Jacques Rousseau, Henry Miller, and Allen Ginsberg—are made public and merge with the topics to which he is drawn in literature. Crumb himself is also frequently an engaging, appealing, and entertaining writer—he has carried on a massive, lively correspondence with many friends, professional associates, and admirers, keeps a compendious notebook chronicling his dreams, and composes the texts of the majority of his narratives—and of course his art is often outrageously humorous. However, Crumb's pervasive, brilliant, and often zany comedy does not obscure the fact that he has also been engaged in a philosophical quest for authentic selfhood. The theme of the falsity and hypocrisy of human institutions, orthodoxies, and political ideologies recurs constantly throughout his oeuvre. While Crumb has garnered attention for his centrality in the development of underground comix, stirred controversy for its putative misogyny and racism, and achieved well-deserved fame for his spectacular draftsmanship and mastery of the intricate craft of combining words and images, I will argue in the following chapters that what has often been ignored in considerations of Crumb's achievements is his deep search for philosophical meaning. Crumb does not arrive at clear "resolutions" to the perennial questions of human existence, but rather he sets up a constant dialogue between competing visions of life and frequently leaves it to the reader/viewer to contemplate the contradictions he exposes.

Crumb differs from other graphic storytellers in that he has produced both adaptations as well as personal, confessional, autobiographical works. He is also unique because literary allusions proliferate throughout to a degree unparalleled in the output of any other contemporary cartoon artist. What Ben Saunders has observed in connection with superhero comics—that they are "a space where traditional distinctions between philosophy, theology, and literature collide and break down"—applies as well to Crumb, whose world, however, is populated by no supermen but rather with his many versions of the antihero. Crumb makes art, but he is often also doing philosophy and literature: he is preoccupied with finding the truth of the inner self, which has led him to consider a variety of spiritual traditions. A complete understanding of his aims as an artist is incomplete without a response to this dimension of his life and work, for Crumb engages with a variety of texts and traditions including Buddhism, Hinduism, existentialism, Gnosticism, and voodoo as well as theosophical, esoteric, and occult sources. Crumb has later in his career become a devotee of meditation and is also intrigued by the possibility of life on other planets, the paranormal, and out-of-body experimentation.

Although as a child Crumb suffered from dyslexia and therefore found reading challenging, he gradually familiarized himself with a wide variety of authors. In a letter composed at age sixteen, he declared his affinity for Charles Dickens—*A Tale of Two Cities*, *The Pickwick Papers*, *A Christmas Carol*—but revealed: "I think my favorite writer is Mark Twain. . . . His work holds a charm and color for me. He puts it down simply and clearly, yet in a pleasant way that I like." He perused Twain's *Autobiography* and was particularly fond of his philosophical classic *What Is Man?*, which supplied him with arguments concerning free will and determinism that would ultimately contribute to what he later called his "heresy"—his break with Catholicism.[1] He thought Upton Sinclair's unrelenting exposé of the horrors of Chicago's meat-packing industry—*The Jungle*—a "good book, but very depressing," and read J. P. Donleavy's *The Ginger Man*, William Golding's *Lord of the Flies*, and Philip Wylie's *An Essay on Morals*. In high school he studied the Faust legend as elaborated by both Johann Wolfgang von Goethe and Christopher Marlowe. However, he evinced distaste for modernism in literature. He was puzzled why William Faulkner's *The Sound and the Fury* had been rendered opaque by the employment of complex narrative techniques; he felt similarly about the work of James Joyce.[2] Later in his career, this preference for authors who—like Mark Twain—expressed themselves "simply and clearly" would continue to define Crumb's aesthetic stance: he admired the lean, muscular prose of Charles Bukowski, the direct writing of contemporary Texas author J. R. Helton, and William S. Burroughs in his pared-down, "documentary" books such as *Junkie* (1953). Crumb has praised Keiji Nakazawa, creator of *Barefoot Gen: A Cartoon Story of Hiroshima*, for similar qualities: "Nakazawa, I'm sure, will be considered one of the great comic artists of this century, because he tells the truth in a plain, straightforward way, filled with real human beings." "Plain" and "straightforward" are for Crumb terms of approbation in both literature and art. Furthermore, this desire to return to a "premodern," "simpler," and more "direct" sensibility may be seen in Crumb's taste in music as well.

The three Crumb brothers—Charles, Maxon, and Robert—formed a kind of "Three Musketeers Art and Literary Club." Robert's older brother Charles and younger brother Maxon were equally absorbed in literature. Charles transcribed passages from Shakespeare, Homer, and Dickens and became obsessed with Robert Louis Stevenson's *Treasure Island* as well as with actor Robert Newton's performance as Long John Silver in Walt Disney's film version of the novel (1950). Sixteen-year-old Charles and fifteen-year-old Robert—inspired by *Mad* magazine—collaborated on a comic entitled "Treasure Island Days," which they published in their series of three magazines entitled *Foo!* (1958) and attempted to sell door to door in their neighborhood in Dover, Delaware, without much success. Robert later recounted his memories of these events in "Treasure Island Days: A True Story" (1978), which opens with the brothers mesmerized watching the Disney version on television in Oceanside, California, in 1955. In one of his masterpieces, "Walkin' the Streets" (begun 1992, completed 2004), Crumb features an inebriated Charles in the dramatic act of reciting to him passages from Shakespeare's *Macbeth* and *Hamlet*. And while Charles declaims Edgar Allan Poe's "The Tell-Tale Heart" to Robert—he knew the narrative by heart—Crumb depicts himself under the covers in bed attempting through the noise to read Golding's *Lord of the Flies*. Charles's comics would gradually devolve into asemic writing in which the content is impossible to decipher. Maxon, on the other hand, has had an abiding interest in Poe, publishing *Maxon's Poe: Seven Stories and Poems by Edgar Allan Poe* (1997). Robert described his younger brother in his preface to this volume as pursuing an "ascetic holyman quest." Maxon spends his time on Market Street in San Francisco, meditating in lotus position complete with beggar's bowl, then returns to his skid row hotel, where he reclines for hours on a bed of nails. Maxon also fasts, periodically passing a twenty-one-foot cotton string through his stomach "to clean the pyloric valve," and is prone to epileptic fits: he views his seizures as "a religious fucking thing, but Western medicine just refuses to deal with them as such."

Another important influence on Crumb's development was his friend Marty Pahls, an aspiring author with whom Crumb would share in apartment in Cleveland when he left home in 1962. Pahls expanded Crumb's literary horizons, urging both Robert and Charles to read J. D. Salinger's *The Catcher in the Rye*.[3] Crumb also read *Franny and Zooey* and *Raise High the Roof Beams, Carpenters, and Seymour: An Introduction*: the latter he enjoyed "every bit as much as *Franny and Zooey*. In some ways, I liked it even more." Salinger's characters' yearning for enlightenment in a fallen world as well as the reclusive author's increasing immersion in Zen Buddhism surely appealed to the young Crumb, who was struggling with his own alienated status as an outsider trapped within conventional 1950s American culture. At age eighteen, he pointed out in a letter: "Academic learning just doesn't lead to true wisdom and understanding. . . . It almost seems, and Salinger agrees with us on this, that you have to push all that you have learned in school aside to get at the true meaning and proportion of things. . . . The Buddhists say that a high point is reached when you take all your books out and burn them."[4] It is noteworthy that already in his late teens with his interest in Buddhism, Crumb had established the trajectory of his later interest in Eastern philosophy. And Salinger's mystical sensibility—as seen in a work such as "Teddy" from *Nine Stories*—clearly spoke to the young Crumb: this desire to move beyond language toward the inner silence of *gnosis* or self-knowledge would become more insistent as his career progressed. Salinger's comedic influence may also be seen in the name Crumb gave to his character "Eggs Ackley": Robert Ackley is an obnoxious classmate of Holden Caulfield's in *The Catcher in the Rye*.

Pahls also encouraged his friend to explore Burroughs's *Junkie* and Jack Kerouac's *On the Road*; Crumb later acknowledged that "Beat literature gave me an alternative point of view about living in America that we weren't getting from our parents, from school, from television, or *Life* magazine." He was struck by Kerouac's essay "The Origins of the Beat Generation" describing the philosophical message of the Beats: "beat" signifies beaten down by suffering, the "beat" of jazz music, and most importantly the beatific vision, the revelation of life's ultimate mystery. Like Crumb, Kerouac had been in his youth a devout Catholic and worshiped his older brother Gerard, who died at age nine—Robert also looked up to Charles for guidance—becoming for Kerouac a sainted religious symbol whom he would memorialize in his novel *Visions of Gerard* (1963). As we shall see in chapter 1, Crumb's artistic journey coincides with the Beat movement: he shared the Beats' opposition to the repressive and life-denying aspects of American consumerist society as well as their quest for a philosophy that would answer to humanity's deepest needs. Crumb expressed these dissatisfactions with the status quo during the sixties with his revolutionary cartoons. European thinkers of the prior generation had also registered their disaffiliation with contemporary "civilization" and commented upon the link between the flourishing art of cartooning and political radicalism. Esther Leslie has observed that for Walter Benjamin and his friends, "cartoons depict a realist—though not naturalist—expression of the circumstances of modern daily life; the cartoons make clear that even our bodies do not belong to us—we have alienated them in exchange for money, or have given parts of them up in war. The cartoons expose the fact that what parades as civilization is actually barbarism."[5] So, too, Crumb became directly involved in the countercultural rebellion against the "barbaric" and destructive aspects of contemporary American life and sought to present alternatives in his constant—and often uproariously humorous—dialectic of asking questions and posing possible answers through his narrative art.

In the following pages, I explore the ways Crumb develops complex themes of solitude, terror, anxiety, dread, despair, sexual desire, and conflict as aspects of personal spiritual development in his engagement with the Beats and Charles Bukowski; blues artists Jelly Roll Morton and Charley Patton; Philip K. Dick; Jean-Paul Sartre; Franz Kafka; and the book of Genesis. The philosophical, theological, and existential questions that preoccupied the counterculture of the fifties, sixties, and seventies—how can I arrive at true knowledge; who am I and what is the meaning of my life; is there a God and why does evil exist; what is the soul and what will happen to me after I die— had been pondered by thinkers throughout history whom Crumb would peruse deeply. The philosophers who composed the Upanishads, Gautama Buddha meditating beneath the Bodhi Tree to achieve nirvana, the Gnostics, African Americans in their relationship to the supernatural and fate through voodoo—all had wrestled with similar questions. Crumb sought what the Gnostics were also after: what is oldest, truest, and deepest within the Self; hence my phrase in this book's title "Quest for Self." It becomes evident that, rather than approaching the mystery of being through institutional, orthodox "religions," Crumb seeks this knowledge within the Self—the Jungian capital "S" signifying the eternal within as well as the notion that our individual selves participate in a greater cosmos beyond our tiny, personal "identity."

Crumb's effort has been to depict the hidden shape of experience through his art. As he has observed:

As far as visual art goes, it has to reveal something about reality that you can't really put into words. Any artist who can explain his work with words is not exactly on the right track. It's tough. You're always probing down in the dark and you reveal things to yourself as you do your art. . . . Comics have their own special take on reality. There are many different approaches to comics, but it doesn't do what literature can do. Comics are different, and when cartoonists try to "elevate" the form, so to speak, it's in danger of becoming pretentious. Comics have always lent themselves to the lurid and the sensational, starting as far back as penny prints of the martyrdom of the saints or battle scenes in the 1500s. . . . There's something rough and working class about comics.

Crumb learned from a number of predecessors and was amazed upon discovering David Kunzle's *The Early Comic Strip: Narrative Strips and Picture Stories in the European Broadsheet from c. 1450 to 1825*, declaring: "Some of them are so crude, those little, tiny postage stamp–sized panels of, like, husband-and-wife squabbles done in Russia or Germany or Czechoslovakia. Incredible stuff, but totally obscure. If you try to inform people in the art world about this history, they know nothing about it. A complete underground, unknown, history of popular art that the general art world knows nothing about." Crumb rebelled against the "pretentious," "genteel" world of "fine art" and found power in the frowned-upon "crude," "lower-class," and "lurid" work of the "underground" artists of the past. These early works of the "working class" of centuries past spoke to the rebellious instincts of American underground artists of the sixties who also were revolting against an "Establishment" whose hypocrisy, racism, repressiveness, humorlessness, and classism they found repellent. If we define comics as "narrative, sequential images," we may trace an ancient, international, historical development beginning with the Paleolithic Neanderthal cave art of Lascaux in France, to the paintings of ancient Egypt, the pictorial script of Mayan codices, the Bayeux Tapestry, stained-glass cathedral windows, and woodblock prints from Japan. My purpose in this book is to demonstrate how Crumb's genius lay in his ability to absorb and synthesize these traditions, thus creating an idiosyncratic, often hyperkinetic, consistently engaging body of work. Crumb was fascinated by narrative styles and I will argue is among the most *literary* of comic book artists, since he desired to tell stories with philosophical depth through a compelling integration of images and words. For example, his virtuosic skill in drawing the letters of the alphabet in a variety of striking styles often serves to highlight the dramatic tension of the texts he illustrates.

In addition, I seek to explore the ways Crumb creates a method of shaping narrative accompanied by images in order to emphasize as well as interrogate particular moments of psychological intensity. The compression of temporality possible through the effective manipulation of technique in graphic storytelling also allows Crumb to at once foreground, explore, and dramatize the sense of timelessness that characterizes psychological, interior experiences.[6]

Robert Crumb has been the first comic book artist to develop an original mode of graphic autobiographical narrative forming an extended record of his emotional and intellectual experiences that reveals his own struggles with belief, disbelief, and skepticism. Like the Beats as well as the "confessional poets"—Robert Lowell, John Berryman, Sylvia Plath, Theodore Roethke, W. D. Snodgrass, Anne Sexton, and others—he makes his art directly from his life and withholds nothing. Françoise Mouly has remarked that Crumb, "the ex-Catholic boy, is deeply in love with the fools and the simple folks and just as overwhelmed by the weight of evil in the world. The only enemy is easy answers. As fallible as the lesser of us, Crumb is endlessly in the confessional, but he's resigned to the fact that no priest is on the other side, that no one is there to give him absolution."[7] Indeed, even when he is ostensibly illustrating the works of writers other than himself, he is also engaging in autobiography, for he employs their work as masks through which to express his own dilemmas. As he declares: "The thing you gotta understand about all my cartoons is that, in a roundabout sort of way, it's all very personal and subjective. . . . It's all about me, basically."[8] He has created an immense gallery of characters rivaling Shakespeare or Dickens in their numbers and diversity, yet each seems to express some aspect of himself, to occupy some symbolic position in his interior dialogue, which he lays bare for the reader/viewer to witness.

As I shall document in the following chapters, Crumb often pursues identical themes both in his literary adaptations and in his "confessional" works. His strength derives from his ability to dramatize his ambivalences, and he strives to uncover meanings in the texts he illustrates that reveal the contours of his own interior landscape. Other graphic storytellers such as Chris Ware in *Jimmy Corrigan: The Smartest Kid on Earth* also mine their personal lives for material, while Daniel Clowes begins "Gynecology" with: "Do you believe in God? In the invisible tyranny of universal order? In the membrane of truth that gives shape to the random and the arbitrary?" Yet Crumb is unique in the ways he continually explores such conflicts from a myriad of different angles and contends with his own multiple contradictions and complexities. As Clowes has revealed, Crumb has been a major influence on him because he has "always grown as an artist, experimented, worked at all his abilities, always tried to struggle with his inner demons in an honest way. That's been a great example for me."[9] Through his skills at caricature, Crumb developed a method to render extreme states of self-questioning, doubt, and despair. He was influenced by the German expressionists as well as Edvard Munch's *The Scream*—which Crumb reformulates in his illustrations to Charles Bukowski's *Bring Me Your Love* as well as *Gilgamesh*. Crumb "modernizes" these European forebears, depicting himself as suffering, meek, sometimes possessed by a violent imagination, wracked by sexual mania and seemingly ungovernable erotic impulses; yet sensitive, innocent, often tender, in search of Romantic love and self-knowledge.

Robert Crumb's affinity for African American culture—he is particularly devoted to jazz and blues—his mystical sensibility, radical politics, and questioning of typical gender/sex roles as dictated by the repressive, Cold War United States in which he grew up, distinguish him as a unique figure in American artistic history. Crumb moves between the influences of popular culture—television, comics, advertising, jazz, erotic "vulgarity," slang—and "high art" as represented by Assyrian sculpture, Pieter Bruegel, and his wide reading in canonical literature. He straddles several worlds simultaneously and like several of the best contemporary graphic storytellers combines in both his style and biography essential oppositions. W. J. T. Mitchell has observed: "Comics and comic artists are now able to leap tall buildings at a single bound, especially all the old boundaries between art and mass culture, juvenile and adult forms of expression, generic distinctions between satire and autobiography, fiction and nonfiction, poetry and philosophy and history." The son of a Marine Corps soldier, Charles Crumb—author of a book entitled *Training People Effectively*—and a mother burdened by mental illness, addicted to amphetamines, who spent her days watching television and reading movie magazines, Crumb had a peripatetic childhood, moving with his family to several states as his father was stationed at a variety of marine bases including Oceanside, California; Ames, Iowa; and Philadelphia. The Crumb family was large, numbering five children: Robert; his brothers Charles, who was born in 1941, and Maxon, in 1945; his elder sister, Carol, born in 1942; and a younger sister, Sandra, in 1946. Crumb endured a traumatic, unstable childhood. In one of his father's frequent bouts of explosive anger, he broke Robert's collarbone when the boy was just five years old, and his parents often engaged in physically violent quarrels. This contributed to his preternatural sensitivity as well as his status as an "outsider" to the "norms" of American society.[10] Crumb from childhood exhibited a crippling, shy, introverted vulnerability, becoming a deeply alienated adolescent, memorably described by

Sharon Waxman as "a sensitive soul locked in the body of a nerd." This was due to a variety of complex factors that enter into the making of any artist: his particular genetic inheritance, the psychological trauma inflicted during childhood, his physical awkwardness. He would shape these various strands into an original artistic style, which derived from his receptivity to popular culture, immense reading, and thoughtful contemplation of the history of spiritual traditions. The African American author Charles Johnson, who studied Sanskrit and took formal vows in the Soto Zen tradition, has spoken of a particular "Aleph-consciousness" or "epistemic skill":

> The term Aleph-consciousness derives from a short story by Jorge Luis Borges called "The Aleph," in which he describes the *aleph* as "the place where . . . all the places of the world, seen from every angle, coexist." It is the first letter of the Hebrew alphabet, and of its shape Borges says that it "is that of a man pointing to the sky and the earth, to indicate that the lower world is the map and mirror of the higher." (Buddha's "one-finger dharma" may come to mind here, as well.) From its vantage point, Borges says, one can see "simultaneous night and day." Historically, black Americans, Asians, and Hispanics had to develop this epistemic skill, and doing so required a lot of work for an entire lifetime.[11]

So, too, Robert Crumb belonged to an ostracized minority of intellectual "misfits" and sought a way out of his challenging familial background as well as the shallowness and meretriciousness of American cultural life through the hard work and rigorous discipline required to become an artist. Friedrich Nietzsche famously declared: "Wir haben die Kunst, damit wir nicht an der Wahrheit zugrunde gehen" (We possess art lest we perish of the truth), and it is understandable—given the severity of the Crumb family psychodrama— that Robert as well as his brothers devoted themselves to constantly drawing comics and turned within themselves to nurture their abundant imaginations as a place of refuge from their wracked emotional life to the solace of music and the balm of literature.

During his childhood, Crumb attended Catholic schools and went through a phase of fervent piety: "I was fanatically Catholic, praying all the time." When passing a church, he made the sign of the cross; upon hearing Jesus's name, he bowed his head.[12] At one point he even considered becoming a priest, believing "that was the best guarantee of getting into heaven." Crumb recalled: "[I] was kind of a mystical idealist when I was 16. Catholic mystic. I studied the lives of guys like St. Francis." Harvey Kurtzman has claimed

that before he decided to be a cartoonist, Crumb contemplated becoming a
Trappist monk.[13] Crumb's work is replete with Christian iconography, and he
demonstrates an impressive knowledge of both the Old and New Testaments.
However, he began to question the doctrines he had been espousing, and
both Crumb and brother Charles eventually broke with the church: "One day
it just came clear to me that the truth about reality is actually something that
is beyond our comprehension. Nobody knows the truth. It's something to be
curious, not dogmatic about." This motto might be said to be a controlling
theme throughout Crumb's life as an artist and seeker: he eschews all forms
of ideological certainty, "dogmas," and orthodoxies, advocating rather a relentless curiosity about the universe and our place within it. However, while
beneath his fierce cynicism he seeks a center in the labyrinth, Crumb does
not settle for easy answers or comforting illusions. Coincidentally, at about
the same time in 1958, cartoonist Justin Green—whose father was Jewish
and mother Catholic—also rejected Catholicism: his struggle with sexuality,
mental illness, and religious faith is depicted in his groundbreaking *Binky
Brown Meets the Holy Virgin Mary* (1972; reissued 2009), which would influence Crumb's confessionalism. Harvey Kurtzman's *Help!*—to which Crumb
contributed—included Kurtzman's "The First Golden Book of God" in the
February 1964 issue, garnering the magazine negative publicity due to its
satirical take on religion. Jack Jackson created *God Nose*—in which God and
Jesus have conversations concerning racism and contraception—from 1963
to 1966. Frank Stack's satirical *The New Adventures of Jesus* (1969) concerning
Christ's return to the modern world—fellow Texan artist Gilbert Shelton
distributed fifty photocopies to friends at the University of Texas at Austin
in 1964—also poked fun at the contradictions and hypocrisies of organized
religion. Stack is considered one of the progenitors of the underground
comix movement, and Crumb contributed an admiring introduction to *The
New Adventures of Jesus: The Second Coming* (2006).[14] Like these satirists
of the hypocrisy of American fundamentalism, Crumb as we shall see also
critiques the Jesus of American evangelical Christianity, whom he sometimes
juxtaposes with his own interpretation of the historical meaning of Christ
as understood within the context of the Gnostic communities of the early
Christian era.

　　Thus Crumb is an ironical, often acerbic and cynical skewer of accepted
truths. As Robert Hughes has observed, Crumb differed in several fundamental ways from the countercultural sensibility: "He is by nature a pessimist
and a skeptic: that is to say, a realist and an honest man, unlike the pretentious messiahs and fuddled creatures who were the accepted leaders of the
pseudorevolution." Yet Crumb's awareness that "the truth about reality"—as

he phrases it—is *something that is beyond our comprehension* becomes a tantalizing motif in his art and also defines his predilection for literary works that suggest this mystery. Indeed, in an interview with Eric Spitznagel, Crumb criticized comedian Bill Maher's takedown of religion in his film *Religulous* (2008)—the title obviously implying in its punning that religions are "ridiculous"—declaring that Maher "dismissed all spirituality in a way that I just don't like. I also don't like it when people completely dismiss the idea of U.F.O.'s as totally nuts. I think that whole phenomenon is something that should be seriously examined. We don't really know, so don't just presume it's some nutty delusion." For Crumb, "we don't know" = *agnostic*, and since we don't actually know whether there is life on other planets or if there is a "God," we'd best admit we do not know. Crumb went further, telling Jean-Pierre Mercier: "I actually believe in God, to tell you the truth. I believe in a superior force in the universe, a superior intelligence. I believe it. It's there. It's in every person. There is a force of intelligence in every person." Mercier then asked how Crumb could reconcile the fact that his stories are often "absurd" with this notion of a greater power and meaning. Crumb responded: "That's no problem at all. (Laughs) Both of those things can exist simultaneously in the universe." Crumb has also acknowledged in several of his interviews and his *Dream Diary*, and has dramatically portrayed in his *Sketchbooks*, the fact that when in extremis, he prays to "God" for help. Finally, as Crumb's career has evolved, his inner life has undergone several stages. When he moved to France and with his increasing fame, Crumb spoke openly about his "spiritual" journey. In dealing with his new notoriety, he realized that "the only way to deal with it was to go toward mysticism. I had to get control of the inner self. To do that, you have to meditate and examine yourself very closely. It's partly self-psychoanalysis. It takes a high degree of motivation to do that without outside help.... It's got to involve something that gives my life meaning.... To get involved in mysticism is a matter of survival for me." Crumb's psychological and spiritual lives are deeply intertwined: to seek a way out of one's inner conflicts is also often to attempt to find a larger meaning, a larger context within which to understand and interpret one's own life.

In Crumb's development, there is a constant struggle between a starkly cynical and satirical view of human existence—his work is pervaded by black humor, sarcasm, parody, irony, and sharp and aggressive, anarchic subversion—and a desire to find some deeper, underlying truth. Indeed, Crumb would publish three *Mystic Funnies* (1997, 2000, 2002), and the juxtaposition of these two words—"mystic" and "funnies"—reveals that within Crumb's artistic imagination, his sense of humor and his spiritual impulses are often inextricably combined. Perhaps the two tendencies are related, for in stripping away the falsities of contemporary life and making fun of them, Crumb is simultaneously seeking something more profound. And of course, great comedians throughout history have often been supreme melancholics and depressives: they use their humor to cheer themselves—and others—up. Indeed, as Carl Barks, one of Crumb's heroes, declared: "I noticed that Crumb's underlying message . . . is that nothing is important enough to be taken seriously. This was a message I often sneaked into my duck stories." It is not my intention in *R. Crumb: Literature, Autobiography, and the Quest for Self* to transform Crumb into a humorless "spiritual seeker" or to force his life and work into some preconceived theory. Indeed, the "two Crumbs"—if one can speak of him in this way—exist in a complementary polarity, and I do not seek to privilege one over the other. All one can do is take Crumb's own recurring statements concerning his attraction to what he calls "mysticism" seriously, and attempt to search out the connecting threads in his evolving philosophy of life. Indeed, as F. Scott Fitzgerald famously declared: "The test of a first-rate intelligence is the ability to hold two opposed ideas in the mind at the same time, and still retain the ability to function."

One of the key moments in Crumb's spiritual life that would profoundly shape the direction of his future career was his encounter with lysergic acid diethylamide—LSD. Robert Wuthnow researched how frequently people in San Francisco and the Bay Area encountered what psychologist Abraham Maslow called "peak experiences," which Wuthnow broke down into three areas by asking his interviewees whether they "ever had the feeling that [they] were in close contact with something *holy* or *sacred*"; whether they had "experienced the *beauty of nature* in a deeply moving way"; and finally, whether they had ever felt that they "were in *harmony with the universe.*" Wuthnow discovered that "just asking about nature experiences and religious experiences showed that all but 12 percent had had at least one of these experiences." Indeed, during the sixties, the spiritual quest that Crumb embarked upon was common among many young people. Like Allen Ginsberg, who recounted seeing a vision of William Blake in 1948, which he later ceaselessly attempted to duplicate through ingesting a variety of entheogens, so too Crumb experienced a fundamental shift in his relationship to reality after his discovery of LSD that would inspire his art for decades to come.[15] Crumb's then-wife Dana obtained LSD from a psychiatrist in June 1965—a time when the entheogen was still legal. The sample originated in the Sandoz laboratories in Switzerland—"a blue liquid in a blue vial"—which Crumb proceeded to mix with some orange juice, describing his trip one Saturday as "a road-to-Damascus experience." Crumb recalled: "When your mind is blinded with this other-worldly experience, that makes you see the whole of life in a completely different and larger way, it makes your everyday life of just struggling to make it seem like a sort of sham."[16] It is significant here that he compares his psychedelic experience with a famous biblical episode, thus underscoring what for him was its fundamentally religious significance. When he returned to work on Monday at the greeting card company where he worked in Cleveland, suddenly the fraudulence of the so-called real world struck him inexorably, and henceforth his artwork would never be the same: he now embarked on an "intensely visionary period."

Crumb's style began to reflect the psychedelic imagery and symbolism prevalent on rock 'n' roll posters and record albums as well as paintings proliferating in San Francisco: distorted wavy lettering, exclamation points boldly slanted to the right, dreamlike compositional techniques, objects and faces in metamorphosis, fluorescent, neon, kaleidoscopic colors, surrealistic perceptual swirling. It was during this period that the work of the great Dutch artist M. C. Escher (1898–1972) was discovered by the counterculture: Escher's games with perspective, mirrors, trompe l'oeil, images that reflect back upon themselves in an infinite feedback loop, and stairways that appear to go up and down simultaneously seemed to evoke the paradoxes of the ancient Greek pre-Socratic philosopher Heraclitus—"The road up is the same as the road down"—and spoke to the hippies' sensation that life held secretly in its symmetrical paradoxical complexity a riddle they believed may have partially revealed itself to them in their hallucinatory inner voyages. In "I Remember the Sixties: R. Crumb Looks Back!" Crumb recounts "a lot of 'religious experiences' on acid. . . . [S]everal times I saw the great white light and heard celestial music. . . . It was quite impressive." In one panel, we note that *The Tibetan Book of the Dead* is depicted, and in another Crumb claims that his "Third Eye" has been opened—the Third Eye in Hindu thought is the vehicle through which one achieves higher consciousness, and, as we shall see, imagery involving the eye and vision is pervasive throughout Crumb's career. Crumb would also subsequently claim that after ingesting LSD, he was unable to create the type of "linear" stories in which one event logically follows what precedes—he could not, as he put it, "keep the linear thread going"—typical of most graphic narratives. Rather, his art became more "iconographic" and "mystical," concentrating on single moments of bizarre or visionary inner experience, or even abandoning words and logic altogether in favor of entire panels composed solely of silent characters who are in constant change and movement, which leads them back to the place where they began.[17]

Indeed, Crumb would differentiate himself from some of his fellow cartoonists, like his close friend, Spain Rodriguez (1940–2002), whose work, Crumb said, was "overtly political": Rodriguez was the author of a book on

Che Guevara entitled *Che: A Graphic Biography* (2008). Crumb claimed that Rodriguez "was much better educated politically than I was. I was more of a mystical, instinctive-type artist. My tendencies were both more religious and mystical than they were political, really, deep down, but I tried, you know, I tried to be political." Crumb would contribute, for example, to the ecologically oriented magazines *Winds of Change* and *CoEvolution Quarterly* (later named the *Whole Earth Review*) and would bemoan the fact that his satirical thrusts were not always welcomed by his "liberal" editors. Crumb's *Sketchbooks* chart the startling evolution of his relatively conventional earlier work to the LSD-inspired visions that followed. We recall that following a severe injury to his head, Jorge Luis Borges began producing the startlingly original, complex, and labyrinthine *Ficciones*, while Charles Bukowski, following a near-death experience induced by his drinking, also embarked on a creatively intense period of poetic composition. Andrew Robinson, in his book *Sudden Genius? The Gradual Path to Creative Breakthroughs*, argues that many scientific and artistic discoveries that appear to be "sudden" are actually the result of a long period of preparation. So too, after years of self-education and training, Crumb's experience with entheogens led his work in a radically new direction, but the way had been prepared by his discipline and fierce dedication to constant practice at drawing. LSD also allowed Crumb's "crazy" side to emerge in all its glory. There is also, of course, a tradition of associating "genius" with "madness" and sometimes "childlike," "impulsive," "irrational" behavior—one thinks of Ludwig van Beethoven, Friedrich Nietzsche, Fyodor Dostoevsky, William Blake, Arthur Rimbaud, and scores of others—and Crumb himself, as we shall see in later chapters, has speculated concerning the link between madness, creativity, and spiritual explorations.[18]

Crumb has often expressed feelings of extreme alienation, that he is a "stranger" on planet earth. As he phrases it in the masthead for *Weirdo*: "A graphic journal for the rootless, alienated, nihilist, post-modern, existentialist masses."[19] As we shall see in chapter 4, this psychological/spiritual state—which is adumbrated in both Albert Camus's *L'Étranger* and Jean-Paul Sartre's *La Nausée*—is of course one of the hallmarks of existentialism. Hans Jonas, in his landmark treatise *The Gnostic Religion* (1958), draws parallels between our contemporary sense of meaninglessness and the beliefs of ancient Gnostics, who thought the world to be a cosmic mistake created by a bungling demiurge, where humanity must seek salvation through *gnosis*, or self-knowledge. In "Can You Stand Alone and Face Up to the Universe?," which appeared in *Hup*, no. 4, in 1992, Crumb confronts "existential terror" and "the void." He declares: "You gotta work at it . . . study it . . . this is what the Gnostics were into . . . So, yeah, I'm, like, a Gnostic."[20] As we shall see in chapter 3, Crumb would trace out these linkages between Gnosticism and the contemporary experience of spiritual emptiness in another of his most compelling works, "The Religious Experience of Philip K. Dick."[21] This relationship between fantasy/hallucination and reality recurs in several Crumb illustrations. In his depiction of Alan Lomax's biography of the great African American musician Jelly Roll Morton, in which Lomax describes an experience the musician underwent with voodoo—"Jelly Roll Morton's Voodoo Curse"—Crumb also asks in the opening panel: "Was it real? Or was it . . . all in his mind?"[22] It is clear that Crumb is seeking—as we have seen above—to explore and question the reality of religious experience, its relationship to mental illness as well as to the use of drugs.

Polemics over whether drugs were the agents of authentic "religious" or "mystical" experiences erupted during the sixties. Robert Charles Zaehner, an eminent Oxford professor of Eastern religions and ethics—following Aldous Huxley's experiments with psilocybin in *The Drugs of Perception*—argued in *Mysticism Sacred and Profane* (1957) and *Zen, Drugs and Mysticism* (1972) for distinguishing between accessing visionary states through natural means and employing entheogens. Zaehner asserted that Huxley's account of his visions should not be placed in the same category as sacred breakthroughs achieved by mystics under "natural" circumstances.[23] Huston Smith, on the other hand, claimed in his essay "Do Drugs Have Religious Import?" that such experiences should be taken seriously as authentic breakthroughs into the divine, cosmic depths of the psyche.[24] A poet Crumb would come to know—Allen Ginsberg—became an enthusiastic advocate of the use of entheogens. Ginsberg believed along with Timothy Leary that entheogens could play a central role in the revolution in consciousness begun during the Beat movement and continued by the hippies. During the early sixties, Ginsberg declared:

> But now everybody's having visions! That's what it boils down to. Really, truly having visions. And now there are these new "wisdom drugs"—lysergic acid, mescaline. Many, many people have taken peyote now—thousands and thousands—and it's legal. And it's freedom of religion. It's inescapable—people are beginning to see that the Kingdom of Heaven is within them. Instead of thinking it's outside, up in the sky and that it can't be here on earth. It's time to seize power in the Universe, that's what I say—that's my "political statement."

Crumb also has asserted that "LSD was one of the main things that turned the leftwing political movement into something religious and visionary." He recalled that Timothy Leary's writings had inspired him to take LSD, "and a lot of other people too. He was like the evangelist of LSD. But then later, I thought he kind of went crazy. All that government persecution. . . . All of that kind of made him crazy."[25] It is noteworthy that Crumb employs the word "evangelist" here: like Ginsberg, he sees that at this point in American history, young people were looking for a breakthrough in consciousness to be achieved by a new kind of sacrament administered by a novel sort of priest.

The spiritual crisis that the counterculture experienced of course has its roots in an earlier historical schism. The classic narrative of modernism's genesis is the fragmented sense of reality that resulted from the crisis of faith precipitated by the Great War of 1914–1918, chronicled in T. S. Eliot's *The Wasteland*. It is commonly understood that artists took to myth—Yeats, Joyce, Lawrence, Pound, Graves, and Eliot himself—to find new ways of belief in a world where faith in the transcendent had vanished. The universe had now been rendered sterile and "non-magical" due to the domination of a materialistic, purely scientific view of life. William S. Burroughs observed: "But it's obvious, I think, that the old, the old gods have fallen, the old beliefs are gone. Gone, crumbling before our eyes, of their own inertia. And when that happens, you look for something new."[26] Robert Crumb—like D. H. Lawrence and the counterculture as a whole—sensed that something had been lost by accepting a purely analytical and "rational" approach to nature, since this attitude inevitably cut humanity off from a deeply felt connection to the cosmos. Ginsberg defined the "new consciousness" that the counter-culture sought, a now buried tradition that must be found anew. Ginsberg asserted in his essay "Prefatory Remarks Concerning Leary's Politics of Ecstasy":

The new consciousness born in these States can be traced back through old gnostic texts, visions, artists and shamans; it is the consciousness of our ground nature suppressed and desecrated. It was always the secret tale of the tribe in America, this great scandal of the closing of the doors of perception of the naked human form divine. It began with the white murder of Indian inhabitants of the ground, the theft and later usurious exploitation of their land, it continued with an assault on all races and species of Mother Nature herself and concludes today with total disruption of the ecology of the entire planet. No wonder black slaves kept for non-human use into this century in tear-gassed ghettoes of megalopolis were the first aliens to sound the horn of change, the first strangers to call the great call through Basilides' many heavens.[27]

Ginsberg and the Beats situated the quest of the young for a new spirituality within the context of the Gnostic mystical practice of *gnosis* or self-knowledge, as well as the otherworldly journeys of the shaman. As we have seen, Crumb also sought wisdom within Eastern religions and experimented with entheogens, which would influence the shape and content of his work. Ginsberg notes here as well the increasing ecological awareness of the counterculture, and Crumb also chronicled the despoiling of the American landscape in "A Short History of America," in twelve panels that first appeared in *CoEvolution Quarterly*, no. 23 (Fall 1979) and was reprinted in *Snoid Comics* (1980). Crumb subsequently added three additional panels with hypothetical future scenarios for our planet—apocalypse through ecological destruction; a world dominated utterly by technology; or his obviously preferred outcome: a planet restored to its natural yin/yang, homeostatic balance. Furthermore, Crumb created illustrations for environmentalist Edward Abbey's (1927–1989) *The Monkey Wrench Gang* (1975), which depicts the employment of sabotage to attempt to put a stop to the depredation of wilderness in the American Southwest. The word "ecology" derives from the ancient Greek *oikos*, or house—ecology is the study of how best to care for our "house," the planet earth—and Crumb would join in the opposition to the despoiling of nature by corporations.

Thus, during the fifties and sixties, a new American revolutionary sensibility was being born. As Robert N. Bellah has noted in "The New Religious Consciousness and the Crisis in Modernity," "the churches were even less well prepared to cope with the new spirituality of the sixties. The demand for immediate, powerful, and deep religious experience, which was part of the turn away from future-oriented instrumentalism toward present meaning and fulfillment, could on the whole not be met by the religious bodies."[28] Comic book artists responded accordingly. In her essay "Comics as Literature? Reading Graphic Narrative," Hillary Chute observed: "In the 1950s, 1960s, and 1970s, comics reflected the seismic cultural shifts—often produced by war—in American culture of those decades; comics bridged the experimentalism of literary and visual modernisms and mass-produced American popular culture."[29] Crumb's work responded to this shift in the zeitgeist and records a plethora of influences. The German expressionists Otto Dix (1891–1969) and Max Beckmann (1884–1950) also supplied Crumb with a method for transcribing extreme states of consciousness. The German encounter with irrationality during the rise of Hitler and fascism—as we noted earlier, a prescient observer such as Walter Benjamin registered these psychic disruptions in his essays—would provide an analogue for Crumb in his exploration of the American unconscious and its roots in violence and racism. One may note in particular Crumb's virtuosic skill with the technique of cross-hatching, which brings out in stark relief the terrifying and dark implications of the text he is illustrating in true expressionist style—one thinks particularly of his interpretations of works by Franz Kafka, which we shall explore in chapter 5.

Among "Cartoonists/Illustrators," Crumb has singled out as primary artistic influences his brother Charles Crumb Jr. as well as John Stanley, Carl Barks, Thomas Nast, Walt Kelly, Harvey Kurtzman, Chester Gould, Will Elder, Norman Rockwell, Jack Davis, Wallace Wood, Justin Green, and his wife Aline Kominsky-Crumb. Among "Fine Artists" he names De Limbourg, Leonardo da Vinci, Hieronymus Bosch, Pieter Bruegel, Albrecht Dürer, Rembrandt van Rijn, Peter Paul Rubens, James Gillray, Francisco Goya, Honoré Daumier, Gustave Doré, Gustave Courbet, Henri de Toulouse-Lautrec, Vincent van Gogh, Pablo Picasso, Edward Hopper, Reginald Marsh, Salvador Dali, George Grosz, Hans Holbein, Alice Neel, and William Hogarth. Hogarth (1697–1764) provided a model for Crumb's illustrations to James Boswell's *London Journal 1762–1763*, and Hogarth's precise eye for detail would influence Crumb's own penchant for sometimes crowding his pages with fascinating visual clues, which tantalize viewers to seek deeper meaning in their interpretations. If Crumb has been influenced by "fine artists," the influence has also gone in the other direction: several scholars have argued that Crumb's work had an impact on the evolution of the style of New York School artist Philip Guston (1913–1980). Crumb has expressed admiration for illustrator and creator of Arrow Shirts advertisements J. C. Leyendecker: "What charm! What warmth! He creates a beautifully sentimental world of fantasy with folkways of America as one ingredient, fairytale symbolism as another ingredient. It's a world of innocence, a world without cynicism"; for Winsor McCay (1869–1934)—creator of *Little Nemo in Slumberland*—whom Crumb considered a "genius"; and for Oregon artist Basil Wolverton (1909–1978), whose weird, surreal, and ghoulish portraits of the fifties were prepsychedelic in their outrageous, mind-blowing humor. Curiously, Wolverton also—like Crumb—produced illustrations to the Old Testament, published posthumously as *Wolverton's Bible* (2009).

Indeed, Crumb's work is in continual dialogue with the history of art—from Assyrian and Sumerian sculptures to medieval Christian iconography to German expressionism—and simultaneously profoundly affected by the popular culture of the 1920s through the 1950s. His family acquired a television set in October 1948, and Crumb recounts watching Milton Berle, Captain Jet, Sheriff John, cartoons, and a variety of comedy shows. He also read *Little Lulu*, *Donald Duck*—Carl Barks (1901–2000) he regarded as "one of the rare cartoonists to combine great art with great storytelling"—*Mickey Mouse*, *Mighty Mouse*, and *Felix the Cat*: of course Crumb's own work would ultimately far surpass the typical American "comic strip" in imaginative depth, scope, and wild, frenetic creativity. At age eleven, he became intrigued by *Dick Tracy*, which "had a very black and weird psycho-vision of the world, which was fascinating, negative and creepy," as well as Walt Kelly's *Pogo*. He began to read *Nancy*, *Peanuts*, and Jules Feiffer, whose "neurotic introspection" he found inspiring. Harvey Kurtzman—who helped produce the Classics Illustrated version of Melville's *Moby-Dick* in 1942—would go on to edit *Mad* magazine from 1952 to 1956. *Mad*'s acerbic, satirical, and often hilarious send-ups of the clichés of American life—a precursor in the fifties to the underground press of the sixties—would shape Crumb's emerging, supremely inventive style. Crumb recalled that, growing up in a small town in Delaware, coming upon *Mad* was a "revelation . . . nothing I read anywhere else suggested there was an absurdity in the culture." This often-unbearable sense of meaninglessness would ultimately lead Crumb toward a study of existentialism as well as Eastern religions.

Crumb recalled that it was at age sixteen—in 1959—that he became serious about dedicating himself to drawing. Kurtzman's *Humbug* (1957–1958) and *Help!* (1960–1965)—where Terry Gilliam, later of *Monty Python* fame, worked and to which Crumb also contributed his early *Fritz the Cat* strips— were significant publications in his artistic development. In issue no. 22 of *Help!* from January 1965, Crumb contributed sketches of Harlem, and illustrations from his trip to Bulgaria appeared in issue no. 25 as well as prototypes of Fritz. *Help!* also featured examples of Italian *fumetti*—photo-comics in which dialogue is superimposed over a photograph—and Crumb would himself experiment with this genre. Just as Crumb moved back and forth between "high art" and "popular culture," writers in Europe such as Italo Calvino (1923–1985) were also navigating the territory between these hitherto mutually exclusive realms. Calvino grew up encountering the Katzenjammer Kids, Felix the Cat, Maggie and Jiggs, and the Happy Hooligan before he was able to read, spending rapt hours contemplating the compelling images before him, often inventing his own permutations of the narrative order, characters, and scenes. Calvino emphasizes the poetic reveries that seeing the images without the accompanying text evoked in him: "But reading the pictures without words was certainly a schooling in fable-making, in stylization, in the composition of the image. For example, the elegant way Pat O'Sullivan could draw the background in a little, square cartoon showing the black silhouette of Felix the Cat on a road that lost itself in a landscape beneath a full moon in a black sky: I think that has remained an ideal for me."[30] Crumb would also strive to attain this elegance through his own idiosyncratic poetics of perception and by means of a disciplined organization of images into a cogent compositional form.

Upon arriving in Haight-Ashbury in San Francisco in 1967, Crumb participated in the birth of underground comix along with Spain Rodriguez, S. Clay Wilson, Victor Moscoso, Robert Williams, Rick Griffin, and Gilbert Shelton. Crumb felt that "there was a sense of urgency, of cosmic possibility in the air there in 1967 . . . a certain magic glow or light about the place that seemed to be saying, 'This is it . . . it's now or never.'" The late sixties and early seventies became a remarkably prolific period for Crumb during which he contributed to countless underground magazines: *Yarrowstalks* and *East Village Other*, as well as *Cavalier*, which serialized an early incarnation of *Fritz the Cat*—"*Fritz Bugs Out*"—in nine issues. Avant-garde illustrators in Europe learned of his work through publications such as *Aloha* (Amsterdam), *Actuel* (Paris), and *Oz* (London). Crumb's connection with the music scene also led to increasing notoriety due to the cover illustration he created for the album *Cheap Thrills* by Janis Joplin with Big Brother and the Holding Company (1968). The first issue of *Zap Comix*—which revolutionized the conservative, staid, "square" "comics" of earlier years, hence the new spelling of the word, *comix*—was published by Don Donahue and printed by Charles Plymell (a Beat poet and thus yet another Crumb connection to the movement): five thousand copies appeared in February 1968. *Zap* nos. 1, 2, 3, and 0 all appeared the same year—but the material Crumb had assembled for *Zap*, no. 1, was stolen before going to print. Fortunately, Crumb had created Xerox copies of the work, so it could be reinked and thus would appear as *Zap*, no. 0.

Crumb learned particularly from S. Clay Wilson (1941–) that he was free to transcribe whatever weird, nightmarish, violent, sexual images arrived in his subconscious. Wilson revealed in an interview his interest in the Austro-German psychiatrist Richard von Krafft-Ebing's (1840–1902) *Psychopathia Sexualis* (1886), a work that Crumb would illustrate. Wilson's work was populated by deviant motorcycle gangs, rotund red devils, libidinous, deranged pirates, Old West reprobates, and heavily made-up damsels sporting prominently erect nipples and cavorting in various conditions of undress. Crumb reported that during this time—like S. Clay Wilson—his "head was spinning with strange visions and this kind of electric animated craziness, it's hard to describe."[31] Indeed, it is precisely the *head* of the human body that is often depicted by Crumb as it implodes, explodes, separates into sections, expands, shoots upward, is reduced to nothingness, liquefies, and transmogrifies in every possible fashion. Grace Slick in Jefferson Airplane's hit song "White Rabbit"—based on Lewis Carroll's surrealistic *Alice's Adventures in*

Wonderland—exhorted her listeners: "feed your head," by which Slick meant not only by means of entheogens but through the expansion of consciousness brought about through knowledge and education, "a call to liberate brains as much as the senses." During the sixties, there were "headshops" filled with paraphernalia catering to the drug culture, while Crumb published his work under the rubric *Head Comix*. The counterculture was studying the head, the brain, the mind, the *psyche*, not only exploring the superego and ego but excavating the dark places of the unconscious as well. As Todd Hignite has eloquently argued concerning Crumb's innovations: "With an absolutely id-emptying cocktail of drug-altered consciousness, anti-conformity, cultural alienation, sublimated sex and violence, and the twin poles of spiritual transcendence and philosophical delusion, Crumb's command of storytelling subtlety, pacing, and characterization made apparent from the outset that the artist was not only a jaw-dropping prodigy but an astute pupil of the form."[32] The *id* is the dark planet of our being, the area that is left often unexplored. Crumb's universe is populated by antiheroes, by solitary spiritual seekers who like the artist himself are often awkward, shy, neurotically self-lacerating, tormented by metaphysical doubts and odd, seemingly overwhelming sexual impulses; who inhabit the night world of the dark unconscious. Crumb's genius opened up a new awareness of the potentials of graphic narrative. Previously relegated to the category of entertainment—usually in bad taste—for children, comics began to be elevated to the status of works of art worthy of exhibition in the great museums of the world. Crumb began to explore the hidden realm of the archetypal unconscious, surfacing from his deep-sea diving with such freakishly funny icons as Eggs Ackley, Mr. Snoid, Flakey Foont, the Vulture Demoness, and Devil Girl. He exposed and often ridiculed his own private sexual compulsions and fetishes, playing as artist in public—as we have noted above—a role similar to the one the "confessional poets" had performed in American poetry.

Crumb was never a somber seeker of the transcendent. Although he has a profoundly interior side to his character, he is alert to the absurdities of too much seriousness, as we see in his characters Fritz the Cat—a libidinous feline—and Mr. Natural, a long-bearded elderly guru who constantly teases and makes life difficult for his disciple Flakey Foont: his paradoxical and gnomic utterances are reminiscent of Zen koans such as, "What is the sound of one hand clapping?; Wash your bowls; Out of nowhere the mind comes forth; What do you call the world?" Crumb seeks "kozmik trooths," as he comically puts it—a phrase likely taken from the rock group the Grateful Dead, who believed that "LSD is a cosmic truth serum." Indeed, both Fritz the Cat and Mr. Natural satirized the hippie culture. Crumb pokes fun with an ironically detached style at the excesses of his generation *from the inside*, so to speak—as a kind of artist/anthropologist who is at once a member of the tribe but also an informant concerning its inner workings—lending his work its lively verisimilitude. Crumb mercilessly deflated the pretensions of the Haight-Ashbury crowd, declaring: "You'd see them skipping through the park with their bamboo flutes and their robes, calling themselves things like Gingerbread Prince. And they had an irritating, smug, superior attitude. If you didn't have long hair, if you didn't have a bamboo flute, they just ignored your existence."[33] Crumb was too much of a skeptical, rational intellectual to abandon himself to any sort of groupthink—hippie or otherwise. As we shall see in chapter 1, Crumb was more respectful toward the earlier generation of American cultural revolutionaries, the Beats.

In 1991, Crumb moved to southern France, where he has continued the philosophical quest he began in his youth. Several European artists were deeply involved with spiritual traditions such as Wassily Kandinsky, author of *Concerning the Spiritual in Art* (1912), and Piet Mondrian, who was influenced by Madame Helena Petrovna Blavatsky and became a member of the Dutch Theosophical Society in May 1909. In America, Robert Motherwell believed that the artist's function was to "guard the spiritual in the modern world." Other abstract expressionists such as Jackson Pollock studied Sir James Frazer's *The Golden Bough* and Joseph Campbell's *The Hero with a Thousand Faces*; Barnett Newman was drawn to Native American art of the Northwest Coast; and Mark Rothko immersed himself in mythology and indigenous art. Although he abjured the abstract expressionists, Crumb revealed that he "was influenced by surrealism a lot" when he was young— "de Chirico and Dali, you know, all those guys." Max Ernst's *Une semaine de bonté* (1934)—considered by art historians an early example of a graphic novel—features bird-headed humans and erotic mayhem, which perhaps inspired Crumb's own human/animal figures such as the Vulture Demoness. George Herriman's *Krazy Kat*—a favorite of Crumb's as well as of poet e. e. cummings—contains many dadaist and surrealistic elements. And of course another beloved artist for Crumb—Hieronymus Bosch (ca.1450–1516)—was a supremely fantastic proto-surrealist. André Breton believed that the surrealists were involved—like the ancient alchemists and Hermetists—in the "Great Work," the *Magnum Opus* in search of the "philosopher's stone." In "Toward the Sociology of Esoteric Culture," Edward Tiryakian's commentary on Breton applies equally to Crumb:

> Breton drew upon various sources of inspiration (including Marx, Freud, and occultism) to formulate a revolutionary consciousness

aimed against the bourgeois world (of utility, reason, realism, and technological society), a consciousness whose intention is always to allow the irruption of "wild" images that will disturb the sensibility by shattering the coherence of those "stable" images that make up, for each individual, the objective world.

André Breton is the subject of one of Crumb's superb portraits, and Crumb's often bizarre and constantly in motion images—like those of the surrealists—strive to expand the limits of our supposedly "normal" perception of "reality" in order to allow the mind to acknowledge the existence of the suppressed, sometimes violent and disruptive elements of the archaic, volcanic unconscious. Crumb has acknowledged in an interview: "We humans with all our intelligence and cleverness are helpless creatures driven by forces over which we have very little control and which we barely understand."[34] Crumb's work is devoted to an exploration of this terra incognita of the human psyche, which needs to be dredged up and brought out into the light of consciousness so that we may more fully understand ourselves.

Crumb is a continuation of a long tradition of artists who have sought out both literary works and spiritual texts for their own edification as well as for purposes of illustration. In our own times, manga artist Osamu Tezuka (1928–1989) between 1972 and 1983 illustrated an eight-volume life of Buddha; Anant Pai launched the comic books series *Amar Chitra Katha* (Immortal Picture Stories), which retells Indian mythical and religious texts such as the Bhagavad Gita; and Grant Morrison with artist Mukesh Singh created *18 Days*—a science fiction and fantasy version of the great Indian epic the Mahabharata (2010). Crumb himself has exhibited a curiosity about a number of traditions including the voodoo of Jelly Roll Morton's French Louisiana; Hinduism (his sketch "The Seven Chakras of R. Crumb"); Buddhism (his comic "Crybaby's Blues" includes a panel featuring the Buddha's Third Noble Truth, "Cessation of desire is the way out"); and the books of Carlos Castaneda, whom he quotes: "The purpose of human life is to increase awareness." In a satirical account of a trip to the Academy Awards in Hollywood published in 1991, Crumb closes with an excerpt from the Trappist monk Thomas Merton: "Keep as far away as you can from the places where they gather to cheat and insult one another, to exploit one another . . . or to mock one another with their false gestures of friendship." This is from Merton's book *Seeds of Contemplation*: Merton corresponded with several members of the American counterculture, including Henry Miller and Lawrence Ferlinghetti, and affirmed the spiritual message of the Beats. The theme of solitude returns in an entry from Crumb's *Sketchbook* (1990) from Henry David Thoreau's *Walden*: "I find it wholesome to be alone the greater part of the time. To be in company, even with the best, is soon wearisome and dissipating. I love to be alone. . . . We are for the most part more lonely when we go abroad among men than when we stay in our chambers. A man thinking or working is always alone, let him be where he will."[35] In this invocation of Thoreau, Crumb returns to the original genius of the American counterculture who closely read the Bhagavad Gita and Buddhist texts, admired and studied the spiritual lives of the Native Americans, and was our first great ecologist.

In chapter 1 of this volume, "On the Road: Beats, Zen Buddhism, and Bukowski," I discuss Crumb's relationship to the Beat writers Allen Ginsberg, Jack Kerouac, and William S. Burroughs as well as Charles Bukowski and the ways Hindu and Buddhist themes enter Crumb's work. In chapter 2, "Jelly Roll Morton, Charley Patton: Blues, Voodoo, and the Devil," I explore Crumb's intense relationship to music, especially blues, and the ways spiritual themes in the form of voodoo/hoodoo are developed. In chapter 3, "Philip K. Dick: Gnostic Travels," I analyze the increasing interest Crumb began to show in Gnosticism and the ways Gnostic themes are portrayed in his illustrations to "The Religious Experience of Philip K. Dick." In chapter 4, "Jean-Paul Sartre and the Existential Quest," I discuss Crumb's illustrations to Sartre's *Nausea* and demonstrate the ways Crumb incorporated existential themes in his autobiographical work. In chapter 5, "Franz Kafka: Allegories of the Soul," I investigate Crumb's collaboration with David Mairowitz in their book *Introducing Kafka* and how Crumb illustrated Jewish mystical themes as well as the ways his interpretation of Kafka is influenced by Christian iconography. In chapter 6, "In the Beginning: *The Book of Genesis Illustrated by R. Crumb*," I discuss Crumb's four-year labor on the book of Genesis and his method of introducing his own interpretations while observing a strict fidelity to the text. In a concluding epilogue, I draw the strands of my argument together, reviewing the ways Crumb has continued in his later years to combine his autobiographical quest for self and authenticity with his meditation and philosophical studies.

There has yet to appear a definitive monograph studying how Crumb treats literary and spiritual themes in relation to his personal, philosophical quest in his work. Jeffrey J. Kripal's *Mutants and Mystics: Science Fiction, Superhero Comics, and the Paranormal* explores how these topics appear in the work of several artists including Grant Morrison, Stan Lee, and Alan Moore. Kennet Granholm's essay "The Occult and Comics" discusses similar terrain, but neither of these works considers Crumb's contribution.[36] Thus, *R. Crumb: Literature, Autobiography, and the Quest for Self* aims to fill a major gap in contemporary scholarship in the humanities. I seek to explore Crumb's adaptations of literary works in his original—and often technically dazzling—art. I argue that Crumb's work has been wrongly interpreted due to its "outrageous" aspects—for example, its putative misogyny and racism—and a failure to understand Crumb's essentially parodic and satirical imagination.[37] Crumb's humor is indeed often "over the top," yet his motive is to undo and critique stereotypes rather than to affirm them. And while Crumb is indeed a dazzling humorist and rapier-witted satirist, he has also been embarked on a serious spiritual quest from childhood. Feelings of extreme alienation, terror, the uncanny, despair, and existential angst recur throughout Crumb's illustrations to the Beats and Charles Bukowski, the biographies of Jelly Roll Morton and Charley Patton, the works of Philip K. Dick, Jean-Paul Sartre, and Franz Kafka, and the book of Genesis, as well as in his magnificent *Sketchbooks*. Crumb's genius lies in his ability to carry on his autobiographical quest for deeper meaning as a continual dialogue with literary and spiritual texts that have intrigued and inspired him, thus making his life and work a seamless fabric in which work speaks to life, and life to work.

ON THE ROAD

Beats, Zen Buddhism, and Bukowski

Robert Crumb, born on August 30, 1943, arrived in the world just as the Beat generation emerged in New York City with the friendships of Jack Kerouac, Allen Ginsberg, William S. Burroughs, Gregory Corso, and Neal Cassady: allusions to Beat literature recur frequently in his work. Crumb has also declared his affinity for the writings of Charles Bukowski, who—while not a "Beat"—shared many of their preoccupations and is the subject of one of Crumb's earliest literary adaptations, "Bop Bop Against That Curtain," published in the Fall 1975 issue of *Arcade*. In this first chapter, I shall trace Crumb's reading of Beat texts such as Kerouac's *On the Road* and *The Dharma Bums*; the ways his familiarity with the biographies of Beats such as Allen Ginsberg and William S. Burroughs intersected with his own philosophical evolution; and how Buddhist themes reappear in Crumb's oeuvre—for example in both his Mr. Natural series and illustrations of *The Zen Teachings of Huang Po*—demonstrating that the fascination of the counterculture with Asian spirituality would become a recurring Crumbian theme. Crumb's close friend Harvey Pekar was influenced by the Beats and—like Crumb—was an autodidact who read widely in authors such as Herman Melville, Mark Twain, Stephen Crane, Frank Norris, and Katherine Mansfield.[1] Pekar contributed much of the text to accompany the illustrations in *The Beats: A Graphic History*, edited by Paul Buhle (2009). The qualities that Crumb was attracted to in Pekar—he "always talked in very plain language and I always admired him for that"—were, as we noted in the introduction, precisely the stylistic features he would admire in the hard-boiled writings of Burroughs and Bukowski.[2] Crumb revealed that he first learned about "beatniks" in 1956 from Jules Feiffer's (1929–) clever satirical cartoons that appeared in the *Village Voice*, founded in 1955.[3] Further evidence of Crumb's awareness of the developing hip scene may be gleaned from a work created when he was nineteen and courting his first wife, Dana, *R. Crumb's Yum Yum Book* (written in 1962; published in 1975). The young bohemian character Oggie, we are told—bored by conventional religion—"became cynical and fell in with a crowd of sensualists." One of these "sensualists" spouts hipster lingo: "Life is short, Oggie! You gotta get your kicks while you can! Do you dig?"

In addition, during the mid-sixties, Crumb contemplated an artistic enterprise to be titled "A Comic Book of the Beat Generation," priced at ten cents, which appears in *Sketchbook, vol. 1, June 1964–September 1968.* The satirical story "Where It's At" features a young woman named Muffy Zimmerman, who desperately seeks to discover "where the action is" by coming to Greenwich Village, New York.[4] Crumb depicts Muffy as a lost soul who has no clear sense of her own identity and therefore hungrily seeks some external definition of what it means to be "cool." Crumb frequently skewered the silly aspects of youth culture; however, he did respond to the Beat philosophy as a primal revolt against America's post–World War II stultifying, conformist, "phony" sensibility—to employ Holden Caulfield's term in Salinger's *The Catcher in the Rye.* For Crumb as for the Beats, the modern world often seemed an absurdist nightmare where contemporary humanity was conditioned and condemned—like Sisyphus in Camus's famous metaphor—to tirelessly perform the same meaningless tasks over and over again in an indifferent universe. The Beats sought to face this existential situation directly, without the delusions fabricated by consumerist, capitalistic society. James J. Farrell in *The Spirit of the Sixties: Making Postwar Radicalism* argues that "the Beat spiritual revolution challenged American religion, rejecting the private pieties, positive thinking, and pubic hypocrisies of the 1950s." As Crumb would declare in his *Sketchbooks*: "The true meaning of 'hip' is not 'cool' or some kind of avant-garde chicness, but a keen state of alertness to the constant onslaught of hype, the sleaze behind the mask, the elaborate con-job that is modern mass culture."[5] Crumb made a clear distinction between what he saw as the superficial, frivolous aspects of the counterculture and the more serious themes of Beat authors, whom he believed were advocating a deconstruction of the "hype" foisted upon the young by the "Establishment." Indeed, Crumb would struggle to separate out within himself the elements that he believed had been meretriciously shaped by the surrounding culture and to find and recover—rather like peeling an onion—whatever might have been left unmolested, pure, and uncorrupted by what he termed the "con-job" of contemporary life.

Crumb's friend Marty Pahls encouraged him to read William S. Burroughs's *Junkie* and Kerouac's *On the Road.* Crumb later acknowledged: "Beat literature gave me an alternative point of view about living in America that we weren't getting from our parents, from school, from television, or *Life* magazine." Another Beat connection was Charles Plymell (1935–)—a poet in the Beat orbit—who would become instrumental in the publication of the first *Zap Comix*. Indeed, the creators of countercultural comix would appear in many of the same underground newspapers as the Beats. When Crumb moved to Cleveland in October 1962 and roomed with Pahls, he "got involved with these beatnik girls who were able to appreciate the quirky guy I was," and he began socializing with a group of poets, artists, college students, and musicians who gathered in the University Circle area of the city. Crumb also met poet d. a. levy—who spelled his name in lowercase letters a la e. e. cummings—while in Cleveland and submitted "Cheesis K. Reist in the Detroit Avenue Story" to levy's *Marrahwanna Quarterly* in 1966. A central figure in the counterculture, levy published Charles Bukowski's *The Genius of the Crowd* with his 7 Flowers Press in 1966. He was a suicide, perishing at age twenty-six from a gunshot wound to the head. Crumb was likely referring to levy when he recalled that Cleveland "was a grim scene. What did I know? Cleveland was a place where a lot of sensitive middle-class kids—outcasts—committed suicide, and this was before LSD! The scene was filled with depression, a beatnik kind of sensibility."[6] Greenwich Village, Berkeley, Cambridge, San Francisco, Ann Arbor are frequently thought of as the centers of the countercultural revolution that began with the Beats in the fifties and continued with the hippies during the sixties, but Cleveland was also an important locus of literary and artistic activity.

Like the confessional poets, the Beats' oeuvre was autobiographical, and they wrote directly out of their own experience without attempting to gloss over their faults and weaknesses. In the past, the genre of autobiography was often distinguished by the fact that when people recollected their experiences, they did not tell the truth about themselves: they glossed over their frailties, exaggerated their virtues, and recast their lives in the form of a heroic narrative. Crumb's goal was not to idealize himself but rather to confess his own life through drawings on paper, to portray all his sins of omission and commission. And just as Henry Miller in *Tropic of Cancer* and *Tropic of Capricorn*, as well as his autobiographical trilogy, *The Rosy Crucifixion: Sexus, Nexus,* and *Plexus*, recounted every unsavory fact about his life—indeed, Miller set out intentionally to depict himself in the worst possible light, even inventing misdeeds of which he was innocent—so too the Beats, many of whom admired Miller, held little back when it came to their poetry, prose, and memoirs. Allen Ginsberg revealed the traumas of his own childhood—his mentally ill mother, struggles with homosexuality, experimentation with drugs, and psychological derangements. Daniel Bell's observation in *The Cultural Contradictions of Capitalism* concerning novelists of the 1960s such as Joseph Heller, J. P. Donleavy, Thomas Pynchon, and Terry Southern is equally true of poets who achieved fame in the 1950s such as Ginsberg and Gregory Corso:

> In reading the novelists who have touched the nerve of the age, one finds that the major preoccupation of the 1960s was *madness*. When the social life has been left behind, and the self, as a bounded subject, has been dissolved, the only theme left is the theme of dissociation, and every important writer of the decade was in one way or another involved with this theme. The novels are hallucinatory in mode; many of their protagonists are schizoid; insanity, rather than normalcy, has become the touchstone of reality.

When Crumb read Ken Kesey's *One Flew over the Cuckoo's Nest*—which satirically and unforgettably portrays an insane asylum in which the staff are clearly deranged while many of the inmates appear normal by comparison— he thought it "was great, just excellent. It came from a time when mental institutions were a big thing in America. There were a lot of them, and a lot of people threw their relatives and kids in these mental institutions at the drop of a hat." Thus "madness" would become a prominent theme throughout Crumb's work, and he sought to reveal himself completely, including his own struggles with keeping his sanity. R. D. Laing, the Scottish psychiatrist who came to fame during the sixties, famously declared: "Insanity is a sane response to an insane world," and Crumb plays throughout his work with the seeming dichotomies of normal/abnormal, sane/mad, real/hallucinatory.

Crumb's colleague Art Spiegelman experienced a mental breakdown in 1968, spending a month in Binghamton State Hospital in upstate New York: his mother committed suicide shortly thereafter, which Spiegelman documented in his four-page "Prisoner on the Hell Planet," completed in 1972, first published in *Short Order Comix*, no. 1 (1973) and later in *Maus*. Spiegelman reveals that, at his mother's funeral, he recited—in true Beat style—from *The Tibetan Book of the Dead*, a favorite text of the counterculture: "O Nobly Born. . . . In your journey through the formless void, remember the unity of all living things." Spiegelman humorously recalled that his experiments with entheogens "shifted" his ambitions "toward becoming At One With the Universe and Achieving Egoless Buddha-hood." Due to their explorations with entheogens, probings of the deep recesses of the unconscious, and struggle for political and sexual freedom, the Beats, Crumb believed, "were all heroes, all those people from the Beatnik-hipster era.... [T]hey were our antecedents and the people we looked to." Crumb had read Ginsberg's *Howl*—"I saw the best minds of my generation destroyed by madness"—which he considered a "great" work as well as "the beatnik manifesto of the '50s":

> [I]t says it all. It's got that beatnik attitude of that time in America. It's quite eloquent. But after that, [Ginsberg] didn't really do anything that struck me as particularly interesting. But he was like a spokesman for the hippies in the '60s too. He would lead the hippies in all those Indian chants. He tried to lead them in the direction of spirituality, an East Indian kind of spirituality with mediation and chanting and all that.

Other artists such as Bill Griffith (1944–) have also paid homage to Ginsberg. In *Invisible Ink: My Mother's Love Affair with a Famous Cartoonist* (2015), Griffith describes himself as a young man taking the train to New York "to escape Levittown and to wander Greenwich Village in search of folksingers and beatniks. . . . I'm seventeen and I'm going to hear Allen Ginsberg do a reading of his poem 'Kaddish,' in a loft in the West Village. I bring my dog-eared copy of 'Howl' for him to sign." Ginsberg went to San Francisco in 1954, where *Howl* was premiered the following year on October 7, and Crumb arrived twelve years later in 1967.[7] Don Donahue printed the second run of *Zap Comix*, no. 1, on a press that Ginsberg himself had originally obtained. Ginsberg responded in kind to Crumb's work, contributing a blurb for the back cover of *Head Comix* (1968): "So far supreme funny underground comicstrip incarnation of the posthistoric flower age," and later Ginsberg would also attend the *Zap Comix* get-together in New York at the Psychedelic Solution Gallery at Saint Mark's Place in 1989. Crumb provided the front and back covers of an issue of *CoEvolution Quarterly* (Winter 1979–1980) featuring the poem "Factory," which excoriates corporate capitalism and the dehumanizing life of factory workers, written by a poet Ginsberg admired, Antler—the pseudonym of Brad Burdick (1946–). Jeffrey Weinberg of Water Row Press in Sudbury, Massachusetts, commissioned Crumb to create a series of three six-by-nine-inch portraits of Ginsberg, Kerouac, and Burroughs, which were published in a limited edition of one hundred copies in 1986. A set of one hundred posters—eleven-by-seventeen-inch posters of Kerouac and Burroughs and twelve-by-eighteen-inch posters of Ginsberg—were also produced. It is clear from the detail and care he lavished on these works that Crumb continued to hold the Beats in high esteem decades after his initial encounter with their writings. As recently as

R. Crumb, Allen Ginsberg, *Meet the Beats*, 1985.

2018, for example, Crumb created a portrait of Charles Plymell entitled "Ol' Charlie" and in the same year provided a cover illustration to *Don't Hide the Madness: William S. Burroughs in Conversation with Allen Ginsberg*. This engagement with the Beat legacy has extended to Crumb's late son Jesse (1968–2018), who made portraits of Diane di Prima, William S. Burroughs, and Tuli Kupferberg of the Fugs.

Hindu and Buddhist iconography recurs throughout Crumb's work, and in his drawing of Ginsberg for Water Row Press, we note that the poet is portrayed holding his right hand aloft with his thumb and index finger touching, which is the *gyana mudra* pose employed in yoga. Crumb's character Shuman the Human (also variously spelled by Crumb "Schuman the Human")—described on *R. Crumb's Trading Cards* as "a bald Flakey Foont"—is also depicted with eyes closed and begging bowl performing cross-legged yoga on a bed of nails (coincidentally just as Crumb's brother Maxon would do later on the streets of San Francisco) with both hands in the *gyana mudra* pose. Shuman is an earnest spiritual seeker who in one nine-panel episode collected in *Head Comix* (1968) goes looking for God, stalking the city streets in the wee hours of the morning, when suddenly a bright light flashes from the sky bellowing "AHEM!" Shuman's hat flies off his head; he perspires profusely, pulls on his collar, and begins to giggle, and in the final two panels his head gradually shrinks to near invisibility.

The Beats were fascinated by Hindu and Buddhist philosophy, and Crumb absorbed these influences of the zeitgeist. Asian spiritual themes influenced other artists, such as Kim Deitch, who studied at the Integral Yoga Institute with Swami Satchidananda, where he chanted mantras. Deitch also created a comic for the *East Village Other* featuring Sunshine Girl, who battled dark forces including Zoroaster the Mad Mouse: however, here Zoroaster is not the heroic Zarathustra of the Good Religion of Persia but rather a dastardly foe. Justin Green, in his series entitled *Zen Time*, narrates a variety of Zen stories, including one 1978 installment concerning the paradoxes involved in the need to know and believe. A hermit named Ngonagpa wants to know the color of Amitabha—the celestial Buddha of Pure Land Buddhism—and is told his color is "ash." This puzzles him his whole life, but as he lies dying he is told that Amitabha is actually the color red, and he dies laughing. Chogyam Trungpa, the guru of Allen Ginsberg, tells the tale in his book *Cutting through Spiritual Materialism*. It is clear that Crumb also was interested in applying the principles he'd learned from Eastern spirituality to his artistic practice. In *Sketchbook*, vol. 7, his imaginary mental companion, who appears often as a small, ornery pig in his drawings and functions as a kind of scolding superego, tells him when he can't think of anything to draw: "Don't think, Bob!! Just draw!!" He does, and then declares: "It's kind of like a Zen meditation practice in spontaneous creativity. . . . I must remember this an' never get 'hung up' about drawing again." And in "Notes for Story for *Arcade* #7, April 10, 1975," Crumb depicts himself struggling to create his drawings and muses to himself: "I know it's a form of yoga, drawing these comics . . . A kind of meditation . . . A spiritual struggle . . ." with two speech bubbles above his head as he places his hand thoughtfully to his temple: "Be spontaneous! Break on through the mental barriers, Bob!!," and "Ommm," the famous mantra chant. Finally, we can witness the pertinacity with which Crumb explored Buddhist ideas in a *Sketchbook* entry dated January 1993: "There is no 'I' . . . The 'observer' is an illusion . . . The 'ego' is a construction." Crumb is persistently engaged throughout his work with one of the basic questions of Eastern thought concerning the Self and its nature. What within us is "real" and what is "illusion"? Where is the "self" located, if it indeed exists at all? While these are questions that have exercised philosophers and thinkers from Gautama Buddha to the present—Derek Parfit (1942–2017) is a recent example, who in his *Reasons and Persons* (1984) questions our stable notions of personal identity—it is clear that for Crumb as well it has been an abiding concern.

Like the Beats, Crumb also—as we saw in the introduction—from childhood had a strong attraction to mysticism. Jared Gardner points out that in his work during the sixties, this strand of Crumb's thought becomes increasingly prominent in comics such as "The Trip" or "Big Freakout on Detroit Ave." Both "follow a similar narrative pattern, providing very little text. . . . [T]hese strips focus on individuals struggling to arrive at an answer to a question that can't be formulated in words." At least some of this affinity for mysticism Crumb inherited from his brother Charles. Robert recalled that during their adolescence, Charles "was the one who first started reading about mysticism and stuff like that when we were teenagers. I didn't know about that stuff. He went through this Catholic mysticism, then he rejected the Catholic church that we were raised in and then went on to Buddhism and stuff like that. He was kind of a young, adolescent mystic." Throughout his work, Crumb often incorporates the language, cultural memes, and mystical symbolism of the Beat movement. Allusions to *The Tibetan Book of the Dead*, karma, and the Chinese concept of yin and yang illustrate that Crumb was thoroughly familiar with the Beat lexicon of spiritual exploration. As early as 1960, for example, at age seventeen, he depicted the chakras—energy centers of the body—and returned to the theme later with "The Seven Chakras of R. Crumb," in which he comically depicts himself slouching over, depressed, "beat," and clearly not exemplifying in any healthy way the centers of physical well-being discovered by the ancient philosophers of India.

Crumb also has created countless drawings depicting the Third Eye of Hindu mystical thought as well as of the eye itself in a variety of amazing permutations. Crumb depicts the moment of visionary insight as weirdly horrific, comic, and simultaneously cosmically intense. In a fantastic drawing from *Sketchbook*, vol. 12, the self has been possessed by a force at once awesome and terrifying, the *mysterium tremendum*. The body is prone and passive while the hand of the prone figure is shaped as a helpless, hanging claw. A whirlpool of energy resembling the funnel clouds of a tornado pour into his eyes, while the heading reads "Oh the Ignorance! The Suffering!!," with three portraits at the bottom of two seemingly eighteenth-century gentlemen facing a less elegant fellow. Another example of ocular imagery is the cover

R. Crumb, "Oh the Ignorance! The Suffering!!," *Sketchbook*, vol. 12.

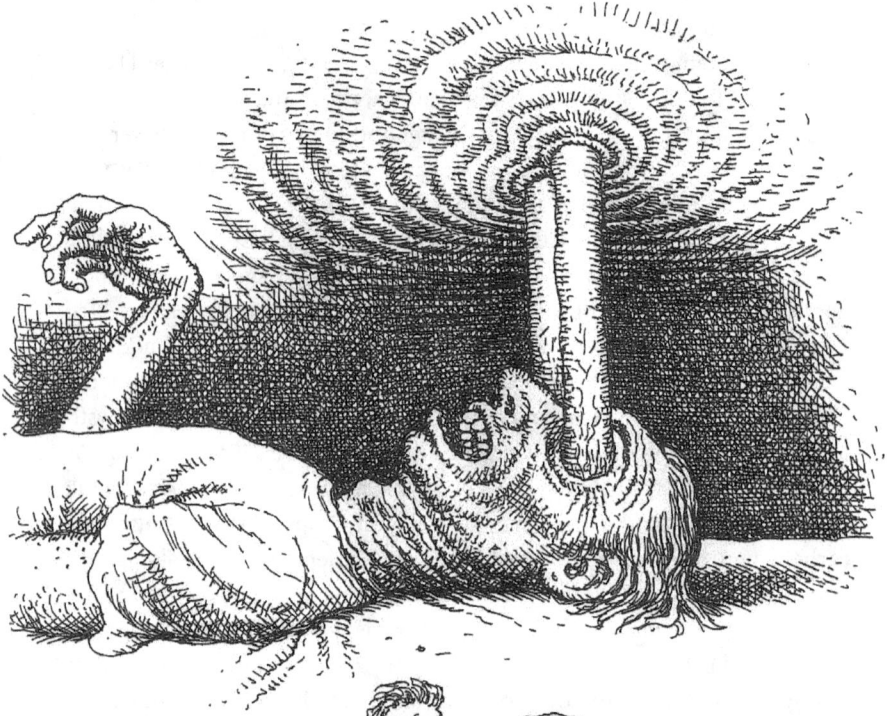

of *Mystic Funnies*, no. 3 (2002); Crumb draws in the night sky overlooking a city street a huge, open eye with golden rays permeating outward looking down upon the proceedings, as if a giant hole had been rent in the cosmic texture through which an awesome, inscrutable, eerie Being/Power were peering at the human comedy below.

Thus one reason Crumb was drawn to the Beats was their spiritual quest, and while Crumb admired Ginsberg's early work, he did not seek to illustrate Ginsberg's poetry, as did Eric Drooker in *Howl: A Graphic Novel* (2010). Rather, he demonstrated greater interest in Kerouac, Burroughs, and Charles Bukowski. Bukowski had several connections to the Beats, although his literary relationship to them has been debated.[8] Crumb was drawn by Kerouac's essay "The Origins of the Beat Generation" describing the philosophical message of the Beats—"beat" means beaten down by suffering, the "beat" of jazz music, and most importantly the beatific vision. As we have seen, Kerouac, like Crumb, had been in his youth a devout Catholic and worshiped his older brother Gerard, who died at age nine, becoming for Kerouac a sainted figure in his personal pantheon. Another connection to Crumb occurs in the same Kerouac essay, in which Kerouac pays his respects to the popular culture of the twenties and thirties. Kerouac argues that one of the sources of the Beat sensibility "goes back to the inky ditties of old cartoons (Krazy Kat with the irrational brick) ... to Popeye the sailor and the Sea Hag and the meaty gunwales of boats, to Cap'n Easy and Wash Tubbs screaming with ecstasy over canned peaches on a cannibal isle, to Wimpy looking X-eyed for a juicy hamburger such as they make no more." Like Crumb, Kerouac was nostalgic for "the glee of America, the honesty of America. ... [L]ike my grandfather this America was invested with wild selfbelieving individuality and this had begun to disappear around the end of World War II with so many great guys dead ... when suddenly it began to emerge again, the hipsters began to appear gliding around saying 'Crazy, man.'" Like Kerouac, Crumb nursed an abiding nostalgia for an America of bygone times, which by contrast to the post-Hiroshima world of the fifties appeared to be innocent and optimistic in ways that seemed irretrievable. The Armenian American writer William Saroyan (1908–1981)—an author Kerouac admired greatly—also depicted in his short story collection *The Daring Young Man on the Flying Trapeze* (1934), his Pulitzer Prize–winning play *The Time of Your Life* (1939), and his novel *The Human Comedy* (1943) an America where childlike joy and love were still able to save humanity from hate and death.

In Crumb's portrait of Kerouac, Crumb clearly captured the pensive, shy, introverted qualities of Kerouac's personality as well as his casual mode of dress: unshaven, with collar opened at the chest looking—as his friends

sometimes noted—a bit like a burly, French Canadian lumberjack. After reading *On the Road*, Crumb was enthralled by several themes in the novel. The
compelling narrative depicting Sal Paradise (Kerouac) and Dean Moriarty
(Neal Cassady) as they sped across America in a nonstop quest for mind-
expanding experience, sexual excitement, and enlightenment was an obvious
attraction. At the time, Crumb felt that he had little access to such pleasures:
"When I was 17, I read *On the Road*, and it sickened me, because my reaction
was, 'Oh God, these guys are out there having so much fun. I'm not having
any fun at all. I'm just sitting here in my parents' house. But them—the girls,
the adventures . . .'" We can see the ways Beat themes began to enter Crumb's
work with "Fritz Bugs Out," published in *Cavalier* (February–October 1968),
featuring Crumb's famous bohemian feline Fritz the Cat. We find Fritz at
the university musing in breathless, nonstop, hip sentences in distinctly
Kerouacian style about "all the stuff to see and all th' kicks an' girls are all out
there an' here you sit under a pile of mouldy ol' textbooks fillin' your head
full of junk . . . an' me a writer and poet who should be havin' adventures an'
experiencing all the diversities and paradoxes and ironies of life and passin'
over all the roads of the world and digging all the cities and towns and rivers
and oceans and making all the chicks . . . by God!" We can see here a classic
example of the ways Crumb's reading of literature influenced his inner life as
well as how he then channels Beat conceptions back directly into his artwork.

   In addition to powerfully portraying the electric enthusiasms of youth, *On
the Road* is replete with Buddhist themes: Jack Kerouac had devoted several
years to a serious study of Buddhism as has been revealed in the posthumous
publication of *Some of the Dharma* (1997). The novel also contains Taoist
allusions: the "road" is obviously Lao-Tzu's *Tao*, or "way of life in accordance
with Nature," and there is also a Gnostic theme in the novel as represented
by the quest for the pearl of self-knowledge: as we shall see in chapter 3,
Crumb would become increasingly attracted by Gnosticism as his career
progressed. Crumb also responded to Kerouac's confrontation with what
Ernest Hemingway called *nada*—the "nothingness" of existence—or what
the Buddha named as one of the Four Noble Truths, *dukkha*: all life is suffering. In *Sketchbook*, no. 2, Crumb depicts the despairing side of Kerouac's
vision of America. A forlorn character looks out over the entry of a house
with cracked, weed-infested sidewalks, a parked car, a lonely, scraggly tree
against a melancholy sky, a quarter moon, and gloomy houses with the script:
"Jack Kerouac was right!" An arrow below points to a darkened dwelling
featuring two illuminated windows, "Denver Doldrums." In part 1, chapter
7, of *On the Road*, "Carlo Marx"—Allen Ginsberg—exclaims "to the sky," "oh,
these Denver doldrums!" In his poem "Last Stanzas in Denver," Ginsberg

declared: "So I enact the Hope I can create / A lively world around my deadly eyes / Sad Paradise it is I initiate, / And fallen angels who lost wings and sighs." The story goes that when reading the poem, Kerouac mistook the phrase "Sad paradise" for "Sal Paradise" and then adopted it in *On the Road* to designate his own name. Surrounding Crumb's Denver scene are several typically Crumbian images—a man slouched asleep in his chair in front of the television; an overweight girl; a hip, nattily dressed dog with an empty alcohol bottle on the ground; two discombobulated men—a sad America filled with Ginsberg's "fallen angels" who wander through an alienating, cold, loveless spiritual wasteland.

Crumb was also most likely attracted to Kerouac due to the central role jazz euphoria plays in *On the Road*: during his time in Cleveland, Crumb often met with Harvey Pekar, Marty Pahls, and other friends to discuss and trade their recordings of jazz and blues. This period is chronicled in Pekar and Crumb's "The Young Crumb Story," which appeared in *American Splendor*, no. 4 (1979). Indeed, it has been argued that jazz greats such as Thelonious Monk, Charlie Parker, and Charles Mingus performed the role of shaman—they set out on imaginative voyages to higher realms and brought therapeutic joy to their listeners—in the counterculture. As we shall see in the following chapter, Crumb considered jazz performers—in particular musicians from the earlier generation such as Jelly Roll Morton, Charley Patton, and Robert Johnson—as conduits to aesthetic ecstasy. Jazz and the speed of postwar American life as represented by the automobile and the new transcontinental system of highways instituted by Dwight D. Eisenhower are obviously connected in Kerouac's imagination, and Crumb's *Sketchbooks* contain innumerable depictions of automobiles: he tries his hand at drawing countless American models. Crumb is at once memorializing in a vivid and lifelike way the power cars assumed in American life, particularly in the period following World War II, as symbol of unlimited mobility and personal freedom, as well as a certain threatening quality he catches in the absurd complexity of some of the designs with their elaborate, menacing tailfins and bizarre body shapes. Kerouac's "jazzy" portrayal of urban American youth and car culture in the post–World War II period influenced Crumb's own prose style as may be seen in one of Crumb's letters dated June 27, 1963, in which the nineteen-year-old describes nightlife in Cleveland: "Outside the night air is hot and thick. . . . Restless people walk around aimlessly . . . sit on doorsteps, porches—lean out of windows. . . . Convertibles tear down 107th Street at breakneck speed—run you down if you don't watch out. . . . Rock 'n' roll comes out of the jukebox in here. . . . Hopeless lost teenage cravings never satisfied."[9] It is evident that key elements of *On the Road*, which Crumb had read three years earlier—both stylistic and spiritual—had remained in his imagination.

As I have argued, there is an interrelationship between Crumb's reading of literature and the ways he then incorporates themes raised by his reading into his own work—sometimes directly through autobiography, and sometimes through the "disguise" of the multitudinous, Shakespearean cast of characters he invented. When we turn from a consideration of *On the Road*, we can see that Buddhist and Hindu themes began to permeate Crumb's work beginning in the late sixties. For example, Crumb first introduced his characters Jippo and Boopsy—"those cute, adorable little Bearzy Wearzies"—in 1968, and in an installment of the series appearing in *CoEvolution Quarterly* (Winter 1979–1980), the first two frames depict Jippo as he ponders life's "big questions." He turns to Boopsy and asks earnestly: "How do you even *begin* to untangle yourself from the big illusion? We are conditioned from birth to accept a certain view of reality! There are layers upon layers of these habitual responses!!" Boopsy counsels him to "practice detachment," and he will then come to realize that he is "in a big movie." The notion of existence as a "movie" in which humans enact roles for the possible amusement of a "higher power" recurs in Crumb's repeated employment of the image of a bunny rabbit with a camera looking down on the usually crazy proceedings of his comics. The illusive quality of a "movie" is underscored here by Crumb's reference to the Hindu concept of Maya—the phenomenal world is illusory—and the struggle to arrive at an "authentic" self that has been liberated from conditioning.

Another example occurs in Crumb's *Sketchbooks* in which he depicts two comical figures dancing a kind of Laurel and Hardy vaudeville act with an epigraph from "an old 1950s Rockabilly Song," "Keep On Dancin' an' Aprancin'": on several *Sketchbook* pages containing "spiritual" or "philosophical" excerpts, Crumb often appends a comical frame from a song as commentary. In a box to the right, we find a quotation from Hayao Kawai's—a Japanese Jungian psychotherapist—*The Buddhist Priest Myoe: A Life of Dreams*, a study of a thirteenth-century Buddhist priest:

In Buddhism, the universe is divided into the realms of desire, form, and formlessness. Those who are filled with lust reside in the realm of desire. Those residing in the realm of form have transcended their attachments to lust and appetite and are said to live in a world of subtle and exquisite substance. This realm is divided into seventeen heavens, with akanistha as the highest. The realm of formlessness transcends all physical existence and is said to be composed of spirit only.

This struggle between flesh and spirit recurs throughout the *Sketchbooks* and Crumb's work as a whole, and it is revelatory that he had obviously read thoroughly Kawai's book on Myoe—a singular figure in the history of Japanese Buddhism—and selected this particular passage for illustration. The Buddhist themes he encountered in the Beats stimulated Crumb to a reading of original texts as well as commentaries on Buddhist thought, and here we find another exemplary case of how he seamlessly incorporated his reading into his art.

Finally, Crumb's masterful comic "Bad Karma" (created 1998; published 1999 in *Mystic Funnies*, no. 2) explores the concept of karma, deriving from the Sanskrit word *karman* meaning literally "action" (the consequences of a person's behavior in past incarnations must be faced in one's present life) within the context of a comical tale depicting an ugly, long-nosed character—his nose obviously phallic in shape and size—named "the Moron." The title on the splash page, "Bad Karma," drips with the identical spooky, viscous liquid that, as we shall see in chapter 4, is featured at the beginning of Crumb's illustrations for Jean-Paul Sartre's *Nausea*. Crumb depicts a series of heads that the Moron must literally walk over to "get ahead"—with the obvious implied pun—in life, thus implying the complex web of causality that the concept of karma involves. The cover of *Mystic Funnies* shows the Moron telling us: "Why do they make me do this?! I don't enjoy it! I really don't!" implying that the suffering he is inflicting on others is beyond his control. Crumb may have been influenced by Samuel Beckett's plays in which only talking heads appear on stage. Beckett's overwhelming sense of absurdity and meaninglessness suffuses "Bad Karma." The Moron wears different clothes as the narrative progresses: at the opening he is in shorts, long-sleeved shirt, and tie, and is wearing huge shoes. As he tramples the heads, he exhibits Crumb's typical erotic voracity. A God-like voice and hand appear from the sky and awakens the Moron from his slumber after he has achieved sexual satisfaction with one of the female mouths in his path. "God" instructs the Moron not to look at him, commanding that he continue his journey for "another thousand miles or so" over the heads, which have now been mysteriously frozen into stone. The Moron gratefully realizes suddenly that he is actually caught in a recurring bad dream, but "God" tells him: "As for what's 'real' and what isn't, *you* figure it out." Here we encounter the recurring Crumbian theme of reality/appearance, and we can see the similarity of the structure of "Bad Karma" and the many dreams Crumb recounts involving initiatory spiritual quests.

The Moron now reaches the edge of a huge abyss. Told by "God" to jump, he faces an existential crisis. In "Can You Stand Alone and Face Up to the

Universe?," the Crumb character arrives at a similar moment of choice, telling us: "I dive head-on into infinity—throw myself on the mercy of the void," and leaps into the blackness. This is at once a "fall" but also a "leap" as in Søren Kierkegaard's "leap of faith" as well as the thrownness—*Geworfenheit*—of Martin Heidegger. So too, in "Bad Karma," the Moron reaches an "abyss" and has to "jump." He is now fed up and confronts "God" and, as he looks in his direction, is pulverized into a dripping mass of gooey liquid with his two eyeballs floating in it, which begins to drip down into the abyss. The narrative is now interrupted: Mr. Natural appears, informing readers that they have now been caught in the fictional reality of the comic book and proceeding to both insult and flatter, cautioning us about "the power of the Media, man." He then tells us: "Okay, let's get back to the Moron now. . . . I wonder how he's going to get out of *this* fix, don't you??" Mr. Natural, the trickster wise guru, thus exhorts us to consider the ways the media today "conditions" us to become the way we are. If we are assenting to the "reality" of the illusion of a comic book that has taken us into its fictional/real world, perhaps we are again being manipulated into believing yet another illusion, but now by the puppeteer controlling the strings beyond the comic strip—R. Crumb himself.

The cycle of reincarnation now begins as the Moron-as-dripping-liquid-mass slowly transforms into a fetus-like creature and then a recognizable infant: he is born again into a new self. Now embraced by a naked, large, and smiling mother figure—identified on the cover of *Mystic Funnies* as "Fairy Godmother"—he delights in her as she takes care of him. Crumb here is depicting his reincarnation, a chance to make amends for his mistakes in his prior life. He emerges naked, swiftly seems to grow in stature as the frames progress, is clothed by his new "mother" in a long, Hindu-like smock, and engages in typically Crumbian sexual hijinx with his voluptuous mate— which goes on for a full twelve pages—at the close of which the Moron is completely naked. Fairy Godmother then has her fill and abandons him, instructing the Moron: "You have to make it through that dark woods over there—the legendary 'impenetrable forest!'" In the recently published *R. Crumb's Dream Diary* (2018), Crumb recounts a similar scenario in a dream in which he struggles through a labyrinth seeking initiation by a guru figure, but ultimately fails this spiritual test. Here too Crumb is alluding to the quest motif in world mythology. Now garbed in "warrior" clothes and equipped with a sword and shears a woman gives him, the Moron reluctantly leaves on his quest as Apollo arrives to pick up the woman, whom we are now told is actually Cassandra. Apollo and Cassandra depart on a horse, and the Moron strives valiantly to cut his way through a labyrinthine forest. The last twenty panels depict the Moron going through the forest, become increasingly smaller and smaller until in the last five panels his face gradually disappears into nothingness as he is submerged by the dense branches. "Bad Karma" also alludes to the myth of Lancelot, Guinevere, and King Arthur, for Lancelot has to make his way through a forest. Before Pentecost, a lovely woman comes to the castle of King Arthur and asks Lancelot to follow her into the woods. So too here, the Moron is clothed like a knight with a sword and the clothing of a warrior. Thus Crumb here at once pays homage and parodies the spiritual quest motif by combining the Hindu/Buddhist concept of karma with the Western myth of Apollo and Cassandra as well as the King Arthur cycle. Is the Moron being "rewarded" or "punished" for the actions of his prior life with his erotic free-for-all with Fairy Godmother/Cassandra? As we lose sight of him in his effort to find his way out of the "impenetrable" forest, will he perish in the attempt and be reborn again to face yet another cycle of karmic challenges?

The idea of karma appears throughout Crumb's work. For example, in one of his *Sketchbooks*, Crumb emphasizes the quest for spiritual progress, declaring that "[e]verything we do has significance. Every action, every thought leaves an imprint—not only on the self, but on the world, on the others, and even on time, on all who come after us. This implies a responsibility for one's thoughts and actions that should be taken most seriously!" Crumb also echoes the language of the Bhagavad Gita here with "thoughts and actions." Crumb alludes to karma in *Sketchbook*, vol. 9, where he depicts himself wide awake in bed, eyes starkly open: "Woke up in the middle of the night. Lay there in the dark thinking . . . about a tedious and irritating dream I just had . . . about how yer karma catches up with you." Crumb's affinity for Hindu thought is confirmed by his masterly depiction in his *Sketchbooks* of A. C. Bhaktivedanta, Swami Prabhupada, who founded the Hare Krishna movement in Los Angeles in 1965: the International Society for Krishna Consciousness.

This respectful portrait of the guru is based on a color photograph that appears as the frontispiece to Bhaktivedanta's translation and commentary on the Sri Isopanisad, one of the briefest of the Upanishads, consisting of eighteen verses. It is clear that Crumb had familiarized himself with this text, for above his drawing, he includes an excerpt: "A living being who lives in the mundane world has four defects: (1) He is certain to commit mistakes, (2) He is subject to illusion, (3) He has a propensity to cheat others, and (4) His senses are imperfect." This excerpt is from Bhaktivedanta's comments on "Mantra One," and the subsequent text reads: "Being conditioned by these four imperfections, one cannot deliver perfect information of all-pervading knowledge. The Vedas are not produced by such imperfect creatures. Vedic

"A LIVING BEING WHO LIVES IN THE MUNDANE WORLD HAS FOUR DEFECTS: (1) HE IS CERTAIN TO COMMIT MISTAKES, (2) HE IS SUBJECT TO ILLUSION, (3) HE HAS A PROPENSITY TO CHEAT OTHERS, AND (4) HIS SENSES ARE IMPERFECT.

~ HIS DIVINE GRACE A.C. BHAKTIVEDANTA SWAMI PRABHUPADA, 1960s

R. Crumb, "His Divine Grace A. C. Bhaktivedanta Swami Prabhupada," 1960s, *Sketchbook*, vol. 10.

knowledge was originally imparted into the heart of Brahma, the first created living being, and Brahma in his turn disseminated this knowledge to his sons and disciples, who have handed down the process through history." Crumb at once sought with this portrait and text both to render homage to Bhaktivedanta, who was a central figure in the dissemination of Hinduism to the counterculture—Allen Ginsberg would seek Bhaktivedanta out and establish a relationship with him—and to draw attention to a recurring theme in his own spiritual quest: the imperfection and fragility of humanity.

Crumb was thus thoroughly immersed in many of the same aspects of spiritual search as the Beats, and he was familiar not only with *On the Road* but also with Kerouac's *The Dharma Bums* (1958), which popularized Zen as well as environmental awareness for the hippie generation. Ginsberg, when he came to California, hiked in the Sierras with poet Gary Snyder, who had become one of the foremost advocates in the nascent ecological movement. Crumb himself would contribute several works to *CoEvolution Quarterly*, which was devoted to environmental topics. He also illustrated Edward Abbey's *The Monkey Wrench Gang*, and of course his famous "A History of America" depicts a country being taken over by ugly cities and rampant pollution. Other "antitechnological" works Crumb contributed to *CoEvolution Quarterly* include—in the Fall 1977 issue—"R. Crumb on Assignment for the CE Goes to the Space Day Symposium (Or Whatever the Hell It Was Called)," which pillories the US space program as a dangerous, militaristic enterprise.[10]

Thus Crumb submitted several important works to *CoEvolution Quarterly*, and he continued with the theme of California Zen in a work published in the magazine entitled "Those Dharma Bhums" in 1979, created a decade after Kerouac's death in 1969. Crumb alters Kerouac's title slightly—"Bhums" for "Bums"—perhaps to create a sly sense of comedy in the repetition of *Dh*arma and *Bh*ums. These are not regular American "bums," but rather their appellation has been translated into Sanskrit to symbolize their pursuit of the Buddhist concept of dharma, or "right living," "cosmic law and order." In Crumb's three-and-three-quarter-page, twenty-two-panel narrative, the male character is named "Jaf," an obvious reference to Kerouac's novel, in which the poet Gary Snyder is named "Japhy Ryder." Jack Kerouac is "Ray Smith" in *The Dharma Bums*, and the two writers engage in dialogue throughout concerning the relative merits of Christianity and Buddhism. The novel is also noteworthy as an important document in the emerging ecological movement of the fifties and sixties: Japhy takes city-dweller Ray on a mountain-climbing trek through the Sierras. Kerouac opens up the theme of preserving the environment as one of the central goals of the counterculture. Crumb had alluded to Zen mountaineers previously in the wildly comic "Ducks Yas Yas," published in *Zap*, no. 0 (October 1967), which features a junkie hipster who narrates a stream-of-consciousness tale of his trip west, where he "wound up on ol' Haight Street. Dropped acid for three weeks. Man, it was intergalactic! Split outa that freak show with a truckload of Zen monks. Doin' the spiritual thing up in the mountains! Whatever's right, man! Wow!"[11]

R. Crumb, "Those Dharma Bhums," *CoEvolution Quarterly* (Summer 1979).

Crumb transforms Kerouac's *The Dharma Bums* plot in several ways while adhering to its essential themes. Jaf and Suzette converse in a hipster café with a wine-bottle candle on the table: the girl wears a turtleneck sweater, while Jaf sports a goatee and mop-top haircut. Paul Morris has observed that in Crumb's work "the characters were so beautifully and uniquely rendered that they could have existed without speech bubbles. Each 'scene' was so well composed that the shifts in scenery from panel to panel resulted in a clear narrative."[12] Crumb here achieves this easy flow through his careful framing and by punctilious employment of details: the burning candle emits a whiff of smoke and casts a halo-like glow. White is contrasted with an encroaching black background emerging and receding at key points in the dialogue to enhance dramatic tension. Sweat flies from Jaf's face at intense moments: motion lines and clouds underline the action as he points repeatedly to his forehead. In "Meatball" (1967), published in *Zap*, no. 0—in which chunks of hamburger arriving unbidden from the skies induce miraculous enlightenment in those who are lucky enough to be struck by the meaty missiles—Crumb had previously depicted a "beatnik who was always high." He snaps his fingers rhythmically, carries a saxophone, and wears sandals and torn pants, while flies and smell signs indicate that he has not bathed recently. He has donned sunglasses and spouts hipster lingo—"crazy man, crazy!," "like cool!," "too much baby! Like, wow!"[13] Here, however, in "Those Dharma Bhums," Jaf discusses with Suzette contemporary issues such as the depredations of oil companies and the threat of nuclear power but then badgers her as a "narcissistic little prancing princess!"

As they drink Burgundy wine, Jaf arises and bites Suzette on the shoulder, declaring in his less than elegant English: "I know . . . I should be locked up in a Zen monastery for five years—Hey! Y'know what? They oughta turn all the prisons inta Zen monasteries!" Suzette then responds: "But, Jaf, I see our problems as basically political rather than religious . . . why d'you think people end up in prisons in th'first place?," and in the next panel: "Well, doesn't it seem like you've got to give people a fair shake in the world before you can expect them to pursue high spiritual states of consciousness?" Jaf returns with: "Talk Talk Talk . . . I think I must go mad!," a variation on Kerouac's famous lines in *On the Road*: "The only people for me are the mad ones, the ones who are mad to live, mad to talk, mad to be saved, desirous of everything at the same time, the ones who never yawn or say a commonplace thing."[14] Jaf now declares that he wants to escape the world's sorrows by backpacking in the Sierras, hoping to "spend about a week up there eating nuts an' raisins an' talking to God." Crumb returns to Suzette's argument in the *Sketchbooks* (September 24, 1975), in which he writes:

> Cessation of desire is a spiritual quest which can obviously only come into the mind of a person who is socially in a position where the physical struggle for survival has been made secure, and the threat of hunger, the need for shelter, economic security, etc. is not a main consideration.... The spiritual aspiration of "cessation of desire" cannot be expected of people who have not secured their basic physical needs and mental security.... Therefore, it does not behoove the man or woman involved in the spiritual quest to lay judgements on the folks who are in a lesser economic class than they.

Thus Crumb recapitulates Suzette's question: "Well, doesn't it seem like you've got to give people a fair shake in the world before you can expect them to pursue high spiritual states of consciousness?" Crumb returns often to this central Buddhist concept, "the cessation of desire": that suffering is related to desire, hence we must try to control our desires. Yet as Suzette points out, this is in a sense a problem that only those who have enough to eat and a warm place to sleep at night have the luxury of confronting. The poor don't worry about "cessation of desire" since only the bourgeois and upper classes don't have to be concerned about where their next meal is coming from: their desire is to eat something or die.

Crumb stays close to the narrative of *The Dharma Bums*, in which Kerouac and Snyder indeed spent time hiking in the Sierras, where they engaged in philosophical discussions. However, before Jaf goes off to the mountains to seek God, Suzette invites him to her place to make love, bringing him down from his idealistic goals to the pleasures of the flesh. Jaf is an emotionally labile comic character, since through the panels he appears variously stunned, angry, bored, apoplectic, and sozzled. He tells her that she is the first person to whom he has ever confessed: "My worst fear, Suzette, is that I might contrive to be authentic ... that I create a myth out of this shoddy existence, instead of looking for the truth!" Suzette again pokes fun at his pretensions, saying: "Truth Truth ... Men are such fools," and takes him home to bed and erotic pleasure. Crumb ends with a statement at the bottom of the final panel: "And Good-Night, Jack, wherever you are!!" Thus Crumb bases his strip on Kerouac's work but also introduces sharply satirical elements, reminding us that Alan Watts famously criticized the Beats in his essay "Beat Zen, Square Zen, and Zen" for misunderstanding the true nature of Zen philosophy. Crumb employs *The Dharma Bums* as a springboard for humorous minidrama—including at the same time some of his own personal fetishes such as biting and climbing on women's backs as he exclaims "women know that Truth is only right here in this animal moment!!"—on the confluence of the ecological, spiritual, and erotic themes of the Beat generation as updated for the hippie generation of the sixties.

Clearly, the Buddhist themes that pervade Beat literature also appear frequently in Crumb's work. During the fifties, Zen began to influence figures in the artistic, musical, and literary worlds. D. T. Suzuki emerged as a significant figure in the dissemination of Zen philosophy, and several American artists and composers—including John Cage—were influenced by his writings. Cage would actually lecture on Huang Po, a Zen thinker who as we shall see would also intrigue Crumb. Zen Buddhists "considered the boundary between self and not-self an illusion to be shattered," and Crumb was always pushing at the limits of the Self.[15] As we have argued previously, Crumb incorporates themes from literature, philosophy, and religious thought into his own oeuvre, and one of his greatest characters—Mr. Natural—has many aspects in common with Zen Buddhist traditions, while his name has its origins in African American culture. In 1966, while staying with Marty Pahls, Crumb was listening to a radio station and recalled: "Some jive instrumental plays and the announcer says, 'That was Mr. Natural.' Based on the natural hairdo, the African natural. I wrote Mr. Natural in my sketchbook and I spontaneously started drawing this little tiny comic strip about this bearded sage." Crumb has revealed that on occasion, "a spontaneous sketchbook drawing would inspire a whole comic-book story, or even a character. Mr. Natural and many other characters started as casual, off-the-cuff sketchbook drawings." Mr. Natural is the epitome of Nature, for he takes no guff from anyone and has the energy and willpower of a Natural Force, yet at the same time is fully aware that he is himself a con artist. Many of the Mr. Natural episodes suggest, as Arthur Berger has observed, that

> there is a great deal that is fraudulent and even silly in mysticism. After all, Mr. Natural is a fake and his disciple Flakey is a fool: so much of a fool, in fact, that he thinks his guru has great powers and refuses to be disillusioned. . . . In fact, Mr. Natural seems to have contempt for Flakey and all that he stands for. . . . Mr. Natural is really a conservative character who is playing the guru for all it is worth; he dupes the well-intentioned but naïve members of the counterculture, who lack discrimination, but seem to have discretionary income. He is the perfect prototype of the *hip capitalist* and seems to have nothing but contempt for those who follow him and are exploited by him.[16]

However, Mr. Natural also has much in common with a Zen Buddhist teacher, and in his first incarnation, he is indeed identified as a "Zen Master" in *Yarrowstalks*, no. 1 (May 5, 1967)—named after the yarrowstalks that are thrown in the Chinese book of divination, the *I Ching*—and in *Zap*, no. 1 (February 1968): in later installments, the "Zen Master" subtitle was removed. Mr. Natural's physical attributes—here he looks a bit like a psychoanalyst but in later versions resembles an avuncular Santa Claus—would change in subsequent renditions. This is true for Fritz the Cat as well, who became progressively more "countercultural" as Crumb's imagination evolved. Yet it is clear from the outset that Mr. Natural represents the tough-minded orientation of a Zen teacher who will not abide any nonsense from his spiritual aspirants. He is named "Mr. Natural" because he indeed strives—as all Zen Buddhists do—to return the mind to its "natural" state of integration within the cosmos rather than only a separate ratiocinative organ that breaks up, analyzes, and attempts to "understand" reality. He also embodies the humor that is typical of Zen training. In one early strip, when his student asks, "Mr. Natural, what's the answer?" he responds, "What's the question." Mr. Natural also counsels, "get the right tool for the job," which is the same idea: ask the right question! For Mr. Natural as for the logical positivists, questions of "meaning"—generalized, vague, "metaphysical" questions—are literally nonsensical unless one asks about the significance of a *specific* thing. In the various incarnations of the series over the years, Flakey Foont—he is "flakey," that is, eccentric and crazy—will become Mr. Natural's pupil, although other characters such as Shuman the Human also seek him out for his wisdom. Crumb tells us in the fantastic biography he invented, filling in the varied details of "Fred" Natural's colorful prior life, that he had traveled in Asia, was a jazz musician, was a faith healer during the 1920s, and also worked in Afghanistan as a taxi driver. Some of this background recalls the Armenian Greek guru G. I. Gurdjieff (1866–1949), whose *Meetings with Remarkable Men* recounts Gurdjieff's travels through Asia in search of esoteric knowledge. Gurdjieff was also known for his wild humor and seemingly nonsensical instructions given to his students, as well as his sometimes-astringent treatment of his followers. Among his well-known pupils was the short-story writer Katherine Mansfield, who attended his meetings at the Institute for the Harmonious Development of Man in Fontainebleau near Paris during the twenties. Henry Miller also became fascinated by Gurdjieff and his philosophy.[17] Mr. Natural is thus a kind of syncretic guru, composed of elements of a Zen Master, Gurdjieff, and a stand-up comedian. Mr. Natural also does not suffer fools gladly. He is not averse—like both Gurdjieff and Zen Masters—to give his disciples such as Flakey a hard blow to the rear end when the disciple fails to learn a lesson.

In *Yarrowstalks*, Mr. Natural instructs his pupil to look out the window, and he obeys. He then asks three questions, which irritates his teacher: "Is there no end to these questions?" The purpose of Zen is precisely to encourage the student to cease asking "why" and to live in the moment without the interference of ego. The discipline of Zen is to bring the mind to an awareness of the *thisness* of reality, to move beyond the traps of language toward the wisdom of silence. In six economical panels, Crumb has encapsulated in a humorous way the essence of Zen teaching. In another strip featuring Shuman the Human entitled "Let's Be Honest," Shuman announces to a crowd of people his brilliant thought: "Let's all stop playing ego games right now!" He is perhaps attempting to implement some of the wisdom imparted to him by his sessions with Mr. Natural. He says the word "GO!" to announce the beginning of the experiment, which is followed by two panels with no speech bubbles depicting Shuman with arms crossed and the crowd waiting for the results. He then declares: "Wow! Now wasn't that a great idea," and the next and final panel shows Shuman abashed and exclaiming "OOPS!" upon realizing that he has violated his own principle by bragging. The very fact that Zen is indeed often *funny* of course would make it attractive to Crumb, who frequently sought to puncture the pretensions of institutionalized, group religious dogma and to arrive closer to some form—however "flawed"—of individual, existential authenticity. Here, Shuman's "honesty" is precisely the sudden realization that he has deceived himself regarding his own ability to be honest: it is in just such a paradox that the "truth" of Zen resides.

In "Mr. Natural: Zen Master," the bare room containing a single window with the sun changing location in each panel suggests that Crumb is alluding to a famous "visual koan" known variously as *Ten Oxherding Pictures* or *Ten Bulls*, which portray the moon as it moves across the night horizon. The text accompanying the illustrations reads: "Both the man and the animal have disappeared, no traces are left, / The bright moon-light is empty and shadowless with all the ten-thousand objects in it; / If anyone should ask the meaning of this. / Behold the lilies of the field and its fresh sweet-scented verdure."[18] Allen Ginsberg noted in a letter to Neal Cassady the impact the *Ten Oxherding Pictures* had on him and began to study D. T. Suzuki's *Introduction to Zen Buddhism*. In a May 14, 1953, letter to Cassady, Ginsberg narrated a number of koans, describing the moment of satori or illumination as "a specific flash of vision that totally changes" one's perception of reality. Ginsberg finds the Zen idea of God fascinating, for "they refuse to have a theology or admit that one exists, or anything verbal at all. That's the point of these anecdotes; to exhaust words. Then the man sees anew the universe." In contradistinction to the more cerebral and intellectualized Buddhistic traditions, Zen seeks an instant radical change in perception through two modes: in *zazen*, or meditation while sitting, the mind is cleared of all extraneous stimuli, and the practitioner concentrates on posture and breathing. In the second method, the koan is utilized to break the student's habit of logical, rational analysis. Ginsberg enjoyed the *Ten Oxherding Pictures* and sent the book to Cassady as a birthday present. The drawings emerged in twelfth-century China and would influence the school of Chan Buddhism. Enlightenment in the ten drawings is illustrated by the struggle to tame the bulls. At first, the bull and tamer are antagonists; in the following four, tamer and bull gradually ignore each other; and in the final two, first the bull disappears and then the tamer, and the final drawing is of a completely open circle: both bull and tamer have vanished. It is a marvelous allegory of the illusory nature of both tamer and bull, and of existence itself, and the final enlightenment is to return to the place from which one began.[19]

Crumb appears to allude to this Zen tradition again in "Mr. Natural's 719th Meditation" (1970), in which Mr. Natural sits in the desert to meditate, and as the "days pass into weeks" a tractor and automobiles appear as "civilization" arrives, with restaurants and a policeman who yells at him to move since he is "obstructin' traffic."[20] As Mr. Natural chants "MMMM"—a variation of course on the famous mantra *Om Mani Padme Om*—gradually the city implodes with earthquakes, floods, and hurricanes until the background returns to its original pristine form, with the sun gradually making its way across the horizon to the same spot at which the narrative begins, thus imitating precisely the structure of the *Ten Oxherding Pictures*.[21] The sequence also previews the concept that Crumb will develop in "A Short History of America" in its depiction of nature being overrun by the ugliness of big-city life.[22] During the progression of Mr. Natural's meditative experience, we enter a kind of timeless realm intended to suggest meditative calm (contrasting with the chaos all about in the real world), which Crumb conveys through his subtle method of conveying atemporal duration. Thierry Groensteen has pointed out that the first image of page 1 occupies a full-width panel, and so is well suited to the evocation of "desolate solitude." The rest of the story is made up of thirty-three rectangular panels of identical format. Mr. Natural remains almost completely still for the entire duration of the story until the last three images, when he finally stands up, stretches, rolls up his mat, and leaves, saying: "Wow, that was a pretty good session, boy." It is impossible to make a precise estimate of the "real" duration of the events represented. Crumb's description of "days pass into weeks" remains deliberately vague and aims only to suggest a protracted time span. We are thereby warned that the two images juxtaposed in space, even with more or less identical content, correspond not to immediately consecutive moments but to moments that are chronologically spaced out.[23]

Crumb is expert at conveying the way the passage of time seems to feel as if no time is passing at all: this is precisely the meditative "zone" that he sought to achieve in his LSD experiences, through his study of literature and world spiritual traditions, and indeed through his intense absorption in constantly creating drawings in his prolific *Sketchbooks*. It is also clear from these early Mr. Natural works that at the very outset of his career, Crumb began to incorporate Zen themes within his work derived from Beat generation literature as well as to invent his own Zen-related character, Mr. Natural, through whom he would expound several of the tenets of Zen thought.

For Crumb, this wordless movement of individual identity through time, which returns the self to zero as at the beginning, is a recurring motif. For example, "Bo Bo Bolinsky: He's the Number One Human Zero," which appeared in *Uneeda Comix* in 1970, is neatly composed on the page in three tiers of three panels. The work opens with Bo Bo sitting in his chair next to a lamp with his hat on, arms folded; and in the following eight panels he is portrayed in full close-up: from the back of his chair; from the left; from the space above him looking down on his hat; from bottom left looking upward; just his shoes; full frontal; and finally a close-up from the right side. He says nothing, his expression remains the same, yet the cumulative effect powerfully conveys a sense of inviolate solitude and the relentless movement of time going forward, yet also time standing utterly still. He remains quiescent, nothing happens, yet everything happens—Crumb here again resembles Samuel Beckett—and there is also a comic element in his stolid imperturbability. As the subtitle informs us, Bo Bo Bolinsky is "the Number One Human Zero": his being begins and ends in the stillness of nonaction, of zero, of nothing—and perhaps as in the *Ten Oxherding Pictures*, Zen wisdom lies in accepting that there is no Self and that a good deal of human activity that passes for meaning is actually meaningless.

A similar effect is achieved through an opposite artistic technique in "I'm a Ding Dong Daddy" from *Zap*, no. 1. The wild, comic energy here jumps off the page, with the big-shoed, whacky figure walking, flying off the pavement, skidding, dancing, banging his head against a wall, flying, breaking into pieces, turning himself into a wordless cloud, then a wordless thought bubble without himself attached, and returning at the end with the empty thought bubble above his head as he began. "I'm a Ding Dong Daddy" is a small masterpiece in eighteen panels, a work that would have been instantly understandable to a Zen monk. Here is the Zen experience of *kensho*, which is the enlightenment that arrives when one realizes that paradise is right now, this moment, and that time is an illusion. In the three-page "R. Crumb Presents R. Crumb," which appeared in *Zap*, no. 7 (1974)—each page containing four neat tiers of three panels each—Crumb depicts himself addressing his audience largely in silence. He opens with "Hi folks!"; however, out of the twenty-four panels on the first two pages, he only begins to speak in the final three on the second page. Before that, he pictures himself either yawning, laughing, picking his teeth, spitting, examining his fingernails, hanging his head, looking sideways, or staring sheepishly. In the first of the final three panels, he finally tells us: "I . . . uh . . . fixed my toilet yesterday . . . and . . . uhhh"; then in the next panel continues: ". . . works good now . . . and . . . uh . . ."; and in the final panel, "And . . . uuuhhh . . ." Crumb begins the final page, first panel, and admits: "What's the use . . . I don't have anything to say . . . It's hard to get up here and—" then "Wait . . . I know what! I'll sing a song!!" and begins to sing Joyce Kilmer's poem "I think I shall never see a poem as lovely as a tree." In the first of the final three panels, he hangs his head and haltingly concludes: "Well . . ."; then ". . . that about wraps it up, I guess . . ."; and the final panel shows him facing the viewer in complete silence. The fact that he has nothing to say is what he wants to say. Art Spiegelman has declared: "Comics are a highly charged medium, delivering densely concentrated information in relatively few words and simplified code-images. It seems to me that this is a model of how the brain formulates thoughts and remembers. We think in cartoons." In Zen, one moves from Point A all the way back to Point A; as T. S. Eliot declared in "Little Gidding" from *Four Quartets*: "We shall not cease from exploring / And the end of all our exploring / Will be to arrive where we started / And know the place for the first time." Crumb's genius is to make such a profound statement but with incredible comic verve.

As we have seen, Mr. Natural also often encounters Shuman the Human as well as Flakey Foont. In an installment published in the *East Village Other* 3, no. 10 (1968), Shuman is engaged in a program of frenetic research on "several projects" to uncover the secret of existence. Mr. Natural informs Shuman that his mother is worried about him: Shuman agrees that she thinks he is "a real mental case." Mr. Natural instructs him to cease his mad quest and asks him if he has "ever investigated a raindrop." Shuman—whose face in the earlier panels is chiseled into shapes resembling a cyborg—takes the advice and with his microscope discovers within a raindrop his own heart: his face now becomes human instead of robot-like. As we noted in the earlier Shuman iteration, when he is on a quest on the streets of San Francisco, his physical head is again the locus of psychological/spiritual transformation. But now, at the moment of enlightenment, he is suddenly approached by two men in white coats who have come to take him away to a mental institution. Mr.

Natural reappears and tells us: "Tsk Tsk! A rotten shame ... But see? That's what happens!" He then farewells the reader with: "So listen, all you smart kids! Get really hip! Come on out and get acquainted! Talk with us! Let us tell you about our easy terms! Long range benefits! No obligations! So long for now!" Shuman appears to have reached an authentic revelatory moment that recalls William Blake's famous "Auguries of Innocence": "To see Heaven in a Grain of Sand / And Heaven in a Wild Flower / Hold Infinity in the palm of your hand / And Eternity in an Hour." But instead of a grain of sand, Shuman finds the hidden mystery of existence inside a raindrop: in esoteric lore, the microcosm contains the macrocosm, as above so below. Finding one's true Self within the heart is of course also a common trope in Hindu and Buddhist literature, and it is possible—given his familiarity with other Hindu and Buddhist texts—that Crumb was acquainted with the Chandogya Upanishad, one of the oldest Upanishads, which counsels:

> There is this city of Brahman (the body), and in it the palace, the small lotus of the heart, and in it that small ether. Now what exists within that small ether, that is to be sought for, that is to be understood. . . . And as here on earth, whatever has been acquired by exertion per- ishes, so perishes whatever is acquired for the next world by sacrifices and other good actions performed on earth. Those who depart from hence without having discovered the Self and those true desires, for them there is no freedom in all the worlds. But those who depart from hence, after having discovered the Self and those true desires, for them there is freedom in all the worlds.

Yet Shuman's discovery literally "cracks him up" in the eyes of the rest of humanity, and Mr. Natural makes of the whole episode a cosmic joke. This is a typical Crumb narrative strategy: to at once appear to recommend undertaking a spiritual quest, to energize his characters to embark on such a search, and then to comically deflate their efforts at the end. Both Flakey Foont/Shuman and Mr. Natural symbolize the twin poles of Crumb's own psychological orientation: on the one hand, the sensitive, "Beat" spiritual seeker; on the other, the cynical and hard-nosed realist who doubts and mocks all efforts to arrive at a final meaning or "answer."

In his more recent work, Crumb has also explored Buddhist literature through a direct adaptation of Zen texts: for example, in *Sketchbook*, vol. 11, he has illustrated *The Zen Teachings of Huang Po*. The *Sketchbooks* allow Crumb to try out ideas, test their feasibility, and consider whether or not to pursue a larger project based on his first attempts. Here Crumb may have

THE ZEN TEACHINGS OF HUANG PO

TRANSLATED BY JOHN BLOFELD

R. Crumb, "The Zen Teachings of Huang Po," *Sketchbook*, vol. 11.

been considering adapting a larger section of Huang Po—a Chinese Zen master thought to have died around 850 CE—but thus far has illustrated just two pages from *The Zen Teachings of Huang Po: On the Transmission of Mind*. Crumb takes his text from "The Wan Ling Record of the Zen Master Huang Po (Tuan Chi)," which is an extract from part 2.[24] As in the Mr. Natural series, Crumb plays on the paradox between Zen teaching and Zen teacher. Again, the relationship between master and pupil is fraught with misunderstanding, for the students are expecting to be passively led toward enlightenment by a wise leader, but of course they have to ultimately arrive there by their own strenuous efforts rather than through the intercession of their master. Northrop Frye includes a cryptic reference in his *Notebooks* to "the iron bar in Zen," which alludes to "the discipline and effort required for enlightenment in Zen Buddhism: the candidate who has been assigned a koan must work at this task 'like a mosquito biting on an iron bar.'" This is a theme that Crumb returns to repeatedly, for example in his illustration to the Indian guru Babaji in which a man seeks "answers" and is rebuffed by Babaji for expecting easy answers to his baffling questions.

On the first page containing four panels, Huang Po is depicted wearing sandals, speaking from a raised dais to an assembled throng of attentive disciples against a backdrop of imposing mountains. Huang Po wears the small cap and goatee of a Chinese sage, his posture bent in the attitude of an elderly wise man. In the first panel, his hands point and gesticulate as he speaks, and his expression remains throughout dispassionate. He tells the assembled students that they are "like drunkards," while in the second panel he emphasizes: "It all seems so easy so why do we have to see a day like this?? Can't you understand that in the whole empire of T'ang there are no 'teachers skilled in Zen'?" Here Crumb has left Huang Po out of the frame with just the speech bubble extended from the first panel indicating that he is still speaking: Crumb now concentrates on the attentive faces of nine of the students. When in the third panel one pupil questions how it can be that Huang Po can make such an assertion, Huang Po declares that he "did not say there is no Zen ... I merely pointed out that there are no teachers!" Here Crumb depicts Huang Po's audience with question marks hovering above their heads. On the second page of four panels, the scene has shifted to a discussion between Wei Shan and Yang Shan concerning the teachings of Huang Po in a simple hut, with a cracked wall and wooden beams on the ceiling. Yang Shan is seated on the ground on a mat, cross-legged, hands folded in his lap, with two bowls and a larger urn in the corner. Yang Shan tells Wei Shan that Huang Po's teaching implies the following: "That swan is able to extract the pure milk from the adulterated mixture. It is very clear that he is not just an ordinary duck!" In the third panel, Wei Shan, touching his beard, exclaims "AH!," and in the fourth: "Yes, the point he made was very subtle." At the conclusion, Yang Shan sits impassively with the same expression in both panels, unmoving and not responding. Crumb has caught in a concise two-page, eight-panel form the essence of Zen Buddhism, pulling the viewer intimately into the vanished spiritual world of China of more than a thousand years ago. The clear and spare presentation, employing the most direct and elemental techniques of draftsmanship and storytelling, demonstrates—as in a piano sonata by Domenico Scarlatti—how much can be achieved by a master artist employing the simplest of materials.

As we have seen, Crumb explored the ecological and Buddhist themes in the work of Gary Snyder and Jack Kerouac and also responded to Kerouac's *On the Road* as an exemplar of the kind of extroverted engagement with experience that he envied. Yet he was also attracted by the transgressive books of William S. Burroughs, which featured the "straight-ahead prose" he preferred:

> Both *Junkie* and *Queer* are great. They're both written in this very dry, prose style. And his little thin book called the *Yage Letters*, which were letters he wrote back to Allen Ginsberg while he was in South America looking for this psychedelic Yage plant. That's a great book; great stuff. But the problem is, there's not enough of that, not enough of his straight-ahead prose. He just didn't think it was any good because he either couldn't get it published or it didn't sell. So then he wrote this gimmicky thing called *Naked Lunch*, which is mostly fantasy stuff and not very interesting to me, and that sold well. He made his reputation on *Naked Lunch*.[25]

Although Crumb has not yet illustrated any complete text by Burroughs, he possesses a wide knowledge of several of his works, even less well-known ones such as *Sidetripping*, which he illustrates in the *Sketchbooks*. The work of other comic writers such as Alan Moore are pervaded with occult and esoteric themes derived from several diverse sources including British Romantic poetry, Aldous Huxley's *The Doors of Perception*, and H. P. Lovecraft. Moore's *Promethea* (1999–2005) is packed with lore alluding to the chakras, Kabbalah, Neoplatonism, and tarot. In addition, Moore has commented upon his fascination with Burroughs:

> I do admire his style, but I suppose the biggest influence is his thinking, his theoretical work, some of which has been wild and extreme,

but the relationship he draws between the word and the image and the importance of both, I think, is significant. Burroughs tends to see the word and the image as the basis for our inner, and thus outer, realities. He suggests that the person who controls the word and the image controls reality. It seems to me a great pity that Burroughs hasn't done more comic-strip work himself given his interest in juxtaposition.

Moore goes on to cite "The Unspeakable Mr. Hart," drawn by Malcolm Mc-Neill, which appeared in the British underground *Cyclops*, no. 2 (August 1970)—"The First English Adult Comic Paper."[26] McNeill also collaborated with Burroughs on a project to illustrate Burroughs's exploration of Maya mythology, *Ah Pook Is Here*.[27] Crumb's friend S. Clay Wilson illustrated several Burroughs works such as "Fun City in Ba'Dan" and created the drawings for the German editions of *The Wild Boys* (*Die Wilden Boys*) and *Cities of the Red Night* (*Die Städte der Roten Nacht*).[28]

In contradistinction to his portraits of Ginsberg and Kerouac, Crumb depicts Burroughs somewhat mysteriously, in keeping with his moniker "L'Hombre Invisible"—the Invisible Man—with his right hand partially obscuring his face wearing his typically inscrutable smile, dressed as usual in his conservative suit with a dapper hat. When asked about his religious beliefs, Burroughs replied that he was a "Gnostic, Manichean, Ishmalian," and as we shall see in chapter 3, Crumb himself would become increasingly attracted to Gnosticism as his career progressed.[29] Crumb has been attracted by Burroughs's interests in the occult and the paranormal and became interested in several books that also intrigued Burroughs, such as Dion Fortune's *Psychic Self-Defense* (1930) and Whitley Strieber's *Communion* (1988) concerning alien abduction. Crumb also quotes or paraphrases from Alfred Korzybski—an author Burroughs admired—in *Sketchbook*, vol. 8: "Humans are different from other animals in that they have the ability to accumulate knowledge over time, and pass it down through generations. 'Time Binders' (Korzybski)"[30] Crumb has frequently recorded his dreams, and these accounts have been published in a number of issues of the magazine *Mineshaft* from 2009 to the present and recently collected in book form as *R. Crumb's Dream Diary* (2018). Robert A. Monroe's *Journeys out of the Body* (1971) was also a favorite book of Burroughs, and in chapter 16, "Preliminary Exercises," and chapter 17, "The Separation Process," Monroe provides techniques for achieving out-of-body states. Crumb records several experiments as well as examples of astral travel throughout *Dream Diary*. For example, in a dream dated July 18, 2002, he recalls "out of body experience followed by lucid dream." Crumb reveals that he "started practicing Robert Monroe's suggestion to focus on a point in front of your eyes, from the third-eye spot, and this seemed to have some effect." As we have noted previously, Crumb portrays the "Third Eye" in a number of his illustrations. Crumb also refers to "Buhlman"—William Buhlman, also an author on paranormal experiences: "I forgot to demand clarity, as Buhlman recommends, but I knew I was out-of-body." Crumb mentions in his *Dream Diary* "'[t]he land of the dead,' as William Burroughs called it in his dream diary"—this is a reference to Burroughs's own book devoted to his nightlife, *My Education: A Book of Dreams*. Crumb viewed Burroughs as

> a very eccentric character; very eccentric ideas and thoughts. He built himself an orgone box based upon the theories of Wilhelm Reich. He later got involved in Scientology and had his E-meter and used it as a way to psychically clear himself. He said it was his electrical Ouija board. He tried other stuff too, like out of body experience. I can relate to all that stuff because I'm interested in all that fringe, psychic experimentation also. But he was very serious about that stuff.

Crumb notes Burroughs's experimentation with Wilhelm Reich's (1897–1957) theories, and he has depicted Burroughs sitting quietly straight up, hands on knees in his orgone box, which presumably increases orgasmic potency.

The *Sketchbooks* contain bits of quotation from a wide variety of authors including Henry David Thoreau, Georges Bataille, and Philip Roth as well as Burroughs. Late in life, Burroughs became increasingly fond of cats, and a quotation from *The Cat Inside* (1992)—Burroughs's meditation on his fleet of feline companions—occurs at the foot of a page from *Sketchbook*, vol. 9: "All relationships are predicated on exchange, and every service has its price."[31] Crumb apparently had even read Ted Morgan's biography of Burroughs, *Literary Outlaw: The Life and Times of William S. Burroughs*, for in "People . . . Ya Gotta Love 'Em!," published in *Weirdo*, no. 26 (Fall 1989), Crumb created a three-page work, each panel crowded with squirming, fighting, angry, and obnoxious humans. As the Crumb character struggles through the crowd, in the final panel he manages to escape into a polluted ocean. The final quotation on a scroll is: "Sure as shit they will multiply their assholes into the polluted seas." This is from Morgan's account of Burroughs's experiences studying Scientology, and it is clear that Crumb has constructed a narrative that will culminate in this apocalyptic Burroughs prediction.

A writer in many ways diametrically opposed to Burroughs—Charles Bukowski—is also a Crumb favorite. It is predictable that due to Crumb's immersion in the Beats and the counterculture and his preference for the direct prose style of William Burroughs and Mark Twain—we recall that he admired Twain because "he puts it down simply and clearly, yet in a pleasant way that I like"—he would admire Bukowski as well. In the late sixties, Crumb created the cover and three illustrations for poet Doug Blazek's *All Gods Must Learn to Kill* (1968): Blazek was one of the earliest advocates of Bukowski's work which he published in his literary magazine *Olé*. Crumb first met Bukowski in the spring of 1972 through artist Robert Williams at a party given by Bukowski's then-girlfriend, Liza Williams. Bukowski told him: "You know, your stuff is good, kid. It's the real thing. Just keep away from the cocktail parties." Three years later, Crumb would complete his first illustration to accompany Bukowski's short story "Bop Bop Against That Curtain," published in *Arcade*, no. 3 (Fall 1975): the story had appeared originally in the *Los Angeles Free Press* (March 23, 1973) and subsequently in the collection *South of No North: Stories of the Buried Life* (1973). "Bop Bop against That Curtain" describes Bukowski's days as a teenager in Los Angeles attending burlesque shows: "There were three of us, me, Baldy, and Jimmy. Our big day was Sunday. On Sunday we met at Baldy's house and took the streetcar down to Main Street. Carfare was seven cents. There were two burlesque houses in those days, the Follies and the Burbank. We were in love with the strippers at the Burbank and the jokes were a little better so we went to the Burbank." The story surely appealed to Crumb, since it again evokes a pre–World War II America when there were still streetcars in Los Angeles, and, though it was the Depression, there were opportunities to experience the simple joys of life. On the splash page, Crumb depicts the smiling stripper entering the stage with the circular spotlight upon her, and on the right side as balance he places a circle cameo of Bukowski's face with his name on a scroll: as we shall see, Crumb would often employ the scroll as a nod to the style of the Classics Illustrated he had read as a young artist. In the audience with their eager faces, we see Bukowski, Baldy, and Jimmy awaiting the beginning of the show.

Crumb's professional association with Bukowski began when Bukowski's publisher, John Martin of Black Sparrow Press, asked Crumb to provide drawings for *Bring Me Your Love* (1983) and *There's No Business* (1984) as well as one of Bukowski's final works, the journal *The Captain Is Out to Lunch and the Sailors Have Taken Over the Ship* (1998). Crumb would also create a Bukowski poster—limited to three hundred copies—for Water Row Press in 1986.[32] Although Bukowski is not considered a member of the Beat generation, as we have seen, his style and philosophy have several links to the movement: his pacifist stance; emphasis on the ecstasy of music—classical music rather than the jazz of the Beats; disaffiliation from the dominant materialistic American culture; and visceral descriptions of sexual experience. Crumb's friend S. Clay Wilson also illustrated several of Bukowski's stories including "Politics and Love" and "A Dirty Trick on God." It is natural that Crumb would be attracted to Bukowski's work. Bukowski—like Crumb—had a tyrannical father and was an outsider due to his severe case of acne vulgaris. He was beaten regularly by his father—as we have seen, Crumb had his collarbone broken by his father—and both struggled with their relationships with women. Both pilloried the motion picture "industry" mercilessly—Crumb in his satirical account of attending the Academy Awards in "R. Crumb, 'The Old Outsider,' Goes to the Academy Awards," which appeared in *Hup*, no. 4 (1991), and Bukowski in his novel *Hollywood* (1989). Both artists' work is highly regarded in Germany, where editions of their work are prized and kept continuously in print. In addition, Bukowski was himself an avid cartoonist, producing hundreds of often clever and funny drawings—he admired the humorous drawings of James Thurber concerning the battle of the sexes—which were included in his "Notes of a Dirty Old Man" series published in the *Los Angeles Free Press*.

Bukowski was aware of the underground comix revolution, since his work appeared in many of the same countercultural publications as Crumb's. For example, Bukowski appeared in Michael Andre's *Unmuzzled Ox*, which also published Burroughs, Corso, and Ginsberg. Crumb contributed several drawings as well as the cover illustration for the February 1972 issue (vol. 1, no. 2). Bill Griffith recalls that he received a letter from Bukowski when the staff of *Arcade* was considering which one of Bukowski's stories to include in their magazine, and Bukowski included the comical declaration: "Underground cartoonists are all a bunch of Baptist ministers in Popeye suits!" Crumb responded to Bukowski's caricature and cynicism: Nothing is sacred. Crumb employs satire as a weapon to expose the lie of the "American Dream," as did Bukowski. He sees falsity and "plastic"—rather like the character in Mike Nichols's film *The Graduate*—taking over the modern world. He attempts to peel away the layers of conditioning by church, state, and parents. In this way, Crumb is similar to many in the counterculture, yet he is different in that he could never accept the hippie lifestyle and often spoke of himself as unable to participate in the "be here now" philosophy. He was the outsider looking in, and his work is often perched in an *observing* posture. Crumb is often in the middle, finding fault—and humor—in the "Establishment" as well as in the opposition to the status quo. And finally, like Bukowski, Crumb is also often "politically incorrect": his sharp parodies and satire puncture many pieties.

As we have seen, Crumb was interested in exploring the boundary lines between literature, "confession," and graphic narrative; thus, it is understandable why the intensely autobiographical Bukowski appealed to him. In an interview, Crumb declared:

> Charles Bukowski is one of my favorite current writers. Generally autobiographical. . . . Some of his best writing is in these letters he writes to people. Real offhand, talking about his life. It's so great, so rich. Since I'm part of the modern American phenomenon myself, I'm attracted to autobiographical diary writing, even from old times, much more than I am to novels or fiction. There's too much bullshit in those things.[33]

This is also why the work of J. R. Helton appeals to Crumb in its tough portrayal of the hardscrabble lives of the American working class in Texas. Crumb considers Helton his "favorite contemporary American writer. He has a gift for writing well in plain language, and he can't seem to help but write with total honesty." Crumb has illustrated several of Helton's book covers including *Below the Line* (2000), *Drugs* (2012), and *The Jugheads* (2014). We can also see why James Boswell's *London Journal* would attract Crumb, for it both exposes Boswell's sexual compulsion to consort with prostitutes even after he is afflicted with a venereal disease and is also precisely "autobiographical diary writing." Yet another example is *My Secret Life* (1888), an erotic book published anonymously under the name "Walter." Crumb has said: "There's a nineteenth century guy who called himself Walter, an Englishman, who kept secret diaries of his sex life that were published recently. They are great. I would love to do some illustration of his diaries but I don't know if I'll ever get to it, it's a huge amount of work. . . . I thought of doing it for ten years but I'm probably not going to do it as it would be too hugely time-consuming." Although Crumb has completed several virtuosic pages, which appear in his *Sketchbooks*, he has not to this date continued with the project. Thus, confessions confided in diary and journal form define Crumb's intent in many of his own works: he is telling us his life in graphic diary form.

Crumb illustrates the transgressive aspects of Bukowski's depiction of sexuality. Crumb had read Georges Bataille (1897–1962), the French fiction writer and philosopher who explored the boundary limits of erotic pleasure and suffering, whom he quotes in his *Sketchbooks*: "The whole business of eroticism is to strike to the inmost core of the living being, so that the heart stands still." As Nadine Hartmann has observed:

> Bataille's aim was to establish a notion of eroticism as a paradigm of the sacred, even as *the* most sacred of all experience. The sacred

unfolds itself in all its ambivalence in erotic experience with those aspects that are considered low and animalistic. . . . For Bataille, transgression constitutes the exceptional moment of a breaking-through the sphere of the profane into the sphere of the sacred. . . . The practices and occurrences of the everyday dictated by utility and capital accumulation belong to the sphere of the profane. The sphere of the sacred is characterized by exceptional states of excess and wastefulness in which alone the subject has the chance to experience its own sovereignty. . . . The banning of eroticism from the sphere of the sacred then is Christianity's offence—to this extent, Bataille seems to agree with the repressive hypothesis. Yet—and this is Bataille's recourse to transgression—any prohibitions Christianity imposes on us ultimately increase the potential for a deeper pleasure.[34]

During the countercultural revolution, there was an emphasis on sacred sexuality, and many of the Beats explored the mystical possibilities of Tantra. Crumb is of course most famous to many people for his graphic—some have accused him of misogyny—depictions of sex. Yet for Crumb, while this ecstatic power of sexual love to bring one to the deepest knowledge of the Self through the Other is certainly present, he combines it with a transgressive power. Sex is violent, an eruption of the unconscious, a primal act of surrender. Bataille famously explored the link between intense sexual experience and mystical illumination, and although Bukowski often appears to depict sex in sordid circumstances, he also clearly saw sexual love as one way—along with classical music and literature—toward self-knowledge and freedom: his cynicism hides an intense romanticism.

In one of Crumb's illustrations for Bukowski's story *Bring Me Your Love*, we observe the German expressionist influence in the drab interior—the film noir quality catching the folds of the blankets and bed linen, an ashtray and liquor bottle on the floor, liquor glasses next to a phone emitting lightning rays of irritating sound, the woman's face turned directly toward the viewer with open mouth and crazed face, with the man crouched above bracing himself up with a hairy, simian arm—which director Barbet Schroeder also employed in the cinematography of the film version of Bukowski's *Barfly*.[35] *Bring Me Your Love* appeared in 1983, and two years later Crumb illustrated Richard von Krafft-Ebing's case studies concerning a variety of bizarre ways people have sought sexual fulfillment, titled *Psychopathia Sexualis* (1886), one of his series of "Klassic Komics." It is clear that Crumb responds to Bukowski's awareness of the eerie strangeness of sexuality and to the challenge to "normalcy" presented by the most common of human activities: Bukowski/

Crumb open the curtain onto what is hidden and secret yet happens every moment of every day.

Another Bukowski work, *The Captain Is Out to Lunch and the Sailors Have Taken Over the Ship*, contains twelve Crumb illustrations as well as a back-cover portrait of Bukowski, depicting the writer in a number of different situations.[36] The work, a journal published posthumously in 1998, consists of a series of entries from August 28, 1991, to February 27, 1993—the final entry a little more than a year before Bukowski's death on March 9, 1994—and again belongs to Crumb's favored genre, the diary/confessional. Bukowski scrupulously notes the time each entry was made for each day: 11:19 p.m., 12:16 a.m., and so on. By this point in his career—after a life spent in poverty and relative obscurity—Bukowski had achieved a measure of fame and financial success due to Barbet Schroeder's film *Barfly* (1987) and the increasing international popularity of his poetry, short stories, and novels, especially in Europe. Crumb reveals Bukowski in a number of different quotidian situations: waking up and putting on his shoes; confronting an obnoxious fan at a bar; observing an angry man screaming at the racetrack; seated at his computer writing; being interviewed by cameramen; sitting in his Jacuzzi; in an unpleasant situation with an angry younger writer; making love to a woman; looking at a series of photographs of potential actors for a television series based on his work; at a reception following a party for *Barfly*; driving to the racetrack.

A variation on the erotic scene discussed above from *Bring Me Your Love* occurs in *The Captain Is Out to Lunch*: again we have cigarettes and an ashtray—this time on the bed instead of the floor—and curtains, but now parted to reveal dull shining lights. The features of the male figure here are clearly meant to suggest Bukowski himself—and perhaps also Mickey Rourke, who played the Bukowski character in *Barfly*—rather than the fictional character in *Bring Me Your Love*, and we see his bookcase in the background covered with books and magazines. The woman again has her head turned in both pleasure and what appears to be abandonment and anguish: bedcovers are wrinkled as she grips the pillow above her head. The walls are busily crosshatched, casting a dark atmosphere in the room. And here, instead of the voice of the narrator as in *Bring Me Your Love*—"They were in the dark, going good when the phone rang"—we have the thoughts of Bukowski himself: "Yet, even during the sex act I'd think, this is another routine. I'm doing what I'm supposed to do. I felt ridiculous but I went ahead anyhow. What else could I do?" In *Sketchbook*, vol. 10, Crumb quotes Moana Pozzi, an Italian pornography star: "Pornography is the representation of our most intimate dreams, our most secret desires. . . . Sex is also black, contorted, corrosive, it isn't always something sunny and joyous. . . . Obscenity is sublime."³⁷ This "contortion" is emphasized in the wrestler-like engagement of these contending bodies, which—as is often the case in pornography—seem to be caught in "another routine."

Another aspect of Bukowski's work that Crumb focuses on is the question of creativity. As we shall see in chapter 5 with Franz Kafka, here he depicts Bukowski in the act of writing. Bukowski's entry for "10/15/91 12:55 AM" is largely concerned with writers and literature. He mentions Maxim Gorky, Turgenev, D. H. Lawrence, and Hemingway. Bukowski then turns to the racetrack and the ways gamblers attempt to get help regarding which horse they should favor, declaring: "Any time you pay somebody to tell you what to do you are going to be a loser. And this includes your psychiatrist, your psychologist, your broker, your workshop teacher and your etc."³⁸ Here again we find a strict existential stance, which Crumb will emphasize in his illustrations of Jean-Paul Sartre. Ultimately, as Bukowski observes in a late poem, "nobody can save you but / yourself." Crumb most likely tried out several possible ways to illustrate this chapter, for in his *Sketchbook*, vol. 10 (August 1992–January 1993), there is a page depicting "Bukowski at the Race Track," and these drawings are based on actual photographs of the poet.³⁹ However, Crumb did not include these sketches in his final choice of illustrations.

In the final sections of the entry, Bukowski now turns to the present and to his writing. Crumb illustrates the phrase: "Old writer puts on sweater, sits down, leers into computer screen and writes about life. How holy can we get?" The frame for the drawing is a *mandorla*—from the Italian for "almond"—the oval-shaped aureola that is employed in Christian art to surround the Virgin Mary and Christ. Crumb further emphasizes an aura of mystery with a circular shape of a white penumbra emanating from an invisible light source intersecting with a much darker background in the upper left side of the drawing.⁴⁰ Yet Bukowski's own text—in particular his use of the word "holy"—simultaneously pokes fun at the pretensions of the artist to special status. The writer's surroundings are totally quotidian, with nothing "holy" in sight: a full ashtray, towel draped over the back of the chair, poster board covered with notes, desk piled high with papers and magazines, beneath more books and magazines. The chair is pockmarked on the left side. The unshaven writer has a cigarette in his left hand, staring grimly into the computer screen. There is a further irony in depicting Bukowski seated at a Macintosh IIsi, a gift from his wife Linda for Christmas in 1990. The sacred, Christian *mandorla* is placed against the modern, technological world. Matthew G. Kirschenbaum in *Track Changes: A Literary History of Word*

R. Crumb, Portrait of Charles Bukowski, *The Captain Is Out to Lunch and the Sailors Have Taken Over the Ship*, 1998.

Processing observes that "by 1995 when R. Crumb produced this drawing of Charles Bukowski, the computer was fully on its way to becoming assimilated into the stock of cultural imagery around writing and authorship."[41] Bukowski himself had been concerned that using a computer would take him away from a direct experience of writing and make it a "consumerist" experience. However, he found to his surprise that he enjoyed writing on the word processor and was enthusiastic about his increased productivity.

Finally, Crumb, in his *Sketchbook*, vol. 11, illustrates a Bukowski poem, "bone palace ballet," which contains the lines: "this / tired / life / this dusty dream, / these April nights, / this thunder in a paper cup, / all the old ladies / alone in rooms / working crossword puzzles, / the dead dogs of forever / crushed with / lolling tongues, / the parched innards of / mountains / aching / to scream, /what is this grueling nonsense? / is it /the worm crawling toward / no paradise? / the scissors in a closed/drawer?"[42] Crumb depicts a pile of newspapers, and if we look closely we see a headline reading "Gunman with bomb kills 7 and himself," a cactus in a pot nearby, and an additional text at the bottom in a similar handwriting suggesting that it is intended as additional commentary: "The Universe is poised to rip us to pieces!"—an apt interpretation of the Bukowski poem, which also juxtaposes daily objects and events with larger metaphysical questions: "thunder in a paper clip," "the worm crawling toward / no paradise?" Crumb also adds a remark concerning his feelings about America during his adolescence: "I always despised the Youth Culture, ever since I first became aware of its existence in the late 1950s, with its silly narcissistic posturing." He clearly finds Bukowski's tough existentialism a bracing antidote to this "posturing."

Thus, we have seen the ways Crumb has been influenced by the Beats and Bukowski as well as how he has adapted their lives and works within the context of his own philosophical itinerary. It is Crumb's practice to explore authors whose themes answer to his own interests, and then to both illustrate their works—they thus supply a kind of metacommentary on his own obsessions—and to employ them as springboards to his own desire to fulfill in his art the Socratic injunction: "The unexamined life is not worth living." The Beats and Bukowski were particularly important to Crumb, for he came of age just as they themselves were reaching their first public successes—Allen Ginsberg's *Howl* in 1956; Kerouac's *On the Road* in 1957; Burroughs's *Naked Lunch* in 1959. Bukowski came to fame in the late sixties and early seventies— his book *Notes of a Dirty Old Man* first appeared in 1969—and published in the underground newspapers as did Crumb, expressing the mood of the Dionysian sixties in the clear prose that Crumb admired. Crumb continued throughout his career to demonstrate his deep love and involvement with both the literature and biographies of writers to whom he responded as well as his ability to faithfully and sensitively translate their key themes into compelling visual form.

Chapter 2

JELLY ROLL MORTON, CHARLEY PATTON

Blues, Voodoo, and the Devil

In interviews, letters, and published essays, Robert Crumb often forcefully declared his idiosyncratic musical tastes. Just as he abjured modernism in literature and painting—he saw little to admire in William Faulkner or James Joyce and found zero of interest in abstract expressionism—so too Crumb evinced no great love for rock 'n' roll, preferring instead the popular music of the early twentieth century and relishing folk music from a variety of world cultures. Crumb credits the soundtrack from Hal Roach's *Little Rascals* (1922–1944)—broadcast later on television to an appreciative generation of baby boomers—as awakening his interest in "old-time" music. At last count in 2013, Crumb possessed an astounding six thousand, five hundred 78 rpm records in his collection. A sign of his obsessiveness may be seen in "I'm Grateful! I'm Grateful!," a work completed in 1989 in which Crumb enumerates all the reasons he has to be thankful for his lot in life. In the second panel, he muses: "I've got a comfortable bathtub, a good book, and time to relax . . . what a miracle!!" Upon closely inspecting the title of the book he shows himself reading in the bathtub, we find that it is *1931 Numerical List of Victor Records*. Crumb has noted that his maternal grandfather, Joseph Hall, was active in vaudeville orchestras as a string musician in Philadelphia, while his grandmother Viola also possessed a lovely singing voice. In "Where Has It Gone, All the Beautiful Music of Our Grandparents?," Crumb depicts himself speaking with his mother, who recollects: "I remember back in the 'Twenties, my mother and father played music with their friends on weekends . . . old string-band music, y' know. . . . On summer evenings they'd play out on the front porch." It is a special moment, for Crumb rarely portrayed his

mother sympathetically or documented many tender exchanges: her recollections of his maternal grandparents' music making in this case creates a
bond between mother and son.

Crumb's affection for blues, jazz, and country began in his youth and has
continued throughout his career: he is himself an amateur musician, com-
petently playing several instruments. He purchased his first plastic ukulele
at age twelve in 1955 and also plays guitar, banjo, and accordion; and he is
a quondam member of the musical group R. Crumb and His Cheap Suit
Serenaders and, in France, of Dominique Cravic's Les Primitifs du Futur. Les
Primitifs have played concerts in Paris, Bourges, and Amsterdam. He has also
appeared frequently with John Heneghan of the East River String Band on
John's Old Time Radio Show, where typical programs have included jazz and
banjo recordings as well as music from Hawaii, North Africa, Martinique,
Turkey, Greece, and Armenia.[1] Like the joy-seeking characters in *On the
Road,* Crumb sought through music to experience "IT," a sense of ecstasy
or—as Kerouac would put it—*beatitude.* This passion for music began at a
very young age, as we see in an endearing drawing, depicting memories of
his life at age four in Philadelphia in 1948. Crumb shows himself as a very
young boy in a rocking chair smiling joyously, gripping the handles of the
chair with his young feet far off the ground with the text: "Musical ecstasy
at age four listening to polka music on the radio, Philadelphia, 1948 and
rocking furiously on the front porch of our house on South 53rd Street."
In *Sketchbook,* vol. 7, Crumb declared: "Listening to a record of 'Pretty Lil''
by Jelly Roll Morton and his Orchestra, I was *sent . . .* into a *jazz ecstasy."*
Crumb—like the Beats—identified with the culture and creative genius of
African Americans: indeed, it was a composition by Blind Boy Fuller (1904
[or 1907]–1941)—"Truckin' My Blues Away"—that was the origin of one of
Crumb's most famous iconic drawings, the ubiquitous "Keep on Truckin'"
figure with his huge legs and feet striding joyously into space. Crumb was
fascinated by the lives of these great musicians, and in this chapter, I shall
turn to his illustrations of biographical texts concerning Jelly Roll Morton
and Charley Patton and the ways their spiritual struggles are portrayed.
Indeed, Son House (1902–1988), the Delta blues singer and guitarist, made
a recording in 1930 entitled "Preachin' the Blues," which featured the verses:
"Oh, I got to stay on the job, I ain't got time to lose / He-e-e-ey, I ain't got no
time to lose / I swear to God I've got to preach the gospel blues." As Robert
Palmer observes in *Deep Blues:* "Blues musicians were well aware that their
singing was comparable to preaching, both in style and in the effect it could
have on an audience."[2] Music of course is intimately connected to humanity's desire for release from suffering and for connection to the rhythms of

nature and the cosmos. Furthermore, music has accompanied sacred rituals throughout world history: from the Dionysian festivals in ancient Greece, to the drumming and singing of indigenous cultures, to the Mass in B Minor by Johann Sebastian Bach.

At age seventeen Crumb read *Jazzmen* (1939), an early jazz history containing chapters on the blues and boogie-woogie scenes in New York, New Orleans, and Chicago as well as portraits of Bix Beiderbecke and Louis Armstrong.[3] Thus Crumb's involvement in jazz and blues, and musical creativity, led him early in his career to investigate their historical roots. The chapter on collecting 78s in *Jazzmen* inspired Crumb to travel door to door in Black neighborhoods in Dover, Delaware, in search of old records: he would memorialize this phase of his youth in "That's Life."[4] A recurrent theme in Crumb's psychological orientation is *nostalgia*—literally, in ancient Greek, the pain or longing, *algos*, to return home, *nostos*. Crumb himself declared: "I yearn for something that is lost—gone forever—never to return—the music of the 1920s, the *look* of the 1920s, the absence of suburbia, the smaller population. . . . Gone, all vanished. . . . What good is it to long for something that can never be again??"[5] This yearning is starkly rendered in Crumb's famous "A Short History of America," which depicts the gradual degradation of the rural United States into the urban horrors of the present: gas stations on every corner, telephone lines blocking the sky, billboards, strip malls, garish neon, smog and water pollution, fast-food joints, vulgarity run rampant. In a sketch from 1975 entitled "No Rest for the Wicked," Crumb depicts himself waking in bed and in the second panel confesses that his "mind is always busy trying to sort out the byzantine entanglements of my overly complex life." He then remarks in the third panel: "As Mark Twain once said about America: It is a civilization which has destroyed the simplicity and repose of life; replaced its contentment, its poetry, its soft romantic dreams and visions with the money fever, sordid ideals, vulgar ambitions, and the sleep which does not refresh." Crumb turned to the "pure" music of "the people" to cleanse his soul of the detritus of contemporary life.

Crumb believed that "folk music" possessed an authenticity absent in the commercial, studio-produced popular commodity marketed to mass audiences of the contemporary world. As he observed in an interview:

> [J]ust go down to Mexico and you'll hear little groups, the most common peasants, do some absolutely beautiful music that's deeply moving. It's very simple, but they're putting so much of themselves into it without any contrivance or self-consciousness at all, or any attempt to get chart-action. . . . So, in that way, music is the first thing to go when

a culture goes down the drain. They just took the music away from the people and sold this fake version of it back to them.[6]

Crumb echoes here art historian John Berger's ideas in *Ways of Seeing* (1972) concerning the ways capitalism through advertising takes and then sells back to us our own bodies:

> The spectator-buyer is meant to envy herself as she will become if she buys the product. She is meant to imagine herself transformed by the product into an object of envy for others, an envy which will then justify her loving herself. One could put this another way: the public-ity images steals her love of herself as she is, and offers it back to her for the price of the product.

So too, Crumb would assert, the contemporary corporate music business has "sold back" to the public a "fake version" of the artistic imagination, which was in fact the public's own original possession. Instead of people learning to play a musical instrument themselves and thus becoming "creative" actors in their own lives—the poet Gary Snyder has made similar arguments—the masses seek to be "entertained" (and must pay money for the privilege) by others. In "Street Musicians" (1996)—an illustration published in the *New Yorker* praising the talented instrumentalists and singers Crumb has encoun- tered on city streets—Crumb declares his admiration for these anonymous performers, who often achieve impressive degrees of musicianship. Crumb has launched frequent polemics against rock 'n' roll and against all contem- porary music. In *Sketchbook*, vol. 8, he complains: "This music doesn't let you think! It is highly aggressive, even in its supposedly 'easy listening' forms.... [I]t is fashioned by very skilled professionals, 'studio sharks' and calculating businessmen. It is a terrible thing they have done to one of the human's best ways of connecting to eternity.... It's a calamity, a tragedy as great as the destruction of the rain forests!! This is no exaggeration!!"[7] It is evident that for Crumb music is a primary way of achieving euphoric states of being, and he is vehement in his condemnation of the cheapening and diluting of this Dionysian form of human creativity, which is "one of the human's best ways of connecting to eternity."

Because jazz and the blues have been so central in Crumb's life, allusions often recur in his stories: for example, "Dirty Dog," which appeared in *Zap* (1968), depicts the adventures of a libidinous canine and opens with the blues lyrics "Rather drink muddy water, Lord / sleep in a hollow log / than be up here in New York City / treated like a dirty dog," originally sung in

1936 by Jimmie Gordon and later performed by musicians such as Lou Rawls. Crumb has also created a series of portraits honoring his favorite jazz and country music heroes, which were published as a book as well as a set of trading cards.[8] The blues of course would become a central aspect of the counterculture. The Beatles, the Rolling Stones, Bob Dylan, Eric Clapton—all have acknowledged their fascination with blues, born of the suffering of African Americans in the South. The film *Easy Rider* derived its title from the eponymous song by Blind Lemon Jefferson (1893–1929), which contains the lyrics "your easy rider died on the road"—foreshadowing the murder of Peter Fonda and Dennis Hopper by southern rednecks at the close of the film. The movie also contains an interesting allusion to comic book history. As John Carlin in *Masters of American Comics* has observed: "The main character in the film, played by Peter Fonda, was called Captain America, ironically reversing the meaning of Jack Kirby's World War II–era super-hero. The combination of these two references showed how sixties youth culture borrowed early twentieth-century folk music at the same time as they rejected the mainstream pop culture they were brought up on." Captain America, the patriotic archetypal fighter against the Axis powers—the first issue featuring his heroic exploits appeared under the Marvel Comics imprint in March 1941—was now an Easy Rider, and Wyatt and Billy were Beat characters riding their Harley-Davidsons across America to the soundtrack of African American blues. Crumb's fascination with these gifted musicians mirrors the reverence that Beat authors of the fifties such as Kerouac and Ginsberg felt for them, and he would revitalize their cultural relevance for our own times. Furthermore, one can connect blues to existentialism, for as Joel Dinerstein has argued in *The Origins of Cool in Postwar America*, "blues is a popular form of existentialism: an accessible, democratic art form focused on sex and violence, desire and imagined freedom."[9] It is in jazz music, after all, that Antoine Roquentin at the close of Sartre's *Nausea* finds a kind of redemption: in the song "Some of These Days" sung by a "Negress." As we shall see in chapter 4, Crumb would make the quest for authenticity in existentialism a central feature of his philosophical quest.

Crumb created two significant works on Charley Patton (ca. 1891–1934) and Jelly Roll Morton (1890–1941). "Patton" was published in *Zap*, no. 11 (1985), while "Jelly Roll Morton's Voodoo Curse" appeared in *Raw*, no. 7 (May 1985).[10] Both were executed with ink and brush, and the stark, spooky black backgrounds render an atmosphere reminiscent of crime comics. A decade earlier, Crumb had created a five-page biography entitled "That's Life" concerning a fictitious blues musician named Tommy Grady from Crystal Springs, Mississippi, which appeared in *Arcade* (Fall 1975). Here Tommy's wife implores him to "join de church an' sing 'long wif me on Sunday!" but she and Tommy engage in a violent quarrel. He leaves home, spends money on liquor, and "gets involved with a woman who has a jealous husband" who kills Tommy at a bar. Decades later, a Robert Crumb–like character at the end discovers Tommy's unknown music during one of his jaunts purchasing old records, and the story concludes ironically with Tommy's music being discovered by a group "of blues collectors and scholars." Crumb includes several of these elements in his adaptations of the biographies of Jelly Roll Morton and Charley Patton, but the narratives are different from "That's Life" in that they dramatize supernatural intervention in the lives of gifted musicians. As Linda Hutcheon has observed, "the act of adaptation always involves both (re-)interpretation and then (re-)creation." Indeed, in the act of transforming these biographies into drawings accompanied by text, Crumb "re-interprets" and "re-creates" them in his own image. As we shall see with Philip K. Dick, Crumb was intrigued by the question of the authenticity of religious experience, and thus the biography of pianist and composer Jelly Roll Morton fascinated him, which inspired "Jelly Roll Morton's Voodoo Curse."

An influence on Crumb's treatment of voodoo was Carl Barks. As early as 1961, Crumb praised Barks's "Voodoo Hoodoo" (1949), first published in Dell's *Four Color*, no. 238; however, he appeared to have been cognizant of the racist stereotypes that mar the work—Barks would later revise it—for Crumb pointed out that "Barks would never be able to do something like 'Voodoo Hoodoo' nowadays."[11] The Marvel comics character "Brother Voodoo"—Jericho Drumm—also first appeared in *Strange Tales*, no. 169, in September 1973, suggesting that the subject of voodoo had entered the imaginations of several American comics artists. Clearly, voodoo must have continued to intrigue Crumb, for twenty-four years after his comments on Barks, Crumb would illustrate an episode from Alan Lomax's biography *Mister Jelly Roll* (1950) in which Lomax describes Morton's relationship to voodoo: we are informed at the close of the narrative that Crumb has taken all the dialogue he employed from Lomax's text. Raised Catholic, Morton grew up in New Orleans and hence was exposed to voodoo practices from childhood, and, as we shall see, these traditions became central to his life. Brought to French Louisiana from West Africa by slaves, *voodoo* or "spirit"—also known as *vaudou*, *vodou*, and *vodoun*—derives from languages spoken in the Fon and Yoruba kingdoms.[12] We learn that the lady who raised Morton—Laura Hunter—was a voodoo witch and that in order to become a witch you must "sell the person you love best to Satan as a sacrifice." Thus Laura gave Morton's soul to Satan, which led to his subsequent terrible fate: his career, business enterprises, and personal life would all end in disaster.

R. Crumb, "Jelly Roll Morton's Voodoo Curse," *Raw*, no. 7 (May 1985).

A point that cannot be emphasized enough regarding Crumb's virtuos-ity as an artist is his close attention to the form and shape of his text. The published handwritten letters Crumb has sent to correspondents reveal an incredibly, scrupulously neat skill at forming each printed letter of the al-phabet. Philip Pullman, in his book chapter "*Maus*: Behind the Masks," has observed: "What shape things have, and in what kind of letters the words are printed, and how a picture is set against its background, are matters we have to think about when we look at comics. A comic is not exactly a novel in pictures—it's something else." And as Gene Kannenberg Jr. has asserted: "The text in comics, known as lettering, plays an important yet often over-looked role in that art form's visual storytelling."[13] We note on the splash page that while the name "PATTON" in Crumb's illustration of the life of Charley Patton is starkly bold with bullet holes, for Jelly Roll Morton he has chosen spooky, melodramatic lettering engulfed in flames on the words "Voodoo Curse," and here we have a placard instead of a scroll containing the introductory biographical material. Crumb also employs fiery lettering for the words "Voodoo Curse," which we see featured in the opening of his Philip K. Dick illustrations, as well as the shadow of a devilish creature with claws for hands menacing the Morton figure as he approaches the corner of Broadway and Forty-Second Street in New York.

The portrait of Morton in the second panel is a transformation of a pho-tograph taken in Chicago in September 1926 at the height of Jelly Roll's career. Morton is posed pensively with head down, his left arm resting on the grand piano's lid, left open hand dangling over the keyboard and right hand clutching the piano bench; he sports bow tie and tuxedo. In Crumb's version, right hand and bench are absent; Jelly Roll is dressed in tie and sus-penders, thus rendering a more quotidian, casual, and weary scene. However, a threatening shadow lurks behind Morton's back: a literal foreshadowing of things to come. The fact that Crumb looked for an actual photograph of Morton when he set about the task of adapting his biography demonstrates his urge to pursue scrupulous research to lend his illustrations historical accuracy and authenticity.

Morton in the first panel reveals: "When I was a young man, these hoodoo people with their underground stuff helped me along." Morton tells of a man whom he made his business partner—"a West-Indian guy"—which subtly suggests that he is familiar with Caribbean supernatural practices. This West Indian also knows a "light-complected old man" who Morton realizes pos-sesses "a book, like an encyclopedia full of charms that never fail." The first tier of page 4 contains three panels arranged to create mounting suspense: in the first, Morton recounts the fact that when people visit his office, they mysteriously appear unable to cross into the room, and Morton wonders how this could be happening. In the second panel, an astonished Morton and his assistant Billy Young pull up the rug that is next to the door, "and there, underneath, were four different colors of powders: gray, white, brown and pink." An increasingly frantic Morton then finds that the powder has been sprinkled throughout his office, even on every piece of his stationery. To discover the source of this puzzling occurrence, Morton attends a sé-ance, which is conducted by one Madame Elise. Morton then takes a bath in the liquids she prescribes to cure himself of what has now been clearly diagnosed as a curse. Madame Elise advises Jelly Roll to burn his clothing, and Morton confesses that he spent large sums of money "to get the spell taken off me." He now experiences difficulty achieving success in the music business and in 1935 moves to Washington, DC, from New York. Anita Gon-zalez, Morton's first wife, states on the final page: "Jelly was a very devout Catholic. But voodoo, which is an entirely different religion, had hold of him too." Gonzalez relates that his godmother, Laura Hunter—formerly known as Eulalie Echo—made a prosperous living with voodoo and became a voodoo witch by selling "the person you love best to Satan as a sacrifice." Thus it is confirmed in the finale that this is the primal curse that indeed led to Jelly Roll Morton's downfall.

The "powders" referenced here are actually employed by "conjurers"—who were called "root doctors"—in "hoodoo," which is to be distinguished from voodoo. Hoodoo is a kind of *conjuring* derived from African traditions and practiced by slaves in the South that pervades blues music: Junior Wells (1934–1998) created an album released in 1965 entitled *Hoodoo Man Blues*, while Curtis Jones in "Black Magic Blues" declared: "I call it black magic, some call it plain hoodoo." As Albert J. Raboteau has observed:

The strongest alternative to Protestantism among the slaves was the tradition of conjure. A combination of religion, medicine, magic, and folklore conjure flourished in the slave quarters. The appeal of conjure depended upon its effectiveness in explaining illness and misfortune and its prescriptions for curing them. Slaves and surprising numbers of white people believed that the conjurer had the power to cure but also to harm. Conjurers, also called root doctors or hoodoo (a word derived from "voodoo") doctors, used materials (such as roots, herbs, bones, and graveyard dirt) whose spiritual power was activated by secret spells known only to the conjurer. A variety of otherwise un-explained illnesses, mental and physical, or a series of accidents were blamed upon conjure.... Christian slaves sometimes spoke of conjure as evil, the tool of the devil. But many conjurers were themselves religious and regarded their skill as a gift from God.[14]

Thus the "powders" employed by Laura Hunter were likely an assortment of dirt from graveyards, herbs, roots or bones, and magic powders with such alluring names as "Attraction Powder," "Uncrossing Powder," "Black Cat Oil," and "Hex-Removing Floor-Wash," which may still be purchased today in specialty shops catering to seekers of hoodoo elixirs. Clearly, Morton had been the victim of a curse by a hoodoo "conjurer." Justin Green—creator of the groundbreaking graphic novel *Binky Brown Meets the Holy Virgin Mary*—when discussing his early career as an artist, declared that he "was on a mystical quest to get a 'crow quill hand,' like the 'Mojo hand' that Muddy Waters sang about. If I ever got one, I'd be able to produce calligraphic marks which would effortlessly register the intention of my mind's eye, in a style that would be like my own handwriting." Green alludes here to Muddy Waters's famous blues song "Got My Mojo Workin'," which contains the verse: "Going down to Louisiana to get me a Mojo hand." A "Mojo hand" is precisely a hoodoo "conjure bag" containing the transformative magical substances—which can help Muddy Waters in his courting of the ladies, and Justin Green in his artistic aspirations—or wreak terrible effects on an unlucky target. A final example of the way hoodoo/Mojo entered into the popular imagination occurs in the song "L. A. Woman," in which Jim Morrison and the Doors sang of driving through the suburbs of Los Angeles, "into your blues. . . . Mr. Mojo Risin,' Mr. Mojo Risin.'" For Crumb, the significance of the Mojo/hoodoo phenomenon lies in the question he asks in the opening panel concerning Morton's terrible curse: "Was it real? Or was it . . . all in his mind?," which correlates exactly—as we shall see in chapter 3—with the question Crumb asks at the outset of "The Religious Experience of Philip K. Dick": "Was it the onset of acute schizophrenia, or was it a genuine mystic revelation, and then again, is there any difference??"

One autobiographical clue to Crumb's fascination with the question of whether a "curse" can render objective harm may lie in a story he has recounted concerning his father Charles, who was stationed with the US Marines in Shanghai in 1938. Crumb reports having an intuition that his father may have committed an unconscionable, brutal act—a "secret sin"—during his tour of duty there, which then wrapped the lives of all the Crumb family in a web of karmic doom and retribution. Crumb and Maxon began referring to it as "the Chinese Curse." Crumb's brother Charles ended up a suicide, while Maxon endured severe mental problems. Although Robert was never able to ascertain what crime, if any, his father committed—he consulted letters his father composed while in China but was unable to find any hard evidence—he however remained haunted by the idea that he may have been "cursed" by some supernatural force that was responsible for his family's suffering. One may also interpret this—apart from any "karmic" interpretation—as a parable of the ways parents or parental figures doom their progeny (as in the sublime ancient Greek tragedies) to terrible lives. This is perhaps one reason why Jelly Roll Morton's "voodoo curse" struck such a sensitive nerve in Crumb, since he suspected that his father might have also been the perpetrator of a mysterious "secret sin"—analogous to Morton's loss of his soul due to the "conjuring" of Laura Hunter—committed during his time in Shanghai.[15]

In 2001, sixteen years after completing "Jelly Roll Morton's Voodoo Curse," Crumb returned to the theme in a fabulous drawing, "Hypnagogic Hoodoo," illustrating that long after hoodoo first appeared in his work, the concept had returned—as he puts it at the left top of his drawing—"from the murky depths" of his unconscious, as we witness the spooked artist pulling back the curtain on a rope-faced man in a hat leading the charge (the speech bubble records him as declaring, "Comin' In!") of four chimpanzee-like creatures. The drawing appears in the *Sketchbooks* as well as in *R. Crumb's Dream Diary* (2018) and is precisely dated "3:00 A.M., Night of March 4, 2001." With the publication of this important text in the Crumb canon, it has become easier to trace lines of influence between Crumb's dream life, his creative imagination, and his art. It is possible that some of his most eerie and weird dreams have their origin in what have been called "LSD flashbacks," in which some of the imagery stored in the unconscious that was created during a person's original LSD trip returns later in life either in conscious flashbacks or in dreams. "Hypnagogic" refers to the appearance of hallucinatory images in the liminal realm between wakefulness and sleep, and Crumb pictures himself in a frightened pose, drawing back the curtain—as it were—of his unconscious with his right hand, with his left hand frozen with fingers parted in terror-stricken apprehension. On the bottom left we are told in a rectangular narrative box that "they were hiding their faces!!" There thus may have been more rope-faced creatures who followed the leader, whose left hand—in contrast to Crumb's—is clenched tightly in purposive forward-moving aggression in close tandem with his left leg, bent in an energetic running pose. Although Crumb cries out to the figures, "Hey!! Wait! No!! You Can't—" his words make no difference as they continue their march out of the darkness, through the curtain, and into Crumb's consciousness. The cumulative power of the composition is undeniable—even the chimpanzee-like child figures are portrayed effectively by Crumb as creatures in manic, unstoppable

R. Crumb, "Hypnagogic Hoodoo," *Sketchbook*, vol. 11.

motion, propelled as if by a demonic force. Finally, the fact that Crumb titles the drawing "Hypnagogic Hoodoo" suggests that he is again exploring the supernatural world that first attracted him in Jelly Roll Morton's spooky and ultimately life-altering episode with his godmother Laura Hunter.

Crumb continued his fascination with the lives of blues musicians in his illustrations concerning Charley Patton. While "Jelly Roll Morton's Voodoo Curse" comprises six pages, "Patton" is twice its length at twelve. Crumb based "Patton" on the second chapter—"Heart Like Railroad Steel"—of Robert Palmer's groundbreaking study *Deep Blues* (1982).[16] Both of these chronicles narrating blues musicians' lives are from the same phase of Crumb's career—they appeared in 1985—and Crumb acknowledged that "you can see a lot of awkwardness when I try to draw realistically. In that 'Patton Story' I had to struggle with that stuff to make it look right. Basically all that early stuff I did was just 'balloon tire' figures. It's all just sausages." As Neil Cohn has observed, underground artists such as Crumb, Harvey Kurtzman, Art Spiegelman, and Harvey Pekar "sought an 'authentic' and idiosyncratic style in contrast to the mainstream styles of superhero comics. This graphic style often uses thicker lines and cartoony—yet deformed and lumpy—figures." What Crumb refers to as his "balloon tire" or "sausage" shaping of his line in his early work, Cohn describes as "deformed" or "lumpy," and in his narratives of Morton and Patton Crumb abandons this method and strives for a more "realistic" style. In both biographical adaptations, Crumb favors the liberal use of black ink backgrounds for the night sky or room interiors, virtuosic displays of his celebrated cross-hatching technique, and a scrupulous ordering of action in each individual frame such that the reader's/viewer's interest is kept through the progress of the narrative. Through Crumb's careful attention to detail—panel by panel, tier by tier—emerges the stark drama of his blues characters caught in their daily struggles and joys.

Patton's music gave Crumb intense pleasure: he describes listening to his compositions in quiet rapture. Crumb pointed out that "no white person had ever heard of Charley Patton until the '50s and he had been dead since 1934. He was only known in Mississippi and some other regions of the South where the few records he made sold OK. No white people knew of those black blues guys at the time . . . no one knew about Patton at all." Singers from the Mississippi Delta did not make recordings until 1926: Tommy Johnson and Charley Patton did not appear on records until 1928 and 1929, respectively. Along with Henry Thomas, Patton is considered to be among the very first "blues" singers—one commentator calls him a "radical Delta blues innovator"—and here again Crumb casts the tale in terms of a spiritual struggle between the powers of musical genius, creativity, and dark forces.[17] It is clear that this trope fascinates Crumb, for he returns to it repeatedly throughout his career. His antiheroes struggle with fate, with their sexuality, with the irrational forces that surround them, with absurdity, with the nihilistic sensation that life has no meaning. His musicians are intensified versions of this character type. Because Crumb has in many ways yearned to be an accomplished musician himself, he admires their gifts and immerses himself completely in their life histories in his illustrations. Music is, as we have seen, one of the routes toward deeper contact with the inner self, and it is not an exaggeration to argue that the careers of composer or performer are to be seen as spiritual paths in which the making of music becomes at once a route out of the prison of individual mortality and into wider harmony with the universe.

The splash page of "Patton" contains a portrait of the musician as well as biographical background on a scroll, a technique that Crumb will employ in the final panel as well. We note bullet holes in the background, which foreshadow Patton's often violent life and also may allude to the infamous and temperamental General George S. Patton of World War II fame, who, as Crumb observes, shares the same last name as his subject. Crumb is faithful to Palmer's text, which informs us that Patton lived on the Dockery Plantation in the Mississippi Delta most of his life. In the case of his adaptation of biographical literature, Crumb is skilled at condensing the more elaborate information supplied by Palmer into succinct summaries. The first panel describes Patton's playing in "juke joints" on the plantation, depicting a dancing couple among a crowd of revelers. Crumb develops his narrative slowly and deliberately, depicting slave labor on the plantations and yet emphasizing in the second panel on the second page that "every farm and every town had its musicians. There were songsters and guitar players, fiddlers and banjo pickers." Patton learned the blues from Henry Sloan, adapting this knowledge to fit his own original style, and W. C. Handy was inspired by Sloan to write "The St. Louis Blues," "Yellow Dog Blues," and "Memphis Blues." As Charley Patton's career progressed, other musicians would learn from him, including Eddie "Son" House, whose life again underscored the connection between the blues and spirituality, for House relinquished his career as a preacher to pursue music. Crumb provides individualized portraits of celebrated musicians such as Howlin' Wolf, Tommy Johnson, and Bukka White, constructing a "genealogy" of the evolution of the blues, which foreshadows his painstaking depictions of the successive biblical generations as we shall see in chapter 6 in *The Book of Genesis Illustrated by R. Crumb* (2009).

Crumb introduces the religion theme as he tells us on the fifth panel of page 4: "Even respectable, church-going blacks considered him and his kind as 'bad niggers' and the blues was looked upon as the 'devil's music.' Patton's father was a hard-working farmer and a devout Christian. He was not pleased when he found out that his young son was playing that sinful music." Crumb again closely follows the account in Palmer's *Deep Blues*: in panels 1 and 2 on page 5 we are told that Charley's father beat him with a bullwhip for playing music with Sloan, but later "softened toward the wayward son, and he bought Charley a guitar." The tale is marked throughout by a stark, expressionistic style of white shadowed heavily by black—for example, in the scene depicting Charley being beaten by his father, the pant legs of his father's overalls are dark and heavy while the belt with which he beats his son glows with white-streaked barbarity against a black sky—to underscore the fights, alcoholism, emotional violence, and agony of Patton's life. Crumb reveals Patton's struggle with drinking and his carousing with women: he would periodically "repent and take up the Bible, and resolve henceforth to put his life in the service of the Lord by preaching the Gospel." Palmer elaborates in *Deep Blues*: "He suffered his dark moods and his occasional repentances and conversions, but he also had fun, or something like it."[18] Crumb devotes the first four panels of page 6 to "lurid"—a word Crumb himself often invokes to describe what he finds attractive in comics art—depictions of Patton's violence toward women, alcoholism, fighting, and an incident in 1931 when an antagonist attempted to cut his throat. Crumb has commented that "the whole blues genre, the world they lived in was the worst, low-life, dangerous, violent environment at that time. The kind of juke joints and dives where those guys played, no decent, churchgoing black people would have anything to do with that. Nothing to do with the blues or those places, and dreaded the idea of their children ever sinking to that level." The five panels of page 7 chronicle the events that Patton memorialized in several songs such as "It Won't Be Long," about his sexual life; "Tom Rushen Blues," concerning drunkenness and time in jail; and "High Water Everywhere," in which Crumb graphically depicts the chaos and drownings of the great Mississippi River flood of 1927.

We learn that the musician Tommy Johnson told his brother Ledell the story of how he became such a splendid player. Here we find another variation of the transaction with the devil concept we encountered in "Jelly Roll Morton's Voodoo Curse." If a musician hoped to acquire extraordinary musical wizardry, they were advised to go to a crossroads just before midnight, where they would sell their soul to the devil. Begin playing your instrument, they were advised, and a large Black man will arrive who will tune your guitar.[19] Blues was considered "the devil's music." Crumb depicts the guitarist against a black sky radiating electric supernatural energy, and this black background will return in the concluding panels depicting the final days of Patton's life. Beginning with Plato's discussions of music's power

HIS LAST RECORDINGS REVEAL HIS AWARENESS THAT HIS LIFE MAY BE CUT SHORT. IN "POOR ME" HE SINGS, "DON'T THE MOON LOOK PRETTY, SHININ' DOWN THROUGH THE TREE, I CAN SEE BERTHA LEE, LORD, BUT SHE CAN'T SEE ME."

HE AND BERTHA LEE SANG TOGETHER ON THE SONG "OH DEATH." ON THIS RECORD YOU CAN VIVIDLY HEAR THE NEARNESS OF DEATH AND CHARLEY'S HORROR IN THE FACE OF IT.

SEVERAL WEEKS AFTER THIS PATTON LAY ON HIS DEATH BED. FOR A WEEK HE LAID THERE PREACHING, REPEATING OVER AND OVER HIS FAVORITE SERMON, RECORDED BY HIM IN 1929 UNDER THE PSEUDONYM ELDER J.J. HADLEY: "WHEN HE COME DOWN HIS HAIR GONNA BE LIKE LAMB'S WOOL AND HIS EYES LIKE FLAMES OF FIRE, AND EVERY MAN GONNA KNOW HE'S THE SON OF THE TRUE LIVING GOD..." 'ROUND HIS SHOULDERS GOIN' TO BE A RAINBOW AND HIS FEET LIKE FINE BRASS..., AND HE'S GONNA HAVE A TREE BEFORE THE TWELVE MANNERS OF FOOD, AND THE LEAVES GONNA BE HEALING DAMNATION, AND THE BIG ROCK THAT YOU CAN SIT BEHIND, THE WIND CAN'T BLOW AT YOU NO MORE, AND YOU GONNA COUNT THE FOUR-AND-TWENTY ELDERS THAT YOU CAN SIT DOWN AND TALK WITH, AND THAT YOU CAN TALK ABOUT YOUR TROUBLE THAT YOU COME.— WORLD YOU JUST COME FROM."

CHARLEY PATTON DIED ON APRIL 28TH, 1934. HIS DEATH WENT UNREPORTED IN THE LOCAL AND NATIONAL PRESS.

A LARGE PORTION OF THE INFORMATION FOR THIS STORY CAME FROM ROBERT PALMER'S FINE BOOK, "DEEP BLUES," PUBLISHED IN 1981 BY VIKING PRESS.

R. Crumb, "Patton," *Zap*, no. 11 (1985).

in *The Republic* and Boethius's *De institutione musica*, philosophers have pondered its tremendous effect on humanity's psychological states. Some "modes"—Lydian, Phrygian, Mixolydian, for example—were considered to cause happy, sad, or other emotional states, just as today we consider "major keys" as appropriate for joyful music and "minor keys" for tragic compositions.[20] Individual musical intervals also had emotional valence.

For example, the blues' melancholy quality—in this case the interval from C to E-flat, or the minor third—is responsible for its association with darkness and depression. This musical interval often appears in the rock 'n' roll of the sixties and exemplifies the influence of Mississippi blues on bands such as the Rolling Stones: for example, in "I Can't Get No Satisfaction," the "blues note" is a prominent part of the main theme. Furthermore, Jim Morrison's and the Doors' "Riders on the Storm" also employs a minor third, as does "Born to Be Wild" by Steppenwolf. During the middle ages, the augmented fourth—the interval from C to F-sharp on the piano—was considered the *diabolus in musica* or "the devil in music" due to its harshly dissonant qualities. So too, the "devil" has also been connected to the dazzling virtuosity of many of these gifted blues musicians: people believed that their genius must be inspired by supernatural forces. The same trope held true for classical musicians: the celebrated nineteenth-century violinist Niccolò Paganini (1782–1840) was considered to be "the demonic virtuoso," and contemporary instrumentalists such as the Canadian pianist Glenn Gould seemed to many possessed by superhuman powers in his interpretations of J. S. Bach.[21]

Thus, Tommy Johnson's tale of the connection between virtuosity and a bargain with the devil has several parallels in musical history. Furthermore, Robert Palmer described the African roots of voodoo:

> The story is at least as old as the blues. Its roots are in the voodoo lore that preserved some African religious beliefs and practices long after the religions themselves had vanished. (In the Caribbean, African religions have survived strongly, and New Orleans, which was part of the French Caribbean until 1803, is the undisputed center of voodoo in the United States.) The "black man" is recognizable as Legba, a Yoruba trickster god who "opens the path" for other supernatural powers and is traditionally associated with crossroads. As the only wholly unpredictable deity in the Yoruba pantheon—the rituals that are virtually guaranteed to bring a desired response from all others do not always work in his case—Legba became identified with the Devil of Christianity early on. Slave lore often depicted the Devil as a trickster figure, more like Legba with his mordant sense of humor

and his delight in chaos than like the more somber and threatening Devil portrayed in hellfire-and-brimstone sermons.

Zora Neale Hurston in her classic study *Tell My Horse: Voodoo and Life in Haiti and Jamaica* confirms the fact that "Legba Attibon is the god of the gate. He rules the gate of the hounfort, the entrance to the cemetery and he is also Baron Carrefour, Lord of the crossroads. The way to all things is in his hands."[22] Thus both Tommy Johnson and Charley Patton were reenacting in the Deep South of America a spiritual tradition that had its roots in African lore: furthermore, the blues singer Peetie Wheatstraw (1902–1941) called himself the "Devil's Son-in-Law" and "The High Sheriff of Hell." Robert Johnson (1911–1938)—widely considered one of the greatest blues musicians who is also said to have met the devil at the crossroads—composed the songs "Cross Road Blues" ("I went to the crossroad, fell down on my knees / Asked the Lord above 'have mercy, now save poor Bob, if you please'") and "Stones in My Passway," which alludes to the hoodoo practice (familiar to us now from "Jelly Roll Morton's Voodoo Curse") of spreading dust on the pathway to the intended victim's doorstep. Ma Rainey's (1882 [or 1886]–1939) "Black Dust Blues" tells the story of a woman accused of stealing another female's man: when she went out one morning, she "found black dust all round my door" and was then stricken with an illness.

In the cases of both Jelly Roll Morton and Charley Patton, their struggles share characteristics in common with the myth of Philoctetes, famously adduced by Edmund Wilson in his essay "Philoctetes: The Wound and the Bow."[23] In the ancient Greek tragedy by Sophocles, Philoctetes's skill as an archer is related to the fact that he was the victim of a snakebite—his talent is thus related to his disability. This is a common trope in studies of creativity: the person of genius is in some sense wounded, and compensates for vulnerability through their gift of creating works of art. Thus selling your soul—or someone else's—to the devil is a similar kind of transaction in which a liability is turned into an ability: something must be sacrificed for a compensatory gain in skill and power. Patton deals with his trauma to an extent through his gift, while Jelly Roll loses his talent and is plunged into tragedy through the intercession of Laura Hunter, who employs her power destructively. We may observe the pervasiveness of this concept of supernatural forces at work in the creative mind in the title of another book on a jazz musician that Crumb has enjoyed reading: *I'd Rather Be the Devil: Skip James and the Blues* by Stephen Calt. And finally, Crumb himself may have been attracted to stories concerning wounding, vulnerability—*vulnus* means "wound" in Latin—and artistic power, since he himself has often remarked that he disciplined himself to become a great artist as a form of compensation for his feelings of inadequacy or "inferiority": his sense of alienation and rejection as a child and young man, and his struggles with being accepted by women, which would be ameliorated if he could achieve fame and recognition for his genius as a creative figure.

The teenage Robert Johnson now appears in the narrative: we are told that he began to spend time with Patton and Son House. Crumb recounts Patton's failing health and, to lend a sense of emotional compression and finality, casts the final page in a striking form: it is composed on only four panels displayed in just two tiers. In the first panel, the lyrics of Patton's song "Poor Me" are inscribed at the top: "Don't the moon look pretty, shinin' down through the tree. I can see Bertha Lee, Lord, but she can't see me." Crumb depicts in striking expressionist style Patton's haunted ghostly face covering the sky, peering down on the scene below, the moon shining behind gnarled tree limbs as Bertha Lee strides through the night. The next panel depicts Patton singing with Bertha Lee, Crumb noting "the nearness of death and Charley's horror in the face of it" as he sings "Somebody is calling me." In the penultimate panel, he continues, and when he sings "Somebody is . . . ," Bertha Lee completes his lyric, chiming in "calling *you*." In back of Patton, a partially clothed skeleton reaches out his bony right hand, placing it upon Patton's shoulder. The final panel depicts Patton on his death bed, repeating his favorite sermon, which Crumb inscribes upon a scroll. Crumb has acknowledged that he was influenced by the design and lettering of the Paramount Record Company's advertisements for its "race records"—recordings by Black musicians. We may observe how the ad for Blind Blake's "Boa Constrictor Blues" features a spooky tree with a frightened lady whose skirt is folded against a dark background similar to the design Crumb chose to depict Bertha Lee. In addition, the lettering is executed in a style that Crumb has closely followed in the Jelly Roll Morton splash panel as well as in other illustrations. Crumb has thus combined several themes concerning the life journey of an artist, the struggle between flesh and spirit, suffering and creativity, including in his tale elements of both Christianity and African religion.

It was not only American blues musicians who were influenced by African and Haitian supernatural practices. So too, the French surrealists André Breton witnessed voodoo rituals in Haiti, and Benjamin Péret, following a stay in Brazil (1929–1931), undertook to describe in his writings "an initiatory journey in the mystical labyrinth of African thought." Crumb's work of course bears the imprint of his knowledge of surrealism—he has cited Giorgio de Chirico and Salvador Dali as early influences—and he includes a striking portrait of Breton in his *Sketchbooks* with the title "Keep it loose,

Paramount Records Advertisement, Blind Blake, "Boa Constrictor Blues," 1928.

spontaneous": an obvious summation of surrealist principles, which advocate opening up the artistic imagination to the volcanic unconscious. Crumb accompanies his portrait with Breton's romantic account of his meeting with Elisa Bindhoff Enet, whom he would marry in 1943. In his *Sketchbooks*, Crumb also depicts a *kujul*, a traditional healer from the Tira, one of the fifty Nuba tribes of Sudan. A *kujul*—also spelled *kujur*—is a shaman who, in the manner of shamans worldwide, undergoes an illness such as madness or epilepsy, recovers, and then incarnates the sacred vision which they have experienced.

There is indeed a historical link between surrealism and African and African American spiritual culture. For Crumb, one of the most attractive features of the "old-time songsters" and blues musicians was the surrealistic element in many of the lyrics. Crumb declared: "The popular arts are a brimming treasure trove of strangeness, weird fantasy, and surrealism." He cites several songs, including "When the Moon Drips into the Blood" by the string band the Taylor-Griggs Louisiana Melody Makers (1928), which includes lyrics from the Bible. Crumb scrupulously analyzes several songs:

> These old-time rural people loved the Book of Revelation and other parts of the Bible with fantastic or grotesque images and visions and used a lot of it in their religious music. Black country preachers and gospel and sanctified singing groups, as well as whites, used surrealistic religious imagery all the time. "Black Diamond Express to Hell" by Rev. A. W. Nix & Congregation or "A Coffin May Be Your Christmas Present" backed by "Death May Be Your Santa Claus" by the Rev. J. M. Gates (1927)—Christmas surrealism. Rev. F. W. McGee & Congregation did "Dog Shall Not Move His Tongue" and "Dead Cat on the Line," both around 1930. There are a couple of surrealistic blues songs that make about as much sense as a Hieronymus Bosch painting. One is "The Duck's Yas Yas Yas" by James (Stump) Johnson and his piano (1929): "Mama bought a rooster / thought it was a duck / brought him to the table / with his legs sticking up / in walks sister with a spoon and a glass / serves up the gravy from his yas yas yas."

Crumb himself made a recording of the song in 1972 with the Good Tone Banjo Boys, and one is reminded of other music that combines blues and surrealism, such as Bob Dylan's "Subterranean Homesick Blues," featuring lyrics as surrealistic as "The Duck's Yas Yas Yas." In *Zap*, no. 0, Crumb included a story entitled "Duck Yas Yas," which contains as an epigraph the first four verses of the lyrics to the song: the narrative is a Kerouacian tale "about big city blues, about the stoned out gurus, hopped-up saints and flunked out hipsters who roam the stark streets and stay up all night and don't watch television." One can thus discern in the development of Crumb's thought the ways he synthesized a wide variety of artistic and spiritual traditions—here surrealism and African American blues—into his own, unique, idiosyncratic style.

Another work in which Crumb combines African American jazz with madcap surrealism is "Hey Boparee Bop" (1967)—the title based on Lionel Hampton's 1946 hit "Hey! Ba-Ba-Re-Bop"—where he combines zany comedy, dreamlike imagery, and an encounter with Christ and ends with Mr. Natural meeting Angelfood McSpade. Crumb declared that it was during this period of the mid- to late sixties after he ingested LSD when his mind crossed fully over into the "surreal zone": "I had no control over it. The whole time I was in this fuzzy state of mind, the separation, the barrier betwixt the conscious and the subconscious was broken open somehow. A grotesque kaleidoscope, a tawdry carnival of dissociated images kept sputtering to the surface." "Dissociated" is precisely how to describe the procession of images in "Hey Boparee Bop," although there is a method to Crumb's madness. The first tiers depict two men getting into a fistfight, and every panel is accompanied by either nonsense rhymes or the conventional sound effects of comics: "Sock," "Pow," "Thud"; an automobile disconnected from the earlier narrative appears next; a precipitous erotic encounter ensues between the two men and a lady pedestrian; the men continue fighting; the mysterious car appears again and in the next frame collides with another car; a new character appears reading a book with the title "Answers" sitting on top of another book labeled "Questions" and his speech bubble reads: "From the heads of ducks and gooses"; on the following page, two new characters appear who light some dynamite and in the next frame blow themselves up; a fleeing fellow in the next frame announces "I Yi Yi! Now I'm paranoid!" followed in the next declaring "Very Funny Mr. Snoid" while we note Mr. Snoid crouching behind a tree; and the man continues to flee before he is apprehended and picked up by the scruff of his neck by a large monster.

Crumb then depicts the screaming—now naked—man head first in the next panel falling through black space, accompanied by the text: "Surrender to the void, cloid"; another character then appears crouching and crawling, saying "Bot I'm lookin for my lost cross, boss!" Christ appears next carrying his cross on his back and tells him: "Ferget this apple sauce, moss!"; in the final six panels, Mr. Natural appears in bed telling us that he has been having a dream about his youth; he then looks at his palm, announcing: "What be this? A strange inscription on my hand!"; a naked breasted Angelfood McSpade appears, and Mr. Natural wonders to her: "It's written in some obscure language"; Angelfood takes Mr. Natural's hand, licks it, and the comic ends with Mr. Natural chasing her: this is the debut appearance of the large, strong, African female in Crumb's work. As is typical in Crumb, he catches our attention with his outrageous comedy, but serious themes are embedded within the horseplay. For example, the appearance of a naked figure falling through black space will recur in other Crumb works such as "Can You Stand Alone and Face Up to the Universe?" in which the existential confrontation with "the void" returns. Second, an inscrutable mystery, which the characters attempt to decipher, is suggested by the man deeply engrossed in reading a book entitled "Answers," while there is also a secret message inscribed on Mr. Natural's hand in an "obscure language" whose meaning he is unable to interpret. Third, even in this playful excursion into nonsense, Crumb includes two panels depicting Jesus Christ on the way to the crucifixion. Finally, we also see the same playful rhyming typical of the surrealist blues Crumb adduces in his explication; a rapid-fire sequence of chaotic happenings that challenge the viewer to construe into logic and sense; and the theme of erotic abandon as symbolized by Angelfood. Crumb has it both ways: on the one hand, he appears to merely be supplying our imaginations with "dissociated" images that defy "meaning" or "significance." The "signs" appear not to "signify." Yet at the same time he speaks in a kind of "code," which he challenges us to "decipher." He plays with chance and determinism, randomness and order, in a supremely effective fashion. Crumb's method here is quintessentially surrealist in his drive to break open our imaginations to the notion that our conventional conceptions of causality may be mistaken: indeed, our dream lives—during which our repressed aggressions and sexual urges reveal themselves—may be truer to "reality" than our conscious "civilized" minds. And here again the reader/viewer has a choice: either we can attempt to "read" the dream for meaning, or we can simply allow the sheer pleasure of beholding each image flowing into the following image to give us aesthetic pleasure, to make us smile, without seeking anything "deeper." Crumb is making psychedelic movies for the page where things "happen" spontaneously, movies that are closer to poetry or music or the paintings of the surrealists than to "rational" prose narrative.

As we have seen in earlier chapters, Crumb often weaves into his autobiographical works the same themes that he explores in his literary adaptations. Crumb's attraction to the ideas of sin and repentance, of prayer and renunciation, in these narratives concerning African American blues may be traced to his childhood, when Crumb was himself intensely pious. In his *Sketchbook*, vol. 8, he declares: "Sure I'm just a big sex degenerate who does nothing but wallow in sordid sensuality in middle age, but a long time ago I was a very different person." In the drawing, Crumb depicts himself kneeling bedside, hands clasped together praying "Hail Mary full of grace the Lord is with thee" as his brother sleeps nearby, oblivious. Although the drawing was created in 1988 and thus memorializes events in Crumb's life stretching decades back to the early fifties when he was a boy, documentary proof of the accuracy of his memory is supplied by his scrupulous eye for evidentiary detail. His notation next to his drawing of his desk chair informs us: "chair my father made in Iowa in 1952." In the panel below, he shows his devoted attendance

R. Crumb, "When I Was a Kid I Used to Pray Alot," *Sketchbook*, vol. 8.

at Holy Communion, with a nun kneeling nearby while the priest officiates at the altar. Crumb has just "gulped" his communion wafer—"swallowing host," he tells us—and he departs in his Sunday suit with prayerful hands, head radiating a nimbus of sacral rays, reporting that he now experienced himself as being "pure and in a state of grace. . . . It was a wonderful feeling."[24]

Crumb wants his audience to know that while he is "a big sex degenerate," he had also within him as a youth the drive toward a sanctified life, which we are to understand is still a central aspect of his being. Crumb has acknowledged having a dream in which he tells a Catholic priest that he had dropped out of the church at age sixteen, and the priest informs him that if he confesses and takes Holy Communion, the church would forgive him and accept him back into the fold. In the dream, Crumb is now overtaken by emotion and agrees to confession: "I was on the verge of weeping. I thought of all the 'sins' I'd committed over the decades. It was partly a sort of nostalgia for the lost innocence of my childhood, when I believed in the Church and its sacraments, a desire to once again have that innocent faith in the cleansing effect of the sacraments." This sense of "sinfulness"—that there exists something within the self that needs to be confessed and accounted for and redeemed—is an obvious remnant of his Catholic upbringing. Yet there is in Crumb's imagination also the sense that there is a deeper "Self" containing occluded within it the "pure" sparks of one's original and ancient divine nature, which would emerge—as we shall see in the following chapter—as Crumb turned more dramatically toward mysticism and Gnosticism as his career progressed.

Crumb also demonstrated his autobiographical connection to the themes of guilt, repentance, and purification, which we observed in his narratives concerning African American blues singers when he devoted a section of one of his masterworks—"Walkin' the Streets" (1992; 2004)—to his encounter during high school with African American spirituality. Crumb and his brother Charles became friends with an African American boy named Tom Freeman, who had been shunned by the Crumb family due to his race. Crumb recalls: "During our religious phase my brother and I attended Sunday services at many different churches to see what they were about, including a small black one. Charles's friend Tom Freeman was the son of the minister of this church." Crumb describes the congregation singing hymns, and music is central to the ecstatic atmosphere as Reverend Freeman preaches a sermon: "[S]oon the whole room was a mass of rocking, clapping, shouting people. Charles and I had never witnessed such behavior in church before."[25] The congregation throws itself into a frenzy to "save" the Crumb brothers; however, Robert notes that he was unable to "believe" and experienced no surge of religious feeling. This Dionysian ecstasy is a far cry from what Crumb had witnessed previously in the white churches of his youth and demonstrates that even in his early years Crumb had already formed a strong psychological connection to the inner lives of African Americans.

There is an irony of course in the fact that Crumb is sometimes accused of both misogyny and racism in his portrayals of women, African Americans, and Jews. Corey K. Creekmur in "Multiculturalism Meets the Counterculture: Representing Racial Difference in Robert Crumb's Underground Comix" has argued that "race remains a blind spot in critical discussions of underground comix, despite a few isolated essays that have addressed the otherwise neglected (if not actively dodged) topic."[26] Crumb obviously deeply admires Black musicians and composers, and as we can see from both "Jelly Roll Morton's Voodoo Curse" and "Patton," he also demonstrates a sensitive appreciation for the history and culture of the South. In Crumb's portrayals of Blacks, Jews, and women, his goal is to send up stereotypes that are lodged in the American subconscious, to bring to light the hidden cauldron of simultaneous fear and attraction that gives birth to stereotypes in the first place. If he shows any person's or group's "positive" qualities—or his own, for that matter—he feels duty bound to also expose the "shadow" or the less appealing side. So too Crumb never viewed "spirituality" as being all "sweetness and light." In a revealing conversation concerning his brother Maxon, who begged on the streets of San Francisco and led an increasingly introverted, bizarre interior life, Crumb declared:

> He's an intense character. There's something you can learn from people like that, if you can take the weird aspects of them. But I think that from knowing him, and knowing other people like gurus, anybody like that who you get involved with has a price. There's always some crazy thing about them that's very heavy. People that have strong things that communicate something spiritual, there's always something crazy about them. It's just a fairy tale that there are perfect, sweet saints who emanate great spiritual vibrations or something. There's always a dark side to all that stuff. Everybody's human. But I've learned a lot from my brother—a lot. When I argue with him, a lot of times later I realize that in some ways he's right about everything.

Crumb's conception here again recalls Carl G. Jung's notion of the Shadow—the "dark" side of the conscious ego that represents the hidden or repressed side of the Self. The "sweet saints" may in fact be tormented souls, but that secret face they do not show to the world. So too, living at the far

R. Crumb, "Walkin' the Streets," *Zap*, no. 15 (2004).

reaches of human potential and striving by necessity may lead to "madness," since pushing at the limits of our being may lead to fragmentation and destruction. Music is perhaps a way to balance the Apollonian and Dionysian, to find a way to live within the polarities of life. Crumb certainly learned from the blues, from being beaten down, from sexual/romantic drama and anguish, loneliness and solitude. The power of music may be likened to the pleasure and freedom attained through meditation. In his *Sketchbook*, vol. 7, Crumb declares: "The act of meditation has the power to slow down, and possibly stop altogether, the onrushing chain of reaction that takes place in the mind … the relentless, ever-deepening tangle of reaction on top of reaction that never ceases until one becomes conscious of making it cease."[27] As an alienated outsider, Crumb identified with the Beats, with Jewish people, with African Americans as fellow alienated Americans, and in each case Crumb responded to the transmuting of suffering into art.

Chapter 3

PHILIP K. DICK

Gnostic Travels

~~~~~~

As we have seen in the previous chapter, during the mid-eighties Crumb turned his attention to biographies of his beloved blues musicians, yet during this phase he also became increasingly interested in illustrating literary works. When during an interview Jean-Pierre Mercier noted the "growing importance of literature" in his output, Crumb responded: "I think at a certain point I had enough skill available to take those things on. I wouldn't have dared take them on when I was young. I was challenged by the idea of doing this kind of realistic style, using a brush and with that sort of dark film-noir style that was popular in comics around 1950. I was very attracted to that and was studying a lot of those comics."[1] This "dark film-noir" approach lent itself well in dealing with the subject uniting Crumb's treatments of Philip K. Dick, Jean-Paul Sartre, and Franz Kafka: human suffering and the quest for psychological and philosophical freedom. And while all of these works borrow elements from the Classics Illustrated comics of his childhood, they often exhibit qualities far beyond the achievements of earlier cartoonists in their virtuosic draftsmanship and their intellectually probing power.

In illustrating the work of Philip K. Dick (1928–1982), Crumb strives to translate the ideas of a modern master of speculative fiction whose works have been recently canonized through inclusion in the prestigious Library of America series.[2] Dick's popularity is due to his skill at elaborating many of the postmodern themes that one also finds in Beat literature: the quest for identity, for the "real Self," for some lost ancient secret wisdom that may provide answers to the eternal riddles of human existence. Other artists such as Art Spiegelman also gravitated toward Dick's work: Spiegelman discovered *The Three Stigmata of Palmer Eldritch* (1964) and *The Zap Gun*

(1965), corresponded with Dick, and finally met the author, spending several days with him in intense discussions. Spiegelman considered Dick "the only person describing accurately the same border problems I was having—not being able to figure out where I ended off and everybody else began—not being able to figure out what I was causing and what was being caused onto me." "Border problems"—a sense of the liminal nature of one's selfhood and a sometimes-overwhelming feeling of vulnerability to the outside world—also define Crumb's psychological orientation.

Crumb's interest in Dick similarly derives from his own struggles with "identity" and quest for the archetypal sources of the Self. Harold Schechter has observed:

> Crumb's imagination is strikingly mythopoeic. . . . [His] comics derive a great deal of their force—not from the social satire they contain—but from the richness of their mythic imagery—from their archetypal symbolism. . . . Of all contemporary cartoonists, the one who seems most closely in touch with "those fluid ever-changing changeless archetypes that gloom and glow in the depths of the archaic psyche" is Crumb. . . . If his comics are brilliant records of contemporary society, they also reflect a very different world—i.e., the collective unconscious, the "timeless and universal" realm of myth.[3]

We observe Crumb's reformulations of myths, legends, and fairy tales—often in parodic versions—throughout his career. In high school, he composed a term paper on the Faust myth, studying both Goethe's and Christopher Marlowe's versions. His first major work—R. Crumb's Yum Yum Book (written in 1962, published in 1975)—is cast in the form of the classic English fairy tale "Jack and the Beanstalk." In 1987, he illustrated "Mother Hulda" by the Brothers Grimm and also created a parody of "Goldilocks and the Three Bears."[4] And even when he illustrates a historical text, Crumb emphasizes the mythic quality of the story. In a superb two-page narrative included in the Sketchbooks entitled "Rough Women of the Dark Ages," Crumb adapts a passage from The History of the Franks by Gregory of Tours (ca. 538–97) depicting a rollicking physical fight involving the daughter of King Chilperic, Rigunth, and her mother, Fredegund, over the deceased king's belongings. Crumb revels in depicting blood flying from angry punches to the face: the maid looks on in horror while, amid the carnage, we note a comic touch as Crumb depicts a crucifix hanging on the wall behind the warring ladies. And at the end, Fredegund traps her daughter's head and neck beneath the lid of a heavy chest containing the king's "jewels and precious ornaments." The whole effect of this wonderful work is to make us feel we have just witnessed a kind of "fractured fairy tale" in which all the elements of a putative historical narrative have been revealed to contain the archetypal elements of myth: dead king, mother/daughter rivalry, violence, and greed.

Schechter goes on to observe that the British psychotherapist Alan Mc-Glashan published an essay, "Daily Paper Pantheon," in 1953, arguing that the drama enacted by contemporary comic characters "sounds the echo of something unimaginably archaic: the adventure cycle of the early gods." Carl Jung, in "On the Psychology of the Trickster Figure," alludes to McGlashan's analysis in his own interpretation and asserts that "the figures in comic-strips have remarkable archetypal analogies."[5] Schechter's citing of Jung is apposite, since Jung's interests prepared the way for the counterculture. Crumb during the late eighties and early nineties studied texts such as Jung's *Man and His Symbols*, commencing a more conscious exploration of his inner life, although as we have seen the signs and symbols of such a quest were already omnipresent in his work. Crumb emphasized that during this period he grew "more interested in 'the journey within,' the great adventure into the unknown inside one's self. Isn't it strange that we are such a mystery to ourselves?"[6] In a sketchbook drawing, Crumb quotes a similar sentiment from Carlos Castaneda's *Tales of Power*: "The world is unfathomable. And so are we, and so is every being that exists in this world." And Crumb's language also echoes that of Joseph Campbell in his popular book and television series *The Power of Myth* (1988)—"the journey within," "the great adventure"—Campbell was himself of course deeply influenced by Jung. Just below the Castaneda quotation, Crumb includes a passage in which Campbell depicts a circle with a square above a line, and beneath the line a dot that symbolizes the true center of the psyche: the unconscious, *not* the ego. This is precisely what Dick is aiming at in his Gnostic mysticism: that the real Self is not the controlling "I" or "ego" but rather a deeper source of knowledge and intuition that contains archetypal, primal, archaic wisdom, which we may fathom and contact under the proper circumstances. Furthermore, many of Crumb's stories—for example "Bad Karma" and "Can You Stand Up against the Universe?"—are cast in the form of the quest narrative in which his antiheroes must undergo a number of initiatory tests in order to achieve some measure of enlightenment regarding their existential situation. Indeed, Crumb's dreams are often transcribed directly onto the page and are actually "initiatory quests." Since around 2010, Crumb has submitted written accounts of his dreams to the underground magazine *Mineshaft*, edited by Everett Rand and Gioia Palmieri, and these—as well as many more—as we have noted were recently collected and published as *R. Crumb's Dream Diary* (2018).

The work of both Crumb and Philip K. Dick emerged from the cultural ferment that characterized California during the sixties: Crumb was living in the Haight-Ashbury district during the same time that Dick was living in Marin County. California had long been a central locus of a panoply of philosophical seekers. In California, Taoism, Vedantism, Hinduism, and Zen Buddhism found a congenial environment. Aldous Huxley, Christopher Isherwood, Gerald Heard, and Swami Prabhavananda—founder of the Vedanta Society—were all living in southern California in the forties, while Jiddu Krishnamurti gave seminars in Ojai, a picturesque town a few hours north of Los Angeles. Paramahansa Yogananda established his Self-Realization Fellowship in southern California in 1925 and authored *The Autobiography of a Yogi*—a favorite book of Crumb's. Shunryu Suzuki Roshi (1904–1971) founded the San Francisco Zen Center with a branch in the city called Sokoji at 1881 Bush Street, as well as a mountain center in Tassajara. The Buddhist community in California began as early as 1905, when—according to Rick Fields in *How the Swans Came to the Lake: A Narrative of Buddhism in America*—the Japanese Zen master Soyen Shaku arrived in San Francisco. D. T. Suzuki—who became a significant influence on Beats such as Gary Snyder—acted as Shaku's interpreter.[7] We have seen in chapter 1 the ways Zen themes permeated Crumb's earliest work and his invention of the wily Mr. Natural character. Furthermore, during the early sixties in Palo Alto, Elaine Pagels (1943–)—who would emerge as a prominent scholar of Gnosticism—became a member of a circle of writers and musicians including Jerry Garcia of the Grateful Dead. Pagels began her spiritual search by first joining in her youth an evangelical Christian community, which she would soon reject due to its dogmatism, turning later in her career to studies of the Nag Hammadi manuscripts and the origins of Gnostic thought.

Moving to the West Coast in 1967 was thus significant in Crumb's development. He gradually combined his unique sensibility with California's spiritual traditions as they expressed themselves within the emergent artistic culture flourishing in the Bay Area as well as Los Angeles and Topanga Canyon in southern California. Denis Johnston in *Precipitations: Contemporary American Poetry as Occult Practice* has pointed out that

> the "funk" artists of the West Coast, including Jess Collins, George Herms, Bruce Conner, and Jay DeFeo drew on a hodgepodge of occult and religious sources, as did the filmmakers Stan Brakhage, Harry Smith, and Kenneth Anger. Likewise, among practitioners of the "New American Poetry" such as Helen Adam, Robert Duncan, Robert Kelly, Philip Lamantia, Diane di Prima, John Wieners, and Allen Ginsberg,

occultism proved a topical source of interest as well as a means by which to define their process.

The orientation of these figures toward political, sexual, and artistic freedom mirrored Crumb's: Jay DeFeo created her celebrated, massive sculpture *The Rose* between 1958 and 1966, while Bruce Conner (1933–2008) declared that he and his fellow artists "were interested in a spiritual quest. It was a time when people would die or go to jail for their art." Conner was speaking of his friend Wallace Berman, editor of the underground magazine *Semina*, which published the Beats as well as authors such as Antonin Artaud and Charles Bukowski. Berman was immersed in the study of Kabbalah, and his Ferus Gallery in Los Angeles was raided by the police for "obscenity." Poet David Meltzer compiled an anthology of Kabbalistic texts, *The Secret Garden*, and, as we shall see, comics artists such as Rick Griffin incorporated Kabbalistic imagery in their work. George Herms was a pioneer in the evolution of California assemblage sculpture who included astrological symbols in his wall-mounted *Saturn Collage* (1960).[8] Underground newspapers such as the psychedelically colorful *San Francisco Oracle* were packed with articles on Hinduism, astrology, the *I Ching*, Buddhism, shamanism, Native American spirituality, and tarot.

Previously, other artists had explored similar territory. During the early sixties, Steve Ditko (1927–) developed esoteric themes in *Dr. Strange*, chronicling the Ancient One—the mentor of Dr. Strange—whose home is in the Himalayas. Dr. Strange wears a magic amulet on his neck—"The Eye of Agamotto"—recalling the All-Seeing Eye of the Buddha worn by Buddhists in northern India. As we have seen, a Cosmic Eye peering spookily upon the shenanigans of humanity below, the Third Eye of Hinduism, and a wide variety of imploding, exploding, or melting eyes pervade Crumb's work. The theosophist Helena Petrovna Blavatsky's (1831–1891) "Tibetan Masters" have been suggested as having influenced these connections in Ditko's work to Buddhism and India. As Bradford W. Wright has pointed out in *Comic Book Nation: The Transformation of Youth Culture in America*: "Inspired by the pulp-fiction magazines of Stan Lee's childhood as well as by contemporary Beat culture, Dr. Strange remarkably predicted the youth counterculture's fascination with Eastern mysticism and psychedelia."[9] Justin Green—who as we have seen in the introduction broke new ground in personal confession with his *Binky Brown Meets the Holy Virgin Mary*—also delved into magical lore. The front and back covers of *Binky* feature modifications of the tarot card symbols: on the front, Strength—a woman opening the mouth of a lion; and on the back, Destruction—lightning striking a sign at Kentucky Fried

Chicken restaurant. John Thompson (1943–) joined with Don Schenker to create *Yellow Dog*, which published twenty-two issues between 1968 and 1973: Crumb contributed his work to the magazine. Thompson as a child already possessed an affinity for Gnosticism and Buddhism, and his work is replete with motifs derived from astrological, alchemical, and mythological sources. Crumb has acknowledged that he derived the cyclops-eyed guitarist that he created for the cover of Janis Joplin's *Cheap Thrills* album from Thompson's work.

Other visionary artists involved with Crumb in the alternative comix scene such as Rick Griffin (1944–1991) were also drawn to esoteric sources: Griffin would ultimately convert to Christianity. Erik Davis has observed that Griffin was

> one of the key rock poster designers of the psychedelic era . . . a heavy and idiosyncratic symbolism that drew from orange crate art, Manly Hall's *Secret Teaching of the Ages*, blobular modernism, and his own intense imagination. Griffin remixed Kabbalistic and esoteric Christian imagery for R. Crumb's *Zap* magazine while the flying eyeball poster he designed for a Jimi Hendrix Fillmore gig remains perhaps the single most iconic image of the era, an unnerving mix of pop Surrealism, eldritch nightmare, and divine invasion.

The stupendous cover Griffin created for *Zap*, no. 3 (December 1968), features a winged beetle-like creature with a speech bubble containing the tetragrammaton enclosing the Hebrew letter *shin* in the middle, which spells Yahshuah or Jesus, thus indicating Griffin's familiarity with the Christian adoption of Kabbalistic knowledge during the Renaissance. The beetle is gesticulating toward a sun creature equipped with flailing hands and feet running up the stairs of a cave toward a beckoning blue sky with skulls on the floor and scampering eyeball creatures also sporting arms and legs.[10] The eyeball/crazy-limbed imagery here reappears in Crumb's stylistic repertoire. Thomas Albright in *Art in the San Francisco Bay Area, 1945–1980: An Illustrated History* connects the poster artists with the development of *Zap*: "The adolescent exuberance, earthiness, and iconoclasm—as well as a sharp commercial instinct—that had found expression in certain aspects of the poster movement reappeared in the underground comic books—or 'comix,' in the fashionable argot."[11] Thus, as early as his groundbreaking contributions to *Zap* in 1967, Crumb's work reflected powerful imagery that shared much in common with the work of other visionary artists in the Bay Area during this period.

Finally, the artist Jay Kinney—publisher of *Occult Laff Parade* (1973), which dealt wittily with themes such as yoga, cults, the astral plane, mantras, and sexuality—also evinced an interest in the writings of Philip K. Dick. Crumb's connection to Kinney originated in the late sixties: they collaborated on *Bijou*—edited by Jay Lynch and Skip Williamson—which appeared in eight issues from 1968 to 1973. Kinney served as editor of *CoEvolution Quarterly* (1983–1984), which began in 1974 as an outgrowth of Stewart Brand's *Whole Earth Catalog* and in which he often featured Crumb's work. In 1975, Art Spiegelman at *Arcade* magazine solicited a story from Philip K. Dick— "The Eye of the Sibyl"—to be illustrated by Kinney for the magazine, but it was never published there. However, when Kinney later became editor of *Gnosis* magazine (1985–1999), his illustrations to "The Eye of the Sibyl" appeared in *Gnosis*, no. 5 (Fall 1987). Furthermore, Kinney based the layout of the first issues of *Gnosis* on *Weirdo*, which Crumb had edited and which appeared between 1981 and 1993. Other magazines to which Crumb contributed during this period include *Yarrowstalks*, published in Philadelphia by Brian Zahn—"Mr. Natural" first appeared here in 1967—and taking its name from the method for casting divination throws with yarrow stalks in the Chinese classic *I Ching*, which had become an immensely popular text among young spiritual seekers: Bob Dylan praised it enthusiastically. Thus we can see how the countercultural spiritual movement was connected to the evolution of underground comics on many levels through a network of personal relationships that prepared the way for Crumb's own involvement.[12]

It was through Kinney that Crumb became intrigued by Philip K. Dick when he read Kinney's essay in the premiere issue of *Gnosis* (Fall–Winter 1985–1986) entitled "The Mysterious Revelations of Philip K. Dick" describing the author's encounter with Gnostic thought in the form of an electrifying visionary interlude. Crumb then resolved to illustrate it: his eight-page "The Religious Experience of Philip K. Dick" appeared in *Weirdo*, no. 17 (1986) and was later included in the volume *The Weirdo Years, 1981–'93*. Crumb queries in the opening panel: "Philip K. Dick was a writer of science fiction. In 1982 he died suddenly of a stroke. His books often dealt with the illusory quality of reality as we know it. In March 1974 Dick saw what he later described as 'a vision of the apocalypse,' and spent the rest of his life trying to understand what he had experienced. Was it the onset of acute schizophrenia, or was it a genuine mystic revelation, and then again, is there any difference??" The massive manuscript that resulted from Dick's epiphany—he would spend eight years until his death recording in an eight-thousand-page, two-million-word notebook his efforts to fathom its meaning—appeared posthumously as *The Exegesis of Philip K. Dick* (2011).[13]

In his *Sketchbooks*, Crumb seemed to wonder the same thing about himself as in his musings concerning his LSD trips: "Most of the time it was terrifying. . . . And what good did it do to me. Am I any less of a *fool* because of that experience??" Interestingly, Crumb pictures himself with a beard—as he does Dick—a haggard face and furrowed brow, his eyes weary, mouth open to a row of unpleasant teeth, an entire turbulent visage communicating the toll that his "mystic revelations" from LSD have taken on his psyche. Crumb also pondered the relationship between spirituality and "insanity": "I've never known very many authentically spiritual people. I think my brother Charles struggled to achieve high spiritual states, and my brother Maxon still does, but both of them were crazy! Where do you draw the line between craziness and spirituality? I don't know. Especially as they are often embodied in the same person." As we shall see in the following chapters, this link between possible madness and transcendence becomes a recurring theme throughout Crumb's oeuvre. Crumb's attraction to Dick is due to the fact that he sees his own experience of a "divine visitation" as equally inscrutable. John Hick has argued that such episodes preserve information deriving from a source he calls "the Real," observing: "As possible indicators of the nature of reality they can either be dismissed as the remarkable hallucinatory projections of religious eccentrics or accepted as manifestations of the Real within the peak experiences of exceptionally sensitive individuals."[14] Dick's epiphany obviously recalled Crumb's own consciousness-expanding experiences with LSD during the mid-sixties and his haunting desire to fathom their meaning and significance. Furthermore, Dick had lived in the Bay Area during the efflorescence of the Beat period, becoming friends with poets Robert Duncan and Jack Spicer, both of whom were fascinated by Gnosticism, Kabbalah, tarot, theosophy, and magic.[15]

It is during this period of the mid-eighties that Crumb's more ostensible turn to "mysticism" may be said to begin. Crumb has described a phase beginning in 1985–1986 after the film *The Confessions of Robert Crumb* was released on BBC Television when he traveled to France and became profoundly depressed due to the increasing publicity resulting from the film. Crumb was undergoing a deep interior crisis:

> You have to get over it, or go under. You have to do one or the other. It could have driven me to suicide. I realized I had to deal with it. And for me, the only way to deal with it was to go toward mysticism. I had to get control of the inner self. To do that, you have to meditate and examine yourself very closely. It's partly self-psychoanalysis. It takes a high degree of motivation to do that without outside help. For me

it can't just be Freudian. It's got to involve something that gives my life meaning. It's almost like Alcoholics Anonymous, when they tell you that you must have connections to some higher power, otherwise, you can't do it. To get involved in mysticism is a matter of survival for me. It's not just a hobby or dilettante thing. I need this. If I didn't have this, I have no idea in what kind of condition I might be. I'm soft and weak, I'm not a tough guy. I can't deal with humanity in a tough way like Picasso could, like Aline can. A lot of things would kill me if I didn't have this way of dealing with them. It's a way of withdrawing in a sense, but I don't think it's unhealthy.[16]

One might speculate concerning the underlying reasons for this "breakdown." Perhaps as Crumb's fame increased, he also felt the pressure of "exposure": his inner self was on full display, and secrets of his troubled family were now known to a wide public. On the one hand, he desires of course for his work as an artist to become recognized and appreciated by the world. However, with renown also comes a lack of privacy, and strangers often become intrusive upon one's time and energy. Crumb himself has remarked: "When I was young I was an observer of life, as an invisible, ghost-like figure. I observed the world as if detached from it. And then, I became the observed. It drives me insane being the observed. I like being invisible. Originally, it felt painful being invisible, unloved and all that, but now I realize that that was a gift I can never get back." It is noteworthy that Crumb abjures a Freudian approach to the psyche, which deals in a materialistic fashion with superego, ego, and id. Crumb, on the other hand, prefers a Jungian approach to the mysteries of the Self, and he associates the archetypal, symbolic world of the unconscious with "mysticism." It was precisely during this period of inner upheaval that Crumb was ready to approach the work of Philip K. Dick.

Crumb, like Dick, was intrigued by the question of the authenticity of religious experience, which—as we have seen in the last chapter—he would dramatize in several other works, such as "Jelly Roll Morton's Voodoo Curse." Crumb strives to provide a faithful version of the literary texts he illustrates while simultaneously interrogating the meaning of epiphanies and their possible relationship to either delusory thinking or mental illness. Crumb perceived the comic side of this cosmic—after all, the words "comic" and "cosmic" differ only by the one letter s—questing. He was well aware of the possibly absurd aspects of "revelations," declaring in an interview:

In all those literary things that I did, I saw something comic in the characters that was probably not intended to be there in the original.

Even Sartre, there was something comical especially in his conversation with the *self-taught man*. There was something that lent itself to a comic book rendition that probably was not intended by him. The same thing with Philip K. Dick and his religious experiences. There's something absurd and comical about his paranoia and his religious visions and how he interpreted them.[17]

"The Religious Experience of Philip K. Dick" comprises eight pages, each containing seven panels save the first, which has three, and pages 6 and 8, each with six. The splash page features the title along with a portrait of Dick's bearded visage and haunted, searching, wide-open eyes. Throughout Crumb's work, the eye—both inner and outer—is often emphasized as the central organ of spiritual perception, the door opening toward visionary experience as well as existential terror. Crumb is particularly skilled at drawing supple lines, depicting faces that reveal interior, psychological turmoil: Dick will appear alternately as fatigued, shocked, worried, hypnotized, exalted, or—as Crumb described above—a victim of "paranoia." As poet Bill Berkson perceptively observed: "Crumb's Rapidograph line quivers with vexation . . . its paroxysms breed perpetual unrest." The lettering of the phrase "The Religious Experience" is tall and thin, while "Of Philip K. Dick" is wider and angled to the right as if italicized, adding to his name a measure of suspenseful allure. Dick's forehead is emblazoned with a fish-like symbol—the significance of which we shall learn later—while the background is packed with swirling, electric, energetic snake-like shapes emanating from all sides of his face and head. One detects here the influence of L. B. Cole's (1918–1995) covers for *Suspense Comics*, featuring spinning vortexes and psychedelic, hellish fires, whose influence Crumb has acknowledged. These sinuous powers suggest some force field containing a potent charge emanating from Dick's consciousness and/or simultaneously impinging upon it. This ambiguity rests at the center of Crumb's approach to Dick's preternatural experience: did some external power "invade" his being—Lawrence Sutin's biography of Dick is subtitled "divine invasions"—or was it an internal psychological delusion? Crumb indicates in an asterisked footnote at the close that most of the dialogue he employed derives from Gregg Rickman's *Philip K. Dick: The Last Testament*—a series of interviews Rickman conducted with the author between April 1981 and February 1982. However, Crumb also includes extracts from Dick's recollections of the episode, which appeared in *Gnosis* (Fall–Winter 1985). Crumb read both these texts with some attention, for he has carefully constructed his narrative by piecing together sections from

THE RELIGIOUS EXPERIENCE
OF PHILIP K. DICK

PHILIP K. DICK WAS A WRITER OF *SCIENCE FICTION.* IN 1982 HE DIED SUDDENLY OF A STROKE. HIS BOOKS OFTEN DEALT WITH THE ILLUSORY QUALITY OF REALITY AS WE KNOW IT. IN MARCH, 1974 DICK SAW WHAT HE LATER DESCRIBED AS "A VISION OF THE APOCALYPSE," AND SPENT THE REST OF HIS LIFE TRYING TO UNDERSTAND WHAT HE HAD EXPERIENCED. WAS IT THE ONSET OF ACUTE SCHIZOPHRENIA, OR WAS IT A GENUINE MYSTIC REVELATION, AND THEN AGAIN, IS THERE ANY DIFFERENCE ??

FULLERTON, CALIFORNIA, MARCH, 1974: "I HAD A WISDOM TOOTH EXTRACTED. THEY GAVE ME A TREMENDOUS AMOUNT OF SODIUM PENTOTHAL. I CAME HOME AND WAS IN GREAT PAIN. HE HADN'T GIVEN ME ANY PAIN MEDICATION AND MY WIFE CALLED THE PHARMACY."

"I WAS IN SUCH PAIN THAT I WENT OUT TO MEET THE GIRL WHEN SHE CAME. SHE WAS WEARING A GOLDEN FISH IN PROFILE ON A NECKLACE. THE SUN STRUCK IT AND IT SHONE, AND I WAS DAZED BY IT."

R. Crumb, "The Religious Experience of Philip K. Dick," *Weirdo*, no. 17 (1986).

Rickman's 241-page compilation of Dick's final conversations as well as material from Jay Kinney's "The Mysterious Revelations of Philip K. Dick."[18]

Comics are often defined as possessing two key elements: they represent the passage of time through panels in sequence as well as image and word in interaction with one another.[19] Crumb is talented at both. One notes the total absence of word or speech bubbles: the first-person narration appears only in boxes above or to the side of each panel, thus giving the sensation of a direct documentary account. Indeed, since Dick is the only speaker, it would be unnecessarily awkward to have each of his statements appear above his head. We are carried immediately and directly into an immersive, engaging encounter with the uncanny. Assaf Gamzou and Ken Koltun-Fromm have emphasized the particular power of comics to achieve this feat: "Through texture, line thickness, time configured as space, and the various tricks comic artists use to engage the reader as active co-creators, graphic narratives can inform how readers imagine and reconstruct the sacred as a material, visual experience." The opening of the narrative proper tells us that while having his wisdom teeth extracted, Dick's dentist administered a "massive" injection of sodium pentothal. When he arrived home in intense pain, Dick's wife phoned the pharmacy to obtain the medication that had been prescribed. Upon answering the door, Dick noticed that the delivery girl "was wearing a golden fish in profile on a necklace. The sun struck it and it shone, and I was dazed by it." In ancient Greek, the word *ichthus* means "fish," and the letters I-C-H-T-H-U-S stand for Iesous Christos Theou Uios Soter, Jesus Christ Son of God Savior—and a fish became the symbol for early Christians in the second century CE. Crumb depicts a beam of light extending from Dick's eye to the necklace, indicating a kind of "X-ray" or supernatural vision, familiar to us from science fiction, comics, and movies, while the girl's sweater on which the fish rests radiates light in several oval patterns, suggesting that her amulet possesses supernatural connections. This preternatural experience, which occurred on February 3, 1974, was so indelible that Dick would henceforth refer to it telegraphically as "2–3–74," incorporating aspects of the drama of that dramatic day into many of his later writings. Crumb develops his story by assembling several separate sections from Rickman's text—on the epiphany itself, Dick's conception of himself as the prophet Elijah, the health crisis involving Dick's infant son, America as a modern version of a corrupt ancient Rome, and the role of the *I Ching* in Dick's attempt to decipher the meaning of his "revelation"—into a single narrative.

In the first panel of the second page, the uncanny elements increase exponentially as virtually the entire background is filled with detailed radiating rings of cross-hatching—repeating imagery from the prior panel of the fish amulet resting on the girl's sweater—indicating some cosmic force emitting discrete quanta of energy. Dick describes himself as being completely oblivious to his physical pain and "hypnotized" by the fish symbol. When Dick asks what the meaning of the fish is, the delivery girl informs him—and her head now is illuminated by rays of light resembling a halo—that "this is a sign worn by the early Christians." Crumb provides an intense close-up—as in the cinema—of Dick's open-eyed face, concentrating the viewer's attention on this central moment: he tells us later that what he had experienced was *anamnesis* (ancient Greek for "loss of forgetfulness"), a term employed by Plato in his *Meno, Phaedo,* and *Phaedrus* to describe the theory that when we learn, we are actually remembering something we already knew previously. Crumb depicts what Rudolf Otto named in *Das Heilige* (1917; translated as *The Idea of the Holy,* 1923) as the *numinous:* the *mysterium tremendum et fascinans.* The experience of the divine is a fearful and fascinating mystery, and Crumb is able to effectively convey the mix of emotions on Dick's face: he is both *awed* and *terrified* by what he has encountered.

In just these six opening panels, we have already witnessed a riveting drama that testifies to Crumb's ability to concentrate in a very brief space an impressive array of details to effectively move his narrative forward. He is careful—as is Alfred Hitchcock in his greatest films—to keep viewers in suspense by not revealing the entire significance of each intense moment, and also to keep them equally intrigued by both image and story. Thierry Groensteen has observed:

> The reader of comics not only enjoys a *story-related* pleasure but also an *art-related* pleasure, an aesthetic emotion founded on the appreciation of the exactness and expressivity of a composition, pose, or line. There also exists, in my opinion, a *medium-related* pleasure. It cannot be reduced to the sum of the other two, but is related to the rhythmic organization in space and time of a multiplicity of small images. Comic art is the art of details, and as such encourages a fetishistic relationship.

Crumb is highly gifted not only at creating the individual panels but at strategically composing each tier in such a way that the entire page presents itself to the viewer as an aesthetically pleasing whole. He carries the plot forward swiftly, emphasizing the fact that Dick was suffering from physical as well as psychological anguish—his life at this point was fraught with financial (the IRS was pursuing him for payment of taxes) and severe personal problems—thus the moment of *anamnesis* arrives at precisely the right time in his personal history.

In panel 4, page 4, we are suddenly catapulted from modern America back to ancient times with Dick now wearing a headscarf, as is the delivery girl, symbolizing their participation in a "secret" Christian community among the Romans: "I remembered who I was and where I was." Although Crumb does not gloss this brief declaration, it alludes to the *Excerpta Ex Theodoto*—fragments preserved in Greek by Clement of Alexandria (150–215 CE) of the works of the Gnostic Theodotus: "What liberates is the knowledge of who we were, what we became; where we were, whereinto we have been thrown; whereto we speed, wherefrom we are redeemed; what birth is, and what rebirth."[20] In his *Exegesis*, Dick analyzed his encounter with the girl as follows: "The [golden] fish sign causes you to remember. Remember what? This is Gnostic. Your celestial origins; this has to do with the DNA because the memory is located in the DNA [phylogenetic memory].... You remember your real *nature*. Which is to say, origins [from the stars].... The Gnostic Gnosis. You are here in this world in a thrown condition, but you are not *of* this world." For Martin Heidegger—as well as for Jim Morrison of the Doors—*into this world we're thrown*. This reference to a Gnostic text supplies the hint that while Dick at this point believes he has encountered a vision of early Christianity, what he has actually experienced is a Gnostic revelation: *gnosis* derives from ancient Greek *gnoein* or "to know." Coincidentally, Grant Morrison—whose work bears the influence of H. P. Lovecraft, Aleister Crowley, Tantra, and Gnosticism—alludes in his series *The Invisibles* (1994–2000) to an episode of "enlightenment" he experienced in Kathmandu and which he explicitly compared to Dick's "vision of the apocalypse." Morrison also, in December 1995, had a near-death vision of a "Gnostic Jesus" who told him: "I am not the god of your fathers. I am the hidden stone that breaks all hearts"—the line appears in *The Invisibles*.

Dick would come to believe that he was "Thomas" as the narrator reveals in his novel *VALIS*: "There's someone else living in me and he's not in this century.... He called the personality in him living in another century and at another place 'Thomas.'" Dick has taken this name from the Gnostic Gospel of Thomas, and another example of the way Crumb's literary and spiritual preoccupations surface in his own drawings as well as evidence of his familiarity with the Gospel of Thomas—which is purported to contain the secret teachings of Jesus—appears in several sketchbook illustrations, most notably in a work from November 2001. Assigning the title of a popular song to the top of the drawing—in this case, "What a Friend We Have in Jesus"—is a common procedure for Crumb in his *Sketchbooks*. A Christian hymn composed originally as a poem in 1855, it was later set to music in 1868. Crumb signs the drawing humorously, "Sy Twombly," obviously after the contemporary American artist Cy Twombly (1928–2011). Kneeling beneath Jesus is "a poor sinner" who reaches out to touch and implore the "kind lord . . . all loving savior . . . please, please . . . deliver me . . ." Crumb quotes from the Gospel of Thomas: "If you bring forth what is within you, what you bring forth will save you. If you do not bring forth what is within you, what do not bring forth will destroy you," and accompanies it with an arresting portrait of Jesus. According to the Gospel of Thomas, Jesus was not God or the "light of the world"—as in the Gospel of John—but rather a human teacher who urged humanity to reveal the transcendent light that dwelled within. Elaine Pagels has remarked that the Gospel of Thomas "offers only cryptic clues—not answers—to those who seek the way to God. Thomas's 'living Jesus' challenges his hearers to find the way for themselves. . . . Jesus encourages those who seek by telling them that they already have the internal resources they need to find what they are looking for." Crumb thus sets up an opposition between the supplicant who seeks "answers" and "salvation" and the Gnostic Jesus who attempts to open the "sinner's" heart and mind to the profound depths of his own inner light and soul. Crumb's Jesus here thus is closer to the Zen master of Buddhism who refuses the role of "teacher" than to the orthodox conception of Jesus as "savior" or the saccharine tune "What a Friend We Have in Jesus," which trivializes and sentimentalizes the fierceness of the spiritual struggle the Gnostic Jesus urges us to confront. Crumb is clearly imitating medieval sculptures of Christ, as in the work from northern France (ca. 1430–1530) (see page 113), in order to emphasize the primal, poetic, ascetic, and mystical/Gnostic Christ rather than the fundamentalist, domesticated, Americanized Jesus whom Crumb finds particularly repellent.[21]

In yet another drawing—also an excerpt from the Gospel of Thomas, "Become Passers-By"—Crumb captures a couple at an Italian restaurant in France with a third figure between them commenting: "He's gorgeous in the nude." Like the Zen koan, there is a deep beauty in this riddling saying— "Become Passers-By"—which opens up to many interpretations. The Gnostic injunction to be *in* the world, but not *of* the world—to observe as a "passerby" the human scene and be ready to move on to a deeper and more significant world—is dramatically communicated with admirable economy in three words. As in Buddhism, it is our attachment to things that leads to suffering, so one needs to learn to keep moving, keep searching, keep wandering, keep passing by. Crumb depicts a daily human scene—with our absorption in food, wine, and sex—and contrasts it to our lives viewed *sub species aeternitatis*. The juxtaposition is of course jarring, which is precisely his intention. Following Crumb's encounter with Dick's epiphany and his exposure to

R. Crumb, "What a Friend We Have in Jesus," *Sketchbook*, vol. 11.

Christ, northern France, 1430–1530.

Gnostic thought, he began to incorporate Gnostic themes in his own work and is able to express the allure of this philosophy with admirable force and economy in his illustrations.

The Gnostic theme in Dick is continued in the next panel, confirming the location as ancient Rome with the additional details of the centurion and Roman buildings: we are informed that Dick "saw the world as the world of the apostolic Christian times of ancient Rome, when the fish sign was in use." We then return to the present: Dick takes the medicine and describes hemorrhaging a great deal of blood. The experience of *anamnesia* returns a month later and continues for a year. Dick later reflected: "I understood that I had not acquired a new faculty of perception but had, rather, regained an old one. For a day or so I saw as we once all had, thousands of years ago." Ingesting the drug and encountering the fish symbol seemingly transform Dick into another person. This recalls Robert Louis Stevenson, for as Vladimir Nabokov has pointed out in his essay in his *Lectures on Literature* on *The Strange Case of Dr. Jekyll and Mr. Hyde*, Jekyll does not *turn into* Hyde—"Hyde" is an obviously camouflaged version of "hide"—but rather the potion allows the self already hidden within Jekyll to emerge. In Stevenson of course it is a hideous Jungian "shadow" that comes forth, whereas in Dick, it is rather the angelic obscured self now coming into being that he is now *remembering* and encountering for the first time.[22]

Seven panels in three tiers occupy the following page, and we note Crumb's intentional creation of a claustrophobic mood in his crowding of text and image, which duplicates Dick's "flooding" of consciousness. The many quotations in rectangular boxes above or to the sides of each panel give the narrative an equal prominence—or sometimes more than equal—to the images, thus compelling the reader/viewer into an immersive experience. Crumb desires us to be with Dick in the moments he undergoes his dislocating sense of "transtemporal constancy," the feeling that he was living in an eternal, Platonic, archetypal world where past, present, and future appeared to be simultaneous. Dick claims that he wasn't "psychotic" during this "divine invasion" and its aftermath: indeed, he was able to deal effectively with the problems of everyday life. In addition, his finances improved and his literary career blossomed. He then introduces a second visitation—and this narrative continues to page 4—which occurred while he was listening to the Beatles' "Strawberry Fields Forever." His little boy—he was informed through another vision—had a life-threatening birth defect, and Dick was instructed to immediately procure him medical help, which is described as "I saw the light." This is brought to vivid reality in the final panel of page 4: here we see the fiery light again that adorned the very opening of the tale crawling up the walls, up the center, and along the edges of the door. Dick begins to attempt to understand his experiences with this "cosmic consciousness"—as Walt Whitman's biographer Richard M. Bucke called it—over the next seven years. He purchases one of the fish symbols and places it in his window. As he is contemplating the sixth letter of ICHTHUS—the Greek letter upsilon—the upper part of the *U* transforms in the following panel's close-up into a palm tree. Dick's imagination now opens to a vision of Mesopotamia, and Crumb employs imagery that he will feature in his *The Book of Genesis Illustrated by R Crumb*: palms trees, desert sands, and ancient dwellings. If we inspect carefully, the word "VALIS" is also visible: the letters can be seen in reverse through the windowpane. Although this is not explained within the text, it alerts us to the fact that Crumb is incorporating additional knowledge he has obtained from Jay Kinney's essay on Dick. VALIS is an acronym for Vast Active Intelligence System—the force that Dick believed had "invaded" his consciousness and that would be the subject of his "Valis" trilogy: *VALIS* (1981), *Divine Invasion* (1981), and *The Transmigration of Timothy Archer* (1982). Dick believes that he has been "taken over" by this ancient doppelgänger, and in the final panel we are returned to the contemporary world.

Crumb packs the panel with his favorite pictorial vocabulary depicting crowded, vulgar, urban America festooned by ubiquitous horrid telephone wires and garish neon signs, yet with subtle details that emerge only upon close inspection indicating the time-shifting to ancient Rome: the nightclub to the left is named "the Forum"; the auto shop sign partially obscured by a telephone pole clearly reads "Appian Way Motors"; a man walking immediately behind Dick and the girl sports a cap emblazoned with his company's logo, "Empire Builders." Through these clever and humorous hints—Forum, Appian Way, Empire—Crumb suggests the confusion and correlation within Dick's mind between the ancient and the modern, between his "two identities." Harvey Pekar has remarked concerning Crumb's affection for "eyeball kicks," which Pekar defines as "humorous effects jammed into the panel in some way or another which are ostensibly secondary to the action of the main characters in a comic book or strip story but which still are, hopefully, quite funny in themselves." This is a technique that Crumb often employs to engage the reader/viewer in deciphering hidden clues in his drawings in order to make them active agents in the uncovering of his meanings, and to make them smile: Crumb's panels are often dense with fascinating detail, very much like the canvases of several of his favorite artists such as Pieter Bruegel, William Hogarth, and Hieronymus Bosch.

John Lennon once remarked that America today "is the Roman Empire and New York is Rome itself," and images of the modern city in juxtaposition with Rome follow in the first and third frames of the following page, where we find on buildings depicted behind Dick, "Cato's Plumbing Fixtures" and "Virgil's T.V." The first alludes to the Roman family of senator and historian Cato the Elder (243–149 BCE) and his great grandson, the Stoic statesman Cato the Younger (95–40 BCE); the second obviously refers to the poet who created the *Aeneid*, Publius Vergilius Maro (70–19 BCE). In each instance Crumb pairs the ancient Roman historical allusion with a contemporary, quotidian American business enterprise: Forum/nightclub; Appian Way/car lot; Empire/construction company; Cato family/plumbing; Virgil/television shop. In the manner of T. S. Eliot and Ezra Pound—and like Beat poets such as Philip Whalen—Crumb employs the modernist literary technique of juxtaposing contemporary and ancient worlds in order to bring to life Dick's double vision. We also note a threatening cop on a motorcycle driving in front of Dick and the girl: police violence was an issue during the volatile sixties and seventies in the United States. In 1968, Martin Luther King Jr. and Robert F. Kennedy were assassinated; police bloodied protestors during the Democratic convention in Chicago; race riots erupted around the country; the Vietnam War escalated; and the antiwar movement intensified with

"THERE IS NO REASONABLE ARGUMENT THAT WOULD ELUCIDATE WHAT THAT WAS THAT WAS FLOWING AROUND THE ROOM LIKE ST. ELMO'S FIRE...AND IT THINKS! IT GOT INTO MY BRAIN AND MADE ME THINK! ...IT DIDN'T THINK WHAT WE THINK ...'"

"...I WAS LOOKING AT MY NOTES—IT'S OVER SEVEN YEARS LATER, AND I'M STILL TAKING NOTES, IN AN EFFORT TO UNDERSTAND. IT DID NOT THINK IN THE SENSE THAT WE THINK. WE THINK IN DIGITAL, SYNTACTICAL, VERBAL INTEGERS... IT DID NOT THINK IN VERBAL TERMS...IT THOUGHT PURE CONCEPTS, WITHOUT WORDS. BUT IT KNEW WITHOUT RATIOCINATION. IT TRANSFERRED TO MY MIND CONCEPTS THAT IN SEVEN YEARS OF TRYING TO ARTICULATE THEM IN WORDS I'VE ONLY NOW BEEN ABLE TO REDUCE THEM—"

"I'VE FINALLY FOUND A MODEL THAT WAS SUGGESTED TO ME BY A PROFESSOR FRIEND. IT WORKED LIKE A BINARY COMPUTER, ON A FLICKER PULSATION OF 'OFF' AND 'ON'. IT JUST WASN'T A MIND LIKE WE HAVE MINDS."

"ONE OF MY EXPERIENCES— IT WAS '74 — I BOUGHT ONE OF THOSE FISH SIGNS WITH THE GREEK LETTERS ON IT, AND PASTED IT UP ON MY WINDOW."

"I WAS SITTING THERE ONE DAY AND THE UPSILON, WHICH LOOKS LIKE A CAPITAL 'Y', SUDDENLY TURNED INTO A PALM TREE, AND THEN OPENED UP INTO THE ENTIRE MESOPATAMIAN WORLD, THE MIDDLE- EASTERN WORLD."

"...THAT PERSONALITY GRADUALLY TOOK ME OVER FOR A MONTH, AND THEN FOR ABOUT A YEAR I WAS THAT OTHER PERSONALITY...IT WAS SO FUNNY—I USED TO BE ABLE TO PICK UP HIS THOUGHTS WHILE I WAS FALLING ASLEEP.... AND I PICKED UP HIS THOUGHTS ONE NIGHT, AND HE WAS THINKING, 'THERE'S SOMEBODY ELSE INSIDE MY HEAD, AND HE'S LIVING IN ANOTHER CENTURY'...MEANING ME."

"I THOUGHT, 'TELL ME ABOUT IT!' I CAN SAY THE SAME THING!' AT FIRST HE THOUGHT HE WAS STILL BACK IN ROME. HE HAD EVERYTHING WRONG. HE THOUGHT THE ROMANS WERE GOING TO COME AND GET HIM, THAT WE HAD TO DEVELOP ELABORATE CODES AND STUFF TO EVADE THE ROMANS."

R. Crumb, "The Religious Experience of Philip K. Dick," *Weirdo*, no. 17 (1986).

student protests at Berkeley, Harvard, and Columbia. Although Crumb's "The Religious Experience of Philip K. Dick" was published in 1986, the events Dick describes took place in the early seventies, and as Matthew Pustz has documented, several graphic storytellers of the 1970s registered the upheavals in American society during this period in their works. Crumb includes these scenes intentionally to indicate Dick's awareness of the correspondence between the decline of the Roman Empire and the moral degradation of the American imperium during the early seventies as the Vietnam War ground slowly to an end and the Watergate scandal spiraled into a full-scale political crisis: "He had the sense of a regime that was murderous, not just oppressive, but murderous! He thought Christianity was an illegal religion. He was afraid of being killed for being a Christian, that's what he was afraid of." Dick is actually fearful of being killed by the Romans for being belonging to an "illegal religion"—a member of a secret community living within the empire—just as he fears being a member of the counterculture within an inimical America. For Dick, ancient Rome and modern America are the agents of the Black Iron Prison that keeps humanity in chains. Dick saw Rome as the acme of materialism that was responsible for oppressing the Gnostics just as today America is enslaved by a militarist, racist, consumerist Establishment. Indeed, Dick even believed that VALIS contacted him in order to help remove Richard Nixon from office.

We can see how Crumb—as did the Beats—combines his political awareness with the new religious consciousness: the Beats and hippies were driven to alternative forms of spirituality due to the materialism, violence, and racism of American society and the dawning of the "Age of Aquarius." Imagery documenting the quelling of freedom in the modern world returns as we shall see on page 8, leading to the account of Dick's "possession" by his ancient alter ego: now the "spirit of Elijah" comes to him at Passover in 1974—"[T]here was some kind of vigorous spirit in me, and it was not me and yet was human and yet more than human." His friend Thomas Disch describes it as *enthusiasmos*, which Crumb defines in a footnote as "entry of the gods into you; receiving the holy spirit." Dick's experiences become increasingly intense as he begins to identify with John the Baptist, Elijah, and their sufferings. On the final page, he turns to the *I Ching* for answers—as we have seen, another popular book for the counterculture—"if indeed the 'Parousia' (the second coming) was here, Christ had returned. I got 'Darkening of the Light,' and the following line, the only time I ever got this line. . . . 'Darkening of the Light Injures Him in the Left Thigh. He gives aid with the strength of a horse. Good fortune.'" Dick continues in the key passage of the text: "Here the lord of light is in a subordinate place and is wounded by the lord of darkness but the injury is not fatal. It is only a hindrance.... [T]herefore he tries with all his strength to save all that can be saved.... There is good fortune. I interpret these words as saying that indeed Christ has returned.... The lord of light is the Christ who has come here and subordinated himself ... the savior, you see?" Here Dick is depicted holding the *I Ching* with radiant light streaming from his head, indicating a "eureka moment." The *I Ching* hexagram to which he refers is number 36, "Ming I, Darkening of the Light," and Dick is quoting directly from the classic Richard Wilhelm translation.[23] We then move, as earlier, to the apocalyptic present in which powerful men hold the fate of the world in their hands—political, ecological, and spiritual—and who need to be continually opposed.

According to Gerard Genette:

> Narrative is a ... doubly temporal sequence.... There is the time of the thing told and the time of the narrative (the time of the signified and the time of the signifier). This duality not only renders possible all the temporal distortions that are commonplace in narratives (three years of the hero's life summed up in two sentences of a novel or in a few shots of a "frequentative" montage in film, etc.). More basically, it invites us to consider that one of the functions of narrative is to invent one time scheme in terms of another time scheme.[24]

We may see that Crumb is quite adept at this method—"three years of the hero's life summed up in two sentences of a novel or in a few shorts of a 'frequentative' montage in film"—in the final three panels, which narrate Dick's suicidal feelings in 1976. Now he felt that the spirit of Elijah had left him, and Crumb depicts him uttering the final words of Christ, "Eloi, Eloi, Lama Sabachthani"—Lord, lord why have you forsaken me?" (Mark 15:34). As we shall see in chapter 5, Crumb will return to this moment in his illustrations of Franz Kafka's "A Hunger Artist." The narrative closes with: "In the last few months of his life Dick finally located what he considered the likeliest candidate for the returned Christ ... the so-called 'Maitreya.' ... [I]n the midst of this last feverish enthusiasm, however, he suffered a stroke, and died sixteen days later, on March 2nd, 1982." Crumb is able to effectively control our experience of a six-year period—1976 to 1982—within a few panels: "the time of the thing told and the time of the narrative."

It is understandable that Crumb would find Dick's work attractive, since from childhood, Crumb had experienced American life as unutterably meretricious. He had been fed an unending diet of television advertisements, inane entertainment, and brainwashing by what Louis Althusser named the Ideological State Apparatus—church, school, family, and media. Crumb recalled about his childhood:

> What we kids didn't understand was that we were living in a commercial, commodity culture. Everything in our environment had been bought and sold. As middle class Americans, we basically grew up on a movie set. The conscious values that are pushed are only part of the picture. The medium itself plays a much bigger part than anyone realizes: the creation of illusion. We are living surrounded by illusion, by professionally created fairy tales. We barely have contact with the real world.[25]

So too, Dick, in his essay "How to Build a Universe," declared:

> But I consider that the matter of defining what is real—that is a serious topic, even a vital topic. And in there somewhere is the other topic, the definition of the authentic human. Because the bombardment of pseudorealities begins to produce inauthentic humans very quickly, spurious humans—as fake as the data pressing at them from all sides. My two topics are really one topic; they unite at this point. Fake realities will create false humans. Or, fake humans will generate fake realities and then sell them to other humans, turning them, eventually, into forgeries of themselves. So we wind up with fake humans inventing false realities and then peddling them to other fake humans.[26]

The popularity of movies such as *The Truman Show* (1998) and *The Matrix* (1999)—both of which depict characters who unbeknown to themselves are actually living in an artificial world controlled by distant puppet masters—suggests that both Dick and Crumb were intuitively aware decades before this meme had permeated popular culture that modern Americans were losing track of "who they were," as the Gnostics would put it: the Gnostic theme of an absent God and a deceptive demiurge is the inspiration for the admonitory message of *The Matrix*. Indeed, it is as if Crumb ingested massive amounts of "illusion" in the form of American mass advertising and cultural pablum in the forties and fifties, and then when he took LSD, the political ferment and sexual openness of the sixties combined with these earlier influences literally "blew his mind"—as we have noted previously, Crumb often depicted his characters with the heterogeneous contents of their minds being blown open and strewn into space, as if he needed to expel all the detritus to which he had been subjected. Like Dick, he sought to purge himself of illusion and strove toward authenticity and to find what is "real." So too, for Dick—as for the French philosopher Jean Baudrillard (1929–2007), who alludes to Dick in his *Simulacres et simulation* (1981) and whose work in turn inspired the directors of *The Matrix*—the central question our world of illusion is therefore: *what is real?* Here lies the threat that preoccupied both Dick and Crumb: the possibility that—as happened to C. G. Jung during his own descent into the unconscious—the self may be fragmented into pieces during the trip. Dick reflected in *VALIS*: "An irruption from the collective unconscious, Jung taught, can wipe out the fragile individual ego. In the depths of the collective the archetypes slumber; if aroused, they can heal or they can destroy. This is the danger of the archetypes; the opposite qualities are not yet separated. Bipolarization into paired opposites does not occur until consciousness occurs."[27]

Thus Crumb's involvement with Dick's writings was likely one influence that led to his trajectory toward a more serious engagement with mystical thought. Just a few years after completing the illustrations for "The Religious Experience of Philip K. Dick," allusions to Gnosticism began to appear with more frequency in his art. For example, in "Can You Stand Alone and Face Up to the Universe?," featured in *Hup*, no. 4 (1992), Crumb addresses the viewer directly at the top of the drawing: "A sincere, heartfelt question to all my dear friends out there." The title follows, below which Crumb has inscribed a poster at the bottom right with another aside—"Getting existential for a few pages here. . . . We'll get back to the fun stuff right after this"—thus assuring his readers that the rest of the thirty-two-page magazine will be less philosophically demanding. On the splash page, Crumb depicts a naked, lone, isolated, vulnerable man, arms and legs awkwardly twisted against the backdrop of cosmic blackness. The man is standing on what appear to be long slats or miles of flat scaffolding—as if he is walking a gangplank on a ship—leading to a modern cityscape. If one looks closely, it appears that spaceships or jets of the future are zipping by, and in the left part of the frame what appears to be a row of four flying saucers—Crumb has had an abiding interest in the possibility of extraterrestrials—are sailing through the darkness. Crumb just beneath the splash panel adds an aside to the reader: "Uh oh, did Crumb finally get religion?? Jack T. Chick, move over!" This is an allusion to the evangelical cartoonist Jack T. Chick (1924–2016), who produced a series of polemical, fundamentalist, fire-and-brimstone, anti-gay, antifeminist, antievolutionist "Chick tracts" in the form of comics—his company claimed that 750 million were published—which promulgated a variety of conspiracy theories and attempted to frighten the reader into an acceptance of Jesus as the only key to salvation. Chick had been preceded in cartoon history by figures such as Ernest J. Pace (1880–1946), a professor at the Moody Bible Institute, who created comics affirming the Bible's absolute authority and celebrating America as a nation that was destined to carry out the will of God. Thus Crumb humorously suggests to his possibly shocked readers—who have known him mainly as the artist whose febrile imagination created "Keep On Truckin'" and gigantic women with big legs and prominent *derrières*—that he may have now lapsed into the same condition as Mr. Chick and become a "true believer."[28]

The naked man then agrees that the cosmic sky is "beautiful" but is suddenly stricken with horror and runs madly with legs aloft, penis dangling, trailing a snake-like motion swirl, exclaiming: "It's kinda terrifying, isn't it?? Th' silence is deafening . . ." This is a close paraphrase of the great French philosopher and mathematician Blaise Pascal's (1623–1662) outcry "Le silence éternel de ces espaces infinis m'effraie" (The eternal silence of these infinite spaces terrifies me). As our anguished man looks up at the night sky, his left eyeball is enlarged with horror, perspiration pouring from his face as he confronts "existential terror" and "the void." In the final panel, he again takes off running—now in precisely the opposite direction as before—as he yells: "You can't face it alone?? Then go! Run! Run!! Oh dear Jeeziz!" This is the signal that the spiritual quest has begun, for this "Jeeziz!"—"Jesus"—prepares us for the journey ahead: many of Crumb's narratives are cast in the form of a pilgrimage or initiatory set of challenges. On the next page, our beleaguered seeker returns in a kind of time machine to the Roman era—as in Philip K. Dick's transportation to ancient times—casting himself at the foot of the cross: we can only see the nailed feet of Christ as two surprised Roman centurions look on puzzled at this strange creature from the future writhing in pain on the ground.

He tries one alternative after another to resolve his anguish: one suggestion is, "Whine to your Krishna! Your Buddha! Your Mohammed!" We then witness an alcoholic drowning his sorrows; depictions of an enlightened Buddha, an ascetic in the act of whipping himself, a pygmy who counsels two anthropologists: "Life is meant to be enjoyed." Crumb then editorializes: "Still, it's every human being's personal responsibility to become as enlightened as possible. . . . No one's excused on grounds of ignorance, poverty, or oppression." The scene then shifts to a group of "cynics" and "intellectuals" who mock the Crumb character, claiming that "it's his heavy Catholic upbringing coming out" in his newfound turn toward the mystical, but Crumb himself now appears and with hand raised like a stop sign asserts: "I don't 'believe in God' either." We note that he places "believe in God" in quotation marks, suggesting that he abjures the conventional ways of thinking about "faith"

R. Crumb, "Can You Stand Alone and Face Up to the Universe?," *Hup*, no. 4 (1992).

and the "divine" but does not rule out conceptualizing "belief" and "God" in a different manner. Crumb pictures himself in the next frames, admitting his carnal weaknesses and then confessing—as he implores the heavens with his hands raised in a sea of naked fellow humans—that when he feels "so lost, so vexed and helpless, that I pray . . . it's true . . . I appeal . . . I entreat some 'higher power' in the universe . . ." This matches Crumb's acknowledgment during interviews in which he admits to looking for guidance at his darkest moments from a "higher power."

In the first tier of the fourth page, Crumb continues his reflections on his psychological and spiritual weakness and opposition to "all governments, organized religions, large corporations, new age cults," which leads to the third panel: "I dive head-on into infinity . . . throw myself on the mercy of the void" as he leaps from the door into a jet-black night—this is the leap of faith or the jump into the abyss in "Bad Karma." Crumb then enters into a science-fiction "space-time mother-fucking continuum, Jack"—thus bringing the evangelist Jack T. Chick back into the narrative—where he declares while making his way through a kind of spooky tunnel of the unconscious strewn with skulls, bones, and odd plumbing festooning the walls: "But there is something—some kinda source of intelligence and compassion out there . . ." And in the first panel of the third tier we reach the climax of the tale, and he begins by reviewing his journey thus far into outer space, through the "space-time continuum," within the self: "Out there?? In there? Up there, down there, who, how, what, when . . . I dunno, I'm just in the early stages of this investigation. . . . You gotta work at it . . . study it. . . . This is what th' Gnostics were into." Crumb now reveals a halting, hip style: "So, yeah, I'm like a Gnostic" to a disinterested lady at the bar. Christ then appears with a scroll on which is written: "Seek and ye shall find . . . Ask, and it shall . . . ," and Crumb then kicks him away because "so many terrible things have been done in your holy name." On the final page, Crumb metamorphoses into a professor explaining to his audience that "connecting with this higher intelligence . . . that interests me . . . not to a fanatic degree or anything . . . I have to do it my own way." Thus both existential and Gnostic ideas are merged in this striking statement of human solitude and yearning, all accomplished in Crumb's inimitable not-too-serious style.

During the nineties, Crumb began identifying himself as a Gnostic in interviews in which he expanded on the concepts expounded in "Can You Stand Alone And Face Up To The Universe?"

> I'm a Gnostic. . . . my rough, crude definition of a Gnostic is someone who's interested in the idea of higher spiritual existence or being or

reality—a greater reality that you could call divine, you could call it God, you can call it the great spirit, all-that-is, whatever you want. But I'm interested in that, and I spend time studying that and seeking that, and seeking communication with it, a connection with it: the higher reality. So I call that Gnosticism. . . . [S]omething in us wants to know, something has a desire for knowledge. That's where "gnosis" actually comes from, "knowledge." So it's seeking after that knowledge that's interesting. We all have some interest in that, but we get stuck in dogmatic, doctrinal thinking, which makes us feel secure. It's like building a wall around yourself, against the unknown, you know? And people feel secure inside that wall. It's familiar, always the same.

The ancient Gnostics believed that within the material human body—for which they often registered a degree of abhorrence—is trapped a cosmic soul that seeks to return to its divine source. As we shall see in chapter 5 in relation to Walter Benjamin's comments on Kafka, Crumb experienced his own body as *Fremde*, or *foreign/alien*. In a 2011 work created with his wife Aline, Crumb acknowledged the disgust he feels concerning his own body: "Basically I don't really like being in this physical body. . . . It gives me the horrors when I think about it . . . all its needs, its appetites . . . food, sex, elimination."[29] Thus, in a sense, in claiming the label "Gnostic," Crumb is able to embark on a "spiritual" quest without acknowledging "belief" in a particular "faith"—or, as he puts it—without getting "stuck in dogmatic, doctrinal thinking." His quest for Self is based on individual contemplation rather than on adherence to any particular "religion." Crumb's readings in Gnostic literature began to be reflected in the personal, autobiographical drawings in his *Sketchbooks*. When Crumb's sister Sandra died on August 2, 1998, at age fifty-one, the following day Crumb included in his *Sketchbook*, vol. 11, his transcription of a text from the Nag Hammadi Library, "The Exegesis of the Soul," with the heading: "Commune with your own heart upon your bed, and be still." The text proper then begins: "Wise men of old gave the soul a feminine name. / Indeed, she is female in her nature as well." Crumb most likely also learned of this Gnostic text from the Fall–Winter 1985 issue of *Gnosis* in which "The Revelation of Philip K. Dick" was followed by "The Exegesis: Previously Unpublished Excerpts from Philip K. Dick's Private Journals." This section of Jay Kinney's article was transcribed from Dick's handwritten journal entries, and, as we have seen, they were later published in book form as *The Exegesis of Philip K. Dick* (2011).

In his attraction to Gnosticism, Crumb was replicating the trajectory of his Beat forebears. Allen Ginsberg and Jack Kerouac first learned of Gnostic ideas while undergraduates at Columbia University studying with Professor Raymond Weaver; William S. Burroughs and Diane di Prima also made serious studies of Gnostic thought. The feeling that humanity is "on a darkling plain, swept by confused alarms where ignorant armies clash by night"—as Matthew Arnold unforgettably put it in "Dover Beach"—drove post–World War II American youth to seek new philosophical conceptions. So too, the Gnostics believed that the world was a cosmic mistake. According to the great authority on Gnosticism Hans Jonas, there are connections between modern existentialism and Gnostic thought. Giovanni Filoramo in *A History of Gnosticism* has also noted similarities between ancient Gnostics and passionately seeking moderns:

> The question must be asked whether, behind the renewed interest in Gnosis, there is not something other than merely a taste for the exotic or the volatile search for the esoteric, whether there is not hidden the intuition of a secret affinity between our age of crisis, riddled with anxiety and at the same time avid for change and thirsting for novelty, and the historical period between the second and third centuries AD when ancient Gnosticism established itself as a religious response to the acute problems of an "age of anxiety," an original and sometimes victorious response.

Thus while it is tempting to write off Dick's experiences as delusions—and it is clear that Crumb is not wholeheartedly endorsing them and indeed perceives the comical aspects of such "revelations"—it is also evident that they parallel several of Crumb's own epiphanies, which he spent his career interrogating and mining for his creative work. And although he had rejected institutional Christianity at age sixteen, Crumb believed that "at the core of Catholicism there is indeed a very interesting and mystical body of religious theory that the most deeply devoted Jesuits or people like that might get into, but most of it is nonsense. The core of any religion has that interesting mystical element, but most of the peasants that belong to any religious group are just going along with a bunch of hocus pocus. They're just being manipulated."[30] Thus, in his turn toward Gnosticism, Crumb was in a sense discovering the "interesting mystical element" that had been removed from "orthodox" Christianity by the church fathers in the early years of the formation of the "official canonical texts" of the Bible—the "Gnostic" texts such as the Gospel of Thomas were not included—and the establishment of Christianity as a state religion.

We should also remember that one of the great psychologists of the twentieth century recorded very similar experiences, which lead us to believe that they may not merely the ravings of a madman—for C. G. Jung in his Gnostic studies replicates many of these themes. Just as Dick ends in a syncretic combination of Plato, Elijah, Gnosticism, and Maitreya in an effort to understand his experience, so too in *The Red Book* (2009) we have the text of Jung's own Gnostic gospel, *Septem Sermones ad Mortuos*, and a very similar combination of a variety of traditions.[31] Jung was the great predecessor in this syncretism through his studies of world mythological traditions and his emphasis on their relevance for his theory of archetypes and his exploration of the psychology of the unconscious. Jung set the precedent for the Beats as well as Crumb in his profound attraction to Eastern thought and his search for a rapprochement between various spiritual traditions. Jung's drawing of Philemon in *The Red Book*—a character from Greek and Roman mythology—depicts a dream from 1913. In the upper left corner of the painting there is a quotation from the Bhagavad Gita, while the text at top is in Greek: PROPHETON PATER POLUPHILOS PHILEMON, and Jung's own script is in German.[32] Here we have a confluence of Judeo-Christian, Indian, and European traditions, illustrating Jung's desire to forge a new syncretic belief system. Jung's fascination with Gnosticism, alchemy, astrology, the *I Ching*, mandalas, synchronicity, flying saucers, and the paranormal find exact parallels in Crumb. Jung's studies of alchemy were continued not only in the work of Diane di Prima but in Kenneth Rexroth, Robert Duncan, Michael McClure, and William Everson (Brother Antoninus) as well. Furthermore, the Eranos conferences in Switzerland presided over by Jung—where Henry Corbin, Mircea Eliade, Gershom Scholem, and Joseph Campbell lectured— set the stage for the Californian Esalen Institute, where ideas of expanded consciousness were explored. Frederic Spiegelberg, Alan Watts, and Aldous Huxley were significant figures in bringing to California what would evolve into the "New Age" or Human Potential movement, which intersected with Crumb's own trajectory when he moved to the West Coast.[33]

Thus, Crumb's involvement with the life and ideas of Philip K. Dick marks a significant stage in his artistic career. In creating the illustrations for "The Religious Experience of Philip K. Dick," Crumb began a deeper engagement with Gnostic philosophy, which he would pursue more systematically over the following decades. In addition, this 1986 work paved the way for his later major drawings to accompany texts by Jean-Paul Sartre (1989), Franz Kafka (1994), and ultimately the book of Genesis (2009). While Crumb appears to retain some skepticism regarding the reality of such "transcendent" experiences and, as he has admitted, perceives the absurd or even humorous aspects of full-blown "mystical" flooding of the psyche, he also remains open to the possibility that such moments do in fact record a glimpse of the frontiers of expanded consciousness. As Crumb himself put it: "I spend time studying that and seeking that, and seeking communication with it, a connection with it: the higher reality."

Chapter 4

JEAN-PAUL SARTRE
AND THE EXISTENTIAL QUEST

As we have seen in chapter 1, the quest for "authenticity" was a dominating feature of the counterculture. Gary Groth in his introduction to a selection of Crumb's correspondence has noted his

> rejection of inauthenticity, especially of the manufactured reality of the mass media. A belief in and search for authenticity, for the real, is, in fact, practically a leitmotiv that runs through these letters. Crumb didn't know it at the time but he was intuitively groping his way to the same conclusions that public intellectuals were reaching at approximately the same time, in David Riesman's *The Lonely Crowd*, in Herbert Marcuse and the Frankfurt School, in Dwight Macdonald's famous animadversions against mass culture.[1]

Crumb was from the beginning politically liberal, advocating for a communal America—he dreamed of "some kind of practical socialism. There should not be private ownership of huge industries and services"—where art was not "consumed" by the masses but rather created by each individual as part of their daily life. Crumb was fully cognizant of living in an America where the mass media had compelled an unconscious and subliminal conformity to an artificial notion of what it is to be a human being. Indeed, as a thoughtful seventeen-year-old, Crumb had already written to his friend Marty Pahls on May 28, 1961: "I want to develop a strong inner life, so that I won't be easily swayed by the outside world and other people's opinions. I want to be something inside. A real person, not just a shell of a human being. That's vague isn't it. . . . I don't want to be a half-baked human being. I want to be a whole person. I want to have faith in myself, in life. At present, I don't. I can sense the lacking, the emptiness of my present state of existence."[2] Crumb's struggle to define and create "a strong inner life" corresponds to the quest for authenticity of the existentialists and—as we have seen previously—the turn toward Eastern mysticism in writers such as J. D. Salinger or Gnosticism in Philip K. Dick. Following World War II, thoughtful young people sought to forge an unhypocritical, "natural," naked self, unconditioned by the conformity and materialism they saw flourishing throughout America, and to develop a more innocent, direct openness to experience.[3]

Crumb first learned of existentialism at age nineteen from his brother Maxon, who had been reading Fyodor Dostoevsky's *The Brothers Karamazov*, which can be discerned in Robert's self-reflections during this period: "I wonder, sometimes, if people as a whole are ever going to start looking within and searching for the true values of life. I have my doubts."[4] He approaches here Martin Heidegger's concept of *Das Man*—the "they"—the majority of people who do not seek true being but are content to rigidly follow the dictates set out for them by their society. Crumb's older brother, Charles, also encouraged Robert in his search. As Crumb later recalled, Charles "was so attuned to the phoniness of popular culture, and how people just bought into it without questioning it. He was always ranting about that stuff. We would read different religious philosophies, different writers, and try to ask questions—what are we doing here? What's this reality about? Why are we here?—and all that. You know, I'm still asking those questions."[5] Crumb has spoken often of his sensation of extreme alienation, the intuition that he is a "stranger" on planet earth, and thus it is logical that he would gravitate toward illustrating Jean-Paul Sartre (1905–1980). As he phrases it in the masthead for *Weirdo* (1981–1993): "A graphic journal for the rootless, alienated, nihilist, post-modern, existentialist masses." Other graphic storytellers have also explored existential themes such as Daniel Clowes in *Ghost World* (2001) and—more humorously—Keshni Kashyap in *Tina's Mouth: An Existential Comic Diary* (2012).[6] This anguished psychological/spiritual state is of course powerfully adumbrated in both Albert Camus's *l'Étranger* and Jean-Paul Sartre's *La Nausée* and also has affinities with the sense of estrangement felt by the early Gnostics. As we observed in the last chapter with Philip K. Dick, Gnosticism provided Crumb with a philosophy with which to interpret the meaning of his experience as an outsider. Hans Jonas in his landmark treatise *The Gnostic Religion* (1958) draws parallels between our contemporary sense of absurdity and the beliefs of ancient Gnostics, who thought that the world was a cosmic mistake created by a bungling demiurge where humanity must seek salvation through *gnosis*, or self-knowledge. Heidegger spoke of *Geworfenheit* (thrownness): humans are "thrown," without consent, into existence and must attempt to make meaning in what appears to be a chaotic universe.

Thus, three years after completing his work on "The Religious Experience of Philip K. Dick," Crumb turned to the work of Jean-Paul Sartre (1905–1980). Crumb had read several Sartre works including his autobiography *Les mots* (1964; translated as *The Words*), which Crumb described as "pretty funny. It's very self-deprecating, and he writes about what a little bourgeois, arrogant shit he was as a kid." He also read Sartre's *Réflexions sur la question juive* (1948)—translated into English as *Anti-Semite and Jew*—which he found compelling: "It observed how popular and even intellectual attitudes about Jews changed before and during the Nazi occupation." For the purposes of illustration, Crumb selected Sartre's novel *La Nausée* (1938), which appeared as *Nausea* in *Hup*, no. 3 (1989), under the rubric "A Klassic Komic."[7] In another work completed in 1989, "The Story o' My Life," *Nausea* makes a cameo appearance as a book the infantilized Crumb—who is being cared for by a huge, voluptuous German lady—is reading while lounging in his baby carriage. While practicing his daily meditation—he began to meditate daily early in 1981—he conceived the idea of creating a magazine entitled *Weirdo* with himself as editor. Sartre's *Nausea* represented Crumb's third foray into creating Klassic Komics: his first effort, "Boswell's *London Journal*"—which exposes the sexual hijinx of the biographer of Samuel Johnson, James Boswell—appeared in *Weirdo* (Fall 1981), while the second—his illustrations to Richard von Krafft-Ebing's *Psychopathia Sexualis* depicting in explicit detail a mind-bending potpourri of bizarre erotic compulsions—appeared in *Weirdo*'s Summer 1985 issue. The use of *K* in the place of *C* in "A Klassic Komic" functions similarly to the use of *x* in comix, serving to alert us to the fact that we are getting something "like" the original, but fundamentally different and subversive. Furthermore, the double *K*'s are a subtle homage to George Harriman's *Krazy Kat*.[8] Created in 1941 by Albert Lewis Kanter (1897–1973) to popularize canonical literature, the first Classic Comics issues were published by the Gilberton Company and were devoted to *The Three Musketeers*, *Ivanhoe*, and *The Count of Monte Cristo*. In March 1947, Kanter changed the series name to Classics Illustrated, eventually releasing 169 individual titles and completing its first print run in 1971. His purpose was to make what were considered by some to be forbidding, complex—and "boring"—classics more accessible to young readers.[9] Of course, there was often an inevitable cheapening and diluting of the depth, style, richness, and force of the original literary source in these adaptations, an eventuality that Crumb was keen to avoid.

Crumb was aware of Classics Illustrated from adolescence, for in a letter from March 1959 he informs a friend that a local store kept the magazine in stock: "I noticed they had the original of *Les Misérables* (no. 9) copyright

1943, up there." But Crumb reports that when he read the Classics Illustrated version of *Oliver Twist*, he was so disgusted that he cast it in the trash bin:

> It certainly didn't do justice to Dickens. The way they went about briefing the story completely ruined it, and lost all the charm and qualities of Dickens works. I kinda think making comic books out of classic literature is a bad idea to begin with. . . . Comics are for Walt Kelly and Harvey Kurtzman, who apply their genius to this field. Dickens and the other great authors applied their genius to the field of words, without pictures, and their accomplishments just aren't meant for comics.

An obvious limitation is that all of the comic versions of literary classics were often confined to brief sections, excerpted from extended novels. Poet Delmore Schwartz in a famous essay objected to Classics Illustrated, yet as Henry John Pratt has argued, the problem was "not that they cannot adapt long, complex works of literature, but that they try to do so within arbitrary length constraints. Perhaps a comic adapting *Crime and Punishment* that ran for several thousand pages (instead of the original 48 pages) would be more to Schwartz's satisfaction." Ari Folman—who with artist David Polonsky has recently created a graphic version of *The Diary of Anne Frank* (2018)—estimates that if he had attempted to adapt the entire book, his graphic novel would have been three and a half thousand pages.[10] By the same token, the argument might be—and was—made that the adaptations published by Classics Illustrated were not meant to *replace* the original texts. Rather, they were intended merely to give young people an introduction to the important books of primarily British and American literature—although world masterpieces such as *Crime and Punishment*, *The Arabian Nights*, *Don Quixote*, *Les Misérables*, and Homer's *Iliad* and *Odyssey* were also published—and to encourage them to read the entire novels by also introducing the catnip of dramatic and thrilling illustrations.

Crumb endeavors to remain faithful to the authors he adapts, precisely because of his desire to preserve "the charm and qualities" of their works, even within the constraints of excerpting, yet he introduces elements that reflect his own personal obsessions and preoccupations: there can be little doubt that the drawings have been executed by Robert Crumb and no one else. Classics Illustrated was attacked for blurring the lines between "high culture" and "popular culture," but as Bart Beaty has observed, "despite the claims to the contrary, the primary concern of these critics was not the subject matter of the comic books, but the actual form which incorporated elements from both literature and the visual arts to create a new form of literacy which was deemed inadequate by the reading experts." Thierry Groensteen echoes this notion in his analysis of the prevailing attitude toward graphic storytelling in France: "For the educators of the first half of the twentieth century, that which is popular is necessarily vulgar. Comics are seen as intrinsically bad because they tend to take the place of 'real books,' an attitude which crystallizes a double confrontation: between the written word and the world of images, on the one hand; between educational literature and pure entertainment on the other."[11] Crumb was of course aware of the backlash against Classics Illustrated as a young artist, and in his own efforts to illustrate canonical literature he was attempting to bring this new art form to the highest level of expressivity and aesthetic power. He also was fond enough of good literature to attempt, as the Hippocratic oath enjoins, *primum non nocere*—"first, to do no harm"—to the texts he selected.

Crumb illustrates the "Self-Taught Man" episode in *Nausea*, which appears approximately halfway through the novel, scrupulously indicating omitted passages with ellipses.[12] He opens with a definition of "Existentialism" from "the American College Dictionary: 'The doctrine that there is no difference between the external world and the internal world of the mind, and that the source and elements of knowledge have their existence in states of mind.' Webster's New World Dictionary: '. . . holds that each man exists as an individual in a purposeless universe, and that he must oppose his hostile environment through the exercise of his free will.'" Crumb also points out humorously that "the whole thing started with this annoying Frenchman named Jean-Paul Sartre." Horace advised in his *Ars Poetica* that the artist should strive to both *docere et delectare*—to teach and delight/entertain— and Crumb frequently follows this dictum in his approach to illustrating literary texts. He seeks a balance—as Groensteen puts it—"between educational literature and pure entertainment." Crumb depicts the definition of existentialism on a scroll in the far left of the opening. At the beginning of "Mother Hulda" (*Weirdo*, no. 19 [Winter 1986–1987])—a fairy tale by the Brothers Grimm—Crumb also employs a scroll: "Once there was a widow who had two daughters . . ." And twice later he hangs a scroll in the midst or to the side of a panel to move the narrative forward. These are all clearly tongue-in-cheek nods to Classics Illustrated. In the Classics Illustrated version of *Hamlet*, for example, the narrative summary is inscribed on a scroll, effectively subordinating the visual elements of the artwork in favor of the textual.[13] Thus at the opening of his Sartre adaptation, Crumb is paying homage to comics style of an earlier time: he acknowledges that he is working within the context and parameters of a specific artistic tradition. But he also

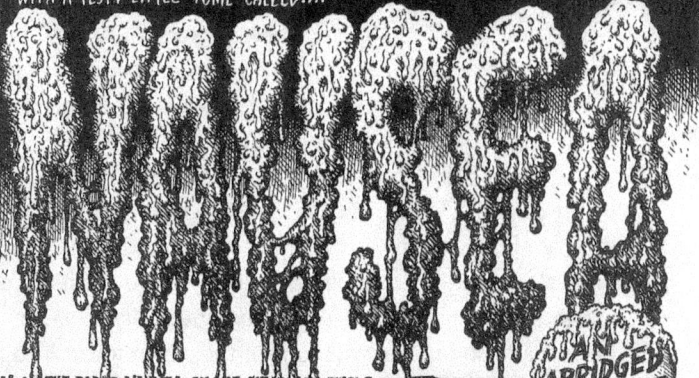

R. Crumb, "Nausea," *Hup*, no. 3 (1989).

injects a note of ironic comedy in his general approach to "this annoying Frenchman" philosopher. Earlier in his career, Crumb would affix to the covers of *Zap* declarations such as "Fair Warning: For Adult Intellectuals Only!" and "Approved by the Ghost Writers in the Sky" to indicate to readers that they are embarking on a different sort of experience that mocks the 1954 Comic Code censors and congressional hearings responsible for harassing EC Comics—Entertaining Comics, founded by Max Gaines in 1944. As Charles Hatfield has pointed out, these "satiric thrusts, influenced by the gleeful cynicism of *Mad* and college humor magazines, were distilled by Crumb into the perfect comic book package, one that kept spiraling in on itself in vertiginous recursions, always aware of its comic book status."[14] Crumb makes works that constantly function as metacommentaries on the history and stylistic conventions of their own form as comics and are also simultaneously homages, parodies, and original creations.

While, as we have seen, "The Religious Experience of Philip K. Dick" is dense with sacral and archetypal imagery, Crumb's drawings to accompany Jean-Paul Sartre's *Nausea* (1938) are decidedly quotidian and "realistic." However, at certain moments of psychological extremity, his style shifts into a hallucinatory realm. Crumb's narrative—which he describes as "an abridged excerpt"—is scrupulously faithful to the text of the New Directions translation of the novel. Unlike the Dick illustrations, pages are broken into two to nine panels each. Furthermore, instead of square or rectangular divisions, the panels are set at an angle beginning on the second page: this forces the viewer into a skewed sense of perspective that intensifies the eerie, menacing mood. The gutters are crooked throughout, lending the impression of a piece of paper ripped apart, thus mirroring the process of psychological disintegration that Antoine Roquentin is undergoing. Were the gutters uniformly symmetrical, the narrative would seem to be describing a "normal" day, and of course Crumb is at pains to underscore the phantasmagoric aspects of the narrator's experiences. Originally titled *Melancholia*—after Albrecht Dürer's famous engraving—*La Nausée* was written from 1932 to 1936 and cast in the form of Roquentin's diary. Sartre reputedly ingested mescaline in September 1935: one of the reasons perhaps that the narrative bears a disjunctive, hallucinatory quality. The technique Crumb favors is rather like that employed by some modern film directors who juggle the camera from side to side when tracking human faces and bodies in motion, giving the spectator a slightly uneasy, seasick sensation, which interrupts our usual expectations of smooth narrative flow. Crumb's lettering of the title *Nausea* also drips with viscous liquid, alluding to the defining famous scene when Roquentin encounters the terrifying absurdity of existence in the spreading roots of a chestnut tree:

"[T]his long serpent, dead at my feet, this wooden serpent . . . I realized that I'd found the key to existence, the key to my nausea, to my whole life. . . . I'd experienced the absolute."

The narrative is conveyed through captions positioned at the top or sometimes to the side of each panel and opens: "Wednesday: There is a sunbeam on the paper napkin. In the sunbeam, there is a fly, dragging himself along, stupefied, sunning himself and rubbing his antennae one against the other. I am going to do him the favor of squashing him." Sartre's sentences move deliberately—"dragging themselves along"—and our sense of time is altered as we slowly attend to one detail after another. Fredric Jameson has observed that from the beginning of *Nausea*, we are aware "that something is about to happen, and soon, and that these details are only apparently unimportant, that they must have meaning and are to be watched attentively."[15] Indeed, Crumb is expert at focusing on just such specifics that only appear to be insignificant—such as the fly on the paper napkin—throughout the novel. Crumb supplies two major visual markers of time's passing. First, the waitress makes seven appearances throughout, a silent witness to the proceedings, coming and going, bringing and removing plates of food. And second, we subtly are allowed to witness the passage of time in Crumb's careful periodic depiction of the windows in the restaurant opening out onto the world. The windows appear twenty-one times from beginning to end, and only twice do we view objects through them: on page 2, panel 3, we see two men leaving the restaurant, and in the following panel, a window with clouds, birds, and Crumb's iconic glum telephone pole and wires. Thus the external world presents itself as blank and empty, concentrating our attention on the drama being played out within the restaurant, which gives us a sense of claustrophobic closeness through the bunching together of panels squashed together within each tier. Crumb also emphasizes the temporal disjunctions of Sartre's text through the effective use of gutters to separate each panel and also by sometimes breaking the image, as in his partial depiction of the right side of Roquentin's face. The somber mood is established immediately as the person we shall learn is the Self-Taught Man tells Roquentin not to kill the fly. Roquentin responds: "I did it a favor." Crumb shows Roquentin's right hand and finger as massively out of proportion to his body—throughout, Crumb emphasizes distortions in correct perspective—as well as to the fly about to be squashed, emphasizing his brute force and the insignificance of the insect's life, and at the moment of impact, the fly's death is accompanied by the sound effect, "scrunch." Crumb also places an asterisk next to the word "Monsieur" in the speech balloon and beneath the panel informs us that this word is "pronounced 'Mis*you*.'" Clearly, Sartre intends for us understand that human life is as fragile and meaningless—"contingent"—as the life of a fly, and Crumb depicts in this panel as well as the following the shocked visage of the Self-Taught Man witnessing this *acte gratuit*.

The second page begins with what may be taken as both a literal and quintessentially existential question: "Why am I here on planet earth—and why shouldn't I be here?"—referring both to why Roquentin is at the restaurant and to why he exists at all. He shall see "Anny" in four days, and she—he confides to us—is the only reason he continues living. Thus killing the fly and Roquentin's indifference to his own life are connected within the opening passages of the novel. Crumb omits a brief section from *Nausea* concerning Anny: "And afterwards? When Anny leaves me? . . ." And when the Self-Taught Man begins to speak, Crumb cuts the unnecessary "he says"—since he is showing the dialogue and not describing it—again indicating the passages he has omitted from the novel by means of ellipses. In the fourth panel, Crumb foregrounds the narrator's severe gaze and varies the lettering of the key sentence: "And then, through the windows, between the white roofs of the bathing-cabins I see the sea, green, compact," with the final phrase smaller in size than the preceding. As with the fly earlier, nature is indifferent and juxtaposed with the human world without comment. Instead of the typical "literary" romantic view of the ocean—*the light was dancing on the blue-green waves as the clouds smiled down*—Sartre supplies just two nondescript adjectives: "green," "compact." As a student of Edmund Husserl's phenomenological method, Sartre wants to pull back from the "normal" way of perceiving objects in order to concentrate solely on what can be perceived: his comments thus sometimes appear singular and idiosyncratic.[16] Crumb adds a few typical touches such as the depiction of sad, drooping telephone poles and wires topped with birds—recalling his famous "A Short History of America," which shows how omnipresent electrical wiring has transformed and vulgarized contemporary landscapes. What is also noteworthy about this moment is that Roquentin is actually not depicted looking through the window but rather facing the viewer, his eyes somnolent and heavy lidded beneath his thick glasses, as if the dullness of his expression mirrors his indifference to the "real world." Crumb effectively portrays him as lost between the internal "world of humanity" of the restaurant and the external "world of nature," unable to connect to either.

Following the sea scene, Crumb cuts three-quarters of a page from *Nausea* describing the restaurant menu as well as several customers but includes the following: "In a moment all these people are going to leave; weighted down by food. . . . They will go to work. I will go nowhere, I have no work." Again, the narrator's disengagement from bourgeois "normality" is emphasized, and

Crumb pulls back his close-up shot of his face to a view from above that takes in several of the surrounding patrons, who are content to be chatting, smoking, eating—one man has an open mouth with fork suspended in the air about to enter it, his hand on his wineglass—reading newspapers, and drinking coffee. Life goes on while Roquentin is wracked by "metaphysical questions." Crumb sustains the reader's/viewer's interest by continually shifting his point of view and perspective in ways that are not obviously indicated by Sartre's text. We pause between each panel to absorb the possible deeper or ambiguous meanings, then go on to the next point in the story to meet a different perspective on the same scene. Crumb is a virtuoso at careful draftsmanship: each separate scene is set in proper relation to what comes before and what follows. He pays close attention not only to each discrete frame but to the pattern of each tier and the whole page as well. In this, he was likely following the example of Winsor McCay, who created *Little Nemo in Slumberland* and whom Crumb regarded as a "genius." Kerry Roeder has noted:

McCay was aware that prior to reading each panel in sequential order, viewers encounter the comic strip in its entirety; consequently, he was concerned with how the page design functioned as an overall image. Like film, comics are concerned with events unfolding in time. However, reading comics and watching films are very different visual experiences. Whereas a director controls how and when a cinematic narrative develops, a comic-strip artist has less power over the reader's temporal experience. The whole page is available to the viewer, who is in command of how quickly the story develops. McCay was interested in demonstrating how the comic strip can allow us to rethink our understanding of time by slowing down the action of a galloping horse or a buzzing mosquito. He imagined the possibilities that comic strips and animation had for revealing a world unavailable in photos or on film.

Art Spiegelman has confirmed this idea, noting that comics "are about time being made manifest spatially, in that you've got all these different chunks of time—each box being a different moment of time—and you see them all at once. As a result, you're always, in comics, being made aware of different times inhabiting the same space."[17] Crumb is attempting to illustrate a key tenet of existentialism: individuals experience time as a forward-moving concept in which they struggle to transform their facticity—their actual state of being—into the transcendence of their potential selves. In effectively supplying the viewer with a simultaneous perception of discrete moments of time, Crumb's panels record this process of sometimes difficult self-discovery and self-creation.

On page 3, Crumb emphasizes a key passage when the narrator says that he is happy to listen to the Self-Taught Man's troubles. He has revealed that he was a prisoner of war in the winter of 1917: "I am all ears: I am only too glad to feel pity for other people's troubles. That will be a change. I have no troubles, I have money like a capitalist, no boss, no wife, no children; I exist, that's all." Again, *existence* is foregrounded, followed by the pregnant phrase "that's all." Is there something more to life than *existence*? And the narrator goes on to reveal: "And that trouble is so vague, so metaphysical that I'm ashamed of it." We are reminded of the earlier question—"why am I here?"—which is now echoed in his "shame" over his philosophical self-analysis. As we have seen, Roquentin is aware that his problems are "metaphysical": "real people"—that is, people who are not philosophers—have "real" problems such as unemployment, ill health, poverty, family tragedies, divorce, and so on. Crumb adds an effective touch here that is not in Sartre's text—the narrator biting down intently on what appears to be a breadstick, again emphasized by a sound effect, "CRUNCH." The striking close-ups in the final three panels of the page echo the close-ups we will find at the end of page 7.

The Self-Taught Man is now depicted eating his radishes—a slightly comic choice of appetizer—and Crumb omits six and a half pages of the novel in order to focus on the narrator's epiphany regarding his fellow patrons: "I glance around the room. What a comedy! All these people sitting there, looking serious, eating . . . Each one of them has his little personal difficulty which keeps him from noticing that he exists . . . But I *know*. I don't look like much, but I know I exist and that they exist." He begins to laugh, telling the Self-Taught Man: "I was just thinking that here we sit, all of us, eating and drinking to preserve our precious existence and really there is nothing, nothing, absolutely no reason for existing." Crumb then omits nine pages of *Nausea*, beginning: "I study the Self-Taught Man with a little remorse. He has been happy all the week imagining this luncheon, when he could share his love of men with another man." As the Self-Taught Man expounds his philosophy of "humanism"—the caring embrace of all humanity—the narrator becomes increasingly agitated: "With difficulty I chew a piece of bread which I can't make up my mind to swallow. People. You must love people . . . I want to vomit—and suddenly, there it is: the Nausea." Here the three images occupying the bottom tier are again increasingly intense close-ups, which lead to the narrator's moment of total disorientation. Crumb moves from a distant side view of the interlocutors, then to a closer frontal view

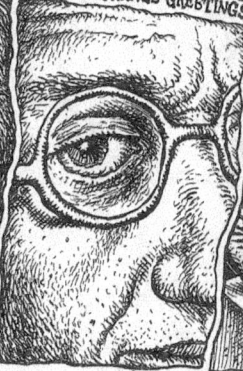

R. Crumb, "Nausea," *Hup*, no. 3 (1989).

R. Crumb, "Nausea," *Hup*, no. 3 (1989).

in which the intensity of the Self-Made Man is emphasized by the radiating light emanating from his head—a technique that Crumb employed in his depiction of Philip K. Dick in his moments of spiritual crisis—culminating in the full frontal close-up of the narrator in a state of severe agitation, his eyeballs swirling in a hypnotized whirlpool daze underneath large circular glasses, face contorted, lips contorted, bulging right cheek, and his head at a slight, quizzical angle. As Scott McCloud observes, "when the content of a silent panel offers no clues as to its duration, it can also produce a sense of timelessness."[18] So too, here Roquentin appears to enter a moment of eternal "nausea" that situates him in a realm beyond space and time. There is also in his dazed look more than a hint of the "comical" that Crumb claims he found in Sartre's text, "something that lent itself to a comic book rendition that probably was not intended by him."

Crumb finds this section of *Nausea* particularly compelling since it dramatizes so effectively many of his own concerns. As we have argued previously, he felt himself from childhood to be an outsider to American life and spent the sixties and seventies undergoing the turbulence of those Dionysian decades. Existential themes appear frequently in Crumb's autobiographical drawings, and one of Crumb's bibliographers, Don Fiene—a professor of Russian language and literature—began his scholarly investigations of Crumb with the intention of pursuing the links between "the great Fyodor Mikhailovich" Dostoevsky and Crumb.[19] The mad search for God depicted in the Russian author's great novels dramatizes the existential quest with the force of unrelenting genius. Crumb himself drew parallels between Dostoevsky, his epileptic brother Maxon, and his own reflections in his journal notation from November 1, 1990: "My mind is so intensely *lucid* today I feel almost on the verge of a seizure of some kind. . . . I guess that's what Dostoievski and Maxon mean by their pre-epileptic state of hyper-awareness, only much more so. . . . Too many realizations crowd the mind at once, building to a state of ecstatic enlightenment, then the fit happens, the convulsions which render you a helpless, quivering, writhing mass on the floor."[20] Dostoevsky was of course an epileptic, and Crumb seeks to underscore the similarities between powerful epiphanies and the convulsive, bodily shakings of epilepsy, which the ancient Greeks—before Hippocrates's medical understanding of the illness—called "the sacred disease" and associated with divinity and genius. Maxon has also confessed to being stricken by epileptic seizures when confronted by naked women. It is not difficult to discern the connection here between erotic ecstasy, possession, and the "fit" of epilepsy: orgasm may also allow a moment of self-transcendence in which the self is for a few minutes "taken over" by an immersive, primal, archaic, instinctive, irresistible power.

Here the climactic moment leads to a recapitulation of the earlier emphasis on the words "exist" and "existence": "So this is nausea: this blinding evidence? I have scratched my head over it! I've written about it! Now I know: I exist—the world exists. That's all. It makes no difference to me." Sartre is clearly playing on René Descartes's famous *Cogito, ergo sum*, "I think, therefore I am." But here there is no causal relationship, no "therefore": I exist, the world exists. This is the moment of the awareness of radical solitude and contingency: *into this world we're thrown.* Crumb skillfully varies our view of the narrator either by himself, with the Self-Taught Man, or with another patron of the restaurant. Crumb also draws the narrator in a slightly different posture in each of the six panels on the page in which he appears. In the first, he is portrayed sitting on the left side frontally; in the second panel, again on the left side, but the right side of his face is in the viewer's direction—the different angle here also allows us to view the reaction of the client seated at the window table witnessing the narrator dropping his knife on his plate—and both the narrator and the observer reveal intense emotion with the lines streaking from their faces. In the third panel, the narrator's face is inclined slightly upward as he bends the knife against the table, then Crumb positions him looking directly at the viewer, seemingly lost and distracted by his own thoughts with bits of perspiration falling from his forehead: the Self-Taught Man is partially cut out of the frame as he queries about ancient Rome. The perspective then shifts so we see both characters together but with the Self-Taught Man now to the left with the narrator showing us the left side of his face. The final panel again portrays both men, but shifting our view clockwise so we now see the table from a forty-five-degree angle to the right. Crumb thus composes page 8 as an entire tableau in which the viewer's eye may visualize the scene from a variety of vantage points, allowing different details to emerge as the perspective shifts. It is the closest thing to having a camera: as we have seen from the outset, Crumb acts like a director filming a scene, but his effects are gained entirely through the skillful manipulation of perspective and point of view. Crumb brings all his skills to bear as a connoisseur of film, a voracious reader of literature, and an expert in the history of comics. As Johanna Drucker has observed, comic artists "synthesize the language of cinema, the sensibilities of contemporary literature, and the appeal of mass media in a format that calls attention to artistry and technique." Crumb brings Sartre's philosophical text to life by employing all the methods at his command.

The narrator is now on electric fire in the final panel, and we note the similarity to the cosmic rays emanating from Philip K. Dick. Crumb deploys a variety of halos or "auras" hovering about the heads and bodies of his

R. Crumb, "Nausea," *Hup*, no. 3 (1989).

characters: on the third page, fourth panel, trembling, curved lines enveloping the face like an electric field; on the sixth panel, straight lines radiating outward; on the first panel of page 8, trembling curved lines; on the fifth panel of page 8, straight lines radiating outward; and on the final panel of page 8 when Roquentin contemplates an *acte gratuit*, a senseless "existential" act of stabbing the Self-Taught Man in the eye with his knife—Edgar Allan Poe's "Imp of the Perverse"—Roquentin is now on fire with flaring, long snake-like sun rays. Throughout, Crumb has supplied foreshadowing of this climactic moment by emphasizing forks and knives being held in the hands or poised in the air by the dining clients, the Self-Taught Man, and Roquentin. The final page is composed of seven panels angled severely up to the right side—so much so that the varying size of the panels compels Crumb to add an arrow (to avoid confusion) leading from panel 3 to 4 to ensure that the reader progresses in proper order to the next panel in the series. We again see the swirling, now whirlpool-like energy about the head of Roquentin as he stands up to take his leave, knife in hand. In the next panel indicated by Crumb's arrow, he casts the knife on the plate on the table, which again radiates cosmic fire, as if he has had to forcibly relinquish the dangerous weapon. The guests have all been startled by the narrator's behavior: arising to depart, he tells us that "everything spins around" him. He takes his leave of the Self-Taught Man, and when he bids goodbye to the clients, "they don't answer. I leave. . . . Now the color will come back to their cheeks, they'll begin to jabber," and the conclusion depicts the narrator strolling along a meticulously rendered cobblestone French sidewalk with awnings, shutters, and a small drainage pipe.

As we have seen, Crumb had long been interested in existentialism, as were many American intellectuals following World War II. Crumb wanted to document—as he put it—"stark reality, the bottom of life," the often absurd contingencies of everyday experience in his drawings: the same goal as the existentialists who sought to communicate the immediacy of lived experience in their literary works. Crumb complained at age twenty-one concerning earlier comics:

> They don't seem to get close enough to reality in human life . . . too idealistic, and stereotyped. Sometimes I think it's impossible to portray reality in a comic-strip. I don't think it's ever been done. . . . All the great strips have either been satire or poetry. . . . I can think of no really outstanding strip which has dealt with real life . . . Can you? [Jules] Feiffer's is, I guess, in a symbolic sort of way. . . . There are so many delicate little things that, when I try to express them in comic

strip form, come out awkward. . . . I consider it a challenge, though, to be as human, and real, but yet interesting and with my personal ideal toward life, as possible in a comic strip. . . . So far, I haven't really gotten at stark reality, the bottom of life (as I see it) in my work. . . . I might end up giving it up and going over to writing alone, if it doesn't seem to be doing any good to try to do it in comic strips.[21]

These are revealing comments, and indeed arriving "at stark reality" is precisely the goal of existentialism. It is also noteworthy that Crumb seems willing to relinquish art in favor of writing—as we have remarked, he is indeed himself a very skilled writer—if he proves unable to attain his aesthetic desire to "portray reality" through drawing. Roquentin thus in many ways stands for Crumb himself in his struggle against the "unreal" and his desire to break free into authenticity, true selfhood. Indeed, as with all the literature Crumb finds engaging, he had several characteristics in common with both characters and author. Sartre, like Crumb, was fond of jazz music—Sartre was also an accomplished classical music pianist—and it is noteworthy that Roquentin does at the close of *Nausea* find a kind of redemption in jazz: in the song "Some of These Days," sung by a "Negress." Sartre, however, was mistaken here—the song was sung by Sophie Tucker, a Jewish woman—not a "Negress." Furthermore, when Roquentin perceives his face in the mirror, he remarks that his "eyes especially are horrible seen so close. They are glassy, soft, blind, red-rimmed, they look like fish scales." So too, Crumb has produced several self-portraits in which he expresses disbelief at the horror of his own face and body. And finally, for Roquentin, the feeling of "Nausea is not inside me: I feel it out there. . . . Everywhere around me . . . I am the one who is within it." Crumb, like Roquentin, is also beset with the Gnostic sensation that it is the cosmos itself that is out of kilter, not just his own fragile psyche: "I am the one who is within it."

In his youth, Crumb also pondered the goals of Eastern philosophy: "I think that gradually I will find peace and acceptance of my existence, and be satisfied to live just for the sake of existence, because it's better to exist than to not exist, even though it is a struggle. I'm constantly wondering whether or not a man can do this. I suppose it is what the Taoists do."[22] Lao-Tzu in the *Tao Te Ching* sought a rapprochement between the yin and the yang—the seemingly opposite contraries of existence—through a recognition of their interdependent nature. Thus this "question of being" had long pervaded Crumb's autobiographical quest, and his illustrations to *Nausea* form a high point in the continuing cycle of his "existential comics." As we have seen in chapter 2, in "Walkin' the Streets," Crumb confronts his intense "feeling of alienation." Jean-Paul Sartre was clearly on his mind as he composed this masterful work, for in one scene, in which he recalls his nocturnal peram- bulations through town with his brother Charles, he appends to the side of a panel one of his trademark hanging scrolls: "Yet did I dream all this? I remember only vaguely the hideous reality.—Jean-Paul Sartre." The quota- tion comes from Sartre's autobiography *Les mots*, with which as we have seen previously Crumb was familiar. In the story, Crumb reveals that he does not belong anywhere in contemporary American society and admits to being "depressed" and "angry." He describes his flirtation with suicide at age nineteen in 1962 as well as his mystical and philosophical conversa- tions with his brother Charles. Crumb chronicles his misanthropy, declaring that he "had nothing but a towering *contempt* for human society"—in his *Sketchbooks*, Crumb cites Jonathan Swift and Mark Twain voicing similar sentiments—but his lust for women is the one thing that draws him toward attempting to mingle with his fellow humans. Yet his cynicism is balanced by his idealistic discussions with brother Charles: "We were throwback mel- ancholy nineteenth century romanticists." Crumb agrees with his brother that "love and beauty are the only things worth living for." But here Crumb comments on his own earlier self in a boxed comment at the bottom with an arrow pointing at his portrait as he holds his left hand aloft in a poetic gesture and face lifted gently forward: "Oh yeah, right! Ten years before 'Big Ass Comics,'" referring to one of Crumb's publications. Crumb also portrays the violent quarrels of his parents: in one panel, he depicts his crazed mother scratching her husband's face with her fingernails, blood spurting plentifully. In the next panel, Crumb's father is shown with a bandaged visage with suit and tie returning to work "dutifully."

In "Walkin' the Streets," literature again plays a central role in the evolution of the brothers' awareness. Charles recites from memory a section from Edgar Allan Poe's "The Raven," as well as passages from Shakespeare: *Macbeth* and the "To be or not to be" soliloquy from *Hamlet*—the quintessential existential text—while Crumb depicts himself absorbed in William Golding's *Lord of the Flies*. Thus, the literary, spiritual, and existential are deeply connected in Crumb's imagination. At one point in the narrative, he asks the ques- tion of *Nausea*—"Why am I here?"—and Crumb is particularly skilled at depicting his adolescent angst: alone reading in his room on his rumpled bed, engaging in auto-eroticism, walking the night city streets stooped over, alone and feeling, rather like the monster in *Frankenstein*, completely cut off from the surrounding human world.[23] The *Nausea* drawings appeared in 1989, while Crumb began creating "Walkin' the Streets" three years later in 1992. However, Crumb did not complete work on the project until 2004: he

R. Crumb, "Walkin' the Streets," *Zap*, no. 16 (2004).

interrupted his labors due to the suicide of his brother Charles. Thus, Crumb clearly imagined the two works as overlapping in their film noir theme and style. The American streets are detailed with the same scrupulous eye as the streets of France: the shark-finned cars resting silent on the night streets recall Robert Lowell's famous poem "Skunk Hour" in which Lowell tells of a dark night of the soul with the cars sitting "hull to hull."[24] The street lamps emit an eerie glow, a television antenna sprouts from a rooftop, sidewalks are shadowed, the sky bleak in its unremitting dark blankness: there is no star in sight. Because "Walkin' the Streets" was created over a long time span—1992 to 2004—Crumb is able to bring his autobiographical quest up to date. And while the *Nausea* narrative ends with Roquentin leaving the restaurant in disgust, Crumb chronicles a measure of spiritual equanimity: here he ends affirmatively, declaring that he has now arrived at an "unalienated" state, has two children, and is at relative peace with his life.

Another dramatic example of the way Crumb has incorporated existential themes in his work may be seen in "Life Certainly Is 'Existential'!" from 1984, which begins with a pensive figure responding to the title with "What makes it get like that?" He then answers his own question: "I dunno . . . it's . . . it's like the sound of somebody flushing a toilet down the hall."[25] Crumb is among the characters depicted—the figure in panels 1 and 8 is clearly Crumb himself—thus counting himself among the mass of suffering humanity: he is by no means above the fray. In this first panel he is in a dark room, shadows on his chest, shadows half covering the door in the background, the cross-hatched walls lending a drab mood. The fact that he can hear a toilet flushing nearby suggests that the room is in an apartment or rooming house, where one is surrounded by the sounds of the daily activities of others. In the next panel a woman's face is depicted frontally speaking directly to the viewer, bemoaning the fact that "people can never think of what to say to each other half the time . . . or something . . ." A typical theme in existential literature as well as the absurdist drama of Samuel Beckett and Eugène Ionesco is the inability to truly communicate with others. This idea became pervasive in the sixties, as can be seen in Simon and Garfunkel's 1965 hit "The Sound of Silence"—"People talking without speaking / People hearing without listening"—or the loneliness the Beatles chronicled in a song that appeared the following year, "Eleanor Rigby." In the fourth panel, we have a direct allusion to Sartre. Here Crumb gives a full-frontal view—as he did with Roquentin—of a despairing man afflicted by "existential nausea": eyes open and mouth agape displaying fearful teeth, his large hand in front of his face. In the next two panels, we switch again from metaphysics—as we did in the opening "existential" question to flushing toilets—to the real

LIFE CERTAINLY IS "EXISTENTIAL"!

©1989 BY R. CRUMB

WHAT MAKES IT GET LIKE THAT??

I DUNNO...IT'S...IT'S LIKE THE SOUND OF SOMEBODY FLUSHING A TOILET DOWN THE HALL...

YEAH...IT'S THE WAY, Y'KNOW, HOW, LIKE, PEOPLE CAN NEVER THINK OF WHAT TO SAY TO EACH OTHER HALF THE TIME...OR SOMETHING...

AND THE WAY THEY LOOK AWAY FROM EACH OTHER IN THOSE AWKWARD MOMENTS OF SILENCE...

OH GOD, THAT CAN BE PAINFUL...THE LONELINESS OF THOSE MOMENTS...I GET EXISTENTIAL NAUSEA JUST THINKING ABOUT IT...

THAT QUEAZY FEELING CAN HIT YOU AT ANY TIME, IN ANY SITUATION... LIKE WHEN YOU'RE COOKING SOME LUNCH OR DINNER...

THE SIZZLING SOUND OF THOSE BURGERS...

SPUTTER CRACKLE SPRIT

...OR WATCHING TV COMMERCIALS...

YOU CAN COUNT ON SEARS!!!

OR LAYING IN BED AT NIGHT, WHEN YOU HEAR THOSE LITTLE MOTORS THAT YOU CAN NEVER HEAR IN THE DAYTIME.

WHIRRRRRRRRRRRRRR

OR EVEN...EVEN SITTING DOWN TO DRAW ANOTHER COMIC PAGE...

GASP...I CAN'T BREATHE...

YEAH, HELL, LIFE'S AN EXISTENTIAL DEAL, AIN'T IT?

SURE AS SHITTIN'!...

END

R. Crumb, "Life Certainly Is 'Existential'," *Weirdo*, no. 14 (1981).

world represented by "that queasy feeling" (Sartre's "nausea" now arrives with "the sizzling sound of those burgers") and the blaring sound of a television commercial. Even Crumb himself as he sits down to draw is afflicted by the inability to breathe. Crumb also employs another technique he summoned for Sartre in the partial figure of the cowboy in the final panel. Yet the work is thoroughly American—not French—with the use of language such as "dunno," "yeah," the references to Sears commercials, frying "burgers" in a pan, and the final comic tableau of the working-class beer drinkers in a bar adding their down-home expletives in their assent to the relevance of that fancy philosophical theory from France. The final image is marvelous, demonstrating the fertility of Crumb's imagination. He typically hones in on specific details that make his work spring to life: the puddles on the bar, an emblazoned Peterbilt logo trucking company cap, the partially invisible cowboy-hatted companion with the tattooed "Nancy" on his arm.

This attention to the telling detail can be found in several of the artists Crumb admires: Bruegel, Bosch, and one of his favorites—William Hogarth (1697–1764)—with whose work he became familiar at age sixteen. In a letter of April 4, 1960, to Marty Pahls, he notes that he has "seen a few cartoons by Hogarth, I wish I could see more! I like his work a lot. . . . It's colorful, and has more bounce and flexibility than most of his crude contemporaries." The adaptation Crumb created of James Boswell's *London Journal* bears witness to Hogarth's influence on his work.[26] In Hogarth's illustrations to Samuel Butler's (1613–1680) satirical poem *Hudibras* (1684), we find an alert cat, a skeleton hanging in the closet with an owl on its shoulder, a mysterious figure exiting through a lit doorway: in details we find the real significance of things. Crumb in a late sketchbook entry speaks of "details, thousands millions and trillions of details . . . and each and every one of them is . . . a clue, a hint, a metaphor. Pay attention!"[27] Thus there is both an aesthetic and a philosophical rationale in Crumb's work for this attention to the seemingly insignificant. First, on the artistic level, this focus on specificity brings the work fully to life, avoiding the generalities of ideology for the actual facts of existence; and second, in this way Crumb emphasizes the famous saying of Hermes Trismegistus—"as above, so below." There may be—if we pay close attention—correspondences to be found between inner and outer worlds, between the manifest world of creaturely being and a hidden world of meaning in camouflage.

One of the central dilemmas of existentialism is of course the question of free will, a question that preoccupies Crumb. He believes that it is

a real subtle matter. I think free will is something you [have] to cultivate. Very few people actually do. We probably have the ability, but

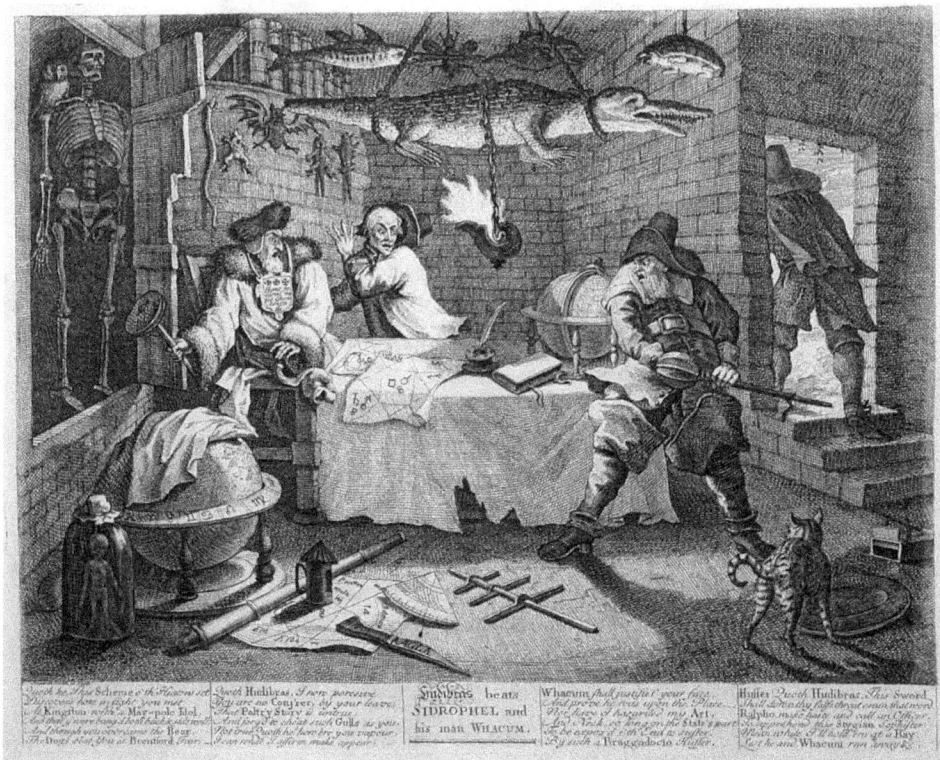

William Hogarth, *Hudibras*, 1726.

that's a really hard thing to get to, the ability to exercise free will. Most people don't use it very much. That's why religions are based on the idea that we're responsible for our actions, and that's what morality is based on. But actually finding and taking that responsibility is a very esoteric matter.[28]

Here Crumb appears to be moving toward a Buddhist orientation regarding achieving liberation from the law of karma, the law of cause and effect, by achieving nirvana, or *kensho* according to the Zen Buddhists. In his illustrations to Sartre, Crumb is dramatizing precisely the ambiguity the narrator faces when confronted with his own "freedom": because the responsibility to "choose" is completely on his own shoulders, the gravity of each situation with which he is faced may have profound consequences. As Sartre memorably said, we are condemned to be free. Existentialism is similar to *gnosis* in that responsibility comes from within, the course of action revealed by considering what is best through individual choice rather than through external authority, institutions, or a mediating figure such as a priest. Sartre in *Existentialism Is a Humanism* gives the famous example of a young man who during World War II must decide whether to fight the Nazis or remain with his ailing mother. Sartre argues that the man cannot find the answer in the Bible or indeed in any outside source: *he* must decide, *he* must choose, *he* must face the consequences of his actions.[29] However, Sartre was an atheist, and we can see that because existentialism puts the emphasis on the individual; it shares similarities with the struggle of the youth culture to define itself apart from the institutions and orthodoxies of American life.

In other works, such as "The Unbearable Tediousness of Being"—the title is a play on Milan Kundera's novel *The Unbearable Lightness of Being* (1984)—Crumb creates an "existential" scene reminiscent of the torture the characters in Sartre's play *Huis clos* (*No Exit*) inflict upon each other. Crumb brilliantly depicts a miserable blind date between two supremely unlikeable characters, admonishing his audience at the opening: "Warning! If you are one of those happy-go-lucky louts who thinks Mel Gibson is the ideal man, then don't bother to read this. You won't like it. This is only for those persons of extreme sensitivity, for whom every second of life on this planet is an excruciating ordeal." And in his later *Sketchbooks*, Crumb develops the connection between existentialism, Eastern philosophy, and the release from karma—the cycle of suffering and causality—which is achieved through nirvana. Crumb declares:

> Everything we do has significance. Every action, every thought leaves an imprint—not only on the self, but on the world, on the others, and even on time, on all who come after us! This implies a responsibility for one's thoughts and actions that should be taken most seriously! And yet one feels helpless, a hapless victim of circumstances beyond one's control, as if one's behavior and thoughts did not originate in the self, but were a product, an accumulation of imprints from the world, from our ancestors, from the people around us. It behooves one to take responsibility, to take the power to decide how one will act, and even how one will think! Not only for the betterment of one's self but for the betterment of the world, all the others, and all who will come after us![30]

This is a remarkable statement, suggesting the depth of Crumb's thought concerning this central question of human existence. It recalls the concept in the theosophy of the Akashic records—we find allusions to this idea in the work of H. P. Lovecraft as well—which posits that every thought and action leaves a record, or an "imprint" as Crumb puts it, catalogued in some sort of infinite cosmic internet. It also echoes the Bhagavad Gita regarding the relationship between thought and action.

Finally, there is a striking page in the Zweitausendeins edition of the *Sketchbooks* that features a scowling pig with dollar signs for eyes pointing his finger accusingly at the viewer with the headline: "Buy 'n' Sell!!" The text reads:

> *Your* lives are bought and sold for profit! *Your* future, *your* children have been bought and sold for profit! *Your* culture! *Your* music! Your art! Your traditions! Your freedom! Your destiny has been bought and sold and bought and sold again and again! Get your head outa yer ass, pal!! Face reality! Awareness of these facts eventually brings one to a set of choices. . . . No longer a dupe, a sucker, a sap & a "mooch," you can either join in the buying and selling yourself, or, you can join the struggle against this disease. The latter choice is a much more difficult road to follow. Temptations to join the forces of exploitation are offered at every turn and twist in the road. The existential question may be asked: how much "choice" is really involved in one's destiny? Can the question ever be satisfactorily answered? Probably not. We have to think in terms of *survival* when dealing with *social* problems. Existential questions bog us down and cause in us an inability to come to grips with the problem. This may be alright for some, but for those struggling near the edge, the deeper questions must wait!![31]

Here we return to a theme we saw adumbrated in chapter 1 in Crumb's illustrations for "Those Dharma Bhums" in which Suzette argues that, in a sense, the "higher, existential" questions are luxuries for those who are economically secure enough to be able to try to free themselves from the grip of "conditioning" through philosophy or spiritual discipline. Those on the bottom of the social hierarchy do not have this freedom. Crumb also returns to his polemics against capitalism, against a society in which everything is for sale and where each of us must make the "existential choice" whether to enter the game of exploitation of our fellow humans or attempt to free ourselves from being chained to the machine, to the robotic daily bazaar of "buying and selling yourself." Thus, we can see how Crumb's engagement with Jean-Paul Sartre incorporates many of the themes that preoccupied him from his youth. In his illustrations to *Nausea*, he brings out the stark nature of the process of self-realization and the difficult road to achieving honesty with one's self and one's own true motives, desires, and potentialities. Crumb also continued in his autobiographical works to explore these themes in a number of different permutations, including the connections between the existential quest and conceptions of Eastern thought.

Chapter 5

FRANZ KAFKA

Allegories of the Soul

Following the completion of his adaptation of Jean-Paul Sartre's *Nausea*, Crumb turned his attention to the work of Franz Kafka (1883–1924), which bore fruit in the volume *Introducing Kafka* (1994) with text by David Mairowitz. Crumb is successful here in forging from the union of literature and image a work more powerful than either individually: his graphic storytelling strengthens, deepens, and transforms our understanding of Kafka's themes. Richard Alleva has argued that "*Introducing Kafka* is a work of art in its own right, a very rare example of what happens when one idiosyncratic artist absorbs another into his world view without obliterating the individuality of the absorbed one." Kafka's style lends itself particularly well to Crumb's illustrations due to his dreamlike imagery and often visceral, violent themes and has attracted other artists such as Peter Kuper.[1] The fact that Crumb's drawings have been exhibited in galleries in New York and London as autonomous masterpieces able to stand on their own supports the notion that they indeed both possess impressive aesthetic power and also aid the viewer toward a deeper understanding of Kafka's life and work.[2]

Crumb undertook the project without knowing a great deal about Kafka's writings before he began, but over the year he spent working he became "deeply immersed" in Kafka's inner world. The degree of self-identification with Kafka Crumb displays is significant: he clearly feels an affinity both intellectually and spiritually to the Czech author. Kafka's dreamlike world answered to Crumb's own emphasis on the importance of dreams, as we see in the recently published *R. Crumb's Dream Diary* (2018). Crumb particularly appreciated *Das Schloss* (*The Castle*): "Reading it closely, you get to another level with it—an incredibly detailed, layered writing that is deceptively under the surface. . . . [I]f you go back and read it slowly, you start discovering the whole other layer of stuff that's going on. It's really strange that way—very strange, dream-like, levels like in dreams." In addition, Kafka's years-long approach/retreat emotional dynamic with his fiancée Felice Bauer echoes Crumb's own complex relationships with women, while Kafka's tortured relationship with his father—wrenchingly described in his famous *Brief an den Vater* (1919)—is replicated by Crumb's fear-ridden connection to his violent Marine Corps father.[3] Furthermore, nightmarish themes of guilt, persecution, and punishment for uncommitted and unspecified crimes; an absent God; loss of identity; and the absurdity of modern life are idées fixes for Crumb as well. Crumb, like Kafka, felt uncomfortable in his own body— an awkward ectomorph—and keenly felt his vulnerability in a frequently brutal, uncaring world, declaring: "Some of the imagery in my work is sorta scary because I'm basically a fearful, pessimistic person. I'm always seeing the predatory nature of the universe, which can harm you or kill you very easily and very quickly, no matter how well you watch your step." Finally, both are frequently quite funny: although known for his dark parables, in private life Kafka was known as the life of the party, and his stories often feature the same ironic, absurdist, mordant edge that characterizes Crumb's work. Kafka, like Jorge Luis Borges, spoke to the counterculture due to his depiction of a labyrinthine world in which one wandered ceaselessly in search of a center to the maze, but no center could be found. Indeed, Max Weber in his essay "Science as a Vocation" (1914) had diagnosed the triumph of the "rational" and "bureaucratic" sensibility that led to the instrumentalization and *Entzauberung*—or "demagification"—of our world, which is precisely the situation Kafka's work so memorably describes.[4] During the sixties and seventies, these conceptions began to influence popular culture in television shows such as *The Prisoner* starring Patrick McGoohan, who plays a British secret agent incarcerated by an unknown power for mysterious reasons.[5] Just as the surveyor in *The Castle* seeks unsuccessfully to journey through a dreamlike landscape dominated by an inscrutable, unresponsive bureaucracy to find his way to his goal, so too modern humanity appeared to be lost in a truly *Kafkaesque*—Kafka is one of the rare writers whose name has been adopted to describe a particularly disoriented modern sensibility—world that made no sense.

Finally, Kafka, as a Jew writing in German in the Austro-Hungarian city of Prague, was the perpetual outsider: as one scholar has observed, "a token Jew among Germans and, after 1918, a token German among Czechs."[6] Crumb makes frequent references to Jewish culture and in often portrayed himself as a *schlemiel*—Yiddish for a vulnerable loser—which may also be said of the antihero Gregor Samsa in *The Metamorphosis* who lives at home with his parents, abandons his job, and transforms into a gigantic insect. Commentators have noted similarities in some of Crumb's characters to Jewish stereotypes. Steven Marx, for example, observed regarding Crumb's character Shuman the Human: "Although wearing different masks in the two strips in which he appears (*Head Comix*, Viking Press, 1968), Shuman the Human has a single identity; he represents man as Jew. . . . He also fits the psychological stereotype of the Jew: super-intellectual, paranoid, anal. But most important, Shuman's relationship with God stems from the Old Testament. He could be Abraham or Jonah or Job."[7] Crumb had never known any Jewish people before moving to Cleveland in 1962, where he met Harvey Pekar—"the first person I ever met who I thot [*sic*] was a genuine 'hipster'"—and helped Pekar publish his work.[8] Crumb's colleague Will Eisner, in *A Contract with God* (1978)—considered one of the first graphic novels—dramatically explored religious themes in connection with Jewish immigrants in New York City during the thirties, and as a misfit and outsider himself, Crumb identified with Jewish people as oppressed and alienated.[9] Several of the major figures in the evolution of American comics were of Jewish ancestry: Jerry Siegel and Joe Shuster created *Superman*; Bob Kane and Bill Finger, *Batman*; Stan Lee, *The Amazing Spider-Man*, *The Hulk*, and *The X-Men*; and Harvey Kurtzman, *Mad* magazine. In addition, Crumb would later marry two Jewish women, Dana Morgan and Aline Kominsky, née Aline Goldsmith, who introduced him to many elements of their culture—such as Yiddish terms and expressions—which began to surface more prominently in his work.[10] Aline's witty humor derived in part from her exposure to the Borscht Belt comedians who plied their trade in the Catskills during her youth, and Crumb claimed that it was due to her influence that he began to perfect the art of self-deprecation:

> To make yourself into a fool like that, it's a defensive measure to try to distance yourself from yourself, from what's bothering you. . . . I really learn a lot about doing that from Aline. It's a Jewish tradition, making yourself an absurd character. Gentiles have a hard time with that. We are raised in a Christian culture, which holds up this ideal of perfection that we're always trying to live up to.[11]

Introducing Kafka contains biographical information, excerpts from Kafka's *Diaries* and *Letters*, and interpretations of *The Judgment*, *The Metamorphosis*, *The Burrow*, *In the Penal Colony*, *The Trial*, *The Castle*, and *A Hunger Artist*. David Mairowitz's text begins—as a grim foreshadowing of what will follow later in the book—with an account from Kafka's *Diaries* in which he imagines himself being dragged by a rope around his neck up through the top of a building "until the last torn-off bits of me drop from the empty noose as it crashes through the tiles and comes to rest on the roof"—which Crumb illustrates with impressive horror. In this chapter I shall explore the ways Crumb illustrates several central spiritual themes as they appear in Kafka's work: the Golem and the Hasidim; the Talmud; his mystical relationship to writing; and the meaning of suffering and martyrdom. To provide background knowledge concerning Kafka's life and works, we are introduced to the famous Rabbi Loew of Prague, who was known to have secretly studied Kabbalah. We know that Kafka possessed Kabbalistic texts such as an extract from the Zohar, "Das Licht des Urquells" ("The Light of the Original Source"), which held "that God concealed the primal light from the eyes of sinful mankind and will reveal it again only when the diverse worlds, into which the creation has disintegrated, are again united." Kabbalistic themes also occur in *Amerika*, while the Shekhinah—the feminine principle in the theology of Kabbalah—figures prominently in *The Castle*.[12] Crumb provides the lettering to accompany a page of Hebrew text from "Title Page of Rabbi Loew's Book of 1578," and Mairowitz explains that in Kabbalah, "the letters of the Hebrew alphabet were imbued with magic powers." He then goes on to quote from the preeminent Kabbalah authority Gershom Scholem, who asserted that although these mystical ideas have largely disappeared among contemporaries—and Mairowitz italicizes the following—"*they still retain an enormous force in the books of Franz Kafka*." Kabbalah was an influence on the California counterculture during the sixties, and Crumb was conversant with the symbolism of Kabbalah, as was his friend Rick Griffin. In his depiction of the Golem, Crumb employs imagery that he will later incorporate in his illustrations to the book of Genesis: his interest in the author of *Der Golem* (1915)—Gustav Meyrink (1868–1932)—is further confirmed by the fact that in *Waiting for Food*, vol. 1, Crumb includes a portrait of the Austrian author. The lettering of the word *Golem* emerges from the torches borne aloft by two observers of the rabbi inscribing the Hebrew letters on the forehead of the Golem.[13] The Golem will return in a later section of the book when the Jews are being persecuted in Prague: Crumb depicts a huge figure with Hebrew letters on his forehead looking down upon the scene. Also striking is Crumb's rendering of R. Israel Ben Eliezer in the section dealing with the Hasidic movement. The portrait is effective, rendering the sensitive and kind face of Eliezer and demonstrating Crumb's virtuosity with careful lettering: he is capable of rendering a wide variety of shapes, sizes, boldness, and intensities. These abilities—in combination with all of his other narrative gifts—give his literary adaptations a status far above the typical "comic book" of the past.

The text explains the philosophy of the Hasidim, which is clearly an element in Crumb's own spirituality: "What excited Kafka, and surely had an impact on his stories, was the mystical, anti-rational side of Hasidism, where earthly reality was continuous with unearthly reality, where mystical value was to be found in the details of everyday life, and where God was everywhere and easily contactable."[14] Ritchie Robertson has further described the doctrine of Eliezer, who asserted that

> the Creator, though not identical with the creation (as in pantheism), was present in its midst, and the created world was a mere garment which the devout could penetrate in order to enjoy *devekut*, or communion with God. Since God was omnipresent, man should be confident and joyful, and allow *devekut* to permeate his entire life. Whereas the Cabala had reserved *devekut* as the reward for extreme spiritual distinction, Hasidism made it freely available to all, thus annulling the division between the sacred and the profane. Man could be united with God, not only in ecstatic prayer, but even in the most mundane details of daily life.

Indeed, one commentator has remarked on Crumb's own "devout, almost religious attention to detail": one thinks of medieval illuminated manuscripts.[15]

Crumb treats this theme in his inimitable manner on the cover of *Mystic Funnies*, no. 1. We note in Eliezer the emphasis on "the mundane details of everyday life," and Flakey Foont asks Mr. Natural: "Whataya MEAN, they're signs and omens everywhere, Mr. Natural?! I don't get it!" In Crumb's drawing, the viewer is cast into the role of a magician who must interpret the hidden meanings or "signatures," since Flakey Foont is totally oblivious to the "signs and omens" that surround him. As one examines the illustration carefully, one notices at the top far right a bunny rabbit in the clouds bearing a movie camera trained on the scene below: the pose of the creature and the position on the tripod of the camera replicate exactly Crumb's rendition of the director rabbit (on the side of his camera is written "The Great Kozmic TV Network in the Sky") in "Dirty Dog" from *Zap*, no. 3 (December 1968), in which the speech bubble has the animal jauntily declaring: "Hi! I'm God! Let's Get Going!" as he observes Dirty Dog going about his obsessive, sex-crazed preoccupations. This figure is clearly intended throughout Crumb's work to stand for the silent, "divine" figure in the sky who functions as a spectator/witness observing the human drama below in the manner of a movie director; a black bird hopping unnoticed in the path; a seven-headed snake (a Buddhist Naga); an angel with trumpet among the clouds to the far left;

R. Crumb, *Mystic Funnies*, no. 1 (1997).

a cosmic Shiva with Third Eye blazing above his eyebrows just beneath the "funnies" logo; and an antler-headed man holding in his hands two sacred staffs to the ground near the trees in the background (this likely alludes to shamanic tradition as well as to Cernunnos, the Celtic god beloved to witch-craft and the Beats—Diane di Prima and Gregory Corso both refer to him). To the right and above the shaman is Shiva, dancing as Nataraja; a discarded diet cola can under a bush beside which an alien creature crouches; a piece of notepaper next to Mr. Natural's left foot bearing the Alpha and Omega symbols; a lost key behind his right foot and in front perhaps a serpent eat-ing its tail—the *ouroboros*, which, according to Jung, is an archaic symbol of eternal becoming in alchemy; a pile of offal that bears a human face; a petroglyph-like creature as well as alien and howling figures among the leaves in the tree to the far left; in the clouds to the far left an angel with trumpet; a mask-like head hanging from a tree limb next to Flakey Foont, whose foot is about to descend upon an ace of spades playing card (there is also a mad-eyed, fanged monster threatening from the tree just above his head); a pterodactyl-like creature flying through the sky; a bat-like creature hidden in the leaves of the bush; and a girl whose appearance gives the knowing viewer a clue that she is a favored Crumb type: schoolgirl dress, chunky leg, and black shoe (perhaps Crumb's method of drawing himself into the picture in the manner of the old masters, or as in an Alfred Hitchcock cameo).

Thus we have a confluence of Buddhist, Hindu, Christian, pagan, prehis-toric, and space-age symbolism, typical of the syncretism of Beat spirituality. Crumb is exemplifying the Hasidic belief that the "world was a mere garment which the devout could penetrate in order to enjoy *devekut*, or communion with God." He is also illustrating the esoteric doctrine that there are two realms of interpretation: the Book of Scripture and the Book of Nature, both of which contain hidden symbols that we are intended to interpret—the concept of "signatures," famously expounded by the German mystic Jakob Böhme in his *De Signatura Rerum*. Stuart Clark has explained: "The idea of 'signatures' also depended on the ability both of the heavens to stamp particular characteristics and uses onto natural things from above and of the natural magician to read them." Alan Moore (1953–), creator of *Watchmen* and *V for Vendetta*, has written appreciatively about Crumb's influence on his own work and has a deep interest in shamanism and the occult. Moore has asserted that "the world is kind of pregnant with revelation if you're somebody who comes equipped with the right kind of eyes and the right kind of phrase book . . . for decoding. Magic is, in a sense, a kind of language with which to read the universe."[16] Mr. Natural here moves beyond his role as a "Zen teacher" in an attempt to open Flakey up to the mysteries that lie under his very nose. Crumb here—as usual—is not "advocating" through Mr. Natural a "belief" in any particular system of interpreting the world, but rather suggesting to Foont that, as Hamlet observes: "There are more things in heaven and earth, Horatio, / Than are dreamt of in your philosophy" (*Hamlet*, 1.5.167–68).

Crumb goes on to depict several examples of anti-Semitism prevalent during Kafka's youth as well as Kafka's debilitating relationship with his father Herman, which leads to his illustrations for *The Judgment*. He employs again the stylistic feature from Classics Illustrated, a hanging scroll with curled-up ends in the opening panel: "In this early story George Bendemann, a young merchant living alone with his aging father since the death of his mother, has been writing to an old friend in Russia."[17] Kafka narrates the suicide of a young man due to the constant abuse of his father. This is of course a recurrent Kafka theme, and Crumb as we have seen was abused by his sadistic Marine Corps father: the father/son relationship mirrors God the Father/ Christ (Humanity). Notably, Crumb illustrates the father in one panel in God-like fashion with arm and finger extended, surrounded by the black energy lines that he will employ in his depictions of God in the Book of Genesis: "Therefore, take note: I hereby sentence you to death by drowning," a sentence that his son then carries out.

Kafka's *The Metamorphosis* may be interpreted as a kind of twisted animal fable: *Investigations of a Dog* and *Report to the Academy*, concerning an ape "which has become more or less human" are two others. Crumb had from the beginning of his career discovered in the tradition of animal cartoons— which have their sources in Aesop's *Fables* and Ovid's *The Metamorphoses*—one of his favorite genres. As we have seen, one of his favorite artists was Carl Barks, who developed the character of Donald Duck, which had been created by the Walt Disney Studios, and Crumb himself possessed a fecund imagination when it came to animals. Brombo the Panda, Diffy the Mouse, Bearzy Wearzies, Fritz the Cat, the Silly Pigeons, Andrea Ostrich, Abigale Alligator, Dirty Dog, Fuzzy the Bunny, Oggie the Frog, Patricia Pig, Smelly Old Cat, Squirrely the Squirrel, Farnsworth the Fox, Vulture Demoness, Wiesenhiemer Weasel: all perform specific allegorical roles throughout Crumb's oeuvre. Art Spiegelman created "The MetaMetamorphosis" (2014) and has acknowledged Kafka's animal fables—such as *Josephine the Singer, or the Mouse Folk*, published in 1924—as inspiration for his own work.[18] In Crumb's illustrations to *The Metamorphosis*, the panels are tilted at an angle—as we saw with Sartre's *Nausea*—instead of arranged in regular rows in order to increase the sense of disequilibrium and anxiety for the viewer. Crumb shows great skill in depicting the gigantic insect into which Gregor

David Mairowitz and R. Crumb, *Introducing Kafka*, 1994.

Samsa has been transformed. There are small, telling details: for example, multiple close-ups of Samsa's sister Grete's shoes—the same type as Crumb's favored clodhoppers. In another illustration, he shows Grete howling in the pose of Edvard Munch's *The Scream*—Crumb employs this iconic image in his illustrations to Charles Bukowski as well as to *Gilgamesh*.[19] Indeed, Crumb excels at depicting the human face, and the relationship of Kafka to Judaism is depicted in several striking portraits. In a biographical section describing Kafka's relationships to the women in his life, Crumb returns to Jewish imagery—again pictured upon a scroll—with a quotation from the Talmud: "A Man without a Wife Is Not a Man." Here a stern rabbi wearing the *kippah* looks down upon Kafka as he peruses the Talmud, with his finger pointed toward the sky and eyes wide open, with Crumb's favored numinous, streaking lines emanating from both Kafka and the rabbi.

Numinous imagery also surrounds Crumb's depiction of what might be termed the transcendence sometimes bestowed upon the writer in the act of writing. Crumb depicts Kafka as struck by a power that takes him over while composing, a condition described often by writers: indeed, Kafka was often possessed by hypergraphia.[20] In his portrait, we see that Kafka's eyes are swirling circles of energy, which also emanate from his head and body as he grips his pen intently over the paper. He is wrapped within and rapt by the silent trance of inspired, creative activity. One notes the stark, compelling energy here, recalling the work of Belgian Frans Masereel (1889–1972), whose wordless, single-image-per-page *Passionate Journey: A Vision in Woodcuts*—published in 1919 in Germany under the title *Mein Stundenbuch* and praised by Thomas Mann—powerfully narrates the daily life of Everyman. Indeed, Crumb has stated his fondness for several expressionist artists such as Otto Dix, and we observe the severe black-and-white etching typical of German woodcut art. Art Spiegelman in his "Prisoner on the Hell Planet" also acknowledged his debt to "the detailed scratchboard drawings" of expressionism. In the subsequent drawing, we have the word bubble: "Every word first looks around in every direction before letting itself be written down by me"—again emphasizing the passive aspects of the creative trance. Indeed, this seems a sacred moment, when Kafka is seized by a higher force and impelled to register the forbidding, awesome, terrifying words he is transcribing from some supernatural power.

Kafka is portrayed again in the following drawing in the act of writing; indeed, it is the same moment, but now portrayed from the left side. We again see his large, awestruck eye open and again gripping his pen over the paper with the inkstand before him, lampshade and lamp and the view of

Prague through the open window: "Writing ... is a deeper sleep than death ... Just as one wouldn't pull a corpse from its grave, I can't be dragged from my desk at night." Stanley Corngold has observed that when Kafka "wrote well, he knew ecstatic moods of extraordinary intensity."[21] Crumb is also speaking here of his own experience as an artist, that it fulfills an essential role. Indeed, Crumb has often said that he exists mainly to create art, that without drawing he is incapable of making sense of his experience and that he feels profoundly depressed if he goes a day without setting pen to paper: he even sketches on placemats while waiting for meals in restaurants, and four volumes of these spontaneous, often extraordinary drawings under the title *Waiting for Food: Restaurant Placement Drawings* (1995, 2000, 2002, 2008) have been published.

Crumb's curiosity regarding the creative process extends beyond Kafka to the practices of the Eskimo. Crumb has been fascinated by books of adventure such as *Kabloona* (1941) by the French author Gontran de Poncins (1900–1962), which recounts the confrontation of a "civilized" Frenchman with the Eskimo people, as well as *The Book of the Eskimos* by Peter Freuchen. Crumb quotes at length in his *Sketchbooks* from Freuchen's account of the ceremony the Eskimo performed during the feasts they held for the soul of the whales. In order to compose new songs for celebrating "the great beast," it was required that

> darkness and stillness were to reign in the festival house. Nothing must disturb them, nothing distract them. In deep silence they sat in the dark, thinking; all the men, old and young, yes, even the youngest of the boys, as long as he was only able to speak. It was the stillness we called Qarrtsiluni, which means that one waits for something to burst. For our forefathers believed that songs are born in this stillness, while all endeavor to think only beautiful thoughts. Then they take shape in the minds of men and rise up like bubbles from the depths of the sea, bubbles that seek the air to burst in the light! That is how the sacred songs are made. ... All songs are born in man out in the great wilderness. Without ourselves knowing how it happens, they come with the breath, words and tones that are not daily speech.

This is a lovely passage illustrating that for the Eskimo—as for Kafka and Crumb himself—the creative artist must wait for the "stillness we called Qarrtsiluni, which means that one waits for something to burst." That Crumb would transcribe such a powerful text at length indicates that his curiosity concerning the creative process extended beyond the field of Western literature as represented by Kafka to the wider context of world traditions as represented in anthropological texts.

Another writerly image that Crumb places later in the book after Kafka meets Dora Dymant—whom Kafka met and fell in love with following his parting from Felice Bauer—again depicts Kafka as he is struggling to compose, but now definitely in the grip of the Furies:

> When he first came to Berlin, Kafka felt he had escaped from those phantoms which had forced him to write: "They keep looking for me, but, for the moment, they can't find me." These were the same ghosts who "drank kisses" written in letters and who seemed to vampyrize his words and thoughts. Soon, he would ask Dora to burn many of his manuscripts. But the phantoms returned and forced him one night to write—appropriately—"The Burrow."[22]

Kafka famously declared that "a book must be the axe for the frozen sea within us. That is my belief."[23] This recalls Crumb's own description of his artistic process as a struggle with the superego and the id, with the binding force of the restricted conscious mind and the volcanic powers of the unconscious: "I still have doubts while I'm doing it. It's my linear mind telling me that. There's always a battle with it; you might call it the ego. That civilized part of you that always wants to be rational and logical. And the real self that wants to be magical."[24] This deep, authentic self is the source of creativity and "magic"—a recurring theme in the counterculture and which may be resuscitated when Kafka's "frozen sea within us" is made to flow again. There was an effort on the part of young people during the Beat and hippie periods in America to preserve the soul from the encroachments of mechanical domination. This also explains Crumb's powerful attraction to pre–World War II American popular culture, which appeared to have enshrined certain qualities of innocence and openness and joie de vivre that had begun to disappear with the triumph of what Martin Heidegger called the *moderne technische Welt*—the modern, technological world. Crumb recalls William Blake's apothegm "energy is eternal delight," for his work often not only exudes stark cynicism but also pulses with joyful exuberance, restoring to the viewer the sense that the world is still a place where magical and supernatural forces surround us. Indeed, as we have seen, depression and delight, doubt and the wish/hope to believe, are inextricably related in Crumb's sensibility.

Some of Crumb's most effective imagery appears in his illustrations to *The Trial*. Here we perceive strong Christian undertones with the condemned man looking upward to a light in the window. This is underscored further

JUST AT THAT MOMENT A WINDOW FLEW OPEN THERE, AND A HUMAN SILHOUETTE, INDISTINCT TO HIM, SUDDENLY LEANED A LONG WAY OUT AND STRETCHED ITS ARMS OUT STILL FURTHER.

WHO WAS IT?? A FRIEND? SOMEONE WHO CARED? SOMEONE WHO WANTED TO HELP? WAS HELP STILL POSSIBLE? WERE THERE OBJECTIONS THAT HAD NOT BEEN VOICED? SURELY THERE WERE...

WHERE WAS THE JUDGE HE HAD NEVER SEEN? WHERE WAS THE HIGH COURT HE HAD NEVER REACHED? RAISING HIS HANDS, HE SPREAD OUT ALL HIS FINGERS.

David Mairowitz and R. Crumb, *Introducing Kafka*, 1994.

by the wide-eyed abandoned look on his face, and in the final panel his two upturned hands open against a bleak sky recalling Christ's mangled hands. Crumb returns repeatedly in his work to two hands held up imploringly or stigmatized. The three images placed diagonally from left to right down the page of a dark house with a man holding outstretched arms at the illuminated window; the man's stricken face radiating fire; and imploring hands reaching out toward the depressed sky placed one above another with the middle circular image (like a halo) between the upper rectangular and bottom square panels possess a cumulative emotional power when seen together in one gaze. The sky is rendered in Crumb's typical striated fashion, with heavy dark lines interrupted down the frame with white spaces that lend a claustrophobic, film noir quality to his depiction of night. These eerie, nocturnal scenes conjure up feelings of apocalypse, as if some great terrible event is occurring. Michel Serres's description of Hergé's *Tintin* applies to Crumb's Kafka: "Comics open up an original path, different to that of language, rhythm, or sound, and allow living beings and things to shine within their own forms, and in their own very singular medium: the mute poetry of clear lines."[25] The power of Crumb's astounding triptych lies in its "mute poetry": the images speak without words, the accompanying words are unnecessary, and we are moved as in great music by a language beyond language. Kafka's *The Trial* depicts every human being's trial by existence, and Crumb effectively portrays the vulnerability and fragility and terror of our final confrontation with death and dissolution.

Among the most stunning illustrations in the book are those accompanying *A Hunger Artist*. Here Kafka explores Crumb's own central themes of spirituality, art, and suffering in one of his greatest works. Interpretations of Kafka's narrative have ranged from viewing it—rather improbably—as a parable for eating disorders such as anorexia nervosa; as a depiction of Kafka's own ordeal with tuberculosis of the throat, which made it impossible for him to eat; or as a cautionary tale concerning the contemporary artist as martyr in a society that ignores his or her creativity. Here, in a striking image, Crumb depicts the hunger artist as if he were Christ being taken down from the Cross accompanied by a weeping Mary and Mary Magdalene—the Apokathelosis or Deposition of Christ. We see in the posture of the *Hungerkünstler*'s legs and feet as well as two hands and inclination of head and body that Crumb intends for us to relate the hunger artist's suffering to that of Christ. Crumb's iconography recalls many paintings of the crucifixion in the history of art, such as Rogier van der Weyden's *The Descent of the Cross* (c. 1435).

THE PERIOD OF FASTING WAS SET BY HIS IMPRESARIO AT FORTY DAYS MAXIMUM, BECAUSE AFTER THAT TIME THE PUBLIC BEGAN TO LOSE INTEREST. SO, ON THE FORTIETH DAY, WITH AN EXCITED CROWD FILLING THE ARENA AND A MILITARY BAND PLAYING, TWO YOUNG LADIES CAME TO LEAD THE HUNGER-ARTIST OUT OF HIS CAGE. WHEN THIS HAPPENED HE ALWAYS PUT UP SOME RESISTANCE...WHY STOP AFTER ONLY FORTY DAYS?!? WHY SHOULD THEY TAKE FROM HIM THE GLORY OF FASTING EVEN LONGER, OF SURPASSING EVEN HIMSELF TO REACH UNIMAGINABLE HEIGHTS, FOR HE SAW HIS ABILITY TO GO ON FASTING AS *UNLIMITED!*

David Mairowitz and R. Crumb, *Introducing Kafka*, 1994.

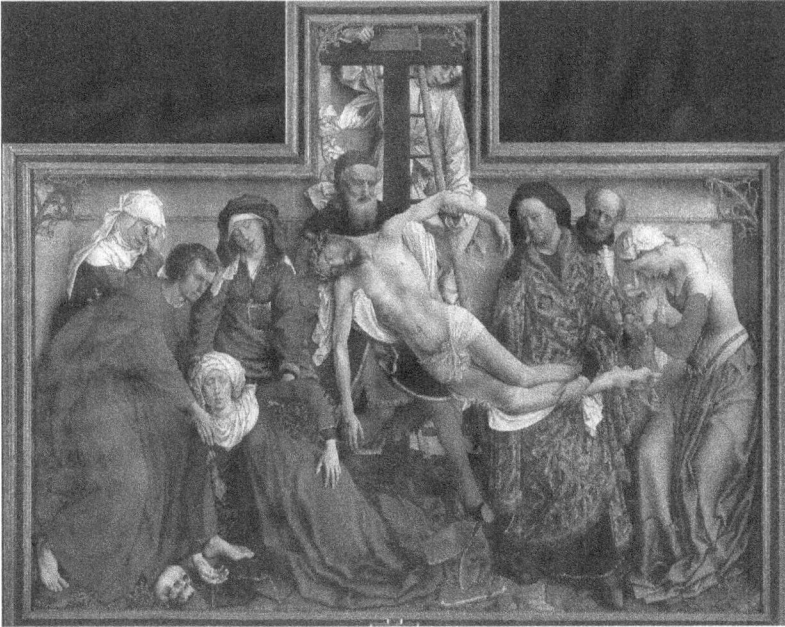

Rogier van der Weyden, *The Descent from the Cross*, ca. 1435.

Furthermore, Kafka's own description—"the period of fasting was set by his impresario at forty days maximum"—obviously echoes biblical language, "forty days and forty nights." Kafka alludes to the crucifixion—"Father, forgive them for they know not what they do"—in a panel in which the *Hungerkünstler* exclaims "Forgive me" to the workers who come by to inspect him in his cage. The workers then say, "Of course we forgive you," intensifying the irony, for of course Christ declares: "Father, forgive them, for they know not what they do" (Luke 23:34). Here the Christ figure apologizes for his own behavior and is "forgiven" by the witnesses of his anguish. We are also told of the "last words" of the Hunger Artist, recalling the final words of Christ: "Eloi, Eloi, Lama Sabachthani" (My God, my God, why have you forsaken me?) (Mark 15:34). These are the famous words we recall that Crumb depicts Philip K. Dick uttering at his own moment of spiritual defeat and transfiguration. The story concludes with the dead body of the Hunger Artist being removed—just as Gregor Samsa's body was taken away—and replaced by a powerful, healthy panther: Samsa's corpse is also symbolically "replaced" by his sister Grete's healthy, young physique. At the beginning of the narrative, Kafka portrays the Hunger Artist's entire body, but as the narrative progresses Crumb is careful not to depict it in the process of decomposing, but rather shows solely the Hunger Artist's head.

At his death, we see only his open eyes and a section of his upper torso, illustrating the thesis of Gotthold Lessing's (1729–1781) famous essay *Laokoön* (1766). Here, Lessing explores the difference between treating a subject through poetry and through art. He discusses Virgil's description of Laocoön in the *Aeneid* (2.195–227) versus the sculptural depiction presently located in the Vatican in Rome. Lessing indicates that the artist should not depict the climactic moment of this dramatic tableau—when Laocoön and his two sons are encircled by gigantic serpents dispatched by the gods—but rather leave it to the imagination of the viewer to complete the scene. James Engell in *The Creative Imagination: Enlightenment to Romanticism* explains that Lessing believed that "the moment the artist selects to depict or to imitate must be when the situation is somewhat developed, but not completely; room must be left for suggestion," and he goes on to quote Lessing:

> Now that only is fruitful which allows free play to the imagination [*was der Einbildungskraft freies Spiel lässt*]. . . . But no moment is so disadvantageous in this respect as the culmination of a course of action. There is nothing beyond, and to present the uttermost to the eye means to bind the wings of fancy and force her . . . to employ herself with feeble images, turning from the given fullness already expressed as her limit.

Engell argues that by "free play of the imagination," Lessing means that the artist "captures a ripe moment when the tension and process between sensuous tumult and final form are most evident. In that moment there is a mediation between the material reality and its ideal shaping spirit; neither dominates, and we see their interplay most clearly."[26] So too, Crumb is able to successfully allow his images to depict yet also go beyond the moment they are intended to illustrate, and he skillfully allows his viewers to fill in intended meanings without having them stated explicitly by either text or image. Crumb had already at the age of fifteen understood this principle, as we see in his comments concerning Harold Gray's *Little Orphan Annie*: "Gray never draws a dead body. . . . He will show a lot of people standing around looking at a corpse, but he never actually shows it. The reader imagines a corpse more terrible than could be drawn. . . . This increases the mood of the story."[27] We remember this technique from Alfred Hitchcock, who at the moments of greatest fear and horror does not actually *show* us the fearful thing but lets us picture in our minds its frightfulness by lingering for example upon the person's hand on the doorknob who is about to open the door to the room that contains the terror, or the shower stabbing scene

David Mairowitz and R. Crumb, *Introducing Kafka*, 1994.

in *Psycho* (1960): we never see the knife strike the woman's body. A similar principle applies in Robert Louis Stevenson's *The Strange Adventures of Dr. Jekyll and Mr. Hyde* in which the details of Jekyll's transformation into the monstrous Hyde are left vague and his terrible appearance left to the reader's imagination to construct.

In the case of Kafka, we can again discern the ways Crumb enters into a reciprocal relationship with the texts he illustrates. He is attracted by a given literary figure because that author delineates themes that reflect his own philosophical orientation. He then often reintroduces these ideas in his own autobiographical work, sometimes in slightly disguised versions: a kind of theme and variations. For example, just as Kafka draws the artist/martyr connection, so too Crumb often depicts himself as an agonized, comical neurotic. In "The Many Faces of R. Crumb" he becomes "Crumb, the long-suffering patient artist-saint," and there are stigmata on the hand that holds his pen: obvious echoes of Kafka's Hunger Artist. In "I Remember the Sixties: R. Crumb Looks Back!," Crumb recalls his LSD trips and "the time I was certain that I was, in fact, Jesus Christ on the Cross, suffering for the sins of all humanity (Catholic upbringing)...Wow, that was powerful acid!!" Crumb is crucified with a crown of thorns and a boxed arrow pointing to himself containing the words "totally crazy."[28] In another drawing, Crumb kneels, head bowed, in a tiny, claustrophobic room—perhaps meant to suggest a padded cell for the criminally or psychotically inclined. There are signs on the walls reading "Get Your Big Fat Ego Out of There & Keep It Out!," and in a parodic, biblical script, "Keep it in the Pants." On the floor are shredded copies of several of the magazines to which he has contributed.

In another drawing, Crumb depicts himself begging forgiveness for his erotic drawings and promising to reform: again we find guilt, repentance, confession—albeit rendered in his inimitable tongue-in-cheek fashion. In a May 28, 2010, sketch, he depicts himself stuck through the chest by a sword to a tree with the thought bubble: "I'm s'posed to be learning something from this."[29] As we have commented previously, Crumb associates his ability to make fun of himself through a method of self-caricature he defines as typical of Jewish comedy:

A lot of Jewish artists and comedians have inherited self-deprecating humor from the Jewish culture. Being able to make fun of yourself is just an ingrained quality that they have. It's real hard for people from Christian, WASP or Catholic backgrounds to do so. For me, it's been a yogic exercise to cop that Jewish thing. Since Christians are taught from birth to strive for perfection, it's very hard to admit that you're

R. Crumb, self-portrait, cover for unpublished *Hup* comics.

not perfect, especially publicly. There's a kind of rigidity in WASP or Catholic people that Jews don't have. The Jews can get under the skin of the goyim by poking fun at their rigidity about self-protection.[30]

In another iteration of this theme with a direct connection to Kafka's Hunger Artist, Crumb depicts a crowd of hip partyers, drinks in hand, smiling and conversing, while a crucified figure nailed to the wall screams in agony. One person in the crowd barely turns to notice, while everyone else at the gathering is totally oblivious to the suffering of the man, whose hands are affixed with huge bolt-like nails, blood dripping down: his body is emaciated and posed in an obvious imitation of the traditions of Christian iconography depicting the Crucifixion. Yet even here, there is black humor in the grotesquerie of the scene—the man is screaming wildly, unlike Christ, who bears his anguish in silence—and in the over-the-top way Crumb juxtaposes the cool, unconcerned sophisticates against the agonized martyr. And just as Crumb's stand-in here is ignored by his audience, so Christ were he to return to earth would be misunderstood and vilified, as Crumb illustrates in many of his drawings. Like Frank Stack in *The New Adventures of Jesus* (1969), Crumb sometimes brings Jesus into present-day America, revealing that he would have been rejected as a hippie communist by the conservative Christians of the times. Were he to have walked among us again, he would be crucified again: and by the very people who claim to revere him. This is also a trope in Beat literature, which we find, for example, in Bob Kaufman, who also mocks the claims of racist and militaristic modern Evangelists to represent the beliefs of Christ.

Another example of Crumb/Kafka symbiosis may be seen in the cover of *Zap*, no. 16 (2014), where Crumb returns to the symbolism of *The Metamorphosis* as well as *A Hunger Artist*. A frail, male musician—in Kafka's *The Metamorphosis*, Grete, Gregor's sister, played the violin for her brother—is here lying prostrate on the ground with his instrument. Crumb often described himself as the proverbial "ninety-eight-pound weakling," a frail ectomorph, and his character is overpowered and crushed by a gargantuan, simian, King Kong–like creature with frightening and massive boots. His added cleats are intended to inflict maximum damage. The violinist's manager/employer/impresario, he is dressed in a three-piece business suit to emphasize his superior social status compared to the impoverished musician, who is collecting coins in his cup. He bellows: "Yeah, play me dat byootiful *Traumerei*, like my mudder yoosta sing ta me! Play it louder! Yer not pullin' in enuff customers! An' play it sweet! That's how dey like it!" Crumb again frames his drawing by alluding to a popular song, "Play Me That Beautiful Traumerei" (1927), which he also recounts hearing during a dream in *R. Crumb's Dream Diary*: "The words of the song tell of a yearning to hear 'that beautiful traumerei,' which reminds the singer of 'things that used to be' when 'mother used to sing me that haunting melody.' ... Arthur Fields sang the chorus in his strident vaudevillian stage style. The band played like an old animated cartoon background.... A silly song." The juxtaposition of the brutal violence of the ape-man manager against a sentimental "silly" song is typical of Crumb's strategy in framing his serious themes. Crumb is also often masterful in his employment of colloquialism, dialect, slang, and voice accents: this unfortunate violinist is confronted by an uneducated, vulgar brute. The musician is "not pullin' in enuff customers," another variation on the theme in *The Hunger Artist* of the man who performs his own hunger and death for a disinterested public. Here he is trampled to death by a figure who symbolizes the craving of the masses for diversion and entertainment: as in Roman times, *panem et circenses*. In Yiddish, a clumsy, inadequate loser

R. Crumb, *Zap*, no. 16 (2014).

is known as a *schlemiel*, while a foolish, negligible person is a *schmendrick*, which is precisely Crumb's way of portraying himself through his stand-in characters.

Joseph Witek points out that Crumb typically appears "thin, stoop-shoul-dered, wear[ing] thick-lensed eyeglasses and old-fashioned suits, with a beak-like nose, unruly cow-licked hair, and a protruding Adam's apple on a long, thin neck." Walter Benjamin in his essay "Franz Kafka: On the Tenth Anniversary of His Death" diagnosed Kafka's understanding that "the most forgotten alien land [*Fremde*] is one's own body."[31] Crumb's alienation from his body precisely mirrors Kafka's. Thus Crumb combines violin-playing Grete, who provided sustenance through music to her rejected brother—whose "own body" had been transformed into the "alien land" of a huge insect—with the image of artist-as-victim and martyr. In his famous *Letter to the Father*, Kafka described the fearful relationship he had with his father and his feeling throughout life that he was constantly a puny, vulnerable creature due to his suffering as a young boy under the thumb of his cruel parent. It is thus possible as well to interpret Kafka's/Crumb's punishment here as a neurotic replaying of the primal violation by the fathers who played such a destructive role in their lives. John Finlay has remarked:

> It is out of this raw material, the primal father whose brutalities have been reinterpreted as justice by his overwhelmed victim-son, that Kafka constructed his mysticism that is gnostic in all its essential fea-tures. In all the gnostic religions, salvation is interpreted as extrication from matter and annihilation of individuality.... Kafka thus executed the orders of his father, and the father's brutalities could be felt as leading to the peace of nothingness.

Given Crumb's own tortured relationship with his violent father, it is clear that Crumb was able to identify in several ways with the sufferings of Kafka as "victim-son."

Crumb is also brilliant here as always at picturing flying fluids: sweat, sperm, the stress signs of physical violence. We note that the shredded body of the violinist recalls the punctured body of the victim portrayed in *In the Penal Colony*, with pieces of bloody, shredded flesh hanging from the terrible instrument of torture, which "recalls the horrors of Gothic and of science fiction." Crumb thus takes upon himself some of the characteristics of the scapegoat/martyr/victim who absorbs the poisons of his society and in exposing them tries to cure both himself and his culture. As Walter Burkert declares in *Creation of the Sacred: Tracks of Biology in Early Religions*:

The *pars pro toto* principle, accepting the small loss in order to save the whole, is even more efficacious in group dynamics. "It is better that one man die than that the whole people should be destroyed," the high priest Kaiphas declares in the Gospel of John; the evangelist is anxious to add that Kaiphas spoke "not on his own but acted as a prophet." This strange balance, salvation of all by the death of one, became one of the fundamental tenets of Christian theology. Yet Kaiphas' prophecy was in fact restating a much older principle, widely understood, accepted, and practiced. It is presupposed already in the Babylonian epic of creation, *Enuma elish*, when sentence is pronounced on a guilty god: "He alone shall perish that mankind shall be fashioned."[32]

As in Kafka, Crumb often elaborates tropes of self-sacrifice in which he at once affirms and mocks his appointed role as the one who "takes on the sins of the world" in order to free his fellow humans from their spiritual shackles.

Thus we can see why Kafka would have been of such interest to Crumb, since he delineates many of the themes of the Beats and American counterculture. In addition, the eerie feeling that we are living in an artificial world recalls *The Matrix*. Indeed, Philip K. Dick's Gnostic vision, Sartre's existentialism, and Kafka all speak to the sense that humanity needs to discover something authentic within and reject the regimentation and falsity of contemporary consumerist society. Kafka's struggle between faith and doubt is of course the same *agon* waged by Crumb throughout his life and work. Erich Heller has remarked: "In Kafka we have the modern mind, seemingly self-sufficient, intelligent, skeptical, ironical, splendidly trained for the great game of pretending that the world it comprehends in sterilized sobriety is the only and ultimate real one—yet a mind living in sin with the soul of Abraham. Thus he knows two things at once, and both with equal assurance: that there is no God, and that there must be God."[33] This doubleness of vision we have seen exemplified in Crumb as well, with his movement between the poles of skepticism and his more recent openness to a Gnostic vision. Crumb's Christian childhood in many ways resurfaced throughout his career as he questioned, reformulated, satirized, and transformed themes of suffering, alienation, sacrifice, and self-realization within the context of his increasingly refined comic art.

Chapter 6

IN THE BEGINNING

The Book of Genesis Illustrated by R. Crumb

Robert Crumb once declared: "I'm a spiritual guy. I'm not an atheist, more an agnostic. I don't doubt the existence of God, I just don't quite know what God is. It's a question that will challenge me until the day I die." At age sixty-six— just a few years short of attaining the biblical three score years and ten—*The Book of Genesis Illustrated by R. Crumb* (2009) appeared, and Crumb now had the opportunity to wrestle with the greatest of all cosmic questions. The artist returned full circle to reexamine from the perspective of maturity his early indoctrination in Christian dogma by illustrating the first of the thirty-six books making up the Old Testament. Yet in choosing Genesis, Crumb was confronting an often-puzzling text. As J. P. Fokkelman has observed: "For at least two reasons Genesis, like other narrative books of the Bible, can be hard to understand. It is very complex, and it exhibits a baffling multiformity."[1] Crumb studied the Torah and had also been fascinated by Mesopotamian mythology—he read widely in the history of the Hittites and Elamites and began studying Sumer seriously in 1994—and carefully examined the As-syrian and Babylonian reliefs in the British Museum. He enjoyed reading the world's first great literary masterwork, *Gilgamesh* (ca. 2100 BCE), which survived on twelve cuneiform tablets composed in Akkadian, noting the ways scholars drew parallels with Genesis. For example, Noah and the building of the ark may be compared with the character Utnapishtim in *Gilgamesh*, who, like Noah, constructs a boat—in the shape of a box—and encounters a cataclysmic flood. One reason for Crumb's immersion in Mesopotamian cultures is that he sought to place Jewish and Christian theology within the larger context of the history of the area in which the events of the Garden of Eden were said to have taken place.

At first, Crumb intended to create a satire on the Adam and Eve narrative but was dissatisfied with this approach: several of these drawings have been published in his *Sketchbooks*. A friend then suggested to him that he illustrate the entire book of Genesis.[2] Approached by the publisher W. W. Norton with a lucrative offer, he now initiated this demanding project, ultimately devoting four years to the task. Crumb retreated to a shepherd's hut in the mountains outside his village in southern France armed with his favorite Rapidograph .035, a brush, crow-quill pen nibs, pencils, Pelikan black drawing ink, bottles of Wite-Out, scholarly texts, and a copy of the Bible. He used Strathmore vellum surface paper, which he asserted "is the best you can get in the Western world for ink line drawing."[3] He selected Robert Alter's translation of the Pentateuch, *The Five Books of Moses: A Translation with Commentary* (2004) as his primary source but also employed the King James Version, since he was fond of the familiar, dramatic, archaic scriptural language such as "Behold!" Crumb states in the introduction that he has "to the best of [his] ability, faithfully reproduced every word of the original text," yet he was fully aware of the inconsistencies in the transmission and redaction of Genesis.[4] Because Crumb illustrated all fifty chapters in an astounding 1,395 separate panels, it will only be possible here to present a broad survey and elaborate upon connections between styles and themes of Crumb's work we have encountered previously. It is evident that Crumb repeats key motifs from his treatments of other literary works and that he has also refined his methods in shaping these themes. Because he illustrates such a variety of dramatic episodes—the primeval history of creation, Adam and Eve, Noah's Ark, Jacob and Esau, Jacob's struggle with the angel, Cain and Abel, the destruction of Sodom and Gomorrah, the epic tale of Joseph and his brothers—he is able to showcase his ability to integrate word and image in a variety of different contexts.

Comic book Bibles have been created for over a century—the first Christian-themed cartoons were published as early as the 1870s—and became commonplace by the beginning of the twentieth century. Max Gaines (1894–1947) published *Picture Stories from the Bible* between 1942 and 1945; and *Outrageous Tales from the Old Testament* appeared in 1987 with illustrations by Alan Moore, Neil Gaiman, and Kim Deitch—the latter contributed the "Story of Job." Basil Wolverton's (1909–1978) art, known for its sometimes wonderfully grotesque imagery, appeared in *Mad* magazine between 1953 and 1979. Wolverton also created hundreds of drawings for the magazines the *Plain Truth* and *Tomorrow's World* published by the Worldwide Church of God—founded by one of the pioneers of fundamentalist radio and television evangelism, Herbert W. Armstrong (1892–1986)—which were later assembled as *The Wolverton Bible* (2009). Like Jack T. Chick, Wolverton emphasized the terrible—nuclear war is strikingly depicted—and apocalyptic aspects of biblical prophecy featured in the book of Revelation. Crumb was thus continuing a long tradition of American artists confronting the Bible, and, after noting that although earlier illustrators have altered and "streamlined" the text that was believed to be "the word of God"—he emphasizes that *Picture Stories from the Bible* contains "pages and pages that have nothing to do with the original text"—Crumb declares that he himself believes that the Bible "is the words of men."[5] As Edmund Leach has noted: "The Bible is not a history book even though many devout believers, both Jewish and Christian, treat it as such. It is a corpus of mythology which provides a justification for the religious performances of believers."[6]

The book begins with a map drawn by Crumb depicting "The World of Abraham circa 2000–1600 B.C.E." and concludes with his "Commentary" and "Comments and Observations on the Chapters." Crumb acknowledged:

> I did not adapt it reverently. I respected the text insofar as I did not want to ridicule it. But I see the text as actually a quite primitive document. It's primitive; it's full of ancient, very old, ritualistic ideas, which are very crude. And there's a lot going on there that is not consciously understood by the people who are telling the stories. And then you have pasted over that this really annoying religious priestly stuff, which is trying to nail the whole thing down so that people can't get out from under it. At a certain point while I was working on it, after about 25 pages, I actually started to despise the text. For a while I went through this phase of hating it. It is really a hateful thing actually. A hateful document that kept people down, kept people in ignorance and darkness, and from advancing intellectually or mentally... . And the same can be said of the New Testament, the Qur'an, all the Western religious stuff. The Eastern thing is different, the Buddhist and Hindu things are very different. They're much more democratic and open, and not as rigid.... You can worship Ganesh, symbolized by an elephant, whatever you want. So it's different, it's very different. But the Western religions are pretty awful, actually. All three of the major Western religions are contentious and antagonistic and aggressive.[7]

However, whether an adapter of the Bible is a believer or not, the resulting work is still an act of *exegesis*. Crumb *interprets* even as he attempts not to interpret and he posits here an opposition between Western and Eastern religions, praising Buddhism and Hinduism for their polytheistic, "democratic" freedom. As Shashi Tharoor has pointed out, in Hinduism there are no dog-mas that are compulsory; more than one "sacred book"; no pope, Vatican, or catechism; many ways to worship; and divine beings to whom to appeal. Furthermore, Hinduism "allows believers to stretch their imaginations to personal notions of the creative Godhead." One might understand, therefore, why Crumb would object to admiring the "primitive," "ritualistic," "crude," "hateful," "contentious," "antagonistic," and "aggressive" Holy Bible.

Yet as we have seen, it was precisely to provocative literary works that Crumb has been attracted, including those of Charles Bukowski and William S. Burroughs; the tortured biographies of blues artists; the works of Philip K. Dick and Jean-Paul Sartre; James Boswell's "pornographic" *London Journal*; Richard von Krafft-Ebing's bizarre sexual case histories reported in *Psychopathia Sexualis*; and the Victorian erotic confessions of *My Secret Life* by "Walter." Crumb has also created a series of portraits of patients at the Surrey County Lunatic Asylum in England, based on photographs taken by the psychiatrist Hugh Diamond (1809–1886). Jeet Heer has ob-served: "Crumb has a common methodology in all his adaptations. He's always drawn to extreme texts, those that offer intense emotional states or unconventional behavior (certainly true of the incest-rich stories in Gen-esis)." Indeed, by virtue of often violent, melodramatic, and tragic narratives, characters, and subject matter, the Bible may also be seen as yet another "extreme" literary work. In this chapter I shall explore how Crumb—while remaining scrupulously faithful to the text—also in several ways questions, undermines, and subverts the conventional understanding of Genesis both in his illustrations and in his commentary. First, he suggests a Gnostic view of God in his way of portraying Yahweh; second, he critiques the "conten-tious and antagonistic and aggressive" aspects of human behavior, as in chapter 34, when the sons of Jacob determine to slay the men of Shechem in revenge for sleeping with their sister Dinah; third, he introduces throughout palpably feminist and ethical themes in his adoption of Savina J. Teubal's thesis in *Sarah the Priestess: The First Matriarch of Genesis* as well as noting the ways Christianity contributed to the institution of slavery in the concep-tion of Ham and his descendants; and finally, he also brings out esoteric elements in his interpretation of Jacob's struggle through the night with a mysterious opponent.

Crumb's "demythologizing" of the Old Testament is thus implied, rather than overt. Although there are places where he winks at the reader—it has been noted that the three peasants depicted on the second page of chapter 6 in the bottom left corner bear a very strong resemblance to Larry, Moe, and Curly of the Three Stooges—Crumb closely follows the biblical text. His relationship to both the Old and New Testaments began in childhood during his religious training in Catholic schools, and he evinces in his work an impressive familiarity with scripture. In order to put into context his relationship to the Bible, one must realize that he had always been in opposition to the prejudice, ignorance, and intolerance that characterize many orthodox, "devout" believers. As we have seen in chapter 3 with his allusion in "Do You Dare Stand Up to the Universe?," Crumb was familiar with the evangelical tracts of Jack T. Chick, which he believed merited mockery. Furthermore, in his satirical portrayal of the ways conservative Americans during the sixties saw Christ himself as a "queer Jew hippie," Crumb depicted the ironic situation of "true believers" who misunderstood and twisted to their own ends the elemental humanitarian, egalitarian, "socialist" message of Jesus: love your enemies, declare your solidarity with the poor and oppressed, and honor the primacy of the spiritual over the material world.

An example of Crumb's righteous indignation over the perversions of fundamentalist Christianity may be seen in his bravura performance in "Jesus People, USA Interviews R. Crumb, Underground Pornographer and All-Around Lost Soul (A Hypothetical Situation) by R. Crumb," which appeared in *Zap*, no. 11. As Jack T. Chick also surely would have done, the members of "Jesus People, USA" in their discussion with one another reveal that they view Crumb and his fellow underground cartoonists Spain Rodriguez, S. Clay Wilson, and Robert Williams—Crumb specifically names these colleagues—as "up to their necks in the corruption of this world": they make an exception for Rick Griffin, who, they concede, "did some beautiful Bible illustrations a few years ago." Griffin, as we recall, renounced his earlier fascination with occult, esoteric, and Kabbalistic knowledge, becoming a "born-again Christian." One of the Jesus People now goes to visit Crumb, desiring to bring him the "hope of salvation." When asked "Who do you think Jesus was, Bob?," Crumb responds: "I dunno . . . A higher being from outer space, maybe . . ." Crumb then impressively quotes several passages consecutively in virtually every panel of the two-page narrative from Mark 9:7, Acts 1:9, Matthew 13:13 and 13:15, Matthew 6:34, Matthew 5:3, Acts 2:14–15, Matthew 5:4, Matthew 21:31, John 8:7, Matthew 23:27, Matthew 22:33 and 22:34, Mark 7:13, and Matthew 23:16. Here again, as with Genesis, the question of whether the Bible is the "word of God" arises. In what amounts to a complete role reversal, Crumb emerges as the person who is thoroughly familiar with the biblical text and is earnestly struggling to extract from his study of the New Testament—Matthew, Mark, Luke, John, and Acts—an authentic meaning divorced from the deadening groupthink of religious orthodoxy, which he can honestly relate to his own personal experience.

Crumb argues testily with his guest over the translation of "Blessed be the humble in Spirit, for theirs is the kingdom of heaven." When his interlocutor attempts to correct him by saying that the text should read "poor in Spirit," Crumb responds: "I take it to mean humble." Crumb attempts to understand the beatitudes from the Sermon on the Mount, to fathom, to interpret the text, even though for him the Bible is "just words on paper, after all . . . WORDS ON PAPER!! . . . An interesting book, though." This interpretation of Jesus is consonant with scores of such portrayals throughout Crumb's work. In many ways, Crumb *identifies* with Christ's sufferings, often depicting himself nailed to the cross like Jesus, and he seeks to rescue the sensitive, "poetic," and sympathetic Jesus from the clutches of those fundamentalists he believes misinterpret his message and example. Crumb's guest is calculated to rouse his ire, for he represents the dogmatic characteristics that the whole-some, "all-American," reactionary "Christian" movement of the 1970s and 1980s represented and that Crumb found most repellent. Crumb becomes increasingly angry as the narrative progresses and finally throws his visitor out of his house, just as he is eager to "throw out" Christianity, Islam, and Judaism, for all three of the major Western religions are "contentious and antagonistic and aggressive."

Thus we can see that Crumb had engaged with the history of Christianity over several decades—from his training in Catholic schools and his intimate familiarity with the New Testament—and was well prepared to "interpret" in his own inimitable way the book of Genesis. His head was already filled with biblical language, symbolism, and imagery, and the art of *The Book of Genesis Illustrated by R. Crumb* has many sources. Immediately on the cover of the book—which depicts God banishing Adam and Eve from the Garden of Eden—Crumb has declared in bold lettering on a scroll: "The first book of the Bible graphically depicted! Nothing left out!" As we have seen previously, Crumb employs the scroll as a nod to earlier comic books, and he is signaling to the reader here that he will—at least in part—be work-ing in a tradition provided by American popular culture. Like many young people of his generation, Crumb received the narratives of our society not only through books but through his passionate devotion to comics and constant exposure to television and movies: *Treasure Island* (1950); *Samson and Delilah* (1950); *Ivanhoe* (1952); *Davy Crockett* (1955); *Sheena: Queen of the Jungle*, a television series that ran during 1955–1956 (Sheena was also a favorite of the literary scholar Edward Said); and *Our Gang*—"The Little Rascals" starring the rambunctious and comical Spanky, Buckwheat, Froggy, Janet, Mickey, and the immortal Pete the dog with the ring around his eye.[8] Crumb acknowledges that he derived some of his images for Genesis from

"Hollywood biblical epics," and he opens chapter 1 with a dramatic rendition of the face of God influenced by Charlton Heston's role in such epics as *The Ten Commandments*.

Crumb emphasizes throughout the patriarchal theme in his illustrations. As Northrop Frye has declared: "God is male because that rationalizes the ethos of a patriarchal male-dominated society. . . . [C]learly one intention in the Eden story is to transfer all spiritual ascendancy of the pre-Biblical earth-goddess to a symbolically male Father-God associated with the heavens." For Crumb, God was portrayed quite literally in the image his own father, Charles, for he acknowledged that "God has a white beard, but he actually ended up looking more like my father. He has a very masculine face."[9] In his interview with the *Paris Review*, Crumb recalled a vison arriving in a dream he experienced in the year 2000 in which God was warning him about a destructive force about to be unleashed on humanity: "When I was trying to figure out how to draw God I remembered that image, which I could look at only for a split second, it was painful to look at this face, it was so severe and yet so anguished."[10] In Crumb's portrait, the lines of God's beard flow into the shape of a swirling black circle as if the creation were an outgrowth of God's own physical being and simultaneously a creation ex nihilo, out of nothing. At the far edges, small dots converge to form more substantial lines of force: from the entire cyclone, energetic rays emanate that are familiar to us from the incandescent moments of Philip K. Dick's spiritual illumination. God appears a kind of magician here, sculpting fire into form through the combined energy of his hands and the power of his vision. God's eyes are stern, his bushy eyebrows raised in creative fervor. His visage bears a striking resemblance to Leonardo da Vinci's self-portrait (1512), and we also note a very similar nose, bushy eyebrows, and flowing mane of white hair and beard in William Blake's awesome *The Ancient of Days* (1794). It is understandable that Genesis would be an attractive theme for Crumb—and for great artists throughout history—for, like God, the artist creates ex nihilo: the image takes form on the page or canvas as the artist adds more and more details, bringing to life his or her creation just as the Creator gradually shapes the cosmos through accretive acts of the imagination.

This portrait, however, by no means came easily, for it grew out of a long process of reflection and experimentation. For Crumb, the depiction of God obviously posed the thorniest problem. People speak about "God" all the time, but what precisely does "God" look like? Is "God" anthropomorphic; is "God" as in pantheism the power and energy that suffuses all of nature, like "the Force" in *Star Wars*? Or can "God" be symbolized by a mathematical idea like $E = mc^2$? As Crumb began work on Genesis, he struggled with this

Chapter 1

WHEN GOD BEGAN TO CREATE HEAVEN AND EARTH, THE EARTH WAS THEN WITHOUT FORM, AND VOID, AND DARKNESS WAS OVER THE DEEP, AND GOD'S BREATH HOVERING OVER THE WATERS.

R. Crumb, *The Book of Genesis Illustrated by R. Crumb*, 2009.

Leonardo da Vinci, self-portrait, 1512.

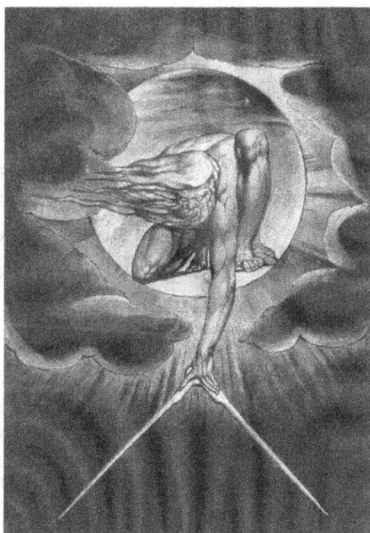

William Blake, *The Ancient of Days*, 1794.

question, revealing: "I had several different approaches to making God. One was a tall thin man with no beard and another was a young looking man with long straight hair that looked more like an angel than like a god. He has pupilless eyes that were beaming light. But I decided to go with the standard, severe patriarchal God. It just felt like the right choice. That just seems to be what the God of Genesis is all about. He's older than the oldest patriarchs." It is noteworthy that in these earlier drafts, which appear in *Sketchbook*, vol. 12, *June 2002–March 2011*, God appears "more like an angel than like a god," and his eyes beam light, suggesting that Crumb was instinctively portraying God as a kind of visitor from another planet—just as he saw Christ as "a higher being from outer space, maybe"—with long robes and hippie long hair down his back typical of the counterculture. Crumb considered not only the possibility of God as a spaceman but also God as a Black woman: again in true Beat fashion, since Gregory Corso composed a poem entitled "God? She's Black."[11] Crumb proclaims "It's time for Bible Studies!," then comments humorously about his own previous effort—"This image of God reveals the white male bias of the artist"—which is followed by the suggestion: "why couldn't God just as easily be depicted as a black woman?" At the top of the page, Crumb sets the playful tone of the entire sketchbook page with an "epigraph" of two verses from "Bib-A-Lolly-Boo" by Chubby Parker (1876–1940), celebrated for his banjo playing and minstrelsy: "Now folks I'll sing you a funny little song / And the whole thing won't detain you long . . ." Because Parker participated in minstrelsy, which involves white performers appearing in blackface, Crumb intended this opening riff as a hint concerning the possibility of a Black divinity. The self-dialogue concludes concerning how best to picture Jehovah: "On the other hand, Adam and Eve were Semitic . . . so their God probably looked Jewish," and thus in yet another series of sketches, we find that Crumb has depicted God as well as Adam and Eve with stereotypically "Jewish" features; God even speaks urban, East Coast colloquial patter to Adam and Eve: "Cut the bickering, you two . . . Stop yelling! Will ya stop?! I'm not finished tawkin' to yiz, awright??" We can see here how Crumb humorously yet seriously entertained a number of different options for his portrayal of God and finally decided to follow the established "Hollywood version" as the best alternative. If most Americans saw God as a severe, patriarchal/father/WASP/chiseled-featured Charlton Heston, then so be it.

Hermann Gunkel observes in *The Legends of Genesis: The Biblical Saga and History* that the myths of Genesis divide into two groups: the world's origins, and historical evolution and the patriarchs of Israel. He argues that

R. Crumb, "Now Folks I'll Sing You a Funny Little Song," *Sketchbook*, vol. 12.

in the latter the divinity appears always enveloped in mystery, un-recognized or speaking out of Heaven, or perhaps only in a dream. In the earlier legends, on the contrary, God walks intimately among men and no one marvels at it: in the legend of Paradise men dwell in God's house; it is assumed that he is in the habit of visiting them every evening; he even closes the ark for Noah, and appears to him in person, attracted by his sacrifice.

Crumb catches this well as he portrays God in the Garden of Eden as he "walks intimately among men." He is also cognizant of the contradictions in the accounts of creation in Genesis 1:1–2:4a and 2:4b–2:25, observing in his "Comments and Observations on the Chapters" that after the first narrative concerning Creation, a different version follows in which first man is created, then animals and woman: scholars believe that Genesis is a combination of "at least three different written sources, maybe more, and that these were 'redacted'—meshed together, abridged, put in a certain order—later by the priests of the Israelite religion, during or just after the 'Babylonian Exile,' circa 600–525 B.C.E."[12] This is yet another example—as we have seen earlier with his scrupulous attention to detail in the texts of Dick, Sartre, and Kafka—of Crumb's desire to examine closely the history, context, and style of the works he selects to illustrate. It also suggests that the Bible itself is not the "Word of God," for the text we now possess has actually been shaped into its present state through a long process of historical evolution and human editing. In-deed, if this "orthodox" tradition may be questioned, the way is obviously open for Crumb to entertain "alternative" versions of the Bible such as the Gnostic Gospel of Thomas. These "unorthodox" versions of the teachings of Christ may lay claim to as much truth as the canonical books of the New Testament.

The fact, however, that God is portrayed primarily as a fierce, brutal ty-rant suggests that Crumb is critiquing both patriarchal masculinity and the violence associated with it. God the Father is not a friendly person for Crumb: we recall that his Marine Corps father broke Crumb's collarbone in one of his frequent rages when the boy was just five years old. Harold Bloom asserts that Crumb's

> disposition toward the story is very refreshing. He is free of stale pi-eties and he properly has no use for the Priestly sentiments preserved in Genesis. The moral insanity of making divine justice an excuse for human suffering is alien to Crumb. Whatever aesthetic unease I feel in regard to his women is more than answered by his healthy wariness

of Yahweh, a sanity I attribute to his graphic exuberance. . . . Yahweh in Genesis, Exodus, and Numbers is Very Bad News. He is human all too human, surpassing Jacob and Joseph, Achilles and Odysseus. As the God he is crafty, daemonic, jealous, curious, brilliant, cruel, irascible, humorous, above all unpredictable.[13]

This God in fact is precisely the Gnostic demiurge who creates a flawed planet and whom the Gnostics rejected. The Gnostics particularly abjured the God of the Old Testament, whom they perceived as arbitrary, violent, unjust, and tyrannical.[14] As Jacques Lacarrière declared in *The Gnostics*:

> The Gospels reveal a God of love and goodness, whose Son has come down to earth for the express purpose of saving men and teaching them fraternity, mercy and love for their neighbors. The Old Testament, on the other hand, shows a God of justice and chastisement who persecutes humanity and always appears surrounded by thunder and lightning. He knows nothing of generosity, clemency, or tolerance. The history of the world and of man, as they appear in the Bible, are made up of crimes, massacres, and blood. They manifest a world which is intrinsically evil and corrupt, a universe that is indisputably a failure, and a mankind that has miscarried. Something is sadly amiss with this creation that Jehovah is constantly forced to punish, and wherein man lives under the permanent threat of taboos, fulminations, and terrorization by the Creator.

God as he is portrayed in the Old Testament becomes proof of the necessity for an alternative explanation of the fallen state of our world, which is supplied by Gnosticism. Indeed, in *Sketchbook*, vol. 12, Crumb depicts God as he begins to create Eve by violently plunging his right hand halfway up the arm into Adam's chest to extract a rib. The drawing is accompanied with sound effects—"SQUISH SQUARCH"—with a speech bubble featuring God exulting in less than formal language: "Creating is a such a hoot! I love it!" Furthermore, Crumb has included a sound bubble with musical notes indicating that the deity is "whistling while he works." On the left side of the panel in a box, Crumb declares: "He's the 'Creator God' of the Gnostic belief system!"[15] Thus it is evident that Crumb interpreted the Old Testament God in terms of the Gnostic demiurge, who is seen as a malevolent rather than benevolent force. Philip K. Dick had reached a similar conclusion. As Jeffrey Kripal has observed:

Dick understood Gnosticism to be an accessible, "already accomplished" truth that was best reflected in a set of early Christian communities and texts that saw the world of matter as corrupt or even evil and that understood the biblical creator-god to be a kind of dumb demiurge or lower creator god.... [T]he true gnostic Godhead, who was entirely beyond this material world, could be reached not through the violent and finally ignorant beliefs and rituals of the orthodox churches, but through a personal *gnosis*, that is, a mystical experience that revealed to one the ultimately illusory nature of the material, social, and religious worlds and the essential divinity of the soul-spark.

Crumb's rejection of a brutal "masculinity" can be seen in his interpretation of other sections of Genesis as well. For example, in his commentary to chapters 39–50 concerning Joseph and his brothers, Crumb argues: "As Jacob was forever pushing up heavy stones, so Joseph is often seen weeping. He is a sensitive man who is moved to tears many times in his life story.... Joseph has learned a much finer humility than the fear-driven kind shown by his barbaric brothers." Crumb indeed remains "faithful to the text" in his illustrations, but in his commentary he reveals his true feelings concerning the unacceptability of the traditional conception of what "being a man" signifies.

As we have seen in chapter 3, Crumb became more attracted to Gnosticism following his illustration of Dick's religious experience, and he desired to find a meaning in human suffering that goes beyond what is offered by the text of Genesis. Whereas the patriarchal God appears bent on the tyrannical and arbitrary infliction of pain, Crumb seeks another way to interpret the spiritual journey. In a 2009 interview, Crumb declared:

Well, the word that comes up all the time in the Gnostic spiritual search is *why*. Why are you putting us through this game and making us suffer? Why are we going through this? Is it just for the excitement of it? Are we just particles of God, some small speck of a greater force of knowledge and understanding in the universe that wanted to hide from itself, that wanted to trick itself and make itself find itself again by creating a barrier that we had to penetrate back through to find our way back? Is that what it's about? ... As a Gnostic, yeah, I would say there's a bigger design. Sometimes you have a split-second glimpse of it. For a second you catch the greater meaning, but then it's lost.[16]

This is one of Crumb's most insightful statements, and we may see implied through his illustrations of Genesis his impatience with such a limited vision of what God is: he prefers to think of human life as a quest toward some primal unity with creation, and he abjures the concepts of sin, punishment, and judgment, which are so central to the dogmas of orthodox Christianity. We recall the imagery of the "impenetrable forest" in "Bad Karma" and Crumb's various restatements throughout his career of the initiatory hero's quest, which entails the struggle through "a barrier that we had to penetrate back through to find our way back." It is also noteworthy that these revelatory perceptions are precisely *momentary*: it is as if at certain privileged instants of heightened receptivity, one is offered a brief but profound intuition into the nature of our true and deepest selves. The curtain of Maya—of illusion—lifts for a split second, and we see into the heart of reality. It is tantalizing and often frustrating that our moments of insight into the inscrutable nature of being occur so seldom and so briefly, but this also provides us with motivation to continue the quest.

If Crumb abjured the patriarchal god in favor of an implied Gnostic philosophy, another pervasive theme in Crumb's "subversion" of the narrative of Genesis occurs in his depiction of violence and destruction. Crumb was strongly influenced by Assyrian art in his illustrations; in *The R. Crumb Handbook* there is a photograph depicting the artist standing in front of Assyrian sculptures in London, and he informs us:

> Recently, I had a chance to look at the Assyrian and Babylonian reliefs in the British Museum. There are large, powerful figures with predatory bird heads, creatures that are truly brutal and scary looking. Here is a warrior holding a sword over a group of prisoners. Here there are defeated warriors being run over by a chariot. In another room there's a relief of a giant mill wheel grinding up the dead enemies of the king after a battle.
>
> It's incredible. They're bragging about all the people they've captured and killed. The king wants everyone to remember how many peoples he conquered and enslaved! It's all a homage to the king's glory. I was very inspired by the lurid, harsh, visual narratives depicted in these early Mesopotamian reliefs. I like them much better than the more refined, stylized Egyptian stuff from the same period. It's more rough and ready, a bit more individualistic, perhaps, than the Egyptian art.[17]

Crumb obviously did his homework in his depiction of Nimrod in the act of hunting in chapter 10, which he bases on one of the tremendously kinetic and powerful Assyrian reliefs.

Chapter 10

AND THESE ARE THE GENERATIONS OF THE SONS OF NOAH, SHEM, HAM, AND JAPHETH. SONS WERE BORN TO THEM AFTER THE FLOOD. THE SONS OF JAPHETH: GOMER AND MAGOG AND MADAI AND JAVAN AND TUBAL AND MESHECH AND TIRAS. AND THE SONS OF GOMER: ASHKENAZ AND RIPHATH AND TOGARMAH. AND THE SONS OF JAVAN: ELISHAH AND TARSHISH, THE KITTITES AND THE DODANITES.

FROM THESE THE SEA PEOPLES BRANCHED OUT.

THESE ARE THE SONS OF JAPHETH, IN THEIR LANDS, EACH WITH HIS OWN TONGUE, ACCORDING TO THEIR CLANS IN THEIR NATIONS.

AND THE SONS OF HAM: CUSH AND MIZRAIM AND PUT AND CANAAN. AND THE SONS OF CUSH: SEBA AND HAVILAH AND RAAMAH AND SABTECA. AND THE SONS OF RAAMAH: SHEBA AND DEDAN. AND CUSH BEGOT NIMROD. HE WAS THE FIRST MIGHTY MAN ON EARTH. HE WAS A MIGHTY HUNTER BEFORE THE LORD. THEREFORE IT IS SAID, "LIKE NIMROD, A MIGHTY HUNTER BEFORE THE LORD."

THE BEGINNING OF HIS KINGDOM WAS BABYLON AND ERECH AND ACCAD, ALL OF THEM IN THE LAND OF SHINAR.

FROM THAT LAND ASSHUR CAME FORTH, AND HE BUILT NINEVEH AND REHOBOTH-IR AND CALAH, AND RESEN, BETWEEN NINEVEH AND CALAH, WHICH IS THE GREAT CITY.

AND MIZRAIM BEGOT THE LUDITES AND THE ANAMITES AND THE LEHABITES, AND THE NAPHTUHITES, AND THE PATHRUSITES, AND THE CASLUHITES, AND THE CAPHTORITES, FROM WHOM THE PHILISTINES CAME FORTH.

AND CANAAN BEGOT SIDON, HIS FIRSTBORN, AND HETH AND THE JEBUSITE AND THE AMORITE AND THE GIRGASHITE AND THE HIVITE AND THE ARCHITE AND THE SINITE AND THE ARVADITE AND THE ZEMARITE AND THE HAMATITE. AFTERWARD THE CLANS OF THE CANAANITE SPREAD OUT.

R. Crumb, *The Book of Genesis Illustrated by R. Crumb*, 2009.

Lion Hunt of King Ashurbanipal, Assyrian relief, ca. 645-635 BC.

Another powerful example occurs in the battle scene from chapter 14. Crumb has taken the bow and arrows, helmets, and shields as well as the inclination of the spears from the Assyrian relief and reproduced its terrific energy. He adapts from the relief from Nineveh during the reign of Sennacherib (700–692 BCE) the brutal depiction of an Assyrian soldier beheading a prisoner from the city of Lachish: indeed, it is the identical scene of the soldier grabbing the victim by the hair. In emphasizing the savagery of war, Crumb conveys the pacifism of the counterculture and highlights the destructive behavior that Genesis appears to condone.[18] As we have seen earlier, "lurid" is a favorite Crumb word, which he often employs to describe a quality he admires in comics and attempts to reproduce in his own work. He observed that Genesis "contains this morality that's so lurid, and it's set in an ancient world that's so grindingly primitive and brutal. It lends itself so well to lurid comic-book types of illustrations. It just invited it." In adapting Assyrian models, Crumb emphasizes this *lurid brutality*: the giant chariot wheels roaring over dead bodies, spears poised to pierce naked bodies, helpless wounded victims reaching their arms up in anguish, dead men lying face down arms at their sides on the ground, spears flying through the air, strung bows pulled back to the greatest degree of tensile strength, a typically bleak, striated Crumbian sky sadly overlooking the carnage.

Another gripping sequence of illustrations occurs in relation to Jacob's struggle in chapter 32 with a mysterious assailant. This episode is brief, yet as J. P. Fokkelman has observed, "the sinister nocturnal story of Jacob's fight and rebirth in 32:22–32 . . . needs only 143 words in 34 cola to develop a formidable intensity."[19] Crumb captured this dramatic wallop by studying a text recommended to him by Justin Green, Eadweard Muybridge's (1830–1904) *Animal Locomotion* (1907)—which features many photographs of naked humans as they move through space as well as of men wrestling—as a source for the scene depicting Jacob as he contends through the long night with his combatant.[20] Indeed, the four panels are effective in conveying the wild energy of the *agon*. Crumb observes the conventions of comic books—stars exploding as Jacob's "hip socket was wrenched" to indicate physical pain. We also note that as the night turns to dawn, larger areas of lit sky appear at the tops of the mountains as Jacob cries: "Let me go, for dawn is breaking!" Jacob is reborn as "Israel," for he has "struggled with divine beings and won out." However, some commentators have faulted Crumb for the way he portrays Jacob's combatant. Peter Sattler remarked:

> The text focuses on what we don't know. The man is unnamed; the man is unseen. And in Alter's translation (but not Crumb's text), Jacob's combatant never claims to be divine: "[Y]ou have striven with God and men, and won out" (32:29). Is this figure "God" or just one of those defeated "men"? Is it an angel? Is it Esau? The script remains silently suggestive.
>
> But Crumb's comic speaks up, (ex)changing the text, making the assailant clearly visible in even the dimmest light, and finally endowing the figure with a placid face and saintly halo. (As the book's endnotes indicate, Crumb is clearly invested in the divinity of this character, but not for reasons of textual fidelity.) Yes, the comic does present this figure as "a man," but by veering away from the letter—and, hence, the ambiguity—of the text, Crumb transforms him into far too particular of a man.[21]

However, Crumb intentionally brought out this interpretation of the text because of his interest in the hidden spiritual meaning of the contest. An example of his close scrutiny of the text is a thoughtful passage in his commentary appended to the close of the volume:

> When Jacob asks the divine being for his name, the reply is "Why should you ask my name?" This is a curious exchange about names. Somewhere I read of one scholar's interpretation, which made sense. The spirit being, who tells Jacob, "You have struggled with divine beings and won out," is giving Jacob *his* name. I have come across references to similar occult experiences such as this in a few different cultures, including the American Indians. The spiritual seeker, in a place of lonely solitude, usually at night, encounters a being, often a dark being who menaces him, and forces him to engage in what seems to be a life-or-death wrestling match, which goes on for the whole night.

R. Crumb, *The Book of Genesis Illustrated by R. Crumb*, 2009.

The seeker often emerges from this struggle injured or traumatized, but a spiritual "ally" has been acquired. The seeker is never the same afterward, but has acquired a "power" of some kind. There's a legend of the old-time blues singer who goes to a deserted "crossroads" at midnight, where he waits until a "big black man" comes and from this "devil" or spirit being he learns to play the guitar. The idea probably hearkens back to some old African spiritual practice or magic ritual, similar to Jacob's struggle with the "divine being."

Here again, Crumb seeks to understand an intense moment in Genesis and sets his interpretation within the context of the Native American and African American traditions we examined in chapter 2. It is noteworthy that he emphasizes solitude, night, and an encounter with a supernatural being, which calls to mind both Saint John of the Cross and *la noche oscura del alma*—the "dark night of the soul"—as well as the shamanistic moment of transformation in Native American culture and figures like bluesman Robert Johnson meeting the devil at the crossroads. Indeed, the fight toward an authentic self requires the death of the old "ego": what the American poet Theodore Roethke called "[d]eath of the self in a long, tearless night."[22] Crumb has described his experience with LSD as leading to a "shattering" of his ego: so too the "old self" must die in order for one to encounter the real Self within.

Another restatement of this theme from Genesis of the "two selves" occurs in Crumb's three-page illustration to William Langland's (ca. 1332–1386) alliterative allegory *Piers Plowman* included in the *Sketchbooks*. Crumb has chosen the passage from book 8—"Thought"—which begins: "So I wandered far and wide, and walked alone over a wild common." The narrator, falling asleep under a tree, continues on the second page:

> Then I dreamt the most marvelous dream, I think, that man has ever dreamt. It seemed to me that a tall man, very like myself, came and called me by my own name. "Who are you?" I said. "And how do you know my name?" "You know me very well," he said, "no man better." "Are you sure I know you?" "I am Thought," he said. "I have followed you for many years. Have you not seen me before?"

Thus again we have the question of knowing one's name and meeting a spiritual double who has a message to bring.[23] Here we have a person on a journey—"So I wandered far and wide, and walked alone over a wild common"—typical of the initiatory psychological/spiritual narratives that are particularly fascinating to Crumb in their several variations throughout world literature and myth. It encapsulates in many ways his own struggle to fathom the mysteries of selfhood and to arrive at a place where the "ego" is no longer the compulsive taskmaster of human behavior, but rather the servant of the impulses of the true inner life. It is also significant that this revelation comes to him in a dream—"Then I dreamt the most marvelous dream, I think, that man has ever dreamt"—during the night as with Jacob, and, as we have seen, dreams are a central source for Crumb's own creative imagination.

A final way Crumb interrogates the traditional interpretation of Genesis and recapitulates an obsessive theme that recurs throughout his work is the portrayal of women. As Claudia Setzer has remarked, feminists agree on two main issues concerning the Bible: "First, the Bible in its canonical form is a patriarchal document that promotes and/or has been used to promote a system that subordinates women. Second, it is an androcentric document that puts the male at the center, in particular in the envisioning of a male God as the ultimate authority."[24] One notes in Crumb's *Sketchbooks* the ways he considered making the women of the Bible—beginning with Eve—more sympathetic as characters. For example, he based one of his several early versions of Eve on Matthaus Merian's *Iconum Biblicarum* (1627). Crumb borrows from Merian's Eve's winsome posture, beauty, gentleness, and innocence. However, instead of the snake curling about the tree trunk as in Merian, Crumb turns him into an upright, human-like figure: the snake's hands are splayed out in a gesture that seems to say—"Why don't you try the apple! You've got nothing to lose!"—while his feet are crossed casually in

"Then I dreamt the most marvelous dream, I think, that man has ever dreamt.

It seemed to me that a tall man, very like myself, came and called me by my own name. 'Who are you?' I said. 'And how do you know my name?'

'You know me very well,' he said, 'no man better.'

'Are you sure I know you?'

'I am Thought,' he said. 'I have followed you for many years. Have you not seen me before?'

'Oh, so you are Thought?' I said. 'Then perhaps you can tell me how to find Do-well.'

R. Crumb, "Piers Plowman," *Sketchbook*, vol. 11.

the stance of a con man in the act of transacting a clever deal. The snake is clearly shown to be a nasty, scheming, conniving, shrewd antagonist. There is nothing "sinful" about Eve in Crumb's portrait: on the contrary, she exudes health, good spirits, and kindness. Indeed, Christianity has foisted upon us an entirely fictitious and destructive narrative concerning the nature of Woman. The British poet and mythographer Robert Graves argued that "Eve's

R. Crumb, "Adam & Eve 'Our First Parents' So the Good Book Says," *Sketchbook*, vol. 12.

Matthaus Merian, *Iconum Biblicarum*, 1627.

creation by God from Adam's rib—a myth establishing male supremacy and disguising Eve's divinity—lacks parallels in Mediterranean or early Middle-Eastern myth."

In his commentary to chapter 3, Crumb reflects on Eve in relation to Inanna in Sumerian myth: "Concerning Eve and the tree of knowledge, it is interesting that among the myths of Sumer there is the story of the goddess Inanna, who nurtures a tree in her 'pure garden.'" Crumb was intrigued enough by Inanna to create a striking portrait of her in 2009, the year he published Genesis. Inanna—or Ishtar—occupies the highest position in Akkadian religious life and is the goddess of love and war. According to Enrico Ascalone, during the second millennium BCE, she also "took on the attributes of the goddess of war, with a bellicose attitude, a greedy character, a virile semblance." Here Crumb portrays her as she appears in the epic of *Gilgamesh*: "It was terrifying, it was terrifying, / The scream of Inanna was terrifying. / The maiden Inanna's scream drew nigh / heaven, the scream drew nigh earth, / Heaven and earth it covered like a blanket, / draped like a cloth. / Who was there could speak to holy / Inanna?"[25] Crumb obviously intends Inanna to resemble Edvard Munch's most famous painting *The Scream*, with the repetition of the word "scream" occurring three times in the verses from *Gilgamesh*. Crumb would also imitate Munch's painting in one of his illustrations for Bukowski's *Bring Me Your Love*.

Crumb also attempts to at least partially undo this "androcentric" tradition of viewing women in a subordinate role, noting in chapter 11 that "some say Sarah, Abraham's wife, was a priestess belonging to the Sumerian matriarchal tradition." In his comments to chapter 12, he observes:

> What is the point of this story? These puzzles and mysteries were cleared up for me by a book called *Sarah the Priestess* by Savina Teubal (1984). She exposes the underlying, buried, hidden, distorted sense of these stories about women—Sarah, Rebekah (Isaac's wife), Rachel and Leah (Jacob's wives)—in a powerfully cogent manner. Suddenly layers of cobwebs are removed, centuries of dust, and some of the earlier lost sense of them is revealed. . . . The historical record shows that in the earlier millennia of this development in Mesopotamia and Egypt, there existed a powerful matriarchal order alongside the patriarchy.

Crumb read Teubal's book with great excitement, then reread it three times. Crumb relates Teubal's argument that Sarah was actually a priestess who engaged in a *hieros gamos* or sacred marriage with the pharaoh. He asserts that "early civilizations were also driven by a strong belief in magic, spiritual powers, dreams, visions, oracles, spells, and curses. Women with powers of this kind were elevated to special, high places. There were temples and rituals and rites that only women were allowed to perform." In chapter 19, Crumb graphically depicts the daughters of Lot plying their father with wine to render him inebriated in order to sleep with him and conceive a child: Lot's wife had been turned into a pillar of salt during the family's flight from Sodom. The older daughter laments to the younger: "Our father is old, and there is no man on earth to come to bed with us like the way of all the world!" In openly showing the sexual reality of the act, Crumb gives the women agency and power. As Melissa Jackson has pointed out, envisioning the biblical text in this manner suggests that "patriarchy was not the status quo, men were seen as fools for being as if they were in total control, and women were valued for motherhood and also for their intelligence, courage, inventiveness, creativity." From their sexual union with their father, the older daughter conceives a son, Moab; the younger a son, Ben-Ami. In his commentary, Crumb argues that the daughters' behavior "is not so shocking in the context of matrilineal descent, in which the father is less significant than the mother." As if to underscore their triumphant power, in the final panel of chapter 19 Crumb depicts the two mothers teaching their young sons the art of archery. They stand strong—with Crumb's signature muscled, impressive legs—with bow and arrows reminiscent of the Assyrian friezes.[26]

Indeed, in response to the frequent charge that he is misogynistic, Crumb has declared: "I'm not antifeminist. I like strong, independent women, like the matriarchs of Genesis—they ordered the men around."[27] Vanessa Davis in her graphic narrative *Make Me a Woman* (2010) offers her interpretation of Crumb's work in the section entitled "Talkin' 'bout My Generation": "And the matriarchs were my favorite. They appear to have been Crumb's too."

There are several other ways that Crumb brings out his "subversive" interpretation, such as in one of the textual cruxes of Genesis. Robert Alter believes that the "and Bethuel" line is "a later scribal or redactorial insertion," and Crumb asserts: "This is one of the few cases in which I took a liberty with the text. I left out 'and Bethuel' altogether. It was just those later scribes trying to shore up the patriarchy!" Indeed, while Crumb does not "editorialize" in his illustrations, his commentary serves to expose the negative repercussions of the biblical text. Another example occurs in chapter 9, where he notes: "Noah curses Ham and Ham's son Canaan—'the lowliest of slaves he shall be to his brothers.' Thus were black Africans later degraded as the descendants of Ham by white Christians, this biblical passage serving as a righteous rationale for their enslavement."[28] Thus Crumb critiques not only the portrayal of women in Genesis but also the ways the Bible has been used to support racist ideology and the oppression of "minorities." On June 14, 2018, the attorney general of the United States, Jeff Sessions, invoked Romans 13: "Let everyone be subject to the governing authorities, for there is no authority except that which God has established. The authorities that exist have been established by God. Consequently, whoever rebels against the authority is rebelling against what God has instituted, and those who do so will bring judgment on themselves." In his defense of separating children of immigrants from their families at the US/Mexico border, Sessions argued that Americans must follow "the clear and wise command" of the Apostle Paul to "obey the laws of the government because God has ordained them for the purpose of order."[29] Thus we can see the relevance of Crumb's critique of the destructive notions of "white Christians," which have been summoned in defense of inhuman political and social policies such as slavery. Crumb responded to the biblical text in a myriad of "objective" ways, but also the ways his personal struggles with belief and doubt played out in his interpretation and the ways he shaped his illustrations. Crumb devoted four years to the project; hence it is fair to say that he believed it to be of great importance in his artistic career.

Crumb has communicated several of the major themes of the counterculture through *The Book of Genesis Illustrated by R. Crumb*: an interior spirituality that may take the form of inner knowledge or *gnosis*; a rejection of the traditional models of male aggression and patriarchy; the celebration of female power; and an antiwar and pacifist stance. Crumb from the beginning of his career was drawn to literature in all its forms: novels, poetry, short stories, plays, biography, history, and the philosophical and spiritual texts of the world. In returning to the opening book of the central text of the Judeo-Christian tradition, Crumb was revisiting his earliest experiences as a child with religion and his training in Catholicism. From adolescence, Crumb exhibited a markedly "mystic" temperament—which he shared with his brothers Charles and Maxon—and sought to move beyond the orthodoxies of institutional religions toward an interior, direct, and authentic encounter with the self and *gnosis*. He indeed was attentive to the original text in his illustrations, yet he was simultaneously—for those who can read between the lines—arguing for an alternative and more tolerant view of human possibility than that advocated in traditional interpretations of Genesis. For Crumb, the goal has always been freedom: freedom to express all the contradictions and complexities of being human.

EPILOGUE

In *R. Crumb: Literature, Autobiography, and the Quest for Self*, I have sought to demonstrate that Crumb from the beginning of his career has been devoted to a continual examination of the intersection between art, literature, and the search for authentic selfhood. Over the years since completing *The Book of Genesis Illustrated by R. Crumb* in 2009, he has continued to create prolifically. His art has also obviously reflected his residence in the south of France, since he has produced many drawings depicting the restaurants, cafés, village streets, and countryside of his adopted French town. A charming work entitled "A Day in the Life" (1995) begins with the Crumb family fleeing from their village, where a battle is taking place, into the woods, where they enter a house as a refuge: the place is said to be haunted. When his daughter Sophie asks her father if he believes in ghosts, he responds: "I'm not sure . . . I tend to believe in everything." We then discover that Crumb has been in his bed and now realize that the story thus far has been only a dream. As he awakens, he says to himself about his dream encounter with the paranormal: "Weird dream . . . Disturbing image of the ectoplasmic ghost." The narrative follows Crumb's thoughts as exciting erotic memories arrive while still abed; he then arises to attend to his household chores. There are several passages in which the Crumb family speak in French—in one amusing episode, Sophie attempts to correct her father's faulty French grammar—and we accompany him as he makes his way to the local post office: en route, he speaks to his neighbors in French. "A Day in the Life" displays Crumb at the peak of his powers, creating a touching portrait of his family life in his new country and even introducing in a casual, offhand way his tendency "to believe in everything" when he reveals his technical knowledge concerning "ectoplasmic ghosts": in spiritualism, this refers to an energy or substance "exteriorized" by physical mediums, a term coined by psychical researcher Charles Richet in 1894.

Crumb has clearly begun to incorporate French life and culture into his work in a seamless fashion, and he has continued to read widely: H. G. Wells's

Outline of History is a favorite, and he enjoys books of adventure such as *Kabloona* by the French author Gontran de Poncins (1900–1962), which as we have noted previously recounts the confrontation of a "civilized" European with Eskimo people. The overarching shape of his career has come into sharper focus with the gradual publication of the complete *Sketchbooks*, the appearance of *Art and Beauty Magazine*, nos. 1, 2, and 3 (2016), as well as *R. Crumb's Dream Diary* (2018). The *Sketchbooks* contain much of Crumb's best work and are essential to understanding the ways his autobiographical quest is centered in a serious search for deeper meaning through his reading of literature. It has been unusually easy for Crumb to immediately transcribe his reflections, for throughout his life, he has constantly had near to hand a variety of journals ranging in length from approximately forty-eight to one hundred pages, which he has filled with the brimming outpourings of his fertile creative imagination.[1] He has acknowledged that when he sees "a nice book with blank pages, I feel a strong compulsion to fill it with drawings and text. I want to transform those blank pages into a book filled with rich visual or literary information. I wish there were twenty of me with nothing but time to fill hundreds of blank books!"[2] We note in this revelatory statement—a perfect description of the contents of the *Sketchbooks*—Crumb's emphasis on "rich visual or literary information," suggesting the equal significance he assigns to images and authors and to the relationship between them. Zweitausendeins in Frankfurt, Germany, commenced publishing the *Sketchbooks* in 1978. Later in 1992, Fantagraphics in Seattle took up the series, and finally in 2012, Taschen, headquartered in Cologne, brought out six hardcover books limited to one thousand numbered sets, and two years later brought out *The R. Crumb Sketchbooks*, vols. 1–6, *1964–1982*. In December 2016, Taschen began to make available less expensive versions of these *Sketchbooks*, and more are planned for the future. As the tumultuous sixties of half a century ago gradually recede from the collective memory, it has become easier to separate the more provocative, "scandalous," and supposedly "obscene" aspects of Crumb's work from the overall shape and meaning of his oeuvre. Just as authors such as Henry Miller have been wrongly categorized as focusing solely on erotic experience—neglecting the fact that the author of *Tropic of Cancer* and *Sexus* spent virtually his whole life reading and studying world spiritual traditions from Lao-Tzu's *Tao Te Ching* to the writings of Ramakrishna and Vivekananda—so too, with the passage of time and the gradual publication of Crumb's complete oeuvre, we are able to see that Crumb was also a seeker and not only an enfant terrible.

Some of the *Sketchbook* pages deal directly with his spiritual battles and bear the mark of personal "confessions" in which he reveals to the reader/

viewer the struggles of his inner life. As we have seen, Crumb is constantly posing questions, supplying tentative answers, and then continuing the process ad infinitum. In a *Sketchbook* entry, he quotes Gertrude Stein's last words: "What is the answer? . . . What was the question?" which serves as a succinct summary of Crumb's continual dialectical process. Some of the entries contain only text, but as always with Crumb, the writing itself is nearly always intriguing, artistically achieved, and aesthetically pleasing. He is able to employ a variety of styles to convey a whole palette of increasing or lessening degrees of emphasis. For example, an entire page of an entry dated "August 24th '96" begins: "It's very hard to . . . FACE THE TRUTH." The style of these last three words is achieved through Crumb's signature shaky line, which emphasizes the existential terror of directly confronting the rigorous struggle toward authenticity. Crumb places a small box at the right bottom of this declaration containing a direct address to the reader/ viewer: "Don't play dumb, you know what I mean!!" This recapitulates a common strategy throughout Crumb's work that aims at breaking down the artificial barrier—or sometimes emphasizing its existence—between artist and viewer, to drop the pose that this is merely "art" or "entertainment" lacking any deeper purpose. Crumb goes on to acknowledge that this direct encounter with "Truth" is indeed "the most difficult thing to do in this life. . . . If you don't know yourself how can you assume to know anything about life, or the world, or other people?" This leads to the central declaration: "The greatest of all mysteries is the SELF"—the word "Self" is emphasized by slanting the letters to the right to suggest italicization—directly echoing C. G. Jung. This is followed in typical Crumb fashion by juxtaposing the cosmic and the comic—he adds "we're all shlubs," quoting his friend Pete Poplaski (*shlub* is Yiddish for a "talentless, unattractive or boorish person"). Crumb admits his inability to resolve the contradiction: at least one reason is, "the spirit is willing but the flesh is weak," alluding to Matthew 26:40–41 and a dramatic moment in the life of Christ: "And he cometh unto the disciples, and findeth them asleep, and saith unto Peter, What, could you not watch with me one hour? Watch and pray, that ye enter not into temptation: the spirit indeed is willing, but the flesh is weak." Here Jesus is in the Garden of Gethsemane, immediately before being arrested. Crumb then admits: "I know what I have to do but I can't get started."

Crumb then adds the puzzling "Shrring": perhaps a meaningless word, or possibly the sound of a bell tolling the necessity to get moving on the path toward selfhood, because the time is late. He wonders who to turn to in his extremity and appears to adopt a Zen Buddhist pose: "Stay still . . . Don't move . . . Take a deep breath"—all aspects of meditative practice—and ends again with "Shrring." In an interview concerning his artistic process, Crumb remarked that

> your conscious mind can never know the truth. It can only know homilies or ideas. What is truth? It's a kind of revelation, it's not a concrete fact like one plus one equals two. That's not truth, that's arithmetic. If you look at a work of art, and there's an identifying spark, that's a revelation. You can't say, "Here's what it's all about; here's what the truth is." Maybe you can't define it. It's just something you experience. ... A person almost has to be crazy to tell the truth. ... The tension and breakthrough is a part of why people can identify with it and why it's appealing, because we all have this struggle of trying to find out who we are and what's really going on.[3]

Is this a "drawing" or a "text"? "Art" or "words"/literature? The whole page is text—and dated "Aug. 24th '96," thus giving the impression of being an actual journal entry—yet due to the creative employment of lettering styles, the use of quotation, and the strategic placement of words on the page, Crumb is straining at the division between "art" and the "written word": he confronts the reader/viewer directly with a revelation concerning his own inner life and employs a mode of communication directly on the boundary *between* illustration and text.

Since his move to France, Crumb has meditated regularly. He first attempted daily mediation early in 1981 but following the birth of his daughter Sophie he found it challenging to continue. He began seriously in June 1996—usually for thirty-five minutes as often as possible—in what is known as the Egyptian pharaoh position: straight in a chair, eyes closed, with hands on knees. Crumb has declared:

> I've had some power meditations from time to time—very powerful. And at times you have revelations that are quite surprising. The inner-self is as profound as the outer-world. The inner universe is as deep and infinite as the outer universe. And humans are different from other animals because we can do that, we can actually go within ourselves in a very conscious, deliberate way. And I think it's very helpful and productive for an individual to practice that. Then again, who really knows what porpoises and whales are capable of?

Crumb asserts that "you don't have to teach yourself; you just sit. Sit down in a chair, close your eyes, breathe, try and relax, you know. Relax and

IT'S VERY HARD TO...

FACE THE TRUTH

DON'T PLAY DUMB, YOU KNOW WHAT I MEAN!!

IN FACT IT MAY BE THE MOST DIFFICULT THING TO DO IN THIS LIFE... IF YOU DON'T KNOW YOURSELF HOW CAN YOU ASSUME TO KNOW *ANYTHING* ABOUT LIFE, OR THE WORLD, OR OTHER PEOPLE...?

THE GREATEST of ALL MYSTERIES IS THE *SELF*...

"WE'RE ALL SHLUBS" (PETE POPLASKI) ~ THE SPIRIT IS WILLING BUT THE FLESH IS WEAK — I KNOW WHAT I HAVE TO DO BUT I CAN'T GET STARTED.

"SHRRING"

WE'RE ALL FUCKED UP. THERE IS NO ULTIMATE STATE OF PERFECTION. FORGET ABOUT IT. RELAX. ABDICATE. YOU ARE AS OF NOW RELIEVED OF YOUR POST. IT'S NO LONGER YOUR PROBLEM.

OH IT'S ALL SO CONFUSING, WHO CAN I TURN TO??

Stay Still... Don't Move... Take a deep breath...

"SHRRING"

R. Crumb, "It's Very Hard to Face the Truth," *Sketchbook*, vol. 10.

breathe—and go from there." As we have seen, Crumb portrayed Mr. Natural in meditative poses, as well as Shuman the Human. As early as January 31, 1976, Crumb began to consider meditation as a practice: "The mind is hooked on stimulation! The mind cannot tolerate even one second of blankness, of being unpre-occupied, except when it's asleep.... The purpose of meditation is to stop the mind at a certain time, and for a certain amount of time, from its usual compulsive habits, to put the mind in a neutral state.... Maybe I should also just meditate."[4] Following his relocation to Europe, Crumb has been able to reconnect with this earlier yearning to integrate more fully a life of artistic and spiritual exploration.

Crumb has also become increasingly immersed in a variety of esoteric sources. In addition to his exploration of Gnostic themes and his fascination with Eastern thought, he has speculated concerning UFOs, aliens, the existence of Bigfoot, and the possibility of out-of-body experiences. Crumb has demonstrated a fondness for the magazine *Fate: True Reports of the Strange and Unknown*, founded by Raymond A. Palmer—who was editor of *Amazing Stories* magazine—and Curtis Fuller in 1948 and publishing articles on the paranormal. The purpose of *Fate* has been "to report honestly the strangest facts of this strange world and the ones that don't fit into the general beliefs of the way things are." Crumb contributed three cover illustrations for *Fate*. The November 2000 issue features a gigantic female Bigfoot striding down a city street; September 2002 depicts a couple in bed at night being visited by a creature from outer space; and January 2003 portrays a Bigfoot couple retreating into a snowy forest. And in his *Sketchbooks*, Crumb created a portrait of one Nicholas Olivas based on an article that appeared in *Fate*'s December 2004 issue. Crumb informs us that Olivas may be "the ghost in the window" at an allegedly haunted house in Ventura, California. With the publication of *R. Crumb's Dream Diary* (2018), we are able to trace the relationship between his dream life and his artistic imagination. Encounters with aliens were clearly on Crumb's mind for the entry dated "Wednesday, June 19, 2002," recounts a "vivid dream about flying saucers and aliens." In the dream, Crumb asks one of the aliens: "I'd love to go see your planet." However, Crumb tells us: "He turned away from me then, mumbling something non-committal, 'We'll see,' or something like that."[5] C. G. Jung in *Flying Saucers: A Modern Myth of Things Seen in the Skies* (1959) explored the significance of humanity's longing for contact with beings from outer space, and we can view Crumb's own interest in this subject within the context of his search for cosmic meaning.[6] In one of his most recent works—a drawing from September 2018 entitled "Self Portrait with Novelty Specs from a Photo"—the book pictured on the table next to a seated Crumb is *Left at East Gate* by

Larry Warren and Peter Robbins: this is an account of a UFO sighting on a military base in rural England.

Crumb's fondness for the occult, esoteric, and paranormal recalls William Burroughs's absorption in these subjects. As we have seen in chapter 1, Burroughs was one of the Beat writers Crumb most admired. Indeed, in describing his life in France, Crumb mentions reading one of Burroughs's favorite books—*Psychic Self-Defense* (1930) by Dion Fortune:

> I have a very strong interest in that [mysticism], and it gets stronger as I get older. I had a big mystic phase in the sixties, when I was taking LSD, a very strong interest in spiritual stuff. I studied Eastern religions and philosophies, but I drifted more into social and political ideas in the early seventies. The interest in mysticism never entirely went away, though; it has gotten stronger since I've lived in France. Partly because I'm culturally free, detached, cut loose. Being a foreigner here, I am really free of cultural pressures. . . . In the south of France, I seem to be more inclined toward that mystic stuff, which I think is good. I like it. I am happy about it. It's a natural tendency that I have. I don't know why. . . . Is it because I was raised Catholic? It has become a very important part of what I spend my time doing. I read all kinds of really nutty books, crazy stuff. I am reading one now called *Psychic Self-Defense*, written in the twenties. . . . Very strange stuff. . . . I also spend a lot of time being alone with nature.[7]

Indeed, many of Crumb's most exquisite recent drawings depicting areas of the French countryside where he goes for walks, for example, "Path in the Mer des Rochers above Sauve Sept. 30th, '96." Crumb has called the Mer des Rochers his "nature refuge from the world."[8] Like the great Romantic poets—Blake, Shelley, Keats, and Wordsworth—for Crumb nature itself becomes a path into deep interiority and compels a confrontation with the essential self. Henry David Thoreau famously announced in *Walden* that his purpose in living in the woods was to "drive life into a corner," to reduce his wants to the essential minimum and learn from nature what it had to teach him:

> I went to the woods because I wished to live deliberately, to front only the essential facts of life, and see if I could not learn what it had to teach, and not, when I came to die, discover that I had not lived. I did not wish to live what was not life, living is so dear; nor did I wish to practice resignation, unless it was quite necessary. I wanted to live deep and suck out all the marrow of life, to live so sturdily and

Spartan-like as to put to rout all that was not life, to cut a broad swath and shave close, to drive life into a corner, and reduce it to its lowest terms, and, if it proved to be mean, why then to get the whole and genuine meanness of it, and publish its meanness to the world; or if it were sublime, to know it by experience, and be able to give a true account of it in my next excursion.

Crumb had avoided urban living in the past—choosing to live in the countryside in Winters, California, for example—and living in rural France has allowed him to pursue a Thoreauvian path in his spiritual life.[9] Crumb is very much in the American tradition of Thoreau, Emerson, and Walt Whitman in his search for the transcendental.

One can also see in Crumb's later work a return to his interest in the Buddhist and Hindu thought—Thoreau hinted in the above quotation about his "next excursion," implying the possibility of reincarnation—that characterized his reading during the sixties. For example, in a drawing completed on March 31, 1997, Crumb includes a portrait of a meditating figure with the description: "Discover the cosmic connection of Kundalini and the Third Eye. Purify your psychic passageways. Tune your awareness to hear the divine sound current. By Earlyne Chaney, former film actress hopeful turned mystic guru in Southern California. 1950s–'80s."[10] Crumb has apparently adapted the drawing of Chaney's book *Kundalini and the Third Eye* (1980). Three decades after Crumb first began to include imagery of the Third Eye in his work of the San Francisco period, he was still intrigued enough by the literature on this subject to include it as the subject matter of his art. The Third Eye also appears in Crumb's continuing interest in out-of-body experiences. In the record of a dream from July 18, 2002, he recalled:

After diligently practicing out-of-body techniques since the beginning of June—much trial and error but persistent effort—this night I finally achieved success and had a real out-of-body experience! . . . I started practicing Robert Monroe's suggestion to focus on a point in front of your eyes, from the third-eye spot, and this seemed to have some effect—I began feeling a strong pull from that spot and stayed with it. It requires a hell of a lot of focus and uninterrupted time. Finally, I began drifting off to sleep and then it happened! I felt myself lift rapidly out of my body![11]

Crumb also created a drawing recording a "hypnagogic" experience that occurred in Paris on June 15, 2002, "in response to my intensely focused endeavor to bring on an out-of-body experience." Here Crumb depicts four "spirits" he encounters during this event: a "very powerful 'alpha male' spirit seemed amused and skeptical, said he'd have me checked out. It was a very brief encounter. Then this serious, stern middle-aged-appearing female spirit seemed to be examining my karmic record, my 'credentials.' She wore a turquoise-blue robe with gold edging. Then this kindly monk-like spirit seemed to be putting my name down on a list." Crumb is finally assigned an African American girl with wings who will be his "angel" or "protector," informing us at the close that "all this took place in a very rapid sequence, in a split second!"[12] We find again the idea of an initiatory sequence in which Crumb is being "tested" to determine whether he has been making spiritual progress. The reference to his "karmic record" is a clear indication that Crumb has been influenced by theosophical literature in which the list of one's deeds are known as the Akashic records, and Crumb created a portrait on December 8, 2001, of Harold W. Percival (1868–1953). Percival was the author of *Thinking and Destiny*—Crumb depicts this fact in his drawing—and helped organize the Theosophical Society of New York.[13]

Another example of Crumb's fascination with Eastern thought is his diagram reflecting his reading of Swami Sri Yukteswar's *The Holy Science* (1894), which Crumb titles as "a description of the workings of the universe." Sri Yukteswar's aim in the book "is to show as clearly as possible that there is an essential unity in all religions; that there is no difference in the truths inculcated by the various faiths; that there is but one method by which the world, both external and internal, has evolved; and that there is but one Goal admitted by all scriptures." Sri Yukteswar was the guru of Paramahansa Yogananda and became a significant figure for the counterculture in part due to the fact that a photograph of him appears on the cover of the Beatles' *Sgt. Pepper's Lonely Hearts Club Band*. In *The Holy Science*, there is included a photograph of Sri Yukteswar with Yogananda, taken in Calcutta in 1935. It is a remarkable diagram, for Crumb has scrupulously translated the Sanskrit terms in the original illustration included in *The Holy Science* into their English equivalents as provided in Sri Yukteswar's text. For example, the book opens: "The Eternal Father, God, Swami *Parambrahma*, is the only Real Substance (*Sat*) and is all in all in the universe." One can see the term *Sat* in the original illustration at the very top, inside a circle, and in Crumb's translation to "the Real Substance." Crumb performs the same translation for the two terms just below *Sat*—*Chit* and *Ananda*, which he correctly translates as "the Omniscient Feeling" and "the Eternal Joy."[14] Crumb does this throughout the diagram, suggesting that he was making the sketch as a mnemonic for his own use as a kind of glossary of the specialized terms

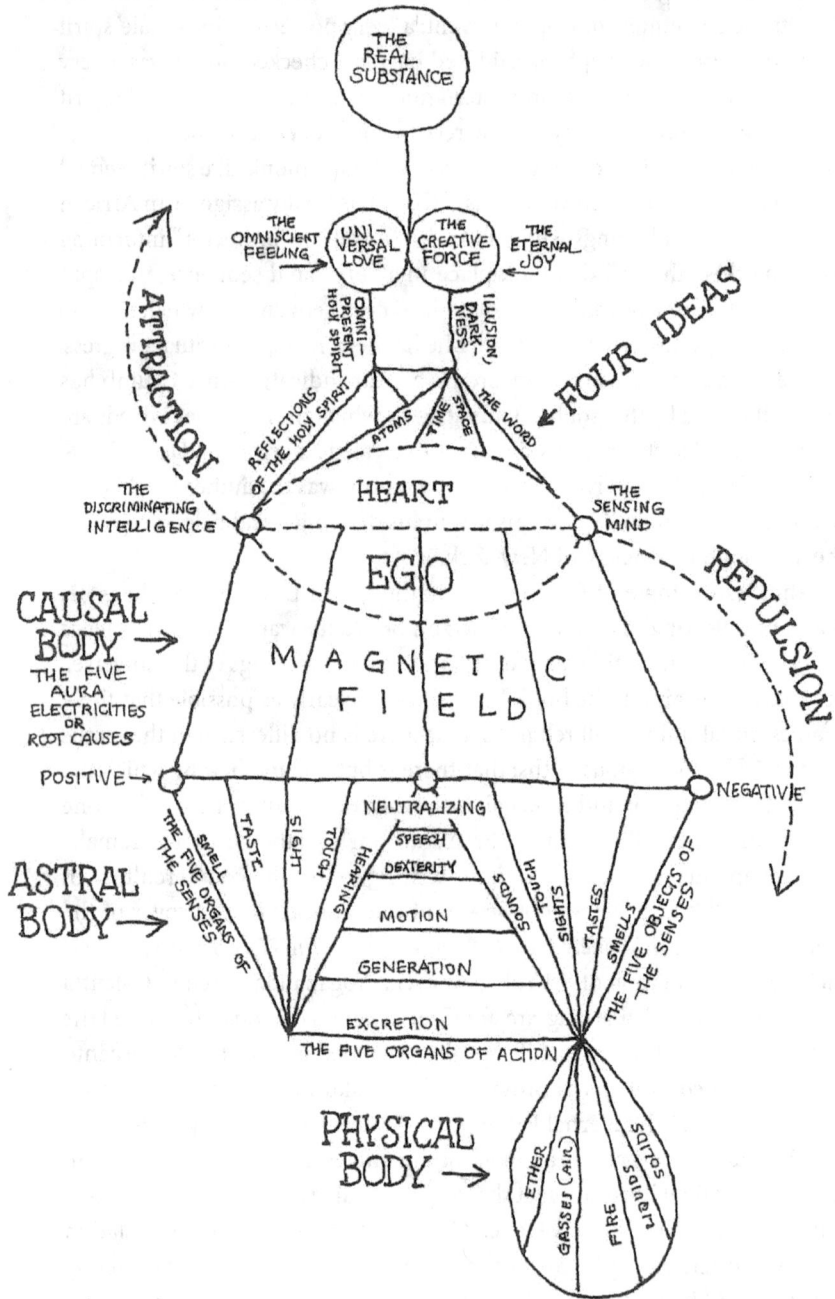

R. Crumb, Swami Sri Yukteswar's "Description of the Workings of the Universe,"
from *The Holy Science* (1894), *Sketchbook*, vol. 12.

employed by Sri Yukteswar. The chart suggests the extent to which Crumb devoted himself to Hindu philosophy, and he also likely took delight in the complex symmetries of the diagram, reminiscent in some respects to the wild designs of Rube Goldberg's nonfunctioning machines, or the improbable going-nowhere factories of Jean Tinguely. Crumb's vision here is—as always—double. He is on an earnest quest for the Self, yet at the same time he stands apart and analyzes, he observes, he ponders, he interrogates, he illustrates. Crumb leaves us here perhaps with a kind of visual koan: diagrams of spiritual liberation appear to go everywhere and nowhere at the same time, which from the truly enlightened point of view is precisely the point. After all our human attempts to "understand," the riddle remains.

In addition to the *Sketchbooks* and *R. Crumb's Dream Diary*, another important recent publication is *Art and Beauty Magazine*, nos. 1, 2, and 3 (2016), in which Crumb offers a myriad of quotations from a variety of authors including Friedrich Nietzsche, Ralph Waldo Emerson, John Berger, John Gardner (*On Moral Fiction*), John Fowles, André Gide, William Blake, Marshall McLuhan, Kenneth Clark, Rudolf Arnheim, and Robert Hughes; and artists Otto Dix, Al Capp, Isamu Noguchi, Vincent van Gogh, and Willem de Kooning. The humor—which as we have seen obtains in the *Sketchbooks* as well in which "serious" drawings are prefaced with lyrics from old-time songs—is achieved through Crumb's method of juxtaposing his often serious quotations with his expert renderings of scantily clad females, whom he describes in the clichéd style of old-fashioned "high-brow" art criticism. This commentary ignores the overtly erotic content of the drawings while extolling the aesthetic qualities of the females in question. For example, a nude is described: "Geraldine Gardner, nightclub performer of the 1950s, in a pose showing the beautiful lines of her body that make her an ideal subject for the artist's pen." Another woman, depicted from the back of her body: "Enchanting grace and supple slenderness of form lend an air divine to this model, whose pose has been captured for immortality." Crumb plays simultaneously here—as he has throughout his career—with the supposed hierarchy dividing "high culture" from "low culture," the "artistic" from the erotic/pornographic, the spirit from the flesh. The constant invocation of famous artists, writers, and philosophers serves to cast a comical aura or veneer of intellectual elitism around the obvious sexual provocation and titillation of Crumb's drawings.

Thus, over the past decades residing in southern France, Crumb has continued to create prolifically. Indeed, some would argue that he is producing work at the highest level of draftsmanship and aesthetic quality: as good or better than work from the earlier phases of his career. However, Crumb has not inhabited an ivory tower, continuing to speak out as an advocate for artistic openness as well as freedom of the press. We recall that Crumb viewed all three of the major monotheistic religions—Christianity, Islam, and Judaism—as "contentious and antagonistic and aggressive," and hence sought wisdom in many other spiritual traditions. Crumb would find his negative view of organized religion confirmed by events in Paris on January 7, 2015, when the offices of the French satirical review *Charlie Hebdo* were attacked by two Islamic gunmen who killed twelve staff members of the magazine in response to its publication of satirical depictions of Mohammed: *Charlie Hebdo* had also been firebombed previously in November 2011. Crumb was asked by the French newspaper *Libération* for his response to the massacre. He considered the matter and decided that he needed to come forward in protest of this attack. Crumb therefore submitted a profusely perspiring, sheepish, and cringing cartoon of himself—described as "A Cowardly Cartoonist"—holding a portrait depicting "The hairy ass of Mohamid!" with speech balloons "Hey Hey," "Just Kidding!" and "Actually it's the ass of my friend Mohamid Bakhsh, a movie producer who lives in Los Angeles, California!" Crumb signed the drawing "R. Crumb—showin' solidarity with my martyred comrads [*sic*]—Jan. 8, '15."

The drawing is interesting for a number of reasons. First, it continues Crumb's satirical thrusts against organized religion; second, it emphasizes humor in the face of ideological fanaticism; and third, it is—as always—autobiographical, since Crumb brings himself directly into the narrative. In order to deflect from the charge that he is actually portraying the posterior of the prophet Mohammed, Crumb tells us that this is actually the rear end of his friend "Mohamid Bakhsh, a movie producer who lives in Los Angeles, California!" This is a hidden joke, because Ralph Bakshi—a person with whom Crumb had quarreled over decades concerning Bakshi's film *Fritz the Cat*, which Crumb disliked intensely—we are intended to understand is the figure to whom Crumb is referring with the name "Mohamid Bakhsh." It is an in-joke, designed to appeal to those who know the facts concerning Crumb's biography, and one would guess that most people would not get the joke. However, that is immaterial, since it serves to deflect—at least partially—the notion that Crumb here is actually depicting something taboo to fervent believers in Islam, and it also emphasizes the irreverence with which Crumb approaches all dogmatism. In opposing groupthink and the humorlessness of ideologies, Crumb affirms the values of free philosophical debate and champions the individual quest for self-knowledge.

Crumb has declared that "as you get older, just the accumulation of your life becomes an inspiration. . . . There's no end to questions. It's like peeling layers off. It becomes more and more interesting. Like I said, my big problem now that I have to struggle with is just clearing the deck so I can work and concentrate on it. It becomes more and more gripping and interesting as I get older. Expressing my life in my work becomes such an interesting, complete, self-contained drama that I could spend three-quarters of my life doing it if I'm allowed to."[15] Crumb in his later work also considers the question of death and preparing for it when it arrives, recalling D. H. Lawrence in his late poem, "Build Your Ship of Death." In a drawing from 1998, Crumb ponders concerning death: "Be prepared to *let go* of *everything* that is of this world—that is, everything you *know* of this world—all connections, all ties must be severed, the biggest one being, of course, the attachment to the *Self!* Start preparing now! Don't be taken *unawares!* Let death be your *advisor— Work on it!* Meanwhile, have a good time!!"[16] In his latest phase, Crumb has continued to critique religious orthodoxy and dogmatism, while also continuing his exploration of his inner life and his intense reading. I hope to have shown in this book that Crumb's intellectual range and depth have been severely underestimated not only by his detractors but by many of his "fans" who have persisted in viewing him through the one-dimensional lens of a sex-and-drug-obsessed enfant terrible. It is evident that throughout his life, Robert Crumb has been involved with a serious and wide-ranging quest to find answers to the complex labyrinth of his own experience.

NOTES

INTRODUCTION

1. Ben Saunders, *Do the Gods Wear Capes? Spirituality, Fantasy, and Superheroes* (London: Continuum, 2011), 6; and R. Crumb, *Your Vigor for Life Appalls Me: Robert Crumb Letters, 1958–1977*, ed. Ilse Thompson (Seattle: Fantagraphics, 1998), 76, 160.

2. Crumb, *Your Vigor for Life Appalls Me*, 123, 196.

3. R. Crumb, blurb on back cover of Keiji Nakazawa, *Barefoot Gen: A Cartoon Story of Hiroshima* (San Francisco: Last Gasp, 2004). Maxon Crumb's account of the Crumb brothers' immersion in *Treasure Island* appears in Tom Pomplun, ed., *Graphic Classics*, vol. 9, *Robert Louis Stevenson* (Mount Horeb, WI: Eureka Productions, 2004), 96–99. Also, C. and R. Crumb, "Treasure Island Days," in *The Complete Crumb Comics*, vol. 1, *The Early Years of Bitter Struggle*, 2nd ed. (1996), 21–42; R. Crumb, "Treasure Island Days," in *Lemme Outa Here* (1978), reprinted in Maxon Crumb, ed., *Crumb Comics: The Whole Family Is Crazy!* (San Francisco: Last Gasp, 1998), 97–98; Edgar Allan Poe, *Maxon's Poe: Seven Stories and Poems by Edgar Allan Poe* (San Francisco: Cottage Classics, 1997); and Anthony Petkovich, "Hardcore Crumb: An Interview with Maxon Crumb," in *Headpress*, no. 17, *Into the Psyche*, ed. David Kerekes (Truro, Cornwall, England: Headpress, 2002), 10, 14, 17, 18. On Maxon, also see most recently Malcolm Whyte, *Maxon: Art out of Chaos; The Illustrated Biography of Maxon Crumb* (Seattle: Fantagraphics, 2018); Sharon Waxman, "The Man Whose Muse Is Misery," *Washington Post*, May 25, 1992, B11; and R. Crumb and Peter Poplaski, *The R. Crumb Handbook* (London: MQ Publications, 2005), 127. On Marty Pahls, see Gary Groth's introduction to Crumb, *Your Vigor for Life Appalls Me*, vii.

4. Crumb, *Your Vigor for Life Appalls Me*, 185, 176. On the fascination for Zen in America during the 1950s, see Arthur C. Danto, "Upper West Side Buddhism," in *Buddha Mind in Contemporary Art*, ed. Jacquelynn Baas and Mary Jane Jacob (Berkeley: University of California Press, 2004), 49–59. The American avant-garde artistic community "felt alienated from rational, technical, bureaucratic modernity in large part because, like generations of their predecessors, they believed that the value systems of contemporary society denied deeper spiritual realities. . . . Some looked to mythology from Western and aboriginal, including Native American, sources to find universal spiritual meanings. Others turned to Eastern religious traditions, especially various forms of Buddhism." See Stuart D. Hobbs, *The End of*

216

the American Avant Garde (New York: New York University Press, 1997), 83. See also Gerald Rosen, *Zen in the Art of J. D. Salinger* (Berkeley, CA: Creative Arts, 1977).

5. Jason Stevens argues that Salinger's fiction "helped to introduce American readers to Eastern religious ideas and motifs that, along with Christian mysticism, became major ingredients of eclectic spirituality." See Jason Stevens, "Religion," in *American Literature in Transition, 1950–1960*, ed. Steven Belletto (New York: Cambridge University Press, 2018), 81. Also, Crumb and Poplaski, *The R. Crumb Handbook*, 129; and Esther Leslie, *Hollywood Flatlands: Animation, Critical Theory and the Avant-Garde* (London: Verso, 2002), 83.

6. R. Crumb, *The R. Crumb Coffee Table Art Book* (Northampton, MA: Kitchen Sink Press, 1997), 247. Crumb's emphasis on the "lurid" and the "grotesque" recalls the theories of Mikhail Bakhtin in *Rabelais and His World* (Bloomington: Indiana University Press, 2009) concerning the "carnivalesque" in Renaissance times—precisely the period of the early popular art Crumb admired—when the conventional hierarchical structure of society was mocked and turned upside down during the carnival by the "lower classes." See Emma Tinker, "R. Crumb's Carnival Subjectivity," in "Identity and Form in Alternative Comics, 1967–2007" (PhD thesis, University College, London, 2009), http://emmatinker.oxalto.co.uk/thesis/; Todd Hignite, *In the Studio: Visits with Contemporary Cartoonists* (New Haven, CT: Yale University Press, 2006), 12, 13; and David M. Ball, "World Literature," in *The Cambridge History of the Graphic Novel*, ed. Jan Baetens, Hugo Frey, and Stephen E. Tabachnick (New York: Cambridge University Press, 2018), 594. The scholarly literature on comics and narrative has grown immensely in recent decades. See, for example, Jeanne C. Ewert, "Comics and Graphic Novel," in *Routledge Encyclopedia of Narrative Theory*, ed. David Herman, Manfred Jahn, and Marie-Laure Ryan (London: Routledge, 2005), 71–73; and Barbara Postema, *Narrative Structure in Comics: Making Sense of Fragments* (Rochester, NY: Rochester Institute of Technology Press, 2013). On the narrative structure of one of Crumb's "Mr. Natural" episodes, see Thierry Groensteen, *Comics and Narration* (Jackson: University Press of Mississippi, 2013), 139–42.

7. See Edward Shannon, "Shameful, Impure Art: Robert Crumb's Autobiographical Comics and the Confessional Poets," *Biography* 35, no. 4 (Fall 2012): 627–49; and Françoise Mouly, "R. Crumb: It's Only Lines on Paper," in *Masters of American Comics*, ed. John Carlin, Paul Karasik, and Brian Walker (New Haven, CT: Yale University Press, 2005), 287.

8. B. N. Duncan, "A Joint Interview with R. Crumb and Aline Kominsky-Crumb," in *R. Crumb: Conversations*, ed. D. K. Holm (Jackson: University Press of Mississippi, 2004), 119.

9. Chris Ware, *Jimmy Corrigan: The Smartest Kid on Earth* (New York: Pantheon, 2000); Daniel Clowes, "Gynecology," in *An Anthology of Graphic Fiction, Cartoons, and True Stories*, ed. Ivan Brunetti (New Haven, CT: Yale University Press, 2006), 375; and Andrea Juno, "Dan Clowes," in *Dangerous Drawings: Interviews with Comix and Graphix Artists*, ed. Andrea Juno (New York: Juno Books, 1997), 111.

10. For an excellent review of Crumb and popular culture, see Kirk Varnedoe and Adam Gopnik, *High and Low: Modern Art/Popular Culture* (New York: Museum of Modern Art, 1990), 213–20; see also Dore Ashton and Art Spiegelman, "The Debate over Popular and Museum Culture: Dore Ashton and Art Spiegelman Visit High and Low at the MoMA," *Art International*, no. 14 (Spring–Summer 1991): 60–64; W. J. T. Mitchell, "Comics as Media: Afterword," in "Comics and Media," ed. Hillary L. Chute and Patrick Jagoda, special issue, *Critical Inquiry* 40, no. 3 (Spring 2014): 255; and Sharon Waxman, "The Man Whose Muse Is Misery," *Washington Post*, May 25, 1992, B10.

11. Charles Johnson, afterword to *The Emergence of Buddhist American Literature*, ed. John Whalen-Bridge and Gary Storhoff (Albany: State University of New York Press, 2009), 235.

12. Friedrich Nietzsche, *The Will to Power*, trans. Walter Kaufmann (New York: Vintage Books, 1968), 435; Susan Goodrick, "Apex Interview: R. Crumb," *R. Crumb: Conversations*, ed. D. K. Holm (Jackson: University Press of Mississippi, 2004), 88; and Crumb and Poplaski, *The R. Crumb Handbook*, 44.

13. Lynda Barry, Ivan Brunetti, R. Crumb, and Gary Panter, "Panel: Lines on Paper," moderated by Hamza Walker, in "Comics and Media," ed. Hillary L. Chute and Patrick Jagoda, special issue, *Critical Inquiry* 40, no. 3 (Spring 2014): 244; Milo George, ed., *The Comics Journal Library*, vol. 3: *R. Crumb* (Seattle: Fantagraphics, 2004), 14; and Harvey Kurtzman, *From Aargh! to Zap! Harvey Kurtzman's Visual History of the Comics* (New York: Prentice Hall, 1991), 65.

14. Jean-Pierre Mercier, "Who's Afraid of R. Crumb?," in *R. Crumb: Conversations*, ed. D. K. Holm (Jackson: University Press of Mississippi, 2004), 196; Goodrick, "Apex Interview: R. Crumb," 88; and Justin Green, *Binky Brown Meets the Holy Virgin Mary* (San Francisco: McSweeny's Publishing, 2009). On Green's influence on Crumb, see Hillary L. Chute, *Graphic Women: Life Narrative and Contemporary Comics* (New York: Columbia University Press, 2010), 18; on Kurtzman's *Help!*, see Jared Gardner, *Projections: Comics and the History of Twenty-First-Century Storytelling* (Stanford, CA: Stanford University Press, 2012), 116–17. Also, Frank Stack, *The New Adventures of Jesus: The Second Coming* (Seattle: Fantagraphics, 2006); and Clay Kinchen Smith, "From *God Nose* to *God's Bosom*; or, How God (and Jack Jackson) Began Underground Comics," in *Graven Images: Religion in Comic Books and Graphic Novels*, ed. A. David Lewis and Christine Hoff Kraemer (New York: Continuum, 2010), 203–17.

15. Robert Hughes, *Things I Didn't Know: A Memoir* (New York: Alfred A. Knopf, 2006), 290; Eric Spitznagel, "Robert Crumb Thinks God Might Actually Be Crazy," *Vanity Fair*, October 22, 2009; Mercier, "Who's Afraid of R. Crumb?," 196–97; F. Scott Fitzgerald, "The Crack-Up," *Esquire*, February 1936; Carl Barks, quoted in Don Fiene, *R. Crumb, Checklist of Work and Criticism* (Cambridge, MA: Boatner Norton Press, 1981), 168; and Robert Wuthnow, *Experimentation in American Religion: The New Mysticisms and Their Implications for the Churches* (Berkeley: University of California Press, 1978), 100, 101. Timothy Leary's advocacy of LSD has been interpreted as a "chemical mystery religion." See Erik Davis, "The Counterculture and the Occult," in *The Occult World*, edited by Christopher Partridge (New York; Routledge, 2015), 639. On Allen Ginsberg's visionary encounter, see David Stephen Calonne, *The Spiritual Imagination of the Beats* (New York: Cambridge University Press, 2017), 85–86. Crumb contributed 175 selections—billed as "sacred drawings"—including "My First LSD Trip," "The Trip Starring Novice Kosher," and "Kozmic Kapers," for inclusion in Cheryl Pellerin, *Trips: How Hallucinogens Work in Your Brain* (New York: Seven Stories Press, 1998).

16. Ted Widmer, "R. Crumb: The Art of Comics no. 1," *Paris Review*, no. 193 (Summer 2010): 41; and Crumb, *The R. Crumb Coffee Table Art Book*, 77. For a recent exploration of LSD, see Michael Pollan, *How to Change Your Mind: What the New Science of Psychedelics Teaches Us about Consciousness, Dying, Addiction, Depression, and Transcendence* (New York: Penguin Press, 2018).

17. An excellent survey of hippie culture is W. J. Rorabaugh, *American Hippies* (New York: Cambridge University Press, 2015). On psychedelia, see Christoph Grunenberg, ed., *Summer of Love: Art of the Psychedelic Era* (London: Tate Publishing, 2005); and R. Crumb, "I

Remember the Sixties: R. Crumb Looks Back!," *Weirdo*, no. 4 (1981), reprinted in R. Crumb, *The Weirdo Years, 1981–'93* (San Francisco: Last Gasp, 2013), 67. On Crumb's drug experiences, also see Brian McHale, *The Cambridge Introduction to Postmodernism* (New York: Cambridge University Press, 2015), 36; on Crumb's new "iconographic" style, see "Comic Con India Special Session with Robert Crumb, Conducted by Gary Groth (Part #1)," https://www.youtube.com/watch?v=S2dm11jHQyI.

18. Hignite, *In the Studio*, 22. Although Crumb acknowledged that during the sixties he "was swept up in the general idealism of the time" and believed that he and others were "creating a new world," he also had trouble once he attempted to get involved in political action. Crumb contributed to *Winds of Change*, a community newspaper in Winters, California, from 1979 to 1984, recalling in an interview with Gary Groth: "They always wanted to present what they thought were positive alternatives to the way things are. It always had this dreary, goody-goody aura of we're-gonna-eat-tofu-and-sit-around-singing-folk-songs-together. Politically I agreed with those people, but working with them was so tedious and annoying, and they were utterly humorless. 'Oh, Crumb, we can't use this cartoon, it's going to alienate the farmers. We can't use this one, it's going to alienate women. . . . I tried to do these really strong political cartoons, like Thomas Nast, putting down agribiz and stuff, and everybody said I was too negative. General agreement that I was too negative. [*Laughter*]." See R. Crumb, "I Remember the Sixties: R. Crumb Looks Back!," in Crumb, *The Weirdo Years*, 64; George, *The Comics Journal Library*, vol. 3, *R. Crumb*, 46; Andrew Robinson, *Sudden Genius? The Gradual Path to Creative Breakthroughs* (New York: Oxford University Press, 2010); and Neil Kessel, "Genius and Mental Disorder: A History of Ideas Concerning Their Conjunction," in *Genius: The History of an Idea*, ed. Penelope Murray (Oxford: Basil Blackwell, 1989), 196–212. Frank Barron has argued: "Creative individuals retain qualities of freshness, spontaneity and joy, as well as a certain lack of cautious reality-testing—openness to the nonrational, if you will. They are in that sense childlike. But this is not regression; it is progression with courage. They bring their childhood along instead of leaving it behind." Frank Barron, "The Creative Personality: Akin to Madness," in *Understanding Mysticism*, ed. Richard Woods (Garden City, NY: Image Books, 1980), 320.

19. See the cover of *Weirdo*, no. 19, collected in Crumb, *The Weirdo Years*, 163.

20. Crumb, *The R. Crumb Coffee Table Art Book*, 176, 177.

21. R. Crumb, "The Religious Experience of Philip K. Dick," *Weirdo*, no. 17, 1986, collected in Crumb, *The Weirdo Years*, 181–88.

22. R. Crumb, "Jelly Roll Morton's Voodoo Curse," *Raw*, no. 7, May 1985, 5–10, reprinted in Ivan Brunetti, ed., *An Anthology of Graphic Fiction, Cartoons, and True Stories*, vol. 1 (New Haven, CT: Yale University Press, 2006), 311–16.

23. R. C. Zaehner, *Mysticism Sacred and Profane: An Inquiry into Some Varieties of Praeternatural Experience* (Oxford: Clarendon Press, 1957); and R. C. Zaehner, *Zen, Drugs and Mysticism* (New York: Pantheon Books, 1972).

24. Huston Smith, "Do Drugs Have a Religious Import?," *Journal of Philosophy* 61, no. 18 (October 1, 1964), reprinted in *The Huston Smith Reader*, ed. Jeffery Paine (Berkeley: University of California Press, 2012), 162–71.

25. David Ossman, *The Sullen Art: Interviews with Modern American Poets* (New York: Corinth Books, 1963), 94. Crumb mocked with great humor and verve the hippies who

claimed superior wisdom based on their experience with LSD: "*I'm* beautiful. *I'm* spiritual. *I've* lost my ego and *you* haven't. We are different from the older generation. We are definitely going to *save the world* because we're so *good and pure*. We took LSD and *we've* seen the light." Crumb argued that "unfortunately, there's no free ride to enlightenment. LSD can show you the other side of reality, can push your face in it, but that doesn't necessarily mean that you'll be able to do anything useful with it, if you're not already working in some direction like that." Ace Backwords, *Acid Heroes: The Legends of LSD* (Scotts Valley, CA: CreateSpace, 2009), 136, 137, 293–64; and Alex Wood, comp., "Crumb on Others, part 3," The Official Crumb Site, https://www.crumbproducts.com/pages/about/crumbonothers3.html. On Leary, see Marcus Boon, *The Road of Excess: A History of Writers on Drugs* (Cambridge, MA: Harvard University Press, 2002), 261–65.

26. Robbie Conal and Tom Christie, "Grandpa from Hell," in *Conversations with William S. Burroughs*, ed. Allen Hibbard (Jackson: University Press of Mississippi, 1999), 224.

27. Allen Ginsberg, "Prefatory Remarks Concerning Leary's Politics of Ecstasy," in *Deliberate Prose: Selected Essays 1952–1995*, ed. Bill Morgan (New York: HarperCollins, 2000), 110.

28. Robert N. Bellah, "The New Religious Consciousness and the Crisis in Modernity," in *The New Religious Consciousness*, ed. Charles Y. Glock and Robert N. Bellah (Berkeley: University of California Press, 1976), 340.

29. Hillary Chute, "Comics as Literature? Reading Graphic Narrative," *PMLA* 123, no. 2 (March 2008): 456.

30. Robert Crumb, "Introduction: Twenty Years Later," in *R. Crumb's Head Comix, Twenty Years Later* (New York: Simon and Schuster, 1988), n.p. On William Hogarth, see David Kunzle, *History of the Comic Strip*, vol. 1, *The Early Comic Strip: Narrative Strips and Picture Stories in the European Broadsheet from c. 1450 to 1825* (Berkeley: University of California Press, 1973), 346–52; and Crumb and Poplaski, *The R. Crumb Handbook*, 432. On Crumb and Philip Guston, see Bill Berkson, "Pyramid and the Shoe: Philip Guston and the Funnies," in *Philip Guston Retrospective*, ed. Michael Auping (New York: Thames and Hudson, 2003), 70–72. See also Hillary L. Chute, *Disaster Drawn: Visual Witness, Comics, and Documentary Form* (Cambridge, MA: Harvard University Press, 2016), 107–8; Crumb, *Your Vigor for Life Appalls Me*, 151; Lisa Eisner and Roman Alonso, "An Eye for the Ladies: Those Who Call Him a Misogynist Don't Know R. Crumb," *New York Times Magazine*, March 30, 2003, 52; and Widmer, "R. Crumb: The Art of Comics no. 1," 30, 32. On Crumb's momentous first encounter with *Mad* magazine and the work of Harvey Kurtzman, see Paul Gravett, *Comics Art* (New Haven, CT: Yale University Press, 2013), 71–73; on Kurtzman's influence on Crumb, see Dan Byrne-Smith, "Harvey Kurtzman and the Influence of *Mad* Magazine," in *The Cambridge History of the Graphic Novel*, ed. Jan Baetens, Hugo Frey, and Stephen E. Tabachnick (New York: Cambridge University Press, 2018), 94–95. See also R. Crumb, "Ode to Harvey Kurtzman," in Harvey Kurtzman, *Harvey Kurtzman's Strange Adventures* (New York: Epic Comics, 1990), 8–9; Abe Peck, *Uncovering the Sixties: The Life and Times of the Underground Press* (New York: Pantheon Books, 1985), 11; Terry Gilliam and Ben Thompson, *Gilliamesque: A Pre-Posthumous Memoir* (New York: HarperCollins, 2015), 64, 72–73; Les Daniels, *Comix: A History of Comic Books in America* (New York: Bonanza Books, 1971), 99; Les Daniels, "Comics Variations," in *The Art of the Comic Strip*, ed. Walter Herdeg and David Pascal (Zurich: Graphis Press, 1972),

63; and Italo Calvino, *Six Memos for the Next Millennium: The Charles Eliot Norton Lectures, 1985–86* (Cambridge, MA: Harvard University Press, 1988), 94.

31. Crumb and Poplaski, *The R. Crumb Handbook*, 142. On the San Francisco scene, see Jay Kinney, "The Rise and Fall of the Underground Comix Movement in San Francisco and Beyond," in *Ten Years That Shook the City: San Francisco 1968–1978*, ed. Chris Carlsson with Lisa Ruth Elliott (San Francisco: City Lights, 2011); and Marjorie Alessandrini, *Robert Crumb* (Paris: Éditions Albin Michel, 1974), 14–24. Steven Heller observes: "The paper with the largest circulation was the *Los Angeles Free Press* with over 120,000; the San Francisco *Oracle* reportedly had 116,000; and New York's *The East Village Other* (*EVO*) reached a peak of around 90,000 copies per week. . . . The Underground Press Syndicate (UPS), the umbrella organization that funneled material to all Undergrounds, estimated that 15 million 'youths' read Underground papers (*Fortune* magazine put the number at one million). But the average number of readers for most other local Undergrounds hovered between 2,000 and 5,000 per issue, with sales fluctuations usually based on the graphics appearing on any given cover." See Steven Heller, *Merz to Émigré and Beyond: Avant-Garde Magazine Design of the Twentieth Century* (London: Phaidon, 2014), 183. See also Walter Madeiros, "Mapping San Francisco 1965–1967: Roots and Florescence of the San Francisco Counterculture," in *Summer of Love: Psychedelic Art, Social Crisis and Counterculture in the 1960s*, ed. Christoph Grunenberg and Jonathan Harris (Liverpool: Liverpool University Press, 2005), 303–48; Peter Plagens, *Sunshine Muse: Art on the West Coast, 1945–1970* (Berkeley: University of California Press, 1999), 94; Jean-François Bizot, *200 Trips from the Counterculture: Graphics and Stories from the Underground Press Syndicate* (London: Thames and Hudson, 2006); and Joost Swarte, "The Independents," in *Drawn Together*, by Aline Kominsky-Crumb and Robert Crumb, ed. Anette Gehrig (Basel: Christoph Merian Verlag, 2016), 72. On Crumb and Joplin, see Alice Echols, *Scars of Sweet Paradise: The Life and Times of Janis Joplin* (New York: Henry Holt, 1999), 106–7, 110, 219, 232; S. Clay Wilson, interviewed in Fred Dortort, ed., *What's Up, Underground!* (Portland, OR: S. K. Josefsberg Studio, 1995), 11; Thomas Albright, *Art in the San Francisco Bay Area, 1945–1980: An Illustrated History* (Berkeley: University of California Press, 1985), 175; and "Robert Crumb Interview: A Compulsion to Reveal," https://www.youtube.com/watch?v=_2ZWrWmypAo&list=PLv2rHgIh3Y9RMNUPf_1mrB2EAB2Vm5NY-&index=1.

32. Rob Hughes, "The Story Behind The Song: White Rabbit by Jefferson Airplane," Classic Rock, March 5, 2019, https://www.loudersound.com/features/the-story-behind-the-song-white-rabbit-by-jefferson-airplane; and Hignite, *In the Studio*, 7.

33. Rock Scully and David Dalton, *Living with the Dead: Twenty Years on the Bus with the Grateful Dead* (Boston: Little, Brown, 1995), 28; Jan Baetens and Hugo Frey, *The Graphic Novel: An Introduction* (New York: Cambridge University Press, 2015), 37; and Peck, *Uncovering the Sixties*, 51.

34. Hans Ulrich Obrist, *Robert Crumb* (Cologne: Walther König, 2006), 9; M. Thomas Inge, *Comics as Culture* (Jackson: University Press of Mississippi, 1990), 41–57; and Edward A. Tiryakian, "Toward the Sociology of Esoteric Culture," in *On the Margin of the Visible: Sociology, the Esoteric, and the Occult*, ed. Edward A. Tiryakian (New York: John Wiley and Sons, 1974), 270. Also see Tessel M. Bauduin, *Surrealism and the Occult: Occultism and Western Esotericism in the Work and Movement of André Breton* (Amsterdam: Amsterdam

University Press, 2014); Maurice Tuchman, *The Spiritual in Art: Abstract Painting, 1890–1985* (New York: Abbeville Press, 1986), 118, 96; Hobbs, *The End of the American Avant Garde*, 83, 85; Catherine Spretnak, *The Spiritual Dynamic in Modern Art: Art History Reconsidered, 1800 to the Present* (New York: Palgrave Macmillan, 2014); and Mats Gustafsson, "Discaholic Interview, R. Crumb, Feb.–March 2013," Discaholic Corner, March 11, 2013, http://matsgus .com/discaholic_corner/?p=2048.

35. Darby Orcutt, "Religion," in *Comics through Time: A History of Icons, Idols, and Ideas*, vol. 2, *1960–1980*, ed. M. Keith Booker (Santa Barbara, CA: Greenwood Press, 2014), 748; and *The R. Crumb Sketchbooks*, vols. 7–12, *1982–2011* (Cologne: Taschen, 2012), 9:59. On the following page, Crumb quotes Thoreau again: "I am convinced, both by faith and experience, that to maintain one's self on this earth is not a hardship but a pastime, if we will live simply and wisely." Crumb and Poplaski, *The R. Crumb Handbook*, 377, 375; "Crybaby Beanhead in Crybaby's Blues," *Arcade*, no. 5 (1976); and "R. Crumb, 'The Old Outsider,' Goes to the Academy Awards," *Hup*, no. 4 (1992), 11–14.

36. Jeffrey J. Kripal, *Mutants and Mystics: Science Fiction, Superhero Comics, and the Paranormal* (Chicago: University of Chicago Press, 2011); and Kennet Granholm, "The Occult and Comics," in *The Occult World*, ed. Christopher Partridge (New York: Routledge, 2015), 499–508. A final text that mentions Crumb briefly but contains no interpretation or analysis is A. David Lewis and Christine Hoff Kraemer, eds., *Graven Images: Religion in Comic Books and Graphic Novels* (New York: Continuum, 2010).

37. Crumb has observed: "I wouldn't judge or condemn work purely because it's misogynistic or racist or anything else; I would judge and condemn it on whether it was interesting or boring, whether it was honest and truthful and real, or whether it was just somebody attempting to pander to some market they think is out there, or trying to imitate something they've seen—someone trying to be successful, or whatever—instead of saying what's really on their minds, dredging up what's really in there. If it's really in there, it ought to come out on paper." See George, *The Comics Journal Library*, vol. 3, *R. Crumb*, 69.

CHAPTER I

1. Joseph Witek, *Comic Books as History: The Narrative Art of Jack Jackson, Art Spiegelman, and Harvey Pekar* (Jackson: University Press of Mississippi, 1989), 132.

2. Paul Buhle, ed., *The Beats: A Graphic History* (New York: Hill and Wang, 2009).

3. Widmer, "R. Crumb: The Art of Comics no. 1," 37; and Jules Feiffer, *The Explainers* (New York: McGraw Hill, 1960).

4. R. Crumb, *The Big Yum Yum Book: The Story of Oggie and the Beanstalk* (Berkeley, CA: Snow Lion Graphics, 1995), n.p.; and *The R. Crumb Sketchbooks*, vols. 1–6, *1964–1982* (Cologne: Taschen, 2014), 1:162–65.

5. James J. Farrell, *The Spirit of the Sixties: Making Postwar Radicalism* (New York: Routledge, 1997), 67; and *The R. Crumb Sketchbooks*, vols. 7–12, 10:52.

6. Crumb and Poplaski, *The R. Crumb Handbook*, 129; *The Comics Journal*, no. 121 (April 1988), 56; John McMillian, *Smoking Typewriters: The Sixties Underground Press and the Rise of Alternative Media in America* (New York: Oxford University Press, 2011), 9; and Charles Plymell, "Curled in Character: R. Crumb and the First *Zap*," in *Hand on the Doorknob: A*

Charles Plymell Reader, ed David Breithaupt (Sudbury, MA: Water Row Press, 2000), 41–48. Harvey Pekar reported that when he first arrived in Cleveland, Crumb "lived a kind of hermit's life. After a while, though, he got to hanging with what I laughingly refer to as 'Cleveland's underground' and started to get Liberated and to get into the Contemporary Scene." Harvey Pekar, "Rapping about Cartoonists, Particularly Robert Crumb," *Journal of Popular Culture* 3, no. 4 (Spring 1970): 681; and Mike Golden, *The Buddhist Third Class Junkmail Oracle: The Selected Art and Poetry of d. a. levy* (New York: Seven Stories Press, 1999), 41.

7. Shannon, "Shameful, Impure Art," 627–49; H. Porter Abbott, *The Cambridge Introduction to Narrative* (New York: Cambridge University Press, 2002), 131; and Daniel Bell, *The Cultural Contradictions of Capitalism* (New York: Basic Books, 1996), 137. On Ken Kesey, see Crumb's comments in Alex Wood, comp., "Crumb on Others, part 7," The Official Crumb Site, http://www.crumbproducts.com/pages/about/crumbonothers7.html; Art Spiegelman, *Maus 1: A Survivor's Tale; My Father Bleeds History* (New York: Pantheon Books, 1993), 102; and Art Spiegelman, afterword to *Breakdowns: Portrait of the Artist as a Young %@*!* (New York: Pantheon Books, 2008), n.p. For Crumb on Ginsberg, see "Robert Crumb's Birthday," The Allen Ginsberg Project, August 30, 2016, http://allenginsberg.org/2016/08/robert-crumbs -birthday-2/. Ginsberg also appreciated Crumb, about whom he declared: "So far supreme funny underground comic strip incarnation of the posthistoric flower age." See Gary Griffith, "Truckin' Along with R. Crumb, or Something," in *R. Crumb: Conversations*, ed. D. K. Holm (Jackson: University Press of Mississippi, 2004), 10. On the literary Beat scene in San Francisco, see Calonne, *The Spiritual Imagination of the Beats*, 16–35; Michael Davidson, *The San Francisco Renaissance: Poetics and Community at Mid-Century* (New York: Cambridge University Press, 1989); and Bill Griffith, *Invisible Ink: My Mother's Affair with a Famous Cartoonist* (Seattle: Fantagraphics, 2015).

8. Ginsberg continued to appear in Crumb's unconscious in later years. In "Second Dream: I Watch Allen Ginsberg Performance, Sauve, Tuesday, April 18, 2004," Crumb reports his dream: "Allen Ginsberg was doing a crazy act on a stage in a small theatre or club. He was his young self, with short, neatly combed hair, black-framed glasses, a suit and tie. It was a surreal performance, supposed to be humorous, with a weird, esoteric meaning. I don't remember the details. I was getting a kick out of it, enjoying it. He bantered with the audience in an open, friendly, good-humored way. I began heckling him, also in a good-humored way, not hostile. 'Hey Allen, is that supposed to be funny? Is it supposed to be surrealistic or what? What're you trying to do up there?' Stuff like that. He responded with wisecracks, I don't remember what." See R. Crumb, *R. Crumb's Dream Diary*, ed. Robert Bronstein and Sammy Harkham (New York: Elara Press, 2018), 191; and Carl Richter, *The Crumb Compendium: The Definitive R. Crumb Bibliography* (Seattle: Fantagraphics, 2018), 203, 209. On Jesse Crumb's Beat portraits, see Maxon Crumb, *Crumb Comics: The Whole Family Is Crazy!*, 80, 84, 83; on Kim Deitch, see Patrick Rosenkranz, *Rebel Visions: The Underground Comix Revolution, 1963–1975* (Seattle: Fantagraphics, 2002), 108, 45. For the Justin Green strip, see James Danky and Denis Kitchen, *Underground Classics: The Transformation of Comics into Comix* (New York: Harry N. Abrams), 74; and Chogyam Trungpa, *Cutting through Spiritual Materialism* (Berkeley, CA: Shambhala, 1973), 117. See also Joseph Witek, "Justin Green: Autobiography Meets the Comics," in *Graphic Subjects: Critical Essays on Autobiography and Graphic Novels*, ed. Michael A. Chaney (Madison: University of Wisconsin Press, 2011), 227–30; *The R. Crumb*

Sketchbooks, vols. 7–12, 7:195; R. Crumb, "Notes for Story for *Arcade 7*," in *The R. Crumb Sketchbook: November 1974–January 1978* (Frankfurt: Zweitausendeins, 1978), 209; Gardner, *Projections*, 119; and Alex Wood, comp., "Crumb on Others, part 8," The Official Crumb Site, http://www.crumbproducts.com/pages/about/crumbonothers8.html. Crumb's allusion to the Chinese yin/yang concept appears in *Yellow Dog*, March 1966. See also Peter Booth Wiley, "Where Did All the Flowers Go? The View from a Street in Bernal Heights," in *Ten Years That Shook the City: San Francisco 1968–1978*, ed. Chris Carlsson with Lisa Ruth Elliott (San Francisco: City Lights, 2011), 107. On Ginsberg and Eric Drooker's *Howl: A Graphic Novel*, see Daniel Morris, "Convergence Cultures: Modern and Contemporary Poetry and the Graphic Novel," in *The Cambridge History of the Graphic Novel*, ed. Jan Baetens, Hugo Frey, and Stephen E. Tabachnick (New York: Cambridge University Press, 2018), 537–39. On Bukowski and his relationship to the Beat movement, see David Stephen Calonne, introduction to *Absence of the Hero: Uncollected Stories and Essays*, by Charles Bukowski, ed. David Stephen Calonne (San Francisco: City Lights, 2010); and Jean-François Duval, *Buk et les Beats: Essai sur la Beat Generation*, rev. ed. (Paris: Éditions Michalon, 2014).

9. Jack Kerouac, "The Origins of the Beat Generation," in *Good Blonde and Others*, by Jack Kerouac, ed. Donald Allen (San Francisco: Grey Fox Press, 1994), 58, 59; see also Hugo Frey, "Beat-Era Literature and the Graphic Novel," in *The Cambridge History of the Graphic Novel*, ed. Jan Baetens, Hugo Frey, and Stephen E. Tabachnick (New York: Cambridge University Press, 2018), 130. On Crumb on Kerouac, see Alex Wood, comp., "Crumb on Others, part 5," The Official Crumb Site, https://www.crumbproducts.com/Crumb-On-Others-Part-5_ep_61.html. See also *The Comics Journal*, no. 121 (April 1988), 55; and "Fritz the Cat in Fritz Bugs Out," in *The Life and Death of Fritz the Cat* (Seattle: Fantagraphics, 2017), 17. On Fritz as "student-poete maudit beatnik rebel," see Jean-Paul Gabilliet, "Fritz the Cat (1972): From Crumb to Bakshi, Betraying the Author and Translating the Zeitgeist," in *Comics and Adaptation*, edited by Benoît Mitaine, David Roche, and Isabelle Schmitt-Pitiot (Jackson: University Press of Mississippi, 2018), 175; Ellis Amburn, *Subterranean Kerouac: The Hidden Life of Jack Kerouac* (New York: St. Martin's Press, 1998), 119; Douglas Malcolm, "'Jazz America': Jazz and African American Culture in Jack Kerouac's *On the Road*," in *Bloom's Modern Critical Interpretations: Jack Kerouac's* On the Road, ed. Harold Bloom (New York: Chelsea House, 2004), 93–114; R. Crumb, "The Heap Years of the Auto, 1946–59," in *Odds and Ends* (New York: Bloomsbury, 2001), n.p.; and Crumb, *Your Vigor for Life Appalls Me*, 215.

10. R. Crumb, "And Now, Those Cute, Adorable Little Bearzy Wearzies," *CoEvolution Quarterly*, no. 24 (Winter 1979–1980), 136–39; and "Keep on Dancin' an' Aprancin'," *The R. Crumb Sketchbooks*, vols. 7–12, 11:57. Crumb's quotation comes from Hayao Kawai, *The Buddhist Priest Myoe: A Life of Dreams* (Venice, CA: Lapis Press, 1991), 86. See also R. Crumb, "Bad Karma," *Mystic Funnies*, no. 2, 1999; and Giorgio Agamben, *Karman: A Brief Treatise on Action, Guilt, and Gesture* (Stanford, CA: Stanford University Press, 2018), 27. Crumb returns to the theme of Buddhist *dukkha*, suffering—but without the possibility of reincarnation—in "Cradle to Grave," which appeared in *Mystic Funnies*, no. 3, 2002. Crumb depicts in twelve concise panels the entire life cycle from birth to childhood, first romantic attraction, sex and marriage, children, career and middle age, old age, and decrepitude, with a final collection of five clown figures who carry the Crumb figure through the last five panels energetically to his burial plot, dropping him directly and unceremoniously into his grave with the final

farewell: "Well, That's That . . . ," with the gravestone "Joe Schmeck R.I.P." It is a bleak, yet—in typically Crumb black humor style—mercilessly accurate view of the tragicomedy of life, depicted economically and with great power; D. K. Holm, *Robert Crumb* (Harpenden, Herts., England: Pocket Essentials, 2005), 133. On Hindu gurus—including Bhaktivedanta—in the West, see Gavin Flood, *An Introduction to Hinduism* (Cambridge: Cambridge University Press, 1996), 269–73; Wendy Doniger, *The Hindus: An Alternative History* (New York: Penguin Books, 2009), 639–40; and "Woke Up in the Middle of the Night," *The R. Crumb Sketchbooks*, vols. 7–12, 9:106. For a portrait of Bhaktivedanta, see *The R. Crumb Sketchbooks*, vols. 7–12, 9:106; and A. C. Bhaktivedanta Swami Prabhupada, *Sri Isopanisad: With Introduction, Translation, and Authorized Reports* (New York: Bhaktivedanta Book Trust, 1974), 5. For an interview between Ginsberg and Bhaktivedanta, see David Stephen Calonne, ed., *Conversations with Allen Ginsberg* (Jackson: University Press of Mississippi, 2019); on Crumb, environmentalism, and *CoEvolution Quarterly*, see Andrew G. Kirk, *Counterculture Green: The Whole Earth Catalog and American Environmentalism* (Lawrence: University Press of Kansas, 2007), 107, 175, 176, 186–87. Crumb and Abbey met on March 24, 1985, at Arches National Park in Utah during a book launch for *The Monkey Wrench Gang*. Abbey recalled the event: "Met Crumb, a very droll delightful fellow—'a true gentleman and a great artist,' as I wrote in his copy of MWG." See James M. Cahalan, *Edward Abbey: A Life* (Tucson: University of Arizona Press, 2001), 230. On Crumb's critique of the American space program, see Neil M. Maher, *Apollo in the Age of Aquarius* (Cambridge, MA: Harvard University Press, 2017), 196–97.

11. R. Crumb, "Those Dharma Bhums," *CoEvolution Quarterly*, no. 22 (Summer 1979): 78–81; and R. Crumb, "Ducks Yas Yas," *Zap*, no. 0 (October 1967): 16–18.

12. Aline Kominsky-Crumb and Robert Crumb, *Drawn Together*, ed. Anette Gehrig (Basel: Christoph Merian Verlag, 2016), 99.

13. R. Crumb, "Meatball," *Zap*, no. 0 (October 1967).

14. Jack Kerouac, *On the Road* (1957; New York: Penguin, 2011), 5.

15. Jane Naomi Iwamura, *Virtual Orientalism: Asian Religions and American Popular Culture* (New York: Oxford University Press, 2011), chap. 2, "Zen's Personality: D. T. Suzuki," 23–62; J. J. Clarke, *Oriental Enlightenment: The Encounter between Asian and Western Thought* (Abingdon, Oxon, England: Routledge, 1997), 103–4; Helen Westgeest, *Zen in the Fifties: Interaction in Art between East and West* (Amstelveen, Netherlands: Waanders Publishers, 1997), 62; Daniel Belgrad, *The Culture of Spontaneity: Improvisation and the Arts in Postwar America* (Chicago: University of Chicago Press, 1998), 162; and Carl T. Jackson, "D. T. Suzuki, 'Suzuki Zen,' and the American Reception of Zen Buddhism," in *American Buddhism as a Way of Life*, ed. Gary Storhoff and John Whalen-Bridge (Albany: State University of New York Press, 2010), 39–56. For a good anthology that includes selections by Ginsberg, Kerouac, Snyder, and Burroughs, see Donald S. Lopez Jr., ed., *A Modern Buddhist Bible: Essential Readings from East and West* (Boston: Beacon Press, 2002).

16. Danny Gregory, *An Illustrated Life: Drawing Inspiration from the Private Sketchbooks of Artists, Illustrators and Designers* (Cincinnati: How Books, 2008), 47; and Arthur Asa Berger, *The Comic-Stripped American: What Dick Tracy, Blondie, Daddy Warbucks, and Charlie Brown Tell Us about Ourselves* (New York: Walker and Company, 1973), 222. On Mr. Natural, also see Edward Brunner, "The Comics as Outsider's Text: Teaching R. Crumb and Underground Comix," in *Teaching the Graphic Novel*, ed. Stephen E. Tabachnick (New York: Modern Language Association of America, 2009), 139–40.

17. On Gurdjieff, see David Stephen Calonne, *The Colossus of Armenia: G. I. Gurdjieff and Henry Miller* (Ann Arbor, MI: Roger Jackson, 1997).

18. R. Crumb, "Let's Be Honest," *East Village Other* 3, no. 12 (February 23–29, 1968), collected in R. Crumb, *R. Crumb's Head Comix* (New York: Viking, 1968).

19. Barry Gifford, ed. *As Ever: The Collected Correspondence of Allen Ginsberg and Neal Cassady* (Berkeley, CA: Creative Arts), 140, 141, 142, 146. For a reproduction of the sequence, see Paul Reps and Nyogen Senzaki, *Zen Flesh, Zen Bones: A Collection of Zen and Pre-Zen Writings* (Boston: Tuttle, 1998), 163–87.

20. "Mr. Natural's 719th Meditation" was first published 1970 and included in R. Crumb, *The Book of Mr. Natural: Profane Tales of That Old Mystic Madcap* (Seattle: Fantagraphics, 1995).

21. On "Om Mani Padme Om," see also "Mr. Natural and Shuman the Human in Om Sweet Om," in R. Crumb, *Carload O' Comics* (New York: Belier Press, 1976).

22. On "The History of America," see Groensteen, *Comics and Narration*, 139–42.

23. Groensteen, *Comics and Narration*, 139ff.

24. Art Spiegelman, "Introduction: Barefoot Gen; Comics after the Bomb," in *Barefoot Gen: A Cartoon Story of Hiroshima*, by Keiji Nakazawa (San Francisco: Last Gasp, 2004), n.p.; R. Crumb, "Bo Bo Bolinksy: He's the Number One Human Zero," *Uneeda Comix* (1970), 7; R. Crumb, "I'm a Ding Dong Daddy," *Zap*, no. 1; R. Crumb, "R. Crumb Presents R. Crumb," *Zap*, no. 7 (1974); and R. Crumb, "Schuman the Human: A Poignant Psychological Drama Featuring Mr. Natural," *East Village Other* 3, no. 10 (1968). Shuman's appearance in the early part of the narrative has been described as "drawn in a distorted way, all angles and knife-edged planes, as if he were an android or animated robot. Even his hands are distorted." See Frank L. Cioffi, "Disturbing Comics: The Disjunction of Word and Image in the Comics of Andrzej Mleczko, Ben Katchor, R. Crumb, and Art Spiegelman," in *The Language of Comics: Word and Image*, ed. Robin Varnum and Christina T. Gibbons (Jackson: University Press of Mississippi, 2001), 113; Lin Yutang, *The Wisdom of China and India* (New York: Modern Library, 1955), 41; and *The R. Crumb Sketchbooks*, vols. 7–12, 11:110–11. The passage Crumb illustrates may be found in Huang Po, *The Zen Teachings of Huang Po: On the Transmission of Mind*, trans. John Blofeld (New York: Grove Press, 1980), 101–2.

25. Robert D. Denham, *Northrop Frye: Religious Visionary and Architect of the Spiritual World* (Charlottesville: University of Virginia Press, 2004), 298; and "Robert Crumb's Birthday," The Allen Ginsberg Project, August 30, 2016, https://allenginsberg.org/2016/08/robert-crumbs-birthday-2/.

26. Christopher Murray, "Alan Moore: The Making of a Graphic Novelist," in *The Cambridge History of the Graphic Novel*, ed. Jan Baetens, Hugo Frey, and Stephen E. Tabachnick (New York: Cambridge University Press, 2018), 224; Christine Hoff Kraemer and A. David Lewis, "Comics/Graphic Novels," in *The Routledge Companion to Religion and Popular Culture*, ed. John C. Lyden and Eric Michael Mazur (London: Routledge, 2015), 221; and Christopher Sharrett, "Alan Moore," in *Alan Moore: Conversations*, ed. Eric L. Berlatsky (Jackson: University Press of Mississippi, 2012), 52–53. On Moore's interest in tarot, Kabbalah, and figures such as Aleister Crowley and John Dee, see Annalisa Di Liddo, "Transcending Comics: Crossing the Boundaries of the Medium," in *A Comic Studies Reader*, ed. Jeet Heer and Kent Worcester (Jackson: University Press of Mississippi, 2009), 325–27.

27. Due to the expense of producing the book, the project never got off the ground during Burroughs's lifetime but has been published recently as Malcolm M. McNeill, *The Lost Art of Ah Pook Is Here: Images for the Graphic Novel* (Seattle: Fantagraphics, 2012).

28. S. Clay Wilson, "Fun City in Ba'Dan," *Arcade*, no. 4 (1975); S. Clay Wilson, *The Mythology of S. Clay Wilson*, vol. 1, *Pirates in the Heartland*, ed. Patrick Rosencranz (Seattle: Fantagraphics, 2014); and S. Clay Wilson, *The Mythology of S. Clay Wilson*, vol. 2, *Demons and Angels*, ed. Patrick Rosencranz (Seattle: Fantagraphics, 2015).

29. Tom H. Dickerson, Paul Dickerson, and Gregory Corso, "Attack Anything Moving," in *Burroughs Live: The Collected Interviews of William S. Burroughs, 1960–1997*, edited by Sylvère Lotringer (Los Angeles: Semiotext(e), 2001), 606. On Burroughs's interest in the occult, see Arthur Versluis, *American Gurus: From Transcendentalism to New Age Religion* (New York: Oxford University Press, 2014), 99–108; and Matthew Levi Stevens, *The Magical Universe of William S. Burroughs* (Oxford: Mandrake of Oxford, 2014).

30. For Crumb on Whitley Streiber, see *The R. Crumb Sketchbooks*, vols. 7–12, 9:28; "Excerpts from *R. Crumb's Dream Diary*," *Mineshaft*, no. 30 (Spring 2014); and Mercier, "Who's Afraid of R. Crumb?," 217. For Crumb on Korzybski, see *The R. Crumb Sketchbooks*, vols. 7–12, 8:209.

31. Alex Wood, comp., "Crumb on Others, part 3," The Official Crumb Site, https://www.crumbproducts.com/pages/about/crumbonothers3.html; Crumb, *R. Crumb's Dream Diary*, 83, 434; and *The R. Crumb Sketchbooks*, vols. 7–12, 9:46.

32. Ted Morgan, *Literary Outlaw: The Life and Times of William S. Burroughs* (New York: W. W. Norton, 2012), 468; Jean-Paul Gabilliet, *R. Crumb* (Bordeaux: Presses Universitaires de Bordeaux, 2012), 97–98; Howard Sounes, *Charles Bukowski: Locked in the Arms of a Crazy Life* (New York: Grove Press, 1999), 125; R. Crumb, "Bop Bop against That Curtain," *Arcade*, no. 3 (Fall 1975), 29–31; and Richter, *The Crumb Compendium*, 209.

33. R. Crumb and Bill Griffith: "As the Artist Sees It: Interviews with Comic Artists," in *Popular Culture in America*, ed. Paul Buhle (Minneapolis: University of Minnesota Press, 1987), 135; and *The Comics Journal*, no. 121 (April 1988), 110. The Raymond Danowski and John Martin Collection of Robert Crumb Material, 1958–2000, is housed at the Stuart A. Rose Manuscript, Archives, and Rare Book Library at Emory University; see https://findingaids.library.emory.edu/documents/crumb1169/.

34. Obrist, *Robert Crumb*, 36. Four of the illustrations Crumb completed from *My Secret Life* by "Walter" appear in a French anthology of several of Crumb's literary adaptations including Richard von Krafft-Ebing, Sartre, Boswell, Philip K. Dick, and Jelly Roll Morton. See R. Crumb, *Nausea* (Paris: Éditions Cornelius, 2011), 33–36; and Nadine Hartmann, "Eroticism," in *Georges Bataille: Key Concepts*, ed. Mark Hewson and Marcus Coelen (Abingdon, Oxon, England: Routledge, 2016), 137, 144.

35. Charles Bukowski, *Bring Me Your Love* (Santa Barbara, CA: Black Sparrow Press, 1983).

36. Charles Bukowski, *The Captain Is Out to Lunch and the Sailors Have Taken Over the Ship* (Santa Barbara, CA: Black Sparrow Press, 1998).

37. *The R. Crumb Sketchbooks*, vols. 7–12, 10:107.

38. Bukowski, *The Captain Is Out to Lunch*, 54.

39. *The R. Crumb Sketchbooks*, vols. 7–12, vol. 10, August 1992–January 1993.

40. Rolf Gran, "Charles Bukowski Illustrated and Drawn by Robert Crumb," *Jahrbuch der Charles-Bukowski-Gesellschaft*, December 13, 2011, 130.

41. Matthew G. Kirschenbaum, *Track Changes: A Literary History of Word Processing* (Cambridge, MA: Belknap Press of Harvard University Press, 2016), 185; see also David Stephen Calonne, "Creative Writers and Revision," in *Revision: History, Theory, and Practice*, ed. Alice Horning and Anne Becker (Anderson, SC: Parlor Press, 2006), 142–76.

42. *The R. Crumb Sketchbooks*, vols. 7–12, vol. 11

CHAPTER 2

1. Clark Peterson, "R. Crumb: Laid Back But Still Truckin,'" *Berkeley Barb*, no. 576 (August 27–September 2, 1976), 12; Melissa Axelrod, "In Search of the Lost Rhythm with R. Crumb," *Pulse!*, no. 187 (November 1999), 60; R. Crumb, "I'm Grateful! I'm Grateful!," in *The Complete Crumb Comics*, vol. 17, *The Late 1980s: Cave Wimp, Mode O' Day, Aline 'n' Bob and Other Stories, Covers, Drawings* (2013), 23; and R. Crumb, "Where Has It Gone, All the Beautiful Music of Our Grandparents?," *Weirdo*, no. 14, reprinted in Crumb, *The Weirdo Years*, 140. For Crumb on his musical grandparents, see "Who Am I?," October 19, 1990, in Maxon Crumb, *Crumb Comics: The Whole Family Is Crazy!*, 143, 144; and Mike Zwerin, "'Oh Boy!': A Robert Crumb Diatribe," *International Herald Tribune*, November 22, 1995, 12. The Serenaders have produced several recordings: *R. Crumb and His Cheap Suit Entertainers* (1974); *R. Crumb and His Cheap Suit Serenaders, no. 2* (1976); and *R. Crumb and His Cheap Suit Serenaders, no. 3* (1978). For a complete listing of Crumb's recordings and illustrations of record jackets, see Richter, *The Crumb Compendium*, 188–94. Crumb has devoted several of his comics to his collecting habit. On his 6,500-record collection, see Gustafsson, "Discaholic Interview, R. Crumb, Feb.–March 2013." Also see Garth Cartwright, "Interview: Robert Crumb," December 5, 2013, http://daily.redbullmusicacademy.com/2013/12/robert-crumb-interview; and Brett Milano, *Vinyl Junkies: Adventures in Record Collecting* (New York: St. Martin's Press, 2003), 72. On the programming on *John's Old Time Radio Show* from July 2012 to November 2017, see Richter, *The Crumb Compendium*, 245–46.

2. *The R. Crumb Sketchbooks*, vols. 7–12, 7:171; and Robert Palmer, *Deep Blues* (New York: Penguin, 1982), 80, 81.

3. Frederic Ramsey Jr. and Charles Edward Smith, eds., *Jazzmen: The Story of Hot Jazz Told in the Lives of the Men Who Created It* (New York: Harcourt Brace and Company, 1939).

4. Widmer, "R. Crumb: The Art of Comics no. 1," 37.

5. *The R. Crumb Sketchbooks*, vols. 7–12, 8:207. After describing Crumb's emotional reaction to listening to "Last Kind Word Blues" by Geeshie Wiley, Hugo Frey observes: "While Crumb is famous and infamous for the lewd and grotesque humor of his underground comix strips, his own oeuvre is punctuated with precisely this same kind of nostalgic historical reflection." Hugo Frey, "Historical Fiction," in *The Cambridge Companion to the Graphic Novel*, ed. Stephen Tabachnick (Cambridge: Cambridge University Press, 2017), 80. In the German edition of *The R. Crumb Sketchbook, November 1974–January 1978* (Frankfurt: Zweitausendeins, 1978), 269, Crumb reflected on his youth and his tendency toward nostalgia on a page dated "Sunday, June 26th, 1977": "I suppose I've always had an inclination towards nostalgia.... Even when I was nine years old I used to recall fondly the innocence of my earlier childhood.... I remember

that when I lived in Oceanside in 1952 to '56 I was always looking back on the time that the family lived on 53rd St. and in the project in Philadelphia, 1947 to 1950. And the period we lived in Ames Iowa, 1950 to Summer '52.... By the time I was eleven years old I looked back on those years as a Golden Age of my life.... When I was totally innocent, unconscious, unknowing, when everything was a wonderment.... The present, which was 1953, '54, '55, seemed dreary, empty and ugly by comparison.... I had already developed, cultivated a strong sense of nostalgia, dwelling on those earlier years." This German Zweitausendeins edition contains material that is not included in the Taschen edition.

6. "No Rest for the Wicked," in *The R. Crumb Sketchbooks*, vols. 1–6, 3:18. Crumb depicts himself in the first panel waking in bed: "I awake from 'the sleep which does not refresh.'" The last phrase comes from a Mark Twain quotation about America, which Crumb quotes in full in panel 3. The source is Mark Twain, *Letters from the Earth*, ed. Bernard DeVoto (New York: Harper and Row, 1962), 88; see also *The Comics Journal*, no. 121 (April 1988), 102.

7. John Berger, *Ways of Seeing* (London: Penguin, 1972). Crumb is clearly familiar with Berger's work: he quotes passages from his writings twice in *Art and Beauty Magazine*, no. 1; see R. Crumb, *Art and Beauty Magazine*, nos. 1, 2, and 3: *Drawings by R. Crumb* (New York: David Zwirner Books, 2016), n.p. R. Crumb, "Street Musicians," *New Yorker*, August 26, 1996; and *The R. Crumb Sketchbooks*, vols. 7–12, 8:223.

8. Robert Crumb, "Dirty Dog," *Zap*, no. 3 (December 1968), reprinted in *The Complete Crumb Comics*, vol. 5, *Happy Hippy Comix* (1990), 74–76; R. Crumb, *R. Crumb's Heroes of Blues, Jazz, and Country* (New York: Harry N. Abrams, 2006); and R. Crumb, *R. Crumb Trading Cards* (Northampton, MA: Kitchen Sink Press, 2010).

9. John Carlin, "Masters of American Comics: An Art History of Twentieth-Century American Comic Strips and Books," in *Masters of American Comics*, ed. John Carlin, Paul Karasik, and Brian Walker (New Haven, CT: Yale University Press, 2005), 175; and Joel Dinerstein, *The Origins of Cool in Postwar America* (Chicago: University of Chicago Press, 2017), 154.

10. "Patton" was reprinted in *The Complete Crumb Comics*, vol. 15, *Featuring Mode O'Day and Her Pals* (2001). Also, "Jelly Roll Morton's Voodoo Curse," in Ivan Brunetti, ed., *An Anthology of Graphic Fiction, Cartoons, and True Stories*, vol. 1 (New Haven, CT: Yale University Press, 2006), 311–16.

11. On the "noir/crime" atmosphere of the Morton and Patton works, see Peter Sattler, "Robert Crumb," in *Comics through Time: A History of Icons, Idols, and Ideas*, vol. 3, *1980–1995*, ed. M. Keith Booker (Santa Barbara, CA: Greenwood Press, 2014), 978; R. Crumb, "That's Life," *Arcade* (Fall 1975); Linda Hutcheon, *A Theory of Adaptation* (London: Routledge, 2006), 8; and Crumb, *Your Vigor for Life Appalls Me*, 158. One historian of Black comics has observed that "'Voodoo Hoodoo' was kept out of circulation for close to 40 years, and when it reappeared American editors carefully adjusted it to suit today's readers. Dialect was altered, sharpened teeth flattened and nose rings plucked from the Africans; Bop Bop, Donald's jazz musician friend back home in Ducksburg, was changed from Black to white. Big lips were also replaced—to grotesque effect for a few characters, whose newly drawn mouths have no lips whatsoever." See Fredrik Strömberg, *Black Images in the Comics: A Visual History* (Seattle: Fantagraphics, 2003), 103.

12. Owen Davies, *Grimoires: A History of Magic Books* (New York: Oxford University Press, 2009), 156; on New Orleans, 190–91.

13. Philip Pullman, *Daemon Voices: On Stories and Storytelling* (New York: Alfred A. Knopf, 2017), 297; see also Gene Kannenberg Jr., "Graphic Text, Graphic Context: Interpreting Custom Fonts and Hands in Contemporary Comics," in *Illuminating Letters: Typography and Literary Interpretation*, ed. Paul C. Gutjahr and Megan L. Benton (Amherst: University of Massachusetts Press, 2001), 165.

14. Paul Garon, *Blues and the Poetic Spirit* (San Francisco: City Lights, 1996), 158; and Albert J. Raboteau, *Canaan Land: A Religious History of African Americans* (New York: Oxford University Press, 2001), 51, 52. As Phil Pastras points out, "[James] Haskins's book, *Voodoo and Hoodoo*, maintains that the term hoodoo, normally a simple variant or synonym for voodoo, should be restricted to the conjurers who deal exclusively in voodoo magic and folk medicine"; Phil Pastras, *Dead Man Blues: Jelly Roll Morton Way Out West* (Berkeley: University of California Press, 2001), 58. Patras also points out that Alan Lomax, Morton's biographer, had "contact with Zora Neale Hurston, whose book *Mules and Men* deals primarily with conjuring practices and prescriptions of what she calls 'hoodoo' in New Orleans, rather than voodoo as a communal, ritualistic religion" (Pastras, *Dead Man Blues*, 64). Ishmael Reed has resuscitated hoodoo as a new, positive, African American religious tradition, a "Lost American Church," and supplies a list of musicians—including Jelly Roll Morton—whom he sees in its historical sweep: "Neo-HooDoo borrows from Haiti, Africa and South America. Neo-HooDoo comes in all styles and moods. Louis Jordon Nellie Lutcher John Lee Hooker Ma Rainey Dinah Washington the Temptations Ike and Tina Turner Aretha Franklin Muddy Waters Otis Redding Sly and the Family Stone B. B. King Junior Wells Bessie Smith Jelly Roll Morton Ray Charles Jimi Hendrix . . ." See Ishmael Reed, "Neo-HooDoo Manifesto/The Neo-HooDoo Aesthetic," in *Symposium of the Whole: A Range of Discourse toward an Ethnopoetics*, ed. Jerome Rothenberg and Diane Rothenberg (Berkeley: University of California Press, 1983), 417, 419. Also see chapter 5, "'We All Believed in Hoodoo': Conjure and Black American Cultural Traditions," in Yvonne P. Chireau, *Black Magic: Religion and the African American Conjuring Tradition* (Berkeley: University of California Press, 2003), 120–49.

15. Garon, *Blues and the Poetic Spirit*, 156; and Justin Green, interviewed in Dortort, *What's Up, Underground!*, 15. For Crumb's account of his family "curse," see "The Chinese Curse," in Maxon Crumb, *Crumb Comics: The Whole Family is Crazy!*, 126–29; and Alex Wood, comp., "Crumb on Others, part 8," The Official Crumb Site, http://www.crumbproducts.com/pages/about/crumbonothers8.html.

16. In an entry from his *Dream Diary* from six years later, dated "Le Vigan, Sunday, June 10, 2007" and entitled "Hypnagogic Demons," Crumb returns to this theme of nightmarish visitations, and his account matches closely the scene depicted in the 2001 drawing. At 4:00 a.m., he reports that as he was "about to fall asleep, I experienced unusually vivid and scary demonic beings imposing themselves on my consciousness, one after another. I willed myself not to be afraid, and at some point I thought of [Carlos] Castaneda's thing about making this menacing dark being into an ally, that you have to fight with it somehow and overcome it. The images shifted and changed, from one hideous, terrifying creature to another. . . . Who are what are these dark, terrifying forces?? Why do they come at that moment, when one is lying in bed about to fall asleep? They take you by surprise. They come quickly, uninvited.

One is both frightened, alarmed and fascinated. . . . One wants to observe them, like a horror show, in all their extreme hideousness, but they quickly shift, or hide, or go away. . . . They don't want to be examined. They thrive in darkness and concealment." See Crumb, *R. Crumb's Dream Diary*, 371–72; and Palmer, *Deep Blues*, 48–92.

17. *The Comics Journal*, no. 121 (April 1988), 112; a portrait of Patton also appears in *The R. Crumb Sketchbooks*, vols. 1–6, 2:393. For Crumb on Patton, see Garth Cartwright, "Interview: Robert Crumb," December 5, 2013, http://daily.redbullmusicacademy.com/2013/12/robert-crumb-interview. See also Neil Cohn, *The Visual Language of Comics: Introduction to the Structure and Cognition of Sequential Images* (London: Bloomsbury, 2013), 143; Allan Moore, "Surveying the Field: Our Knowledge of Blues and Gospel Music," in *The Cambridge Companion to Blues and Gospel Music*, ed. Allan Moore (Cambridge: Cambridge University Press, 2002), 2; W. T. Lhamon Jr., *Deliberate Speed: The Origins of a Cultural Style in the American 1950s* (Washington, DC: Smithsonian Institution Press, 1990), 43; and Luc Sante, "1903: The Invention of the Blues," in *A New Literary History of America*, ed. Greil Marcus and Werner Sollors (Cambridge, MA: Harvard University Press, 2009), 481.

18. Crumb recalls: "I did comic stories about old musicians because I thought it was far superior to anything being done currently. In this case, I had done a comic story about Charley Patton, one of the great fathers of the blues, and the guy who published it was over at my house. So I took out one of my favorite 78s, Charley Patton's 'Down the Dirt Road,' and I put it on. So I'm sitting there, having this great experience listening to this record, and he's sitting there quietly, patiently. And after I took it off, he looks at me and says, 'So what did you like about that?'" Crumb laughs. "I mean, he wasn't trying to be insulting, just curious, but what can you say to that? So I don't try to convert people anymore." See Milano, *Vinyl Junkies*, 71; and Palmer, *Deep Blues*, 57.

19. Alex Wood, comp., "Crumb on Others, part 3," The Official Crumb Site, https://www.crumbproducts.com/pages/about/crumbonothers3.html; and Palmer, *Deep Blues*, 58.

20. See Francesco Pelosi, *Plato on Music, Soul and Body*, trans. Sophie Henderson (Cambridge: Cambridge University Press, 2010).

21. Mai Kawabata, *Paganini: The "Demonic" Virtuoso* (Woodbridge, Suffolk, England: Boydell Press, 2013).

22. Palmer, *Deep Blues*, 60. Erik Davis similarly emphasizes this aspect of Legba: "In Haiti, where the orisha are known as the loa and their worship known as vodoun, Legba went through other drastic changes. He remains lord of the crossroads, the *grand chemin*"; Erik Davis, *Nomad Codes: Adventures in Modern Esoterica* (Portland, OR: Yeti Publishing, 2010), 147. Also, Zora Neale Hurston, *Tell My Horse: Voodoo and Life in Haiti and Jamaica* (New York: Harper and Row, 1990), 128.

23. Garon, *Blues and the Poetic Spirit*, 196; and Debra DeSalvo, *The Language of the Blues: From Alcorub to Zuzu* (New York: Billboard Books, 2006), 87. Robert Johnson's "Cross Road Blues" is considered one of his masterpieces and emphasizes several Crumbian themes: "In the rural South, the crossroad, leading to and from many places, was itself an important place for travel and commerce, and therefore also a place of possibilities and danger. Johnson plunges us into a mood of anxiety and even desperation, without telling us exactly why. In the first stanza, the crossroad seems like a point of fateful, perhaps spiritual encounter; this recalls the folk theme of a crossroad as the scene of a Faustian meeting with the Devil." See Graeme

M. Boone, Fred McDowell, Miles Pratcher, and Fanny Davis, "Twelve Key Recordings," in *The Cambridge Companion to Blues and Gospel Music*, ed. Allan Moore (Cambridge: Cambridge University Press, 2002), 66; and Edmund Wilson, *The Wound and the Bow: Seven Studies in Literature* (Athens: Ohio University Press, 1997), 223–42.

24. Stephen Calt, *I'd Rather Be the Devil: Skip James and the Blues* (Chicago: Chicago Review Press, 1994). In his blurb for Calt's book, Crumb writes: "This is the real thing. I drink up every word. This and Calt's life of Charley Patton are the best books ever written on the subject of old-time blues. Calt cuts through the bullshit with cold precision, punctures the romanticism that coats these blues legends like congealed chicken fat. But hell, I'll still be romantic about old music even *after* Calt is finished with it—I can't help it when I listen to the records. The more I know the truth about it, the better I like it, actually: It makes it all the more interesting. Also, there's a hidden, extremely *dry* humor in Calt's writing that I greatly enjoy. I can imagine some people missing this and being annoyed at the—shall we say—'*down beat*' mood. For me it's *just right*." Crumb clearly admired Stephen Calt's writing, because he also included a story by him entitled "The Tunnel of Love" in *Weirdo* and created three illustrations to accompany it. See *Weirdo*, no. 19 (Winter 1986–1987), 44–47. Crumb points out that Paramount Records, located in Wisconsin, went out of business in 1932. Crumb believed that the design of their ads "is really tops and I've wondered whether there were different artists that did the drawing and lettering, but I just don't know. I've stolen lots of design ideas from these, I use them a lot. Steal from the best, that's my motto." See Hignite, *In the Studio*, 35; Patrick Lepetit, *The Esoteric Secrets of Surrealism: Origins, Magic, and Secret Societies* (Rochester, VT: Inner Traditions, 2014), 109; R. Crumb, "Crazy Music," in Paul Buhle, ed., *Popular Culture in America* (Minneapolis: University of Minnesota Press, 1987), 108, 110; R. Crumb, "Hey Boparee Bop," in *R. Crumb's Head Comix* (1968), 47–48 (first appeared in *Yarrowstalks*, no. 2, 1967); R. Crumb, introduction to *The Complete Crumb*, vol. 4, *Mr. Sixties!* (1997), viii; Pekar, "Rapping about Cartoonists," 683–84, 686; and *The R. Crumb Sketchbooks*, vols. 7–12, 9:123.

25. Crumb, *R. Crumb's Dream Diary*, 261; and Robert Crumb, "Walkin' the Streets," *Zap*, no. 15 (2004). The earlier, incomplete, four-page 1992 version was titled "Days O' My Youth" and has been published in *Die vielen Gesichter des Robert Crumb*, ed. Severin Heinisch (Krems an der Donau, Austria: Karikatur Museum Krems and St. Pölten, 2002), 64–67.

26. Corey K. Creekmur, "Multiculturalism Meets the Counterculture: Representing Racial Difference in Robert Crumb's Underground Comix," in *Representing Multiculturalism in Comics and Graphic Novels*, ed. Carolene Ayaka and Ian Hague (New York: Routledge, 2015), 19.

27. *The Comics Journal*, no. 121 (April 1988), 54; and *The R. Crumb Sketchbooks*, vols. 7–12, 7:202.

CHAPTER 3

1. Mercier, "Who's Afraid of R. Crumb?," 207–8.

2. For a thoughtful review of the Library of America's first two volumes covering Dick, see Stephanie Burt, "Kick Over the Scenery," *London Review of Books* 30, no. 13 (July 3, 2008): 23–25.

3. Joseph Witek, ed., *Art Spiegelman: Conversations* (Jackson: University Press of Mississippi, 2007), 177–79; and Harold Schechter, "Deep Meaning Comix: The Archetypal

World of R. Crumb," *San José Studies* 3, no. 3 (November 1977): 8, 9, 18. Schechter has coauthored, with Jonna Gormely Semeiks, a book of essays on popular culture organized according to Jungian archetypes, and he includes works by Crumb in two of his chapters: "The Shadow" (a selection from the "Whitman" series), "The Trickster" ("Squirrely the Squirrel"), "The Temptress," "The Mother," "The Wise Old Man," "The Helpful Animal and the Holy Fool," "The Quest," and "Rebirth." See Harold Schechter and Jonna Gormely Semeiks, *Patterns in Popular Culture: A Sourcebook for Writers* (New York: Harper and Row, 1980). One can easily see that many of Crumb's works would fit neatly into one or more of these eight categories.

4. "Mother Hulda," in *Weirdo*, no. 19 (Winter 1986–1987); and "Goldilocks," in *Weirdo*, no. 11 (Fall 1984).

5. "Rough Women of the Dark Ages," in *The R. Crumb Sketchbooks*, vols. 7–12, 11:77–78; the illustration is based on Gregory of Tours, *The History of the Franks*, trans. Lewis Thorpe (London: Penguin, 1974), 521–22. See also Schechter, "Deep Meaning Comix," 8, 9; and Carl G. Jung, *Four Archetypes: Mother, Rebirth, Spirit, Trickster* (Princeton, NJ: Princeton University Press, 1970).

6. Crumb and Poplaski, *The R. Crumb Handbook*, 394, 390. In a fascinating January 1975 entry in his *Sketchbooks*, Crumb includes a page entitled "Reality Is Limited by the Experience of the Senses." Crumb is exploring the question of the quest for knowledge beyond the physical realm and invokes Jung's collective unconscious: "There's a barrier limiting my perception of reality.... The barriers of sight, sound, taste, touch, smell.... What other senses are there? ... There is the subtler level of psychic sensing of reality.... It is something that is difficult to pin-down and affects most of us only on a deep unconscious level.... Some people's psychic sense is stronger than others.... Mine isn't that strong, I don't think.... It's a sense I'm not very tuned into.... What does the psychic sense perceive? Only the minds of other humans? The collective unconscious? Is the psychic sense the key to breaking the barrier of the five senses? How does one develop and strengthen the psychic sense?" See *The R. Crumb Sketchbook, November 1974–January 1978* (Frankfurt: Zweitausendeins, 1978), 53.

7. Erik Davis, *The Visionary State: A Journey Through California's Visionary Landscape* (San Francisco: Chronicle Books, 2006); Jeffrey J. Kripal, *Esalen: America and the Religion of No Religion* (Chicago: University of Chicago Press, 2008); David Stephen Calonne, *Henry Miller (Critical Lives)* (London: Reaktion Books, 2014), 88; Harry Oldmeadow, *Journeys East: 20th Century Western Encounters with Eastern Religious Traditions* (Bloomington, IN: World Wisdom, 2004), 271; and David Schneider, *Crowded by Beauty: The Life and Zen of Poet Philip Whalen* (Oakland: University of California Press, 2015), 52. Robert S. Ellwood has chronicled the shifts in American consciousness in *The Fifties Spiritual Marketplace: American Religion in a Decade of Conflict* (New Brunswick, NJ: Rutgers University Press, 1997) and *The Sixties Spiritual Awakening: American Religion Moving from Modern to Postmodern* (New Brunswick, NJ: Rutgers University Press, 1994), which led to the spiritual revolution of the Beats and the hippies. On the spiritual ferment in the Bay Area, also see Hugh McLeod, *The Religious Crisis of the 1960s* (New York: Oxford University Press, 2007), 132–34; and Rick Fields, *How the Swans Came to the Lake: A Narrative History of Buddhism in America* (Boston: Shambhala, 1992), 168–70. On Suzuki, see Lopez, *A Modern Buddhist Bible*, 127–37.

8. On Pagels in California, see Elaine Pagels, *Why Religion? A Personal Story* (New York: HarperCollins, 2018); Denis Johnston, *Precipitations: Contemporary American Poetry as*

Occult Practice (Middletown, CT: Wesleyan University Press, 2002), 12; Rebecca Peabody, ed., *Pacific Standard Time: Los Angeles Art, 1945–1980* (Los Angeles: Getty Research Institute, 2011), 89; and Michael Duncan and Kristine McKenna, *Semina Culture: Wallace Berman and His Circle* (New York: Distributed Art Publishers, 2005), 104, 108, 109. On Berman, see Thomas Crow, *The Rise of the Sixties: American and European Art in the Ear of Dissent* (New Haven, CT: Yale University Press, 2004), 70–71.

9. Blake Bell, *Strange and Stranger: The World of Steve Ditko* (Seattle: Fantagraphics, 2008), 75; and Bradford W. Wright, *Comic Book Nation: The Transformation of Youth Culture in America* (Baltimore: Johns Hopkins University Press, 2001), 2013.

10. Rosenkranz, *Rebel Visions*, 171. See also John Thompson, *Yellow Dog: Robert Crumb and Origin of Comix* (Lexington, KY: Satya Designs, 2017). On Thompson, also see Mark James Estren, *A History of Underground Comics* (Oakland: Ronin Publishing, 2012), 167–75, 215; Monte Beauchamp, ed., *The Life and Times of R. Crumb: Comments from Contemporaries* (New York: St. Martin's Press, 1988), 64; and Davis, "The Counterculture and the Occult," 640–41. See also Erik Davis, "Pop Arcana (6): Rick Griffin, Superstar," HiLoBrow, July 24, 2012, http://hilobrow.com/2012/07/24/pop-arcana-6/. On Griffin, see Danky and Kitchen, *Underground Classics*, 75, 76.

11. Albright, *Art in the San Francisco Bay Area*, 175.

12. Kinney, "The Rise and Fall of the Underground Comix Movement."

13. Crumb, "The Religious Experience of Philip K. Dick"; Philip K. Dick, *The Exegesis of Philip K. Dick*, ed. Pamela Jackson and Jonathan Lethem (New York: Houghton Mifflin Harcourt, 2011); and Victoria Nelson, *The Secret Life of Puppets* (Cambridge, MA: Harvard University Press, 2001), 175–76.

14. Crumb and Poplaski, *The R. Crumb Handbook*, 44; and John Hick, *An Interpretation of Religion: Human Responses to the Transcendent* (New Haven, CT: Yale University Press, 1989), 166–67.

15. Lewis Ellingham and Kevin Killian, *Poet Be Like God: Jack Spicer and the San Francisco Renaissance* (Hanover, NH: University Press of New England, 1998), 21, 22; Lisa Jarnot, *Robert Duncan, the Ambassador from Venus: A Biography* (Berkeley: University of California Press, 2012), 112; and Gregg Rickman, *To the High Castle, Philip K. Dick: A Life, 1928–1962* (Long Beach, CA: Fragments West/Valentine Press, 1989), 174–77.

16. Mercier, "Who's Afraid of R. Crumb?," 217–18. Crumb also discusses this difficult period in "R. Crumb's Cavalcade of Sketches," *Weirdo*, no. 21 (Fall 1987). Crumb reveals: "All these drawings and cartoon strips were done in a period of my life when I was heavily depressed. . . . More than my usual normal level of depression. It was a hard year, from early '85 to mid '86. . . . What's interesting though is how my drawing reached a level of seething intensity during this time when things looked black. They shook me down, wrung me out, drained my blood . . . stripped me bare and left only the bones bleaching in the sun. . . . They loved me to death, smothered me with attention . . . Thousands of them . . . Their smiling faces. . . . It makes me shudder to think back on it."

17. Mercier, "Who's Afraid of R. Crumb?," 207–8.

18. Berkson, "Pyramid and the Shoe," 72; Hignite, *In the Studio*, 17; and Gregg Rickman, *Philip K. Dick: The Last Testament* (Long Beach, CA: Fragments West/Valentine Press, 1985).

Crumb assembled his narrative by ranging back and forth in Rickman's book to select his extracts: chapter 9, 35–36; chapter 10, 43–45; chapter 9, 37, 39–40; chapter 13, 60–61; chapter 34, 217–18; chapter 28, 173; chapter 31, 193; chapter 29, 179; and chapter 32, 222. Two brief passages are taken from Jay Kinney, "The Mysterious Revelations of Philip K. Dick," *Gnosis*, no. 1 (Fall–Winter 1985), 7. For a recent reflection on Dick's experiences, see Kyle Arnold, *The Divine Madness of Philip K. Dick* (New York: Oxford University Press, 2017).

19. Brian Tucker, "Gotthold Ephraim Lessing's *Laocoön* and the Lessons of Comics," in *Teaching the Graphic Novel*, ed. Stephen E. Tabachnick (New York: Modern Language Association of America, 2009), 28.

20. Assaf Gamzou and Ken Koltun-Fromm, "Introduction: Comics and Sacred Texts," in *Comics and Sacred Texts: Reimagining Religion and Graphic Narratives*, ed. Assaf Gamzou and Ken Koltun-Fromm (Jackson: University Press of Mississippi, 2018), xii–xiii; Erik Davis, *TechGnosis: Myth, Magic and Mysticism in the Age of Information* (London: Serpent's Tail, 2004), 332; Samuel J. Umland, "To Flee from Dionysus: *Enthousiasmos* from 'Upon the Dull Earth' to *VALIS*," in *Philip K. Dick: Contemporary Critical Interpretations*, ed. Samuel J. Umland (Westport, CT: Greenwood Press, 1995), 82; Thierry Groensteen, "Why Are Comics Still in Search of Cultural Legitimization?," in *A Comic Studies Reader*, ed. Jeet Heer and Kent Worcester (Jackson: University Press of Mississippi, 2009), 10; and Hans Jonas, *The Gnostic Religion: The Message of the Alien God and the Beginnings of Christianity* (Boston: Beacon Press, 1970), 37, 45. See also Kurt Rudolph, *Gnosis: The Nature and History of Gnosticism* (New York: HarperCollins, 1987), 71.

21. Lawrence Sutin, ed., *In Pursuit of Valis: Selections from the Exegesis* (Novato, CA: Underwood-Miller, 1971), 102, quoted in Kripal, *Mutants and Mystics*, 273, 21. Crumb met Jim Morrison through the poet Michael McClure but was unimpressed by him. See Alex Wood, comp., "Crumb on Others, part 3," The Official Crumb Site, https://www.crumbproducts. com/pages/about/crumbonothers3.html. See also Granholm, "The Occult and Comics," 504; and Philip K. Dick, *VALIS* (New York: Bantam Books, 1981). For two slightly different translations, see the Gospel of Thomas in *The Gnostic Bible*, ed. Willis Barnstone and Marvin Meyer (Boston: New Seeds, 2006), section 70: "Yeshua said, / If you bring forth what is within you, what you have will save you. / If you have nothing within you, / what you do not have within you will kill you"; and section 42, "Yeshua said, / Be passersby," 62, 54. Elaine Pagels, *Beyond Belief: The Secret Gospel of Thomas* (New York: Vintage Books, 2003), 53. On images of Christ in the medieval period, see Alison Milbank, "Seeing Double: The Crucified Christ in Western Mediaeval Art," in *The Oxford Handbook of Christology*, ed. Francesca Aran Murphy (Oxford: Oxford University Press, 2015), 215–32. One of the most popular, omnipresent—and highly sentimentalized, "idealized," and historically dubious—images of Jesus against which Crumb is likely reacting in his own depictions is Warner Sallman's *Head of Christ*. See David Morgan, *Visual Piety: A History and Theory of Popular Religious Images* (Berkeley: University of California Press, 1998).

22. Philip K. Dick, "If You Find This World Bad, You Should See Some of the Others," in *The Shifting Realities of Philip K. Dick: Selected Literary and Philosophical Writings*, ed. Lawrence Sutin (New York: Vintage Books, 1995), 252; and Vladimir Nabokov, *Lectures on Literature* (San Diego: Harcourt, 1980).

23. Pekar, "Rapping about Cartoonists," 682. On comics artists' responses to the "malaise" of the American seventies, see Matthew Pustz, "'Paralysis and Stagnation and Drift': America's Malaise as Demonstrated in Comic Books of the 1970s," in *Comic Books and American Cultural History: An Anthology*, ed. Matthew Pustz (New York: Continuum, 2012), 136–51. See also Richard Wilhelm, trans., *The I Ching or Book of Changes: The Richard Wilhelm Translation* (Princeton, NJ: Princeton University Press, 1971), 139–42.

24. Gérard Genette, "Narrative Discourse," in *Literature in the Modern World: Critical Essays and Documents*, ed. Dennis Walder (Oxford: Oxford University Press, 1990), 142.

25. Crumb and Poplaski, *The R. Crumb Handbook*, 56. In his *Sketchbooks*, Crumb returns to this thesis: "Mass media is almost entirely garbage. A tiny percentage of it has any value beyond the lowest level of passing entertainment, distraction, propaganda. Millions of lives are squandered, their potential for a high level of consciousness derailed, their chance to appreciate the real wonder and mystery of the world thrown away, shoved aside, smashed to smithereens by the powerful onslaught of the media. . . . I know because I'm one of them. My memory is filled with mass media junk—worthless, cheap, tacky, manipulative crap from television, movies, radio, magazines, newspapers, comic books." *The R. Crumb Sketchbooks*, vols. 7–12, 10:185.

26. Philip K. Dick, "How to Build a Universe," in *The Shifting Realities of Philip K. Dick*, 263–64.

27. Dick, *VALIS*, sec. 10, 164.

28. Christopher Grau, ed., *Philosophers Explore* The Matrix (New York: Oxford University Press, 2005); Umland, "To Flee from Dionysus," 84; and Robert Crumb, "Can You Stand Alone and Face Up to the Universe?," *Hup*, no. 4 (1992). For examples of Chick tracts, see Chick Publications, https://www.chick.com/reading/tracts/0001/0001_01.asp; Jason C. Bivins, *Religion of Fear: The Politics of Horror in Conservative Evangelicalism* (New York: Oxford University Press, 2008), 45–51; Jason A. Hentschel, "The King James Only Movement," in *The Oxford Handbook of the Bible in America*, ed. Paul C. Gutjahr (New York: Oxford University Press, 2017), 232–33; Andrew T. Coates, "The Bible and Graphic Novels and Comic Books: Telling Bible Stories with Images," in *The Oxford Handbook of the American Bible*, ed. Paul C. Gutjahr (New York: Oxford University Press, 2017), 457; and Orcutt, "Religion," 746–47.

29. Blaise Pascal, *Pensées*, trans. A. J. Krailsheimer (London: Penguin, 1995). Krailsheimer translates: "The eternal silence of these infinite spaces fills me with dread," 66. Interview by Gary Groth, in Michael Dean, ed., *The Comics Journal Library*, vol. 9, *Zap, The Interviews* (Seattle: Fantagraphics, 2015); and Robert Crumb and Aline Kominsky-Crumb, "Aline and Bob in 'A Constipated Life,'" in *Drawn Together*, 149.

30. R. Crumb, "The Exegesis of the Soul," in *The R. Crumb Sketchbooks*, vols. 7–12, 11:40–41; and Giovanni Filoramo, *A History of Gnosticism* (Oxford: Blackwell, 1996), xvi–xvii. See also Wouter J. Hanegraaff, "Gnosis," in *The Cambridge Handbook of Western Mysticism and Esotericism*, ed. Glenn Alexander Magee (Cambridge: Cambridge University Press, 2016), 381–92; and George, *The Comics Journal Library*, vol. 3, *R. Crumb*, 15.

31. Carl G. Jung, *The Red Book*, ed. Sonu Shamdasan (New York: W. W. Norton, 2009).

32. Jung, *The Red Book*.

33. Kripal, *Esalen*.

CHAPTER 4

1. Gary Groth, introduction to *Your Vigor for Life Appalls Me: Robert Crumb Letters, 1958–1977*, ed. Ilse Thompson (Seattle: Fantagraphics, 1998), ix.

2. Goodrick, "Apex Interview: Robert Crumb," 13.

3. George Cotkin, *Existential America* (Baltimore: Johns Hopkins University Press, 2003), 212–13.

4. Crumb, *Your Vigor for Life Appalls Me*, 209, 153.

5. Groth, introduction to *Your Vigor for Life Appalls Me*, x.

6. See Laura Canis and Paul Canis, "Jean-Paul Sartre Meets Enid Coleslaw: Existential Themes in *Ghost World*," in *Comics as Philosophy*, ed. Jeff McLaughlin (Jackson: University Press of Mississippi, 2005), 130–52. Keshni Kashyap narrates her experiences studying philosophy in a southern California high school and begins her tale: "Dear Mr. Jean-Paul Sartre, I know that you are dead and old and also a philosopher. So, on an obvious level, you and I do not have a lot in common." Keshni Kashyap, *Tina's Mouth: An Existential Comic Diary*, illustrated by Mari Araki (New York: Houghton Mifflin Harcourt, 2012), 3. For commentary on Kashyap, see Leah Hochman, "The Ineffability of Form: Speaking and Seeing the Sacred in *Tina's Mouth* and *The Rabbi's Cat*," in *Comics and Sacred Texts: Reimagining Religion and Graphic Narratives*, ed. Assaf Gamzou and Ken Koltun-Fromm (Jackson: University Press of Mississippi, 2018), 43–55.

7. Alex Wood, comp., "Crumb on Others, part 5," The Official Crumb Site, http://www.crumbproducts.com/pages/about/crumbonothers5.html; and Robert Crumb, *Nausea, Hup*, no. 3 (1989).

8. See Will Pritchard, "New Light on Crumb's Boswell," *Eighteenth-Century Studies* 42, no. 2 (Winter 2009): 300, 306. On *Weirdo*, see George, *The Comics Journal Library*, vol. 3, *R. Crumb*, 11; Jon B. Cooke, ed., *The Book of Weirdo* (San Francisco: Last Gasp, 2018); and Crumb, *The Weirdo Years*.

9. William B. Jones Jr., *Classics Illustrated: A Cultural History* (Jefferson, NC: McFarland, 2011); and Monika Schmitz-Emans, "Graphic Narrative as World Literature," in *From Comic Strips to Graphic Novels: Contributions to the Theory and History of Graphic Narrative*, ed. Daniel Stein and Jan-Noël Thon (Berlin: Walter de Gruyter, 2015), 397.

10. Crumb, *Your Vigor for Life Appalls Me*, 24, 91. Although Crumb was disappointed by modern efforts to adapt Dickens, J. Hillis Miller has commented concerning Dickens's own original illustrators and the symbiosis between text and image: "A new branch of the interpretation of fiction has recently been opened up by the recovery, for example, of the graphic tradition to which Dickens's illustrators belonged and by the study of Dickens's novels as multi-media collaborative productions. . . . Ours is a visual and a multi-media age, the age of cinema and television. This, it may be, has led to a new recognition that nineteenth-century novels also combined two kinds of signs." See J. Hillis Miller, *Illustration* (London: Reaktion Books, 1992), 61; Delmore Schwartz, "Masterpieces as Cartoons," *Partisan Review* 19, no. 4 (July–August 1952): 461–71, reprinted in Jeet Heer and Kent Worcester, eds., *Arguing Comics: Literary Masters on a Popular Medium* (Jackson: University Press of Mississippi, 2004), 52–62; Henry John Pratt, "Comics and Adaptation," in *The Routledge Companion to Comics*, ed. Frank Bramlett, Roy T. Cook, and Aaron Meskin (New York: Routledge, 2017), 235;

and Ari Folman, *Anne Frank's Diary: The Graphic Adaptation*, illustrated by David Polonsky (New York: Pantheon Books, 2018).

11. Bart Beaty, "Featuring Stories by the World's Greatest Authors: Classics Illustrated and the 'Middlebrow Problem' in the Postwar Era," *International Journal of Comic Art* 1, no. 1 (Spring–Summer 1999): 124; and Groensteen, "Why Are Comics Still in Search?," 5.

12. Crumb employs the text of the following edition: Jean-Paul Sartre, *Nausea*, trans. Lloyd Alexander (New York: New Directions, 1969).

13. Beaty, "Featuring Stories by the World's Greatest Authors," 133.

14. Charles Hatfield, *Alternative Comics: An Emerging Literature* (Jackson: University Press of Mississippi, 2005), 12.

15. Fredric Jameson, "The Rhythm of Time," in *Jean-Paul Sartre: Modern Critical Views*, ed. Harold Bloom (New York: Chelsea House, 2001), 27.

16. Estren, *A History of Underground Comics*, 38; and Ronald Hayman, *Sartre: A Biography* (New York: Simon and Schuster, 1987), 102.

17. *A New Literary History of America*, 497; Spiegelman quoted in Michael Silverblatt, "The Cultural Relief of Art Spiegelman," *Tampa Review* 5 (1995), 35.

18. Scott McCloud, *Understanding Comics: The Invisible Art* (Northampton, MA: Tundra Publishing, 1993), 102.

19. Fiene, *R. Crumb, Checklist of Work and Criticism*, v.

20. Maxon Crumb, *Crumb Comics: The Whole Family Is Crazy!*, 130. On Maxon Crumb, see Bob Levin, "Alone in the Western World: The Saga of Maxon Crumb," *The Comics Journal*, no. 217 (November 1999), 78–97.

21. Johanna Drucker, "What Is Graphic about Graphic Novels?," *English Language Notes* 46, no. 2 (Fall–Winter 2008): 39; and Crumb, *Your Vigor for Life Appalls Me*, 159, 174.

22. On Sartre's mistaken attribution of the singer of "Some of These Days," see Cotkin, *Existential America*, 162; and Crumb, *Your Vigor for Life Appalls Me*, 189.

23. Robert Crumb, "Walkin' the Streets," *Zap*, no. 15 (2004).

24. *The R. Crumb Sketchbooks*, vols. 1–6, vol. 1, June 1964–September 1968, contain page after page of cityscapes, caricaturized faces in the style of George Grosz, his obsessive practicing in rendering buildings from a number of angles. Startling drawing depicts a building from a dizzying perspective above and renders details looking down deeply into its dizzying interior as well as sketches of automobiles. See also Crumb, "The Heap Years of the Auto, 1946–59," in *Odds and Ends*, n.p.

25. R. Crumb, "Life Certainly Is 'Existential'!," *Weirdo*, no. 14 (Fall 1985). Crumb created an earlier version of "Life Certainly Is 'Existential'" in his *Sketchbooks*. This version follows the same three panels per three-tier format but features a few "existential" situations missing from the final version. Panel 3 reads: "Waiting for someone on a cold night under a bright street light . . . Watching the cars go by wishing your ride would come." In addition, the phrasing of the second panel in the second tier of the original is different in the first panel of the second tier of the sketchbook version, which reads: "It's . . . that queezy [*sic*] feeling you get at those moments when you have to accept that life's a lot more tedious and complicated than you'd like it to be." The characters are merely sketched out, without the virtuosic draftsmanship and elaborate shading of the final version. This is an example of the ways the *Sketchbooks* provide an intriguing glimpse into the various choices Crumb made and the problems he confronted during the creative process. See *The R. Crumb Sketchbooks*, vols. 7–12, 7:53.

26. Crumb, *Your Vigor for Life Appalls Me*, 121.

27. Crumb and Poplaski, *The R. Crumb Handbook*, 375.

28. Crumb, *Your Vigor for Life Appalls Me*, xi.

29. Jean-Paul Sartre, *Existentialism Is a Humanism*, trans. Carol Macomber (New Haven, CT: Yale University Press, 2007).

30. R. Crumb, "The Unbearable Tediousness of Being," *McSweeney's Quarterly*, no. 13 (Spring 2004); Crumb, drawing, March 25, 1997, in *The R. Crumb Sketchbooks*, vols. 7–12, 10:173, August 1992–January 1998; and Crumb and Poplaski, *The R. Crumb Handbook*, 378.

31. *The R. Crumb Sketchbook, November 1974–January 1978* (Frankfurt: Zweitausendeins, 1978), 268.

CHAPTER 5

1. Richard Alleva, "Comic Erudition: R. Crumb Meets Kafka," *Commonweal* 129, no. 13 (July 12, 2002): 19. One critic, in his review of the exhibition of Crumb's drawings at the Galerie St. Etienne in New York, takes a contrary view: "The inadvisability of spelling out in images of any sort Kafka's logocentric cosmos does not seem a close call. Yes, Kafka stirs a positive ache for visualization, but to requite the ache, turning on the lights in his darkness, is to wreck his art." Peter Schjeldahl, "Crumb Does Kafka!," *Village Voice*, December 27, 1994, 49. Schjeldahl fails to explain how it is the case that illustrations intended to accompany a biographical and literary introduction to Kafka—executed with great aplomb and skill—end in "wrecking" Kafka's power. David Carrier has correctly observed that the Mairowitz/Crumb collaboration "presents a seriously original theme in a comic," while Stephen E. Tabachnick emphasizes the ways "Crumb's powerful sequential art adaptations, using panels, are one with his illustrations of Kafka's life and show the continuity between his life and art." David Carrier, *The Aesthetics of Comics* (University Park: Pennsylvania State University Press, 2000), 110; and Stephen E. Tabachnick, *The Quest for Jewish Belief and Identity in the Graphic Novel* (Tuscaloosa: University of Alabama Press, 2014), 117. See also Peter Kuper, *Kafkaesque: Fourteen Stories* (New York: W. W. Norton, 2018).

2. "R. Crumb: Kafka Drawings from the Book *Kafka* by Robert Crumb and David Zane Mairowitz," Past Exhibition at Tony Shafrazi Gallery, May 6–July 29, 2011, Artnet, http://www .artnet.com/galleries/tony-shafrazi-gallery/r-crumb-kafka-drawings-from-the/; and Tom Murphy, "Proving that Comics Cross Borders, the 'K: Kafka in Komiks' Exhibition Reaches London," Broken Frontier, November 27, 2014, http://www.brokenfrontier.com/kafka-in -komiks-goethe-institut-london-franz-kafka-comics-exhibition-robert-crumb-jaromir-99/. On the gradual acceptance of Crumb's work by distinguished art museums, see Bart Beaty, *Comics versus Art* (Toronto: University of Toronto Press, 2012), 198–209.

3. George, *The Comics Journal Library*, vol. 3, *R. Crumb*, 99; and Franz Kafka, *Letter to the Father/Brief an den Vater*, trans. Ernst Kaiser and Eithne Wilkins (New York: Schocken Books, 2015).

4. Crumb and Poplaski, *The R. Crumb Handbook*, 364; and Max Weber, "Science as a Vocation," in *From Max Weber: Essays in Sociology*, ed. Hans Heinrich Gerth and Charles Wright Mills (Oxford: Oxford University Press, 1958), 129–56.

5. Allusions to *The Prisoner* appear in graphic novels by Grant Morrison and Alan Moore: in Morrison's *The Invisibles* and Moore's *Watchmen*, *The League of Extraordinary Gentlemen: The Black Dossier*, and *V for Vendetta*.

6. Stanley Corngold, "1914, July: Ecstatic Release from Personality," in *A New History of German Literature*, ed. David E. Wellbery and Judith Ryan (Cambridge, MA: Harvard University Press, 2004), 703.

7. Steven Marx, "R. Crumb: The Sacred and the Profane, part 1," *Columbia Daily Spectator*, March 27, 1969, 4.

8. Witek, *Comic Books as History*, 129; and Robert Crumb, introduction to *American Splendor: The Life and Times of Harvey Pekar*, by Harvey Pekar (New York: Ballantine Books, 2003), n.p.

9. Will Eisner, *A Contract with God* (New York: W. W. Norton, 2006).

10. Coates, "The Bible and Graphic Novels and Comic Books," 455. Crumb and Aline have long collaborated on a joint comic. On Crumb's relationship to Jewish culture, see Miriam Libicki, "Jewish Memoir Goes Pow! Zap! Oy!," in *The Jewish Graphic Novel: Critical Approaches*, eds. Samantha Baskind and Ranen Omer-Sherman (New Brunswick, NJ: Rutgers University Press, 2008), 253–74.

11. Mercier, "Who's Afraid of R. Crumb?," 197.

12. David Suchoff, *Kafka's Jewish Languages: The Hidden Openness of Tradition* (Philadelphia: University of Pennsylvania Press, 2012), 139, 113–15, 193–95; and Ritchie Robertson, *Kafka: Judaism, Politics, and Literature* (Oxford: Oxford University Press, 1985), 126.

13. David Zane Mairowitz and R. Crumb, *Introducing Kafka* (New York: Totem Books, 1997), 11. The iconography of this scene recalls expressionist director Paul Wegener's film *The Golem* (1915). See Monika Schmitz-Emans, *Literatur-Comics: Adaptionen und Transformationen der Weltliteratur* (Berlin: Walter de Gruyter, 2012), 185.

14. Mairowitz and Crumb, *Introducing Kafka*, 19; and Robertson, *Kafka: Judaism, Politics, and Literature*, 148.

15. Steven Heller, *Comics Sketchbooks: The Private Worlds of Today's Most Creative Talents* (New York: Thames and Hudson, 2012), 64.

16. Di Liddo, "Transcending Comics," 326; and Stuart Clark, *Thinking with Demons: The Idea of Witchcraft in Early Modern Europe* (Oxford: Oxford University Press, 1999), 219. For Alan Moore's comments on Crumb's work, see Beauchamp, *The Life and Times of R. Crumb*, 71–82.

17. Mairowitz and Crumb, *Introducing Kafka*, 29.

18. See Chute, *Disaster Drawn*, 157. Spiegelman has remarked: "I liked Kafka when I was growing up as a kid. I read Kafka. That was important to me. . . . For philosophers—well, I read a lot of existentialism when I was in high school, that helped shape me." See Witek, *Art Spiegelman: Conversations*, 139.

19. Witek, *Art Spiegelman: Conversations*, 44, 50.

20. See Alice W. Flaherty, *The Midnight Disease: The Drive to Write, Writer's Block, and the Creative Brain* (New York: Houghton Mifflin Harcourt, 2004), 82–83.

21. On Masereel, see David A. Berona, *Wordless Books: The Original Graphic Novels* (New York: Harry N. Abrams, 2008), 14–39. On Crumb and German expressionism, see Paul Buhle, "Questions for . . . R. Crumb," *Cultural Correspondence, Underground Cartoonists: Ten Years*

Later, no. 5 (Summer–Fall 1977), 54; and Art Spiegelman, afterword to *Breakdowns*, n.p. The development of the woodcut novel has been traced "to the combined inspiration provided by German expressionism, the silent cinema, and the comics in newspapers and magazines." See Barbara Postema, "Silent Comics," in *The Routledge Companion to Comics*, ed. Frank Bramlett, Roy T. Cooke, and Aaron Meskin (New York: Routledge, 2017), 202; and Corngold, "1914, July: Ecstatic Release from Personality," 704. Kafka's "religious" attitude toward his writing is confirmed in an interesting interview Kafka had with the theosophist Rudolf Steiner in 1911. Kafka in his *Diary* states that, while writing, he experienced "states described by you [Dr. Steiner] . . . in which I felt not only at my own limits, but at the frontiers of the human altogether." See Walter H. Sokel, "Between Gnosticism and Jehovah: The Dilemma in Kafka's Religious Attitude," in *The Allure of Gnosticism: The Gnostic Experience in Jungian Psychology and Contemporary Culture*, ed. Robert Segal (Chicago: Open Court, 1995), 152.

22. *The R. Crumb Sketchbook, November 1974–January 1978* (Frankfurt: Zweitausendeins, 1978), 302; Dagmar Freuchen, ed., *Peter Freuchen's Book of the Eskimos* (Cleveland: World Publishing Company, 1961), 280–81; and Mairowitz and Crumb, *Introducing Kafka*, 142.

23. Franz Kafka, letter to Oskar Pollak (January 27, 1904), in *Letters to Friends, Family and Editors* (New York: Schocken Books, 2016), 16.

24. Thomas Albright, "Zap, Snatch and Crumb," *Rolling Stone*, March 1, 1969, 25.

25. Michel Serres, "Light," *Yale French Studies*, nos. 131–32 (2017): 220.

26. James Engell, *The Creative Imagination: Enlightenment to Romanticism* (Cambridge, MA: Harvard University Press, 1981), 235; and Gotthold Ephraim Lessing, *Laocoön: An Essay on the Limits of Painting and Poetry*, trans. Edward Allen McCormick (Baltimore: Johns Hopkins University Press, 1984). On Lessing, see also Daniel Albright, *Untwisting the Serpent: Modernism in Music, Literature, and Other Arts* (Chicago: University of Chicago Press, 2000).

27. Crumb, *Your Vigor for Life Appalls Me*, 49.

28. R. Crumb, "The Many Faces of R. Crumb," *XYZ Comics* (1972),18; and R. Crumb, "I Remember the Sixties: R. Crumb Looks Back!," in Crumb, *The Weirdo Years*, 66.

29. *The R. Crumb Sketchbooks*, vols. 7–12, 12:218.

30. George, *The Comics Journal Library*, vol. 3, *R. Crumb*, 56.

31. Joseph Witek, "Comic Modes: Caricature and Illustration in the Crumb Family's *Dirty Laundry*," in *Critical Approaches to Comics: Theories and Methods*, ed. Matthew J. Smith and Randy Duncan (New York: Routledge, 2012), 36; and Crumb, *R. Crumb's Dream Diary*, 63. Crumb includes four pages starring a character named "Shmendrik" in his *Sketchbooks*. In the first drawing, he admires an attractive female but then laments that "she's only looking for some big, powerful 'alpha male.'" In the second, three-page narrative, "Shmendrik Is Such a 'Basket Case,'" he is taken to a hospital and put in bed by orderlies, to whom he complains: "I can't cope . . . It's too much . . . I'm so embarrassed . . . sniff . . ." The story concludes with Shmendrik possessed by anger: "How I despise th' human race . . . hateful species . . . I hope there's a nuclear war just so I can have a few moments of pleasure knowing all these assholes are getting vaporized into oblivion . . . hhnyeah . . ." *The R. Crumb Sketchbooks*, vols. 7–12, 8:217, 219–21. Also Walter Benjamin, "Franz Kafka: On the Tenth Anniversary of His Death," in *Illuminations*, ed. Hannah Arendt (New York: Schocken Books, 1973), 132; and Miriam Hansen, "Of Mice and Ducks: Benjamin and Adorno on Disney," *South Atlantic Quarterly* 92, no. 1 (Winter 1993): 45. Hansen speaks of "the forgotten alien that is part of oneself," which

precisely describes Crumb's relationship to his own body and thus to his inner spirituality that he strives to recover.

32. John Finlay, *Hermetic Light: Essays on the Gnostic Spirit in Modern Literature and Thought*, ed. David Middleton (Santa Barbara, CA: John Daniel, 1994), 135; Angus Fletcher, *Allegory: The Theory of a Symbolic Mode* (Ithaca, NY: Cornell University Press, 1982), 275; and Walter Burkert, *Creation of the Sacred* (Cambridge, MA: Harvard University Press, 1996), 51.

33. Erich Heller, *Franz Kafka* (New York: Viking, 1974), 105.

CHAPTER 6

1. David Colton, "Illustrator R. Crumb Is Drawn to God with His Latest Project," *USA Today*, October 18, 2009, https://www.dcoltonnow.com/r-crumb/; and J. P. Fokkelman, "Genesis," in *The Literary Guide to the Bible*, ed. Robert Alter and Frank Kermode (Cambridge, MA: Harvard University Press, 1987), 36.

2. See *The R. Crumb Sketchbooks*, vols. 7–12, 8:214, for a drawing depicting "1500 B. C. The Hittites Push into Assyria, Thence down the Euphrates to Babylon." Crumb also created a striking portrait of the goddess Inanna from *Gilgamesh* in 2009; for source material in *Sketchbook*, vol. 11, Crumb employed Jeremy Black and Anthony Green's *Gods, Demons and Symbols of Ancient Mesopotamia: An Illustrated Dictionary* (London: British Museum Press, 1998), 52. Crumb writes: "Ancient Mesopotamia: 'A worshipper pours a libation before a god, (probably Iskur) riding in his chariot, drawn by a winged lion-dragon. A naked goddess stands on the back of the beast.' Akkadian period, (2390–2210 B.C.)." See *Sketchbook*, vol. 11, 79. On the same page of *Sketchbook*, vol. 11, Crumb copies a "stone relief in the royal palace of the Assyrian King Assurnasirpal II (Reigned 883–58 B.C.)," which bears a striking resemblance to the head and face of his infamous "Vulture Demoness" character. The source for this image is Black and Green, *Demons and Symbols of Ancient Mesopotamia*, 100; see also Allen Salkin, "Sketching His Way through Genesis," *New York Times*, October 18, 2009, 21. Crumb refers to creation stories from ancient Babylonian and Sumerian tablets and also creates a humorous four-panel narrative entitled "Just Like Mickey Finnegan, You Must Begin Again," in which he depicts "circa 2500 B.C., in the mountains just above the new civilization of Sumer, in Mesopotamia," two bearded figures in sandals who are members of a neighboring tribe discussing their discovery of the strange "cuneiform clay tablet" that they stole "out of a house down in Sumer last week when we made that raid." They puzzle over the strange writing on the tablet, and one man asks the other: "What is the purpose of this thing??," and the other responds: "I tell you I don't know, but I know one thing, they have men in those cities of theirs who do nothing all day but sit and make those things . . . They are pale, sheltered men, like old children! They ran from us like frightened rabbits!!" *The R. Crumb Sketchbooks*, vols. 7–12, 12:163, 55; J. R. Porter, *The Illustrated Guide to the Bible* (Oxford: Oxford University Press, 1995), 33; *The Comics Journal*, no. 301, 26; and Françoise Mouly, "Comic Strip by R. Crumb: The Book of Genesis," *New Yorker*, June 8 and 15, 2009, 90. On *Gilgamesh*, see James B. Pritchard, *Archaeology and the Old Testament* (Princeton, NJ: Princeton University Press, 1958), 170–83. For a recent illustrated version of *Gilgamesh* that is influenced by Crumb, see Kent H. Dixon and Kevin H. Dixon, *The Epic of Gilgamesh* (New York: Seven Stories Press, 2018).

3. Widmer, "R. Crumb: The Art of Comics no. 1," 25.

4. R. Crumb, introduction to *The Book of Genesis Illustrated by R. Crumb*.

5. Coates, "The Bible and Graphic Novels and Comic Books," 456, 458; Emily Laycock, "Graphic Apocalypse and the Wizard of Grotesque: Basil Wolverton, the Worldwide Church of God, and Prophecy," in *The End Will Be Graphic: Apocalyptic in Comic Books and Graphic Novels*, ed. Dan W. Clanton Jr. (Sheffield, England: Sheffield Phoenix Press, 2012), 20; and interview by Gary Groth, in Dean, *The Comics Journal Library*, vol. 9, *Zap*, 38.

6. Edmund Leach, "Fishing for Men on the Edge of the Wilderness," in *The Literary Guide to the Bible*, ed. Robert Alter and Frank Kermode (Cambridge, MA: Harvard University Press, 1987), 580. Also see Edmund Leach, "Genesis as Myth," in *Myth and Cosmos: Readings in Mythology and Symbolism*, ed. John C. Middleton (Garden City, NY: Natural History Press, 1967), 1–13.

7. Interview by Gary Groth, in Dean, *The Comics Journal Library*, vol. 9, *Zap*, 31. A reviewer of the 207 drawings from Crumb's *Genesis* exhibited at the David Zwirner Gallery commented: "Mr. Crumb may be irreverent, but in his attention to every detail of word and image he is as devout as any medieval manuscript illuminator." Ken Johnson, "The Bible Illuminated: R. Crumb's Book of Genesis," *New York Times*, March 19, 2010.

8. Beth Davies-Stofka, "The Bible in Comics: Genesis," *Sacred Matters: Religious Currents in Culture*, March 5, 2014, https://sacredmattersmagazine.com/the-bible-in-comics-genesis/. Arthur W. Frank points out that "Crumb's text is Robert Alter's scholarly translation, but when the words are paired with the images, the telling is anything but the kind of verbatim rendering . . . typical of biblical readings." See Arthur W. Frank, *Letting Stories Breathe: A Socio-Narratology* (Chicago: University of Chicago Press, 2010), 186. Shashi Tharoor, "How Hinduism Has Persisted for 4,000 Years," *Wall Street Journal*, January 17, 2019, https://www.wsj.com/articles/how-hinduism-has-persisted-for-4-000-years-11547770953; and R. Crumb, "Jesus People, USA Interviews R. Crumb, Underground Pornographer and All-Around Lost Soul (A Hypothetical Situation) by R. Crumb," *Zap*, no. 11. Crumb's concern about Christian fundamentalists has surfaced in a dream that he has entitled "Dream of Right-Wing Christians; I Am Murdered." In the dream, Crumb observes a Black woman attempting to purchase a present for her children. In Crumb's dream, "the white clerks in the store had some objection to this thing based on some alleged anti-Christian message it carried." Crumb comes to the woman's defense and argues with the clerks, believing that "their attitudes were based on ignorant, backwards thinking." The present the woman was buying had "cartoon images on it done in a modern Disney style, figures from myths or gothic-type tales that looked bland and harmless to me, but perhaps could be interpreted as treating religious subjects too humorously." Crumb intervenes with the clerks and angrily objects to their behavior, while the "black woman spoke up again, asserting her right to purchase the thing if she wanted to." At the end of the dream, three Christian fundamentalists—two girls and a young man—threaten Crumb, and one of the girls fires a gun at him "point blank," killing him. At that point, he wakes up from the dream. See Crumb, *R. Crumb's Dream Diary*, 191–95. Crumb's impressive knowledge of the Bible is also exhibited in *The R. Crumb Sketchbook: November 1974–January 1978* (Frankfurt: Zweitausendeins, 1978), 290, where he quotes Ecclesiastes 10:20, Ecclesiastes 12:12, and Timothy 1:5–8. On June 9, 1975, he quotes Isaiah 64:6, Mark 4:22, and Romans 3:10 (106). Jeet Heer, "Genesis Revisited," *The Comics Journal*, no. 301, 113; and Crumb, *Your Vigor*

for Life Appalls Me, 45. For Said on Sheena, see Edward Said, "Introduction: Homage to Joe Sacco," in *Palestine,* by Joe Sacco (Seattle: Fantagraphics, 2004), ii.

9. Northrop Frye, *The Great Code: The Bible and Literature* (New York: Harcourt Brace Jovanovich, 1982), 107, 191; and David Hajdu, "God Gets Graphic," *New York Times,* October 25, 2009, 17.

10. Widmer, "R. Crumb: The Art of Comics no. 1," 23.

11. Spitznagel, "Robert Crumb Thinks God Might Actually Be Crazy"; and *The R. Crumb Sketchbooks,* vols. 7–12, 12:57.

12. Hermann Gunkel, *The Legends of Genesis: The Biblical Saga and History* (New York: Schocken Books, 1964), 13. The second chapter of Genesis presents the story of creation in two different versions: the first employs "Elohim" for the deity and the second "Yahweh." See John B. Gabel and Charles B. Wheeler, *The Bible as Literature: An Introduction,* 2nd ed. (Oxford: Oxford University Press, 1990), 88. See also Robert Graves and Raphael Patai, *Hebrew Myths* (New York: Doubleday, 1989), 24.

13. Harold Bloom, "Yahweh Meets R. Crumb," *New York Review of Books,* December 3, 2009, 24.

14. Northrop Frye describes "the Gnostic tendency to think of Christianity as totally discontinuous with Judaism, even to think of the Old Testament God as an evil being." See Frye, *The Great Code,* 84.

15. Jacques Lacarrière, *The Gnostics* (San Francisco: City Lights, 1989), 101; and *The R. Crumb Sketchbooks,* vols. 7–12, vol. 12.

16. Kripal, *Mutants and Mystics,* 201; and Spitznagel, "Robert Crumb Thinks God Might Actually Be Crazy."

17. For Crumb on Assyrian art, see Crumb and Poplaski, *The R. Crumb Handbook,* 363. Crumb also was alert to comparisons between ancient Assyrian culture and the modern world. In the *Sketchbooks,* he quotes an Assyrian text: "Our earth is degenerate in these latter days; there are signs that the world is speedily coming to an end; bribery and corruption are common; children no longer obey their parents; every man wants to write a book, and the end is evidently approaching—Assyrian stone tablet, 2800 B.C." See *The R. Crumb Sketchbooks,* vols. 7–12, 8:35.

18. On Assyrian warfare, see Enrico Ascalone, *Mesopotamia* (Berkeley: University of California Press, 2007), 186–201.

19. Spitznagel, "Robert Crumb Thinks God Might Actually Be Crazy"; and Fokkelman, "Genesis," 39.

20. Widmer, "R. Crumb: The Art of Comics no. 1," 26; and *The Comics Journal,* no. 301, 24.

21. Peter Sattler, "Crumb's Limited Literalism: Seeing and Not Seeing in Genesis," Hooded Utilitarian, http://www.hoodedutilitarian.com/2010/08/crumbs-limited-literalism/.

22. Theodore Roethke, "In a Dark Time," in *The Far Field* (New York: Doubleday, 1964); and Fokkelman, "Genesis," 50–51.

23. "Piers Plowman," *The R. Crumb Sketchbooks,* vols. 7–12, vol. 11.

24. Claudia Setzer, "Feminist Interpretation of the Bible," in *The Oxford Handbook of the American Bible,* ed. Paul C. Gutjahr (New York: Oxford University Press, 2017), 164.

25. *The R. Crumb Sketchbooks,* vols. 7–12, 12:38; and Graves and Patai, *Hebrew Myths,* 69. On matriarchy, see Graves and Patai, *Hebrew Myths,* 13; and Ascalone, *Mesopotamia,* 142.

26. "But Rachel has strong qualities that would incline one to suspect that she was some kind of priestess. The household gods were these things belittled as idols by the patriarchal priestly cast who wrote down the stories in the Bible. But Rachel steals an idol from her father's house when they are leaving. These idols found in archaeological digs are almost all entirely female, little female goddess figures, and these things were in the hands of women." See Allen Salkin, "Sketching His Way through Genesis," *New York Times*, October 18, 2009, 21; and Melissa Jackson, quoted in Scott S. Elliott, "Transrendering Biblical Bodies: Reading Sex in *The Action Bible* and *Genesis Illustrated*, in *Comics and Sacred Texts: Reimagining Religion and Graphic Narratives*, ed. Assaf Gamzou and Ken Koltun-Fromm (Jackson: University Press of Mississippi, 2018), 143.

27. Widmer, "R. Crumb: The Art of Comics no. 1," 51; and Reed Johnson, "The Creation of R. Crumb's Genesis," *Los Angeles Times*, October 29, 2009. "The brawny, big-boned women he's been drawing for decades are re-purposed here as pneumatic, iron-willed Old Testament matriarchs." Although frequently attacked as a misogynist, Crumb should rather be interpreted as being in awe of female power. In *Sketchbook*, vol. 8, he quotes Mara Freeman: "The female is not only the guardian of mysteries—she is the mystery herself," on a page in which he memorializes several of his favorite high school girls. Crumb's drawing alludes to Mara Freeman, "The Crucible of the Goddess and the British Mystery Tradition," *Gnosis* 9 (Fall 1988), 14–15; see also *The R. Crumb Sketchbooks*, vols. 7–12, 8:159.

28. Vanessa Davis, *Make Me a Woman* (Montreal: Drawn and Quarterly, 2010); and Crumb, *The Book of Genesis*, commentary, n.p.

29. Casey Strine, "What the Bible's Romans 13 Says about Asylum—and What Jeff Sessions Omitted," The Conversation, June 19, 2018, http://theconversation.com/what-the-bibles-romans-13-says-about-asylum-and-what-jeff-sessions-omitted-98483.

EPILOGUE

1. R. Crumb, "A Day in the Life, *Self-Loathing Comics*, no. 1 (February 1995), 3–18; and Richter, *The Crumb Compendium*, 117. The *Sketchbooks* present an astonishing cornucopia of allusions to sources as diverse as Paramahansa Yogananda's *Autobiography of a Yogi*, from which Crumb quotes: "Do not allow yourself to be thrashed by the provoking whiplash of a beautiful face" (from chapter 12, "My Years in My Master's Hermitage," 128); the Jain philosopher Chitrabhanu; Richard P. Feynman, *Six Easy Pieces*; *Alice's Adventures in Wonderland*; *Tales of Power* by Carlos Castaneda; C. S. Lewis, *The Screwtape Letters*; Colin Wilson; T. S. Eliot; William Burroughs, *Queer*; Marshall McLuhan; Louis-Ferdinand Céline; Carlos Castaneda, *A Separate Reality*; Albert Camus; Ben Hecht, *A Child of the Century*; Alice Neel; Samuel Johnson; Jean Rhys; Terence McKenna; Robert Burton's *The Anatomy of Melancholy*; Mark Twain, *The Adventures of Huckleberry Finn*; Keith Roberts's biography of Pieter Bruegel; Brendan Behan; Sigmund Freud; George Orwell, *The Road to Wigan Pier*; the guru Mahavatar Babaji; Whitley Strieber's *Communion*; a quotation from the biologist Carl Sauer's "Theme of Plant and Animal Destruction in Economic History"; Rumi; Thomas Hart Benton, *An Artist in America*; a *Newsweek* essay by Boaz Huss on the popularity of Kabbalah among celebrities; B. Traven, *The Death Ship*; Simone de Beauvoir, *The Second Sex*; Aldous Huxley's novel *The Devils of Loudon* as well as his essay "A Case of Voluntary Ignorance";

Lenny Bruce, *How to Talk Dirty and Influence People*; *The History of the Franks* by Gregory of Tours; Jacques Vallée, *Dimensions: A Casebook of Alien Contact*; Henry Miller's *Sexus*; Philip Roth's *My Life as a Man*; *Seth Speaks: The Eternal Validity of the Soul* by Jane Roberts; *The Urantia Book*; Georges Bataille; Pablo Picasso; Philip Larkin; Ernest Hemingway, *A Movable Feast*. What is clear is that Crumb selects carefully what to read and, indeed, exhibits an unerring instinct for what many would consider "high culture." Yet he also as we have seen immediately seeks to puncture intellectual pretension. If it feeds his spirit, he gravitates naturally toward it. An autodidact, Crumb clearly has read a wider range of literature than many American university graduates and—what is more—creatively employed what he has learned in his art and life.

2. Gregory, *An Illustrated Life*, 45.

3. Interview with Gary Groth in George, *The Comics Journal Library*, vol. 3, *R. Crumb*, 60, 61.

4. Alex Wood, comp., "Crumb on Others, part 10," The Official Crumb Site, https://www .crumbproducts.com/pages/about/crumbonothers10.html; Dan Nadel, "An Interview with Robert Crumb," *The Believer*, January 1, 2015, https://believermag.com/an-interview-with -robert-crumb/; and *The R. Crumb Sketchbook, November 1974–January 1978* (Frankfurt: Zweitausendeins, 1978), 179.

5. Crumb, *R. Crumb's Dream Diary*, 79, 81; and *The R. Crumb Sketchbooks*, vols. 7–12, 12:133. Two other references to *Fate* magazine appear in *Sketchbook*, vol. 12: in one, Crumb transcribes a long letter to the editor (October 2005) containing a vivid account of one Joanna T. Peacher regarding an "after death" experience she had following an automobile accident in which she saw "the light" (161–63). And in the second, Crumb illustrates yet another feature from *Fate* magazine (the December 2005 issue), "The Lady Who Paints Angels": "Milli Oden, 63 years of age, living in a sedate apartment complex in Hopkins, Minnesota, a suburb of Minneapolis, . . . refers to herself as 'a visionary artist' inspired by direct communication with angelic beings." Crumb depicts a smiling lady with angel winds holding a wand (March 6, 2006, 165).

6. Carl G. Jung, *Flying Saucers: A Modern Myth of Things Seen in the Skies* (London: Routledge and Kegan Paul, 1959).

7. Mercier, "Who's Afraid of R. Crumb?," 217.

8. *The R. Crumb Sketchbooks*, vols. 7–12, 10:141; and Crumb, *R. Crumb's Dream Diary*, 184.

9. Henry David Thoreau, *Walden*, in *The Portable Thoreau*, ed. Carl Bode (New York: Viking, 1967), 343–44.

10. R. Crumb, *Sketchbook*, March 31, 1997. In "A Highly Spiritual Discussion between Flakey Foont and Shuman the Human," Flakey and Shuman are exploring a concept Flakey says Mr. Natural has shared with him: "He—um—told me to look at a point off in the distance—the far distance—If I looked long enough and hard enough I'd see the 'Eckt Ack.'" Shuman tells Flakey that Mr. Natural is teasing him and that "what he's telling you to do is something that takes years of disciplined Yogic practice . . . hours of meditation every day until the Third Eye opens. . . . Then my friend, you see things quite differently. . . . You see in a new way!" When Flakey asks Shuman if he has "opened the Third Eye? Have you seen the Eckt Ack??," Shuman responds: "Sure . . . lots of times." Flakey bemoans the fact that he is "too earth bound" to achieve this state of being, and Shuman concludes: "Well, don't fret over it . . . Maybe in your next life . . . Heh Hey . . . More tea?" The sketch is dated November 15, 1996, indicating that Crumb continued to explore characters and themes he had first

introduced three decades earlier. Here Flakey and Shuman meet and discuss their experiences with their guru-in-common Mr. Natural, and Crumb also returns to his earlier engagement with the concept of the Third Eye, which also reflects his own recent dedication to regular meditation four months before completing this drawing in June 1996. See *The R. Crumb Sketchbooks*, vols. 7–12, 10:150.

11. Crumb, *R. Crumb's Dream Diary*, 83–84.

12. Crumb, *R. Crumb's Dream Diary*, 82.

13. *R. Crumb, Sketchbooks*. Another reference to theosophical concepts appears in a drawing titled "What a Hoot!," which features a man "forcing his 'etheric double' to come out!" The etheric body is part of the physical body, but it extends beyond the body to form the aura. See *The R. Crumb Sketchbooks*, vols. 7–12, 11:161.

14. Sri Yukteswar, *The Holy Science* (Los Angeles: Self-Realization Fellowship, 1972), vi, 11, 1.

15. George, *The Comics Journal Library*, vol. 3, *R. Crumb*, 63.

16. *The R. Crumb Sketchbooks*, vols. 7–12, 11:70.

BIBLIOGRAPHY

BOOKS BY R. CRUMB

Crumb, R. *R. Crumb's Head Comix*. New York: Viking, 1968.

Crumb, R. *R. Crumb's Fritz the Cat: 3 Big Stories!* New York: Ballantine Books, 1969.

Crumb, R. *Fritz Bugs Out*. New York: Ballantine Books, 1972.

Crumb, R. *Fritz the Cat: Secret Agent for the C. I. A.* New York: Ballantine Books, 1972.

Crumb, R. *Fritz the No-Good*. New York: Ballantine Books, 1972.

Crumb, R. *Carload O' Comics*. New York: Belier Press, 1976.

Crumb, R. *The Complete Fritz the Cat*. New York: Belier Press, 1978.

Crumb, R. *R. Crumb's Head Comix, Twenty Years Later*. New York: Simon and Schuster, 1988.

Crumb, R. *R. Crumb Comics*. Santa Rosa, CA: Black Sparrow Press, 1990.

Crumb, R. *The Complete Dirty Laundry Comics*. San Francisco: Last Gasp, 1993.

Crumb, R. *R. Crumb's America*. London: Knockabout, 1994.

Crumb, R. *The Book of Mr. Natural: Profane Tales of That Old Mystic Madcap*. Seattle: Fantagraphics, 1995.

Crumb, R. *The Big Yum Yum Book: The Story of Oggie and the Beanstalk*. Berkeley, CA: Snow Lion Graphics, 1995.

Crumb, R. *Waiting for Food: Restaurant Placemat Drawings*. Amsterdam: Oog and Blik, 1995.

Crumb, R. *R. Crumb's Carload O' Comics: An Anthology of Choice Strips and Stories, 1968–1976*. Northhampton, MA: Kitchen Sink Press, 1996.

Crumb, R. *The R. Crumb Coffee Table Art Book*. Northampton, MA: Kitchen Sink Press, 1997.

Mairowitz, David Zane, and R. Crumb. *Introducing Kafka*. New York: Totem Books, 1997.

Crumb, R. *Crumb Family Comics*. San Francisco: Last Gasp, 1998.

Crumb, R. *Your Vigor for Life Appalls Me: Robert Crumb Letters, 1958–1977*. Edited by Ilse Thompson. Seattle: Fantagraphics, 1998.

Crumb, R. *R. Crumb Draws the Blues*. San Francisco: Last Gasp, 2000.

Crumb, R. *Waiting for Food*, no. 2: *More Placemat Drawings*. Amsterdam: Oog and Blik, 2000.

Crumb, R. *Odds and Ends*. New York: Bloomsbury, 2001.

Crumb, R. *Waiting for Food*, no. 3: *More Placemat Drawings*. Amsterdam: Oog and Blik, 2002.

Crumb, R. "The Unbearable Tediousness of Being." *McSweeney's Quarterly*, no. 13 (Spring 2004).

Crumb, R., and Peter Poplaski. *The R. Crumb Handbook*. London: MQ Publications, 2005.

Crumb, R. *R. Crumb's Heroes of Blues, Jazz, and Country*. New York: Harry N. Abrams, 2006.

Crumb, R. *Waiting for Food*, no. 4: *Yet More Restaurant Placement Drawings by R. "Keep on Drawin'" Crumb*. Amsterdam: Oog and Blik, 2008.

Crumb, R. *The Book of Genesis Illustrated by R. Crumb*. New York: W. W. Norton, 2009.

Crumb, R. *R. Crumb Trading Cards*. Northampton, MA: Kitchen Sink Press, 2010.

Crumb, R. *Nausea*. Paris: Éditions Cornelius, 2011.

Crumb, R. *The Complete Record Cover Collection*. New York: W. W. Norton, 2011.

Crumb, R. *The Weirdo Years, 1981–'93*. San Francisco: Last Gasp, 2013.

Crumb, R. *The Complete Zap Comix*. Seattle: Fantagraphics, 2014.

Crumb, R. *Art and Beauty Magazine*, nos. 1, 2, and 3. *Drawings by R. Crumb*. New York: David Zwirner Books, 2016.

Crumb, R. *The Life and Death of Fritz the Cat*. Seattle: Fantagraphics, 2017.

Crumb, R. *Bible of Filth*. New York: David Zwirner Books, 2017.

Crumb, R. *R. Crumb's Dream Diary*. Edited by Ronald Bronstein and Sammy Harkham. New York: Elara Press, 2018.

The Complete Crumb Comics

Crumb, R. *The Complete Crumb Comics*, vols. 1–17. Edited by Gary Groth, et al., Seattle: Fantagraphics, 1987–2013.

Vol. 1, *The Early Years of Bitter Struggle*.

Vol. 2, *Some More Early Years of Bitter Struggle*.

Vol. 3, *Starring Fritz the Cat*.

Vol. 4, *Mr. Sixties!*

Vol. 5, *Happy Hippy Comix*.

Vol. 6, *On the Crest of a Wave*.

Vol. 7, *Hott 'n' Heavy*.

Vol. 8, *The Death of Fritz the Cat*.

Vol. 9, *R. Crumb Versus the Sisterhood*.

Vol. 10, *Crumb Advocates Violent Overthrow*.

Vol. 11, *Mr. Natural Committed to a Mental Institution!*

Vol. 12, *We're Livin' in the Lap o' Luxury!*

Vol. 13, *The Season of the Snoid*.

Vol. 14, *The Early '80s and Weirdo Magazine*.

Vol. 15, *Featuring Mode O'Day and Her Pals*.

Vol. 16, *The Mid 1980s: More Years of Valiant Struggle*.

Vol. 17, *The Late 1980s: Cave Wimp, Mode O'Day, Aline 'n' Bob and Other Stories, Covers, Drawings*.

Sketchbooks

The R. Crumb Sketchbook, November 1974–January 1978. Frankfurt: Zweitausendeins, 1978.

The R. Crumb Sketchbook, 1966–1967. Frankfurt: Zweitausendeins, 1981.

The R. Crumb Sketchbook, July 1978–November 1983. Frankfurt: Zweitausendeins, 1984.

The R. Crumb Sketchbook, Late 1967–Mid-1974. Frankfurt: Zweitausendeins, 1986.

The R. Crumb Sketchbook, November 1983–April 1987. Frankfurt: Zweitausendeins. 1989.

The R. Crumb Sketchbook, May 1987–April 1991. Frankfurt: Zweitausendeins, 1993.

The R. Crumb Sketchbook, April 1991–September 1996. Frankfurt: Zweitausendeins, 1998.

The R. Crumb Sketchbook. Vol. 1, *1964–Mid-1965*. Seattle: Fantagraphics, 1992.

The R. Crumb Sketchbook. Vol. 2, *Mid-1965–Early 1966*. Seattle: Fantagraphics, 1992.

The R. Crumb Sketchbook. Vol. 3, *1966*. Seattle: Fantagraphics, 1993.

The R. Crumb Sketchbook. Vol. 4, *Late 1966–Mid 1967*. Seattle; Fantagraphics, 1994.

The R. Crumb Sketchbook. Vol. 5, *Late 1967 and Early 1968*. Seattle: Fantagraphics, 1995.

The R. Crumb Sketchbook. Vol. 6, *Mid 1968–Mid 1969*. Seattle: Fantagraphics, 1997.

The R. Crumb Sketchbook. Vol. 7, *Mid 1969–End of 1970*. Seattle: Fantagraphics, 1999.

The R. Crumb Sketchbook. Vol. 8, *Fall 1970–Fall 1972*. Seattle: Fantagraphics, 2000.

The R. Crumb Sketchbook. Vol. 9, *October 1972–June 1975*. Seattle: Fantagraphics, 2002.

The R. Crumb Sketchbook. Vol. 10, *June 1975–February 1977*. Seattle: Fantagraphics, 2005.

The R. Crumb Sketchbooks. Vols. 1–6, *1964–1982*. Cologne: Taschen, 2014.

The R. Crumb Sketchbooks. Vols. 7–12, *1982–2011*. Cologne: Taschen, 2012.

ANTHOLOGIES CONTAINING WORK BY CRUMB

Brunetti, Ivan, ed. *An Anthology of Graphic Fiction, Cartoons, and True Stories*. Vol. 1. New Haven, CT: Yale University Press, 2006. Contains "A Short History of America," 299–302; "Uncle Bob's Mid-Life Crisis," 303–10; "Jelly Roll Morton's Voodoo Curse," 311–16; and "Where Has It Gone, All the Beautiful Music of Our Grandparents?," 317–21.

Brunetti, Ivan, ed. *An Anthology of Graphic Fiction, Cartoons, and True Stories*. Vol. 2. New Haven, CT: Yale University Press, 2008.

Burns, Charles, ed. *The Best American Comics, 2009*. New York: Houghton Mifflin Harcourt, 2009.

Callahan, Bob, ed. *The New Comics Anthology*. New York: Collier Books, 1991.

Callahan, Bob, ed. *The New Smithsonian Book of Comic Book Stories: From Crumb to Clowes*. Washington, DC: Smithsonian Books, 2004.

Crumb, Maxon, ed. *Crumb Comics: The Whole Family Is Crazy!* San Francisco: Last Gasp, 1998.

Davidson, Steve, ed. *Gung Ho! All American Comicks*. Amsterdam: OM-Arcanum Productions, 1970.

Dean, Michael., ed. *The Comics Journal Library*. Vol. 9, *Zap, The Interviews*. Seattle: Fantagraphics, 2015.

Donahue, Don, and Susan Goodrick, eds. *The Apex Treasury of Underground Comics*. New York: Links Books, 1974.

Fantagraphics. *The Best Comics of the Decade*. 2 vols. Seattle: Fantagraphics, 1990.

Gaiman, Neil, ed. *The Best American Comics, 2010*. New York: Houghton Mifflin Harcourt, 2010.

George, Milo, ed. *The Comics Journal Library*. Vol. 3, *R. Crumb*. Seattle: Fantagraphics, 2004.

Katz, Harry, ed. *Cartoon America: Cartoon Art in the Library of Congress*. New York: Harry N. Abrams, 2006.

Kick, Russ, ed. *The Graphic Canon*. Vol. 1, *From the Epic of Gilgamesh to Shakespeare to Dangerous Liaisons*. New York: Seven Stories Press, 2012.

Kick, Russ, ed. *The Graphic Canon*. Vol. 3, *From Heart of Darkness to Hemingway to Infinite Jest*. New York: Seven Stories Press, 2013.

Kurtzman, Harvey. *Harvey Kurtzman's Strange Adventures*. New York: Epic Comics, 1990.

Lynch, Jay, ed. *The Best of Bijou Funnies*. New York: Links Books, 1975.

Pekar, Harvey, ed. *The Best American Comics, 2006*. New York: Houghton Mifflin Harcourt, 2010.

Poe, Edgar Allan. *Maxon's Poe: Seven Stories and Poems by Edgar Allan Poe*. San Francisco: Cottage Classics, 1997.

Portfolio of Underground Art. San Diego: Schanes and Schanes, 1980.

Rakezic, Sasa, and Bob Kathman, eds. *Flock of Dreamers: An Anthology of Dream Inspired Comics*. Northampton, MA: Kitchen Sink Press, 1997.

Rand, Everett, and Gioia Palmieri, eds. *The Mineshaft Reader*. Durham, NC: Mineshaft Publishing, 2017.

Rip Off Press. *The Best of the Rip Off Press*. San Francisco: Rip Off Press, 1973.

Snatch Sampler. San Francisco: Keith Green, 1977.

Ware, Chris, ed. *The Best American Comics, 2007*. New York: Houghton Mifflin Harcourt, 2007.

Whyte, Malcolm. *Maxon: Art out of Chaos; The Illustrated Biography of Maxon Crumb*. Seattle: Fantagraphics, 2018.

CATALOGS

De l'underground à la Genèse. Paris: Musée d'Art Modern de la Ville de Paris, 2012.

Heinisch, Severin, ed. *Die vielen Gesichter des Robert Crumb*. Krems an der Donau, Austria: Karikatur Museum Krems and St. Pölten, 2002.

Kominsky-Crumb, Aline, and Robert Crumb. *Drawn Together*. Edited by Anette Gehrig. Basel: Christoph Merian Verlag, 2016.

Mercier, Jean-Pierre. *Qui a peur de Robert Crumb? / Who's Afraid of Robert Crumb?* Angoulême, France: Musée de la Bande Dessinée, 2000.

R. Crumb. Paris: Musée d'Art Modern de la Ville de Paris, 2012.

R. Crumb Retrospective. New York: Alexander Gallery, 1994.

The World According to Crumb / Le monde selon Crumb. Angoulême, France: Musée de la Bande Dessinée, 1992.

Yeah, But Is It Art? Cologne: Museum Ludwig and Walter König, 2004.

SECONDARY SOURCES

Abbey, Edward. *The Monkey Wrench Gang*. Salt Lake City: Dream Garden Press, 1990.

Abbott, H. Porter. *The Cambridge Introduction to Narrative*. New York: Cambridge University Press, 2002.

Agamben, Giorgio. *Karman: A Brief Treatise on Action, Guilt, and Gesture*. Stanford, CA: Stanford University Press, 2018.

Agamben, Giorgio. *Nudities*. Stanford, CA: Stanford University Press, 2011.

Ahearn, Edward. *Visionary Fictions: Apocalyptic Writing from Blake to the Modern Age*. New Haven, CT: Yale University Press, 1996.

Albright, Daniel. *Untwisting the Serpent: Modernism in Music, Literature, and Other Arts.* Chicago: University of Chicago Press, 2000.

Albright, Thomas. *Art in the San Francisco Bay Area, 1945–1980: An Illustrated History.* Berkeley: University of California Press, 1985.

Alessandrini, Marjorie. *Robert Crumb.* Paris: Éditions Albin Michel, 1974.

Alleva, Richard. "Comic Erudition: R. Crumb Meets Kafka." *Commonweal* 129, no. 13 (July 12, 2002): 18–19.

Amburn, Ellis. *Subterranean Kerouac: The Hidden Life of Jack Kerouac.* New York: St. Martin's Press, 1998.

Armstrong, David. *A Trumpet to Arms: Alternative Media in America.* Los Angeles: J. P. Tarcher, 1981.

Arnold, Kyle. *The Divine Madness of Philp K. Dick.* New York: Oxford University Press, 2017.

Ascalone, Enrico. *Mesopotamia.* Berkeley: University of California Press, 2007.

Ashton, Dore, and Art Spiegelman. "The Debate over Popular and Museum Culture: Dore Ashton and Art Spiegelman Visit High and Low at the MoMA." *Art International*, no. 14 (Spring–Summer 1991): 60–64.

Auping, Michael, ed. *Philip Guston Retrospective.* New York: Thames and Hudson, 2003.

Backwords, Ace. *Acid Heroes: The Legends of LSD.* Scotts Valley, CA: CreateSpace, 2009.

Baetens, Jan, and Hugo Frey. *The Graphic Novel: An Introduction.* New York: Cambridge University Press, 2015.

Bails, Jerry, and Hames Ware. *The Who's Who of American Comic Books.* Detroit: Simpson, 1973.

Bakhtin, Mikhail. *Rabelais and His World.* Translated by Hélène Iswolsky. Bloomington: Indiana University Press, 2009.

Ball, David M. "World Literature." In *The Cambridge History of the Graphic Novel*, edited by Jan Baetens, Hugo Frey, and Stephen E. Tabachnick, 591–608. New York: Cambridge University Press, 2018.

Barnstone, Willis, and Marvin Meyer, eds. *The Gnostic Bible.* Boston: New Seeds, 2006.

Barron, Frank. "The Creative Personality: Akin to Madness." In *Understanding Mysticism*, edited by Richard Woods, 312–20. Garden City, NY: Image Books, 1980.

Barry, Lynda, Ivan Brunetti, R. Crumb, and Gary Panter. "Panel: Lines on Paper." Moderated by Hamza Walker. In "Comics and Media," edited by Hillary L. Chute and Patrick Jagoda. Special issue, *Critical Inquiry* 40, no. 3 (Spring 2014).

Baskind, Samantha, and Ranen Omer-Sherman, eds. *The Jewish Graphic Novel: Critical Approaches.* New Brunswick, NJ: Rutgers University Press, 2008.

Bauduin, Tessel M. "The Occult and the Visual Arts." In *The Occult World*, edited by Christopher Partridge, 429–45. New York: Routledge, 2015.

Bauduin, Tessel M. *Surrealism and the Occult: Occultism and Western Esotericism in the Work and Movement of André Breton.* Amsterdam: Amsterdam University Press, 2014.

Beaty, Bart. *Comics versus Art.* Toronto: University of Toronto Press, 2012.

Beaty, Bart. "Featuring Stories by the World's Greatest Authors: Classics Illustrated and the 'Middlebrow Problem' in the Postwar Era." *International Journal of Comic Art* 1, no. 1 (Spring–Summer 1999): 122–39.

Beaty, Bart, and Stephen Weiner, eds. *Critical Survey of Graphic Novels: Independent and Underground Classics.* Ipswich, MA: Salem Press, 2012.

Beaty, Bart, and Benjamin Woo. *The Greatest Comic Book of All Time: Symbolic Capital and the Field of American Comic Books*. New York: Palgrave Macmillan, 2014.

Beauchamp, Monte, ed. *The Life and Times of R. Crumb: Comments from Contemporaries*. New York: St. Martin's Press, 1998.

Belgrad, Daniel. *The Culture of Spontaneity: Improvisation and the Arts in Postwar America*. Chicago: University of Chicago Press, 1998.

Bell, Blake. *Strange and Stranger: The World of Steve Ditko*. Seattle: Fantagraphics, 2008.

Bell, Daniel. *The Cultural Contradictions of Capitalism*. New York: Basic Books, 1996.

Bellah, Robert N. "The New Religious Consciousness and the Crisis in Modernity." In *The New Religious Consciousness*, edited by Charles Y. Glock and Robert N. Bellah, 333–52. Berkeley: University of California Press, 1976.

Benjamin, Walter. "Franz Kafka: On the Tenth Anniversary of His Death." In *Illuminations: Essays and Reflections*. Edited by Hannah Arendt. New York: Schocken Books, 1973.

Berger, Arthur Asa. *The Comic-Stripped American: What Dick Tracy, Blondie, Daddy Warbucks, and Charlie Brown Tell Us about Ourselves*. New York: Walker and Company, 1973.

Berger, John. *Ways of Seeing*. London: Penguin, 1972.

Berkson, Bill. "Pyramid and the Shoe: Philip Guston and the Funnies." In *Philip Guston Retrospective*, edited by Michael Auping, 65–73. New York: Thames and Hudson, 2003.

Berona, David A. *Wordless Books: The Original Graphic Novels*. New York: Harry N. Abrams, 2008.

Bhaktivedanta, A. C., Swami Prabhupada. *Sri Isopanisad: With Introduction, Translation, and Authorized Reports*. New York: Bhaktivedanta Book Trust, 1974.

Bivins, Jason C. *Religion of Fear: The Politics of Horror in Conservative Evangelicalism*. New York: Oxford University Press, 2008.

Bizot, Jean-François. *200 Trips from the Counterculture: Graphics and Stories from the Underground Press Syndicate*. London: Thames and Hudson, 2006.

Black, Jeremy, and Anthony Green. *Gods, Demons and Symbols of Ancient Mesopotamia: An Illustrated Dictionary*. London: British Museum Press, 1998.

Bloom, Harold, ed. *Jean-Paul Sartre: Modern Critical Views*. New York: Chelsea House, 2001.

Booker, M. Keith, ed. *Comics through Time: A History of Icons, Idols, and Ideas*. 4 vols. Santa Barbara, CA: Greenwood Press, 2014.

Boon, Marcus. *The Road of Excess: A History of Writers on Drugs*. Cambridge, MA: Harvard University Press, 2002.

Boone, Graeme M., Fred McDowell, Miles Pratcher, and Fanny Davis. "Twelve Key Recordings." In *The Cambridge Companion to Blues and Gospel Music*, edited by Allan Moore, 61–88. Cambridge: Cambridge University Press, 2002.

Brackett, Jeffrey M. "Religion and Comics." *Religion Compass* 9, no. 12 (December 2015): 493–500.

Bramlett, Frank, Roy T. Cook, and Aaron Meskin, eds. *The Routledge Companion to Comics*. New York: Routledge, 2017.

Brunner, Edward. "The Comics as Outsider's Text: Teaching R. Crumb and Underground Comix." In *Teaching the Graphic Novel*, edited by Stephen E. Tabachnick, 137–46. New York: Modern Language Association of America, 2009.

Buhle, Paul, ed. *The Beats: A Graphic History*. New York: Hill and Wang, 2009.

Buhle, Paul, ed. *Jews and American Comics: An Illustrated History of an American Art Form*. New York: New Press, 2008.

Buhle, Paul. "Questions for ... R. Crumb." *Cultural Correspondence, Underground Cartoonists: Ten Years Later*, no. 5 (Summer–Fall 1977).

Bukowski, Charles. *Bring Me Your Love*. Santa Barbara, CA: Black Sparrow Press, 1983.

Bukowski, Charles. *The Captain Is Out to Lunch and the Sailors Have Taken Over the Ship*. Santa Barbara, CA: Black Sparrow Press, 1998.

Burkert, Walter. *Creation of the Sacred*. Cambridge, MA: Harvard University Press, 1996.

Burt, Stephanie. "Kick Over the Scenery." *London Review of Books* 30, no. 13 (July 3, 2008): 23–25.

Byrne-Smith, Dan. "Harvey Kurtzman and the Influence of *Mad* Magazine." In *The Cambridge History of the Graphic Novel*, edited by Jan Baetens, Hugo Frey, and Stephen E. Tabachnick, 92–106. New York: Cambridge University Press, 2018.

Cahalan, James M. *Edward Abbey: A Life*. Tucson: University of Arizona Press, 2001.

Calonne, David Stephen. *Charles Bukowski*. London: Reaktion Books, 2012.

Calonne, David Stephen. *The Colossus of Armenia: G. I. Gurdjieff and Henry Miller*. Ann Arbor, MI: Roger Jackson, 1997.

Calonne, David Stephen, ed. *Conversations with Allen Ginsberg*. Jackson: University Press of Mississippi, 2019.

Calonne, David Stephen. "Creative Writers and Revision." In *Revision: History, Theory, and Practice*, edited by Alice Horning and Anne Becker, 142–76. Anderson, SC: Parlor Press, 2006.

Calonne, David Stephen. *Henry Miller (Critical Lives)*. London: Reaktion Books, 2014.

Calonne, David Stephen. Introduction to *Absence of the Hero: Uncollected Stories and Essays*, by Charles Bukowski. Edited by David Stephen Calonne. San Francisco: City Lights, 2010.

Calonne, David Stephen. *The Spiritual Imagination of the Beats*. New York: Cambridge University Press, 2017.

Calt, Stephen. *I'd Rather Be the Devil: Skip James and the Blues*. Chicago: Chicago Review Press, 2008.

Calt, Stephen, and Gayle Wardlow. *King of the Delta Blues: The Life and Music of Charlie Patton*. Newton, NJ: Rock Chapel Press, 1988.

Calvino, Italo. *Six Memos for the Next Millennium: The Charles Eliot Norton Lectures, 1985–86*. Cambridge, MA: Harvard University Press, 1988.

Canis, Laura, and Paul Canis. "Jean-Paul Sartre Meets Enid Coleslaw: Existential Themes in *Ghost World*." In *Comics as Philosophy*, edited by Jeff McLaughlin, 130–52. Jackson: University Press of Mississippi, 2005.

Carlin, John. "Masters of American Comics: An Art History of Twentieth-Century American Comic Strips and Books." In *Masters of American Comics*, edited by John Carlin, Paul Karasik, and Brian Walker, 25–175. New Haven, CT: Yale University Press, 2005.

Carlin, John, Paul Karasik, and Brian Walker, eds. *Masters of American Comics*. New Haven, CT: Yale University Press, 2005.

Carlsson, Chris, with Lisa Ruth Elliott, eds. *Ten Years That Shook the City: San Francisco 1968–1978*. San Francisco: City Lights, 2011.

Carrier, David. *The Aesthetics of Comics*. University Park: Pennsylvania State University Press, 2000.

Caws, Mary Ann, ed. *Surrealism*. London: Phaidon, 2004.

Chaney, Michael A., ed. *Graphic Subjects: Critical Essays on Autobiography and Graphic Novels*. Madison: University of Wisconsin Press, 2011.

Chireau, Yvonne P. *Black Magic: Religion and the African American Conjuring Tradition*. Berkeley: University of California Press, 2003.

Chute, Hillary L. "Comics as Literature? Reading Graphic Narrative." *PMLA* 123, no. 2 (March 2008): 452–65.

Chute, Hillary L. *Disaster Drawn: Visual Witness, Comics, and Documentary Form*. Cambridge, MA: Harvard University Press, 2016.

Chute, Hillary L. *Graphic Women: Life Narrative and Contemporary Comics*. New York: Columbia University Press, 2010.

Chute, Hillary L. *Why Comics? From Underground to Everywhere*. New York: HarperCollins, 2017.

Cioffi, Frank L. "Disturbing Comics: The Disjunction of Word and Image in the Comics of Andrzej Mleczko, Ben Katchor, R. Crumb, and Art Spiegelman." In *The Language of Comics: Word and Image*, edited by Robin Varnum and Christina T. Gibbons, 97–122. Jackson: University Press of Mississippi, 2001.

Clanton, Dan W., Jr. *The End Will Be Graphic: Apocalyptic in Comic Books and Graphic Novels*. Sheffield, England: Sheffield Phoenix Press, 2012.

Clark, Alan, and Laurel Clark. *Comics: An Illustrated History*. London: Green Wood, 1991.

Clark, Stuart. *Thinking with Demons: The Idea of Witchcraft in Early Modern Europe*. Oxford: Oxford University Press, 1999.

Clarke, J. J. *Oriental Enlightenment: The Encounter between Asian and Western Thought*. Abingdon, Oxon, England: Routledge, 1997.

Clowes, Daniel. "Gynecology." In *An Anthology of Graphic Fiction, Cartoons, and True Stories*, edited by Ivan Brunetti, 375–96. New Haven, CT: Yale University Press, 2006.

Coates, Andrew T. "The Bible and Graphic Novels and Comic Books: Telling Bible Stories with Images." In *The Oxford Handbook of the American Bible*, edited by Paul C. Gutjahr, 451–67. New York: Oxford University Press, 2017.

Cohn, Neil. *The Visual Language of Comics: Introduction to the Structure and Cognition of Sequential Images*. London: Bloomsbury, 2013.

Conal, Robbie, and Tom Christie. "Grandpa from Hell." In *Conversations with William S. Burroughs*, edited by Allen Hibbard, 220–26. Jackson: University Press of Mississippi, 1999.

Cooke, Jon B., ed. *The Book of Weirdo*. San Francisco: Last Gasp, 2018.

Corngold, Stanley. "1914, July: Ecstatic Release from Personality." In *A New History of German Literature*, edited by David E. Wellbery and Judith Ryan, 703–7. Cambridge, MA: Harvard University Press, 2004.

Cotkin, George. *Existential America*. Baltimore: Johns Hopkins University Press, 2003.

Coupe, Laurence. *Beat Sound, Beat Vision: The Beat Spirit and Popular Song*. Manchester: Manchester University Press, 2007.

Crawford, Hubert H. *Crawford's Encyclopedia of Comic Books*. New York: Jonathan David, 1978.

Creekmur, Corey K. "Multiculturalism Meets the Counterculture: Representing Racial Difference in Robert Crumb's Underground Comix." In *Representing Multiculturalism in Comics and Graphic Novels*, edited by Carolene Ayaka and Ian Hague, 19–33. New York: Routledge, 2015.

Crow, Thomas. *The Rise of the Sixties: American and European Art in the Ear of Dissent.* New Haven, CT: Yale University Press, 2004.

Crumb, R. "Crazy Music." In *Popular Culture in America*, edited by Paul Buhle, 108–16. Minneapolis: University of Minnesota Press, 1987.

Crumb, R. Introduction to *American Splendor: The Life and Times of Harvey Pekar*, by Harvey Pekar. New York: Ballantine Books, 2003.

Crumb, R., and Bill Griffith. "As the Artist Sees It: Interviews with Comic Artists." In *Popular Culture in America*, edited by Paul Buhle, 132–38. Minneapolis: University of Minnesota Press, 1987.

Daniels, Les. "Comics Variations." In *The Art of the Comic Strip*, edited by Walter Herdeg and David Pascal. Zurich: Graphis Press, 1972.

Daniels, Les. *Comix: A History of Comic Books in America.* New York: Bonanza Books, 1971.

Danky, James, and Denis Kitchen. *Underground Classics: The Transformation of Comics into Comix.* New York: Harry N. Abrams, 2009.

Danto, Arthur C. "Upper West Side Buddhism." In *Buddha Mind in Contemporary Art*, edited by Jacquelynn Baas and Mary Jane Jacob, 49–59. Berkeley: University of California Press, 2004.

Davidson, Michael. *The San Francisco Renaissance: Poetics and Community at Mid-Century.* New York: Cambridge University Press, 1989.

Davies, Owen. *Grimoires: A History of Magic Books.* New York: Oxford University Press, 2009.

Davis, Erik. "The Counterculture and the Occult." In *The Occult World*, edited by Christopher Partridge, 635–45. New York: Routledge, 2015.

Davis, Erik. *Nomad Codes: Adventures in Modern Esoterica.* Portland, OR: Yeti/Verse Chorus Press, 2010.

Davis, Erik. *TechGnosis: Myth, Magic and Mysticism in the Age of Information.* London: Serpent's Tail, 2004.

Davis, Erik. *The Visionary State: A Journey through California's Visionary Landscape.* San Francisco: Chronicle Books, 2006.

Davis, Vanessa. *Make Me a Woman.* Montreal: Drawn and Quarterly, 2010.

Denham, Robert D. *Northrop Frye: Religious Visionary and Architect of the Spiritual World.* Charlottesville: University of Virginia Press, 2004.

DeSalvo, Debra. *The Language of the Blues: From Alcorub to Zuzu.* New York: Billboard Books, 2006.

Dick, Philip K. *The Exegesis of Philip K. Dick.* Edited by Pamela Jackson and Jonathan Lethem. New York: Houghton Mifflin Harcourt, 2011.

Dick, Philip K. *The Shifting Realities of Philip K. Dick: Selected Literary and Philosophical Writings.* Edited by Lawrence Sutin. New York: Vintage Books, 1995.

Dick, Philip K. *VALIS.* New York: Bantam Books, 1981.

Dickerson, Tom H., Paul Dickerson, and Gregory Corso. "Attack Anything Moving." In *Burroughs Live: The Collected Interviews of William S. Burroughs, 1960–1997*, edited by Sylvère Lotringer, 603–8. Los Angeles: Semiotext(e), 2001.

Di Liddo, Annalisa. "Transcending Comics: Crossing the Boundaries of the Medium." In *A Comic Studies Reader*, edited by Jeet Heer and Kent Worcester, 325–39. Jackson: University Press of Mississippi, 2009.

Dinerstein, Joel. *The Origins of Cool in Postwar America*. Chicago: University of Chicago Press, 2017.

Dixon, Kent H., and Kevin H. Dixon. *The Epic of Gilgamesh*. New York: Seven Stories Press, 2018.

Doniger, Wendy. *The Hindus: An Alternative History*. New York: Penguin Books, 2009.

Dortort, Fred, ed. *What's Up, Underground!* Portland, OR: S. K. Josefsberg Studio, 1995.

Dowd, D. B., and Todd Hignite, eds. *Strips, Toons, and Bluesies: Essays in Comics and Culture*. New York: Princeton Architectural Press, 2004.

Drucker, Johanna. "What Is Graphic about Graphic Novels?" *English Language Notes* 46, no. 2 (Fall–Winter 2008): 39–55.

Duncan, B. N. "A Joint Interview with R. Crumb and Aline Kominsky-Crumb." In *R. Crumb: Conversations*, edited by D. K. Holm, 117–32. Jackson: University Press of Mississippi, 2004.

Duncan, Michael, and Kristine McKenna. *Semina Culture: Wallace Berman and His Circle*. New York: Distributed Art Publishers, 2005.

Duncan, Randy, Matthew J. Smith, and Paul Levitz. *The Power of Comics: History, Form, and Culture*. London: Bloomsbury, 2015.

Duval, Jean-François. *Buk et les Beats: Essai sur la Beat Generation*. Rev. ed. Paris: Éditions Michalon, 2014.

Echols, Alice. *Scars of Sweet Paradise: The Life and Times of Janis Joplin*. New York: Henry Holt, 1999.

Eisner, Will. *A Contract with God*. New York: W. W. Norton, 2006.

Elam, Kimberley. *Expressive Typography: The Word as Image*. New York: Van Nostrand Reinhold, 1990.

Ellingham, Lewis, and Kevin Killian. *Poet Be Like God: Jack Spicer and the San Francisco Renaissance*. Hanover, NH: University Press of New England, 1998.

Elliott, Scott S. "Transrendering Biblical Bodies: Reading Sex in *The Action Bible* and *Genesis Illustrated*." In *Comics and Sacred Texts: Reimagining Religion and Graphic Narratives*, edited by Assaf Gamzou and Ken Koltun-Fromm, 132–48. Jackson: University Press of Mississippi, 2018.

Ellwood, Robert S. *The Fifties Spiritual Marketplace: American Religion in a Decade of Conflict*. New Brunswick, NJ: Rutgers University Press, 1997.

Ellwood, Robert S. *The Sixties Spiritual Awakening: American Religion Moving from Modern to Postmodern*. New Brunswick, NJ: Rutgers University Press, 1994.

El Refaie, Elisabeth. *Autobiographical Comics: Life Writing in Pictures*. Jackson: University Press of Mississippi, 2012.

Engell, James. *The Creative Imagination: Enlightenment to Romanticism*. Cambridge, MA: Harvard University Press, 1981.

Estren, Mark James. *A History of Underground Comics*. Oakland: Ronin Publishing, 2012.

Ewert, Jeanne C. "Comics and Graphic Novel." In *Routledge Encyclopedia of Narrative Theory*, edited by David Herman, Manfred Jahn, and Marie-Laure Ryan, 71–73. London: Routledge, 2005.

Farber, David, and Beth Bailey. *The Columbia Guide to America in the 1960s*. New York: Columbia University Press, 2001.

Farrell, James J. *The Spirit of the Sixties: Making Postwar Radicalism*. New York: Routledge, 1997.

Feiffer, Jules. *The Explainers*. New York: McGraw Hill, 1960.

Fields, Rick. *How the Swans Came to the Lake: A Narrative History of Buddhism in America*. Boston: Shambhala, 1992.

Fiene, Don. *R. Crumb, Checklist of Work and Criticism*. Cambridge, MA: Boatner Norton Press, 1981.

Filoramo, Giovanni. *A History of Gnosticism*. Oxford: Blackwell, 1996.

Finlay, John. *Hermetic Light: Essays on the Gnostic Spirit in Modern Literature and Thought*. Edited by David Middleton. Santa Barbara, CA: John Daniel, 1994.

Finn, Julio. *The Bluesman: The Musical Heritage of Black Men and Women in the Americas*. London: Quartet Books, 1986.

Fitzgerald, F. Scott. "The Crack-Up." *Esquire*, February 1936.

Flaherty, Alice W. *The Midnight Disease: The Drive to Write, Writer's Block, and the Creative Brain*. New York: Houghton Mifflin Harcourt, 2004.

Fletcher, Angus. *Allegory: The Theory of a Symbolic Mode*. Ithaca, NY: Cornell University Press, 1982.

Flood, Gavin. *An Introduction to Hinduism*. Cambridge: Cambridge University Press, 1996.

Fokkelman, J. P. "Genesis." In *The Literary Guide to the Bible*, edited by Robert Alter and Frank Kermode, 36–55. Cambridge, MA: Harvard University Press, 1987.

Folman, Ari. *Anne Frank's Diary: The Graphic Adaptation*. Illustrated by David Polonsky. New York: Pantheon Books, 2018.

Frank, Arthur W. *Letting Stories Breathe: A Socio-Narratology*. Chicago: University of Chicago Press, 2010.

Freeman, Mara. "The Crucible of the Goddess and the British Mystery Tradition." *Gnosis* 9 (Fall 1988): 14–15.

Freuchen, Dagmar, ed. *Peter Freuchen's Book of the Eskimos*. Cleveland: World Publishing Company, 1961.

Frey, Hugo. "Beat-Era Literature and the Graphic Novel." In *The Cambridge History of the Graphic Novel*, edited by Jan Baetens, Hugo Frey, and Stephen E. Tabachnick, 124–38. New York: Cambridge University Press, 2018.

Frey, Hugo. "Historical Fiction." In *The Cambridge Companion to the Graphic Novel*, edited by Stephen Tabachnick, 80–96. Cambridge: Cambridge University Press, 2017.

Frye, Northrop. *The Great Code: The Bible and Literature*. New York: Harcourt Brace Jovanovich, 1982.

Gabel, John B., and Charles B. Wheeler. *The Bible as Literature: An Introduction*. 2nd ed. Oxford: Oxford University Press, 1990.

Gabilliet, Jean-Paul. "Fritz the Cat (1972): From Crumb to Bakshi, Betraying the Author and Translating the Zeitgeist." In *Comics and Adaptation*, edited by Benoît Mitaine, David Roche, and Isabelle Schmitt-Pitiot, 172–85. Jackson: University Press of Mississippi, 2018.

Gabilliet, Jean-Paul. *Of Comics and Men: A Cultural History of American Comic Books*. Jackson: University Press of Mississippi, 2009.

Gabilliet, Jean-Paul. *R. Crumb*. Bordeaux: Presses Universitaires de Bordeaux, 2012.

Gamzou, Assaf, and Ken Koltun-Fromm, eds. *Comics and Sacred Texts: Reimagining Religion and Graphic Narratives.* Jackson: University Press of Mississippi, 2018.

Gamzou, Assaf, and Ken Koltun-Fromm. "Introduction: Comics and Sacred Texts." In *Comics and Sacred Texts: Reimagining Religion and Graphic Narratives,* edited by Assaf Gamzou and Ken Koltun-Fromm, xi–xxi. Jackson: University Press of Mississippi, 2018.

García, Santiago. *On the Graphic Novel.* Translated by Bruce Campbell. Jackson: University Press of Mississippi, 2015.

Gardner, Jared. *Projections: Comics and the History of Twenty-First-Century Storytelling.* Stanford, CA: Stanford University Press, 2012.

Garon, Paul. *Blues and the Poetic Spirit.* San Francisco: City Lights, 1996.

Genette, Gérard. "Narrative Discourse." In *Literature in the Modern World: Critical Essays and Documents,* edited by Dennis Walder, 142–51. Oxford: Oxford University Press, 1990.

Gifford, Barry, ed. *As Ever: The Collected Correspondence of Allen Ginsberg and Neal Cassady.* Berkeley, CA: Creative Arts.

Gilliam, Terry, and Ben Thompson. *Gilliamesque: A Pre-Posthumous Memoir.* New York: HarperCollins, 2015.

Ginsberg, Allen. "Prefatory Remarks Concerning Leary's Politics of Ecstasy." In *Deliberate Prose: Selected Essays 1952–1995,* edited by Bill Morgan, 108–12. New York: HarperCollins, 2000.

Glessing, Robert J. *The Underground Press in America.* Bloomington: Indiana University Press, 1971.

Glover, David, and Scott McCracken, eds. *The Cambridge Companion to Popular Fiction.* Cambridge: Cambridge University Press, 2012.

Golden, Mike. *The Buddhist Third Class Junkmail Oracle: The Selected Art and Poetry of d. a. levy.* New York: Seven Stories Press, 1999.

Goodrick, Susan. "Apex Interview: R. Crumb." In *R. Crumb: Conversations,* edited by D. K. Holm, 84–91. Jackson: University Press of Mississippi, 2004.

Gordon, Ian. *Comic Strips and Consumer Culture, 1890–1945.* Washington, DC: Smithsonian Institution Press, 2002.

Gran, Rolf. "Charles Bukowski Illustrated and Drawn by Robert Crumb." *Jahrbuch der Charles-Bukowski-Gesellschaft,* December 13, 2011.

Granholm, Kennet. "The Occult and Comics." In *The Occult World,* edited by Christopher Partridge, 499–508. New York: Routledge, 2015.

Grau, Christopher, ed. *Philosophers Explore "The Matrix."* New York: Oxford University Press, 2005.

Graves, Robert, and Raphael Patai. *Hebrew Myths.* New York: Doubleday, 1989.

Gravett, Paul. *Comics Art.* New Haven, CT: Yale University Press, 2013.

Gravett, Paul. *Cult Fiction: Art and Comics.* New York: Hayward Publishing, 2007.

Gravett, Paul. *Graphic Novels: Everything You Need to Know.* New York: Harper Design, 2005.

Green, Justin. *Binky Brown Meets the Holy Virgin Mary.* San Francisco: McSweeny's Publishing, 2009.

Greenfield, Robert. *Timothy Leary: A Biography.* Orlando: Harcourt, 2006.

Gregory, Danny. *An Illustrated Life: Drawing Inspiration from the Private Sketchbooks of Artists, Illustrators and Designers.* Cincinnati: How Books, 2008.

Gregory of Tours. *The History of the Franks.* Translated by Lewis Thorpe. London: Penguin, 1974.

Griffith, Bill. *Invisible Ink: My Mother's Affair with a Famous Cartoonist.* Seattle: Fantagraphics, 2015.

Griffith, Gary. "Truckin' Along with R. Crumb, or Something." In *R. Crumb: Conversations,* edited by D. K. Holm, 6–15. Jackson: University Press of Mississippi, 2004.

Groensteen, Thierry. *Comics and Narration.* Jackson: University Press of Mississippi, 2013.

Groensteen, Thierry. "Why Are Comics Still in Search of Cultural Legitimization?" In *A Comic Studies Reader,* edited by Jeet Heer and Kent Worcester, 3–12. Jackson: University Press of Mississippi, 2009.

Groth, Gary. Introduction to *Your Vigor for Life Appalls Me: Robert Crumb Letters, 1958–1977.* Edited by Ilse Thompson. Seattle: Fantagraphics, 1998.

Groth, Gary, and Robert Fiore, eds. *The New Comics.* New York: Berkley Books, 1988.

Grunenberg, Christoph, ed. *Summer of Love: Art of the Psychedelic Era.* London: Tate Publishing, 2005.

Gunkel, Hermann. *The Legends of Genesis: The Biblical Saga and History.* New York: Schocken Books, 1964.

Hajdu, David. *The Ten-Cent Plague: The Great Comic-Book Scare and How It Changed America.* New York: Farrar, Straus and Giroux, 2008.

Hanegraaff, Wouter J. "Gnosis." In *The Cambridge Handbook of Western Mysticism and Esotericism,* edited by Glenn Alexander Magee, 381–92. Cambridge: Cambridge University Press, 2016.

Hansen, Miriam. "Of Mice and Ducks: Benjamin and Adorno on Disney." *South Atlantic Quarterly* 92, no. 1 (Winter 1993): 27–61.

Hartmann, Nadine. "Eroticism." in *Georges Bataille: Key Concepts,* edited by Mark Hewson and Marcus Coelen, 136–47. Abingdon, Oxon, England: Routledge, 2016.

Hatfield, Charles. *Alternative Comics: An Emerging Literature.* Jackson: University Press of Mississippi, 2005.

Hayman, Ronald. *Sartre: A Biography.* New York: Simon and Schuster, 1987.

Heer, Jeet, and Kent Worcester, eds. *Arguing Comics: Literary Masters on a Popular Medium.* Jackson: University Press of Mississippi, 2004.

Heer, Jeet, and Kent Worcester, eds. *A Comics Studies Reader.* Jackson: University Press of Mississippi, 2009.

Heller, Erich. *Franz Kafka.* New York: Viking, 1974.

Heller, Steven. *Comics Sketchbooks: The Private Worlds of Today's Most Creative Talents.* New York: Thames and Hudson, 2012.

Heller, Steven. *Merz to Émigré and Beyond: Avant-Garde Magazine Design of the Twentieth Century.* London: Phaidon, 2014.

Hentschel, Jason A. "The King James Only Movement." In *The Oxford Handbook of the Bible in America,* edited by Paul C. Gutjahr, 229–41. New York: Oxford University Press, 2017.

Herdeg, Walter, and David Pascal, eds. *The Art of the Comic Strip.* Zurich: Graphis Press, 1972.

Hick, John. *An Interpretation of Religion: Human Responses to the Transcendent.* New Haven, CT: Yale University Press, 1989.

Hignite, Todd. *In the Studio: Visits with Contemporary Cartoonists*. New Haven, CT: Yale University Press, 2006.

Hobbs, Stuart D. *The End of the American Avant Garde*. New York: New York University Press, 1997.

Hochman, Leah. "The Ineffability of Form: Speaking and Seeing the Sacred in *Tina's Mouth* and *The Rabbi's Cat*." In *Comics and Sacred Texts: Reimagining Religion and Graphic Narratives*, edited by Assaf Gamzou and Ken Koltun-Fromm, 43–55. Jackson: University Press of Mississippi, 2018.

Holm, D. K., ed. *R. Crumb: Conversations*. Jackson: University Press of Mississippi, 2004.

Holm, D. K. *Robert Crumb*. Harpenden, Herts., England: Pocket Essentials, 2005.

Horn, Maurice. *The World Encyclopedia of Comics*. New York: Chelsea House, 1976.

Huang Po. *The Zen Teachings of Huang Po: On the Transmission of Mind*. Translated by John Blofeld. New York: Grove Press, 1980.

Hughes, Robert. *Things I Didn't Know: A Memoir*. New York: Alfred A. Knopf, 2006.

Hurston, Zora Neale. *Tell My Horse: Voodoo and Life in Haiti and Jamaica*. New York: Harper and Row, 1990.

Hutcheon, Linda. *A Theory of Adaptation*. London: Routledge, 2006.

Inge, M. Thomas. *Comics as Culture*. Jackson: University Press of Mississippi, 1990.

Iwamura, Jane Naomi. *Virtual Orientalism: Asian Religions and American Popular Culture*. New York: Oxford University Press, 2011.

Jackson, Carl T. "D. T. Suzuki, 'Suzuki Zen,' and the American Reception of Zen Buddhism." In *American Buddhism as a Way of Life*, edited by Gary Storhoff and John Whalen-Bridge, 39–56. Albany: State University of New York Press, 2010.

Jameson, Fredric. "The Rhythm of Time." In *Jean-Paul Sartre: Modern Critical Views*, edited by Harold Bloom, 23–40. New York: Chelsea House, 2001.

Jarnot, Lisa. *Robert Duncan, the Ambassador from Venus: A Biography*. Berkeley: University of California Press, 2012.

Johnson, Charles. Afterword to *The Emergence of Buddhist American Literature*, edited by John Whalen-Bridge and Gary Storhoff. Albany: State University of New York Press, 2009.

Johnston, Denis. *Precipitations: Contemporary American Poetry as Occult Practice*. Middletown, CT: Wesleyan University Press, 2002.

Jonas, Hans. *The Gnostic Religion: The Message of the Alien God and the Beginnings of Christianity*. Boston: Beacon Press, 1970.

Jones, William B., Jr. *Classics Illustrated: A Cultural History*. Jefferson, NC: McFarland, 2011.

Jung, Carl G. *Flying Saucers: A Modern Myth of Things Seen in the Skies*. London: Routledge and Kegan Paul, 1959.

Jung, Carl G. *Four Archetypes: Mother, Rebirth, Spirit, Trickster*. Princeton, NJ: Princeton University Press, 1970.

Jung, Carl G. *The Red Book*. Edited by Sonu Shamdasan. New York: W. W. Norton, 2009.

Juno, Andrea. "Dan Clowes." In *Dangerous Drawings: Interviews with Comix and Graphix Artists*, edited by Andrea Juno, 99–113. New York: Juno Books, 1997.

Kafka, Franz. *Letter to the Father/Brief an den Vater*. Translated by Ernst Kaiser and Eithne Wilkins. New York: Schocken Books, 2015.

Kafka, Franz. *Letters to Friends, Family and Editors*. New York: Schocken Books, 2016.

Kannenberg, Gene, Jr. "Graphic Text, Graphic Context: Interpreting Custom Fonts and Hands in Contemporary Comics." In *Illuminating Letters: Typography and Literary Interpretation*, edited by Paul C. Gutjahr and Megan L. Benton, 163–92. Amherst: University of Massachusetts Press, 2001.

Kaplan, Arie. *From Krakow to Krypton: Jews and Comic Books.* Philadelphia: Jewish Publication Society, 2008.

Kashyap, Keshni. *Tina's Mouth: An Existential Comic Diary.* Illustrated by Mari Araki. New York: Houghton Mifflin Harcourt, 2012.

Kawabata, Mai. *Paganini: The "Demonic" Virtuoso.* Woodbridge, Suffolk, England: Boydell Press, 2013.

Kawai, Hayao. *The Buddhist Priest Myoe: A Life of Dreams.* Venice, CA: Lapis Press, 1991.

Kennedy, Jay. *The Official Underground and Newave Comix Price Guide.* Cambridge, MA: Boatner Norton Press, 1982.

Kerouac, Jack. *On the Road.* New York: Penguin, 2011. First published, New York: Viking, 1957.

Kerouac, Jack. "The Origins of the Beat Generation." In *Good Blonde and Others*, by Jack Kerouac. Edited by Donald Allen, 55–68. San Francisco: Grey Fox Press, 1994.

Kessel, Neil. "Genius and Mental Disorder: A History of Ideas Concerning Their Conjunction." In *Genius: The History of an Idea*, edited by Penelope Murray, 196–212. Oxford: Basil Blackwell, 1989.

Kinney, Jay. "The Mysterious Revelations of Philip K. Dick." *Gnosis*, no. 1 (Fall–Winter 1985): 6–11.

Kinney, Jay. "The Rise and Fall of the Underground Comix Movement in San Francisco and Beyond." In *Ten Years That Shook the City: San Francisco 1968–1978*, edited by Chris Carlsson with Lisa Ruth Elliott, 272–84. San Francisco: City Lights, 2011.

Kirk, Andrew G. *Counterculture Green: The Whole Earth Catalog and American Environmentalism.* Lawrence: University Press of Kansas, 2007.

Kirschenbaum, Matthew G. *Track Changes: A Literary History of Word Processing.* Cambridge, MA: Belknap Press of Harvard University Press, 2016.

Knowles, Christopher. *Our Gods Wear Spandex: The Secret History of Comic Book Heroes.* San Francisco: Red Wheel/Weiser, 2007.

Kovacs, George, and C. W. Marshall, eds. *Classics and Comics.* New York: Oxford University Press, 2011.

Kraemer, Christine Hoff, and A. David Lewis. "Comics/Graphic Novels." In *The Routledge Companion to Religion and Popular Culture*, edited by John C. Lyden and Eric Michael Mazur, 210–27. London: Routledge, 2015.

Kripal, Jeffrey J. *Esalen: America and the Religion of No Religion.* Chicago: University of Chicago Press, 2008.

Kripal, Jeffrey J. *Mutants and Mystics: Science Fiction, Superhero Comics, and the Paranormal.* Chicago: University of Chicago Press, 2011.

Kunzle, David. *History of the Comic Strip.* Vol. 1, *The Early Comic Strip: Narrative Strips and Picture Stories in the European Broadsheet from c. 1450 to 1825.* Berkeley: University of California Press, 1973.

Kunzle, David. *The History of the Comic Strip.* Vol. 2, *The Nineteenth Century.* Berkeley: University of California Press, 1990.

Kuper, Peter. *Kafkaesque: Fourteen Stories*. New York: W. W. Norton, 2018.

Kurtzman, Harvey. *From Aargh! to Zap! Harvey Kurtzman's Visual History of the Comics*. New York: Prentice Hall, 1991.

Lacarrière, Jacques. *The Gnostics*. San Francisco: City Lights, 1989.

Laycock, Emily. "Graphic Apocalypse and the Wizard of Grotesque: Basil Wolverton, the Worldwide Church of God, and Prophecy." In *The End Will Be Graphic: Apocalyptic in Comic Books and Graphic Novels*, edited by Dan W. Clanton Jr., 20–34. Sheffield, England: Sheffield Phoenix Press, 2012.

Leach, Edmund. "Fishing for Men on the Edge of the Wilderness." In *The Literary Guide to the Bible*, edited by Robert Alter and Frank Kermode, 579–99. Cambridge, MA: Harvard University Press, 1987.

Leach, Edmund. "Genesis as Myth." In *Myth and Cosmos: Readings in Mythology and Symbolism*, edited by John C. Middleton, 1–13. Garden City, NY: Natural History Press, 1967.

Lepetit, Patrick. *The Esoteric Secrets of Surrealism: Origins, Magic, and Secret Societies*. Rochester, VT: Inner Traditions, 2014.

Leslie, Esther. *Hollywood Flatlands: Animation, Critical Theory and the Avant-Garde*. London: Verso, 2002.

Lessing, Gotthold Ephraim. *Laocoön: An Essay on the Limits of Painting and Poetry*. Translated by Edward Allen McCormick. Baltimore: Johns Hopkins University Press, 1984.

Lewis, A. David. *American Comics, Literary Theory, and Religion: The Superhero Afterlife*. New York: Palgrave Macmillan, 2014.

Lewis, A. David, and Christine Hoff Kraemer, eds. *Graven Images: Religion in Comic Books and Graphic Novels*. New York: Continuum, 2010.

Lhamon, W. T., Jr. *Deliberate Speed: The Origins of a Cultural Style in the American 1950s*. Washington, DC: Smithsonian Institution Press, 1990.

Libicki, Miriam. "Jewish Memoir Goes Pow! Zap! Oy!" In *The Jewish Graphic Novel: Critical Approaches*, edited by Samantha Baskind and Ranen Omer-Sherman, 253–74. New Brunswick, NJ: Rutgers University Press, 2008.

Lomax, Alan. *Mister Jelly Roll: The Fortunes of Jelly Roll Morton, New Orleans Creole and "Inventor of Jazz."* Berkeley: University of California Press, 1973.

Lopes, Paul. *Demanding Respect: The Evolution of the American Comic Book*. Philadelphia: Temple University Press, 2009.

Lopez, Donald S., Jr. *A Modern Buddhist Bible: Essential Readings from East and West*. Boston: Beacon Press, 2002.

Lyden, John C., and Eric Michael Mazur, eds. *The Routledge Companion to Religion and Popular Culture*. London: Routledge, 2015.

Madeiros, Walter. "Mapping San Francisco 1965–1967: Roots and Florescence of the San Francisco Counterculture." In *Summer of Love: Psychedelic Art, Social Crisis and Counterculture in the 1960s*, edited by Christoph Grunenberg and Jonathan Harris, 303–48. Liverpool: Liverpool University Press, 2005.

Magee, Glenn Alexander, ed. *The Cambridge Handbook of Western Mysticism and Esotericism*. Cambridge: Cambridge University Press, 2016.

Magnussen, Anne, and Hans-Christian Christiansen, eds. *Comics and Culture: Analytical and Theoretical Approaches to Comics*. Copenhagen: Museum Tusculanum Press, 2000.

Maher, Neil M. *Apollo in the Age of Aquarius.* Cambridge, MA: Harvard University Press, 2017.

Malcolm, Douglas. "'Jazz America': Jazz and African American Culture in Jack Kerouac's *On the Road*." In *Bloom's Modern Critical Interpretations: Jack Kerouac's* On the Road, edited by Harold Bloom, 93–114. New York: Chelsea House, 2004.

Marwick, Arthur. *The Sixties: Cultural Revolution in Britain, France, Italy, and the United States, c. 1958–c. 1974.* Oxford: Oxford University Press, 1998.

McCloud, Scott. *Understanding Comics: The Invisible Art.* Northampton, MA: Tundra Publishing, 1993.

McHale, Brian. *The Cambridge Introduction to Postmodernism.* New York: Cambridge University Press, 2015.

McLain, Karline. *India's Immortal Comic Books: Gods, Kings, and Other Heroes.* Bloomington: Indiana University Press, 2009.

McLaughlin, Jeff, ed. *Comics as Philosophy.* Jackson: University Press of Mississippi, 2005.

McLeod, Hugh. *The Religious Crisis of the 1960s.* New York: Oxford University Press, 2007.

McMillian, John. *Smoking Typewriters: The Sixties Underground Press and the Rise of Alternative Media in America.* New York: Oxford University Press, 2011.

McNeill, Malcolm M. *The Lost Art of Ah Pook Is Here: Images for the Graphic Novel.* Seattle: Fantagraphics, 2012.

Mercier, Jean-Pierre. "Who's Afraid of R. Crumb?" In *R. Crumb: Conversations*, edited by D. K. Holm, 191–222. Jackson: University Press of Mississippi, 2004.

Meskin, Aaron, and Roy T. Cook, eds. *The Art of Comics: A Philosophical Approach.* Malden, MA: Wiley-Blackwell, 2012.

Messent, Peter B. *Literature of the Occult: A Collection of Critical Essays.* Englewood Cliffs, NJ: Prentice Hall, 1981.

Milano, Brett. *Vinyl Junkies: Adventures in Record Collecting.* New York: St. Martin's Press, 2003.

Milbank, Alison. "Seeing Double: The Crucified Christ in Western Mediaeval Art." In *The Oxford Handbook of Christology*, edited by Francesca Aran Murphy, 215–32. Oxford: Oxford University Press, 2015.

Miller, J. Hillis. *Illustration.* London: Reaktion Books, 1992.

Mitaine, Benoît, David Roche, and Isabelle Schmitt-Pitiot, eds. *Comics and Adaptation.* Jackson: University Press of Mississippi, 2018.

Mitchell, W. J. T. "Comics as Media: Afterword." In "Comics and Media," ed. Hillary L. Chute and Patrick Jagoda. Special issue, *Critical Inquiry* 40, no. 3 (Spring 2014): 255–65.

Molotiu, Andrei. *Abstract Comics: The Anthology.* Seattle: Fantagraphics, 2009.

Monroe, Robert A. *Journey out of the Body.* New York: Broadway Books, 2001.

Moore, Allan, ed. *The Cambridge Companion to Blues and Gospel Music.* Cambridge: Cambridge University Press, 2002.

Moore, Allan. "Surveying the Field: Our Knowledge of Blues and Gospel Music." In *The Cambridge Companion to Blues and Gospel Music*, edited by Allan Moore, 1–12. Cambridge: Cambridge University Press, 2002.

Morgan, David. *Visual Piety: A History and Theory of Popular Religious Images.* Berkeley: University of California Press, 1998.

Morgan, Ted. *Literary Outlaw: The Life and Times of William S. Burroughs.* New York: W. W. Norton, 2012.

Morris, Daniel. "Convergence Cultures: Modern and Contemporary Poetry and the Graphic Novel." In *The Cambridge History of the Graphic Novel*, edited by Jan Baetens, Hugo Frey, and Stephen E. Tabachnick, 526–42. New York: Cambridge University Press, 2018.

Mouly, Françoise. "R. Crumb: It's Only Lines on Paper." In *Masters of American Comics*, edited by John Carlin, Paul Karasik, and Brian Walker, 276–89. New Haven, CT: Yale University Press, 2005.

Murray, Christopher. "Alan Moore: The Making of a Graphic Novelist." In *The Cambridge History of the Graphic Novel*, edited by Jan Baetens, Hugo Frey, and Stephen E. Tabachnick, 219–34. New York: Cambridge University Press, 2018.

Nabokov, Vladimir. *Lectures on Literature*. San Diego: Harcourt, 1980.

Nakazawa, Keiji. *Barefoot Gen: A Cartoon Story of Hiroshima*. San Francisco: Last Gasp, 2004.

Nelson, Victoria. *The Secret Life of Puppets*. Cambridge, MA: Harvard University Press, 2001.

Nietzsche, Friedrich. *The Will to Power*. Translated by Walter Kaufmann. New York: Vintage Books, 1968.

Nyberg, Amy Kiste. *Seal of Approval: The History of the Comics Code*. Jackson: University Press of Mississippi, 1998.

Oakley, Giles. *The Devil's Music: A History of the Blues*. New York: Da Capo Press, 1997.

Obrist, Hans Ulrich. *Robert Crumb*. Cologne: Walther König, 2006.

Orcutt, Darby. "Religion." In *Comics through Time: A History of Icons, Idols, and Ideas*. Vol. 2, *1960–1980*, edited by M. Keith Booker. Santa Barbara, CA: Greenwood Press, 2014.

Oropeza, B. J., ed. *The Gospel According to Superheroes: Religion and Popular Culture*. New York: Peter Lang, 2005.

Ossman, David. *The Sullen Art: Interviews with Modern American Poets*. New York: Corinth Books, 1963.

O'Sullivan, Judith. *The Great American Comic Strip: One Hundred Years of Cartoon Art*. Boston: Little, Brown, 1990.

Pagels, Elaine. *Adam, Eve, and the Serpent*. New York: Vintage Books, 1989.

Pagels, Elaine. *Beyond Belief: The Secret Gospel of Thomas*. New York: Vintage Books, 2003.

Pagels, Elaine. *The Gnostic Gospels*. New York: Vintage Books, 1989.

Pagels, Elaine. *Why Religion? A Personal Story*. New York: HarperCollins, 2018.

Palmer, Robert. *Deep Blues*. New York: Penguin, 1982.

Pascal, Blaise. *Pensées*. Translated by A. J. Krailsheimer. London: Penguin, 1995.

Pastras, Phil. *Dead Man Blues: Jelly Roll Morton Way Out West*. Berkeley: University of California Press, 2001.

Peabody, Rebecca, ed. *Pacific Standard Time: Los Angeles Art, 1945–1980*. Los Angeles: Getty Research Institute, 2011.

Peck, Abe. *Uncovering the Sixties: The Life and Times of the Underground Press*. New York: Pantheon Books, 1985.

Pekar, Harvey. *American Splendor: The Life and Times of Harvey Pekar*. New York: Ballantine Books, 2003.

Pekar, Harvey. "Rapping about Cartoonists, Particularly Robert Crumb." *Journal of Popular Culture* 3, no. 4 (Spring 1970): 677–88.

Pellerin, Cheryl. *Trips: How Hallucinogens Work in Your Brain*. New York: Seven Stories Press, 1998.

Pelosi, Francesco. *Plato on Music, Soul and Body*. Translated by Sophie Henderson. Cambridge: Cambridge University Press, 2010.

Perry, George, and Alan Aldridge. *The Penguin Book of Comics*. London: Penguin, 1971.

Petkovich, Anthony. "Hardcore Crumb: An Interview with Maxon Crumb." In *Headpress*, no. 17: *Into the Psyche*, ed. David Kerekes. Truro, Cornwall, England: Headpress, 2002.

Plagens, Peter. *Sunshine Muse: Art on the West Coast, 1945–1970*. Berkeley: University of California Press, 1999.

Plymell, Charles. "Curled in Character: R. Crumb and the First *Zap*." In *Hand on the Doorknob: A Charles Plymell Reader*, edited by David Breithaupt, 41–48. Sudbury, MA: Water Row Press, 2000.

Pollan, Michael. *How to Change Your Mind: What the New Science of Psychedelics Teaches Us about Consciousness, Dying, Addiction, Depression, and Transcendence*. New York: Penguin Press, 2018.

Pomplun, Tom, ed. *Graphic Classics*. Vol. 9, *Robert Louis Stevenson*. Mount Horeb, WI: Eureka Productions, 2004.

Porter, J. R. *The Illustrated Guide to the Bible*. Oxford: Oxford University Press, 1995.

Postema, Barbara. *Narrative Structure in Comics: Making Sense of Fragments*. Rochester, NY: Rochester Institute of Technology Press, 2013.

Postema, Barbara. "Silent Comics." In *The Routledge Companion to Comics*, edited by Frank Bramlett, Roy T. Cooke, and Aaron Meskin, 201–8. New York: Routledge, 2017.

Pratt, Henry John. "Comics and Adaptation." In *The Routledge Companion to Comics*, edited by Frank Bramlett, Roy T. Cook, and Aaron Meskin, 230–38. New York: Routledge, 2017.

Preece, Julian, ed. *The Cambridge Companion to Kafka*. Cambridge: Cambridge University Press, 2001.

Pritchard, James B. *Archaeology and the Old Testament*. Princeton, NJ: Princeton University Press, 1958.

Pritchard, Will. "New Light on Crumb's Boswell." *Eighteenth-Century Studies* 42, no. 2 (Winter 2009): 289–307.

Pullman, Philip. *Daemon Voices: On Stories and Storytelling*. New York: Alfred A. Knopf, 2017.

Pustz, Matthew, ed. *Comic Books and American Cultural History: An Anthology*. New York: Continuum, 2012.

Pustz, Matthew. "'Paralysis and Stagnation and Drift': America's Malaise as Demonstrated in Comic Books of the 1970s." In *Comic Books and American Cultural History: An Anthology*, edited by Matthew Pustz, 136–51. New York: Continuum, 2012.

Raboteau, Albert J. *Canaan Land: A Religious History of African Americans*. New York: Oxford University Press, 2001.

Ramsey, Frederic, and Charles Edward Smith, eds. *Jazzmen: The Story of Hot Jazz Told in the Lives of the Men Who Created It*. New York: Harcourt Brace and Company, 1939.

Reed, Ishmael. "Neo-HooDoo Manifesto/The Neo-HooDoo Aesthetic." In *Symposium of the Whole: A Range of Discourse toward an Ethnopoetics*, edited by Jerome Rothenberg and Diane Rothenberg, 417–21. Berkeley: University of California Press, 1983.

Reps, Paul, and Nyogen Senzaki. *Zen Flesh, Zen Bones: A Collection of Zen and Pre-Zen Writings*. Boston: Tuttle, 1998.

Richter, Carl. *The Crumb Compendium: The Definitive R. Crumb Bibliography*. Seattle: Fantagraphics, 2018.

Richter, Carl. *Crumb-Ology: The Works of R. Crumb, 1981–1984*. Sudbury, MA: Water Row Press, 1995.

Rickman, Gregg. *Philip K. Dick: The Last Testament*. Long Beach, CA: Fragments West/Valentine Press, 1985.

Rickman, Gregg. *To the High Castle, Philip K. Dick: A Life, 1928–1962*. Long Beach, CA: Fragments West/Valentine Press, 1989.

Robertson, Ritchie. *Kafka: Judaism, Politics, and Literature*. Oxford: Oxford University Press, 1985.

Robinson, Andrew. *Sudden Genius? The Gradual Path to Creative Breakthroughs*. New York: Oxford University Press, 2010.

Roethke, Theodore. *The Far Field*. New York: Doubleday, 1964.

Rorabaugh, W. J. *American Hippies*. New York: Cambridge University Press, 2015.

Rosen, Gerald. *Zen in the Art of J. D. Salinger*. Berkeley, CA: Creative Arts, 1977.

Rosenkranz, Patrick. *Rebel Visions: The Underground Comix Revolution, 1963–1975*. Seattle: Fantagraphics, 2002.

Royal, Derek Parker. *Visualizing Jewish Narrative: Jewish Comics and Graphic Novels*. London: Bloomsbury, 2016.

Rudolph, Kurt. *Gnosis: The Nature and History of Gnosticism*. New York: HarperCollins, 1987.

Sabin, Roger. *Adult Comics: An Introduction*. New York: Routledge, 1993.

Sabin, Roger. *Comics, Comix and Graphic Novels: A History of Comic Art*. London: Phaidon, 1996.

Said, Edward. "Introduction: Homage to Joe Sacco." In *Palestine*, by Joe Sacco. Seattle: Fantagraphics, 2005.

Sante, Luc. "1903: The Invention of the Blues." In *A New Literary History of America*, edited by Greil Marcus and Werner Sollors. Cambridge, MA: Harvard University Press, 2009.

Sartre, Jean-Paul. *Existentialism Is a Humanism*. Translated by Carol Macomber. New Haven, CT: Yale University Press, 2007.

Sartre, Jean-Paul. *Nausea*. Translated by Lloyd Alexander. New York: New Directions, 1969.

Sattler, Peter. "Robert Crumb." In *Comics through Time: A History of Icons, Idols, and Ideas*. Vol. 3, *1980–1995*, edited by M. Keith Booker. Santa Barbara, CA: Greenwood Press, 2014.

Saunders, Ben. *Do the Gods Wear Capes? Spirituality, Fantasy, and Superheroes*. London: Continuum, 2011.

Schechter, Harold. "Deep Meaning Comix: The Archetypal World of R. Crumb." *San José Studies* 3, no. 3 (November 1977): 6–21.

Schechter, Harold, and Jonna Gormely Semeiks. *Patterns in Popular Culture: A Sourcebook for Writers*. New York: Harper and Row, 1980.

Schmitz-Emans, Monika. "Graphic Narrative as World Literature." In *From Comic Strips to Graphic Novels: Contributions to the Theory and History of Graphic Narrative*, edited by Daniel Stein and Jan-Noël Thon, 385–406. Berlin: Walter de Gruyter, 2015.

Schmitz-Emans, Monika. *Literatur-Comics: Adaptionen und Transformationen der Weltliteratur*. Berlin: Walter de Gruyter, 2012.

Schneider, David. *Crowded by Beauty: The Life and Zen of Poet Philip Whalen*. Oakland: University of California Press, 2015.

Schwartz, Barry. *The New Humanism: Art in a Time of Change*. New York: Praeger, 1974.

Schwartz, Ben, ed. *The Best American Comics Criticism*. Seattle: Fantagraphics, 2010.

Schwartz, Delmore. "Masterpieces as Cartoons." *Partisan Review* 19, no. 4 (July–August 1952): 461–71.

Scully, Rock, and David Dalton. *Living with the Dead: Twenty Years on the Bus with the Grateful Dead*. Boston: Little, Brown, 1995.

Segal, Robert A., ed. *The Allure of Gnosticism: The Gnostic Experience in Jungian Psychology and Contemporary Culture*. Chicago: Open Court, 1995.

Serres, Michel. "Light." *Yale French Studies*, nos. 131–32 (2017): 215–21.

Setzer, Claudia. "Feminist Interpretation of the Bible." In *The Oxford Handbook of the American Bible*, edited by Paul C. Gutjahr, 163–83. New York: Oxford University Press, 2017.

Shannon, Edward. "Shameful, Impure Art: Robert Crumb's Autobiographical Comics and the Confessional Poets." *Biography* 35, no. 4 (Fall 2012): 627–49.

Sharrett, Christopher. "Alan Moore." In *Alan Moore: Conversations*, edited by Eric L. Berlatsky, 44–60. Jackson: University Press of Mississippi, 2012.

Singer, Marc. *Breaking the Frames: Populism and Prestige in Comics Studies*. Austin: University of Texas Press, 2018.

Skinn, Dez. *Comix: The Underground Revolution*. New York: Thunder's Mouth Press, 2004.

Smith, Clay Kinchen. "From God Nose to God's Bosom; or, How God (and Jack Jackson) Began Underground Comics." In *Graven Images: Religion in Comic Books and Graphic Novels*, edited by A. David Lewis and Christine Hoff Kraemer, 203–17. New York: Continuum, 2010.

Smith, Huston. "Do Drugs Have a Religious Import?" In *The Huston Smith Reader*, edited by Jeffery Paine, 162–71. Berkeley: University of California Press, 2012.

Smith, Matthew J., and Randy Duncan, eds. *Critical Approaches to Comics: Theories and Methods*. New York: Routledge, 2012.

Smolderen, Thierry. *The Origins of Comics: From William Hogarth to Winsor McCay*. Translated by Bart Beaty and Nick Nguyen. Jackson: University Press of Mississippi, 2014.

Sokel, Walter H. "Between Gnosticism and Jehovah: The Dilemma in Kafka's Religious Attitude." In *The Allure of Gnosticism: The Gnostic Experience in Jungian Psychology and Contemporary Culture*, edited by Robert Segal, 147–66. Chicago: Open Court, 1995.

Sounes, Howard. *Charles Bukowski: Locked in the Arms of a Crazy Life*. New York: Grove Press, 1999.

Spiegelman, Art. *Breakdowns: Portrait of the Artist as a Young %@*!* New York: Pantheon Books, 2008.

Spiegelman, Art. "Introduction: Barefoot Gen; Comics after the Bomb." In *Barefoot Gen: A Cartoon Story of Hiroshima*, by Keiji Nakazawa. San Francisco: Last Gasp, 2004.

Spiegelman, Art. *Maus 1: A Survivor's Tale; My Father Bleeds History*. New York: Pantheon Books, 1993.

Spretnak, Catherine. *The Spiritual Dynamic in Modern Art: Art History Reconsidered, 1800 to the Present*. New York: Palgrave Macmillan, 2014.

Sri Yukteswar. *The Holy Science*. Los Angeles: Self-Realization Fellowship, 1972.

Stack, Frank. *The New Adventures of Jesus: The Second Coming*. Seattle: Fantagraphics, 2006.

Stein, Daniel, and Jan-Noël Thon, eds. *From Comic Strips to Graphic Novels: Contributions to the Theory and History of Graphic Narrative*. Berlin: De Gruyter, 2015.

Stephens, Mitchell. *The Rise of the Image, the Fall of the Word*. New York: Oxford University Press, 1998.

Stevens, Jason. "Religion." In *American Literature in Transition, 1950–1960*, edited by Steven Belletto, 73–86. New York: Cambridge University Press, 2018.

Stevens, Matthew Levi. *The Magical Universe of William S. Burroughs*. Oxford: Mandrake of Oxford, 2014.

Strömberg, Fredrik. *Black Images in the Comics: A Visual History*. Seattle: Fantagraphics, 2003.

Suchoff, David. *Kafka's Jewish Languages: The Hidden Openness of Tradition*. Philadelphia: University of Pennsylvania Press, 2012.

Sutin, Lawrence. *Divine Invasions: A Life of Philip K. Dick*. New York: Harmony Books, 1989.

Sutin, Lawrence, ed. *In Pursuit of Valis: Selections from the Exegesis*. Novato, CA: Underwood-Miller, 1971.

Swarte, Joost. "The Independents." In *Drawn Together*, by Aline Kominsky-Crumb and Robert Crumb, edited by Anette Gehrig. Basel: Christoph Merian Verlag, 2016.

Tabachnick, Stephen E., ed. *The Cambridge Companion to the Graphic Novel*. Cambridge: Cambridge University Press, 2017.

Tabachnick, Stephen E. *The Quest for Jewish Belief and Identity in the Graphic Novel*. Tuscaloosa: University of Alabama Press, 2014.

Tabachnick, Stephen E., ed. *Teaching the Graphic Novel*. New York: Modern Language Association of America, 2009.

Teubal, Savina. *Sarah the Priestess: The First Matriarch of Genesis*. Athens, OH: Swallow Press, 1984.

Thompson, John. *Yellow Dog: Robert Crumb and Origin of Comix*. Lexington, KY: Satya Designs, 2017.

Thoreau, Henry David. *Walden*. In *The Portable Thoreau*. Edited by Carl Bode. New York: Viking 1967.

Tinker, Emma. "R. Crumb's Carnival Subjectivity." In "Identity and Form in Alternative Comics, 1967–2007." PhD thesis, University College, London, 2009. At http://emmatinker.oxalto.co.uk/thesis/.

Tiryakian, Edward A. "Toward the Sociology of Esoteric Culture." In *On the Margin of the Visible: Sociology, the Esoteric, and the Occult*, edited by Edward A. Tiryakian, 257–80. New York: John Wiley and Sons, 1974.

Trungpa, Chogyam. *Cutting through Spiritual Materialism*. Berkeley, CA: Shambhala, 1973.

Tuchman, Maurice. *The Spiritual in Art: Abstract Painting, 1890–1985*. New York: Abbeville Press, 1986.

Tucker, Brian. "Gotthold Ephraim Lessing's *Laocoön* and the Lessons of Comics." In *Teaching the Graphic Novel*, edited by Stephen E. Tabachnick, 28–35. New York: Modern Language Association of America, 2009.

Twain, Mark. *Letters from the Earth*. Edited by Bernard DeVoto. New York: Harper and Row, 1962.

Umland, Samuel L., ed. *Philip K. Dick: Contemporary Critical Interpretations*. Westport, CT: Greenwood Press, 1995.

Umland, Samuel L. "To Flee from Dionysus: *Enthousiasmos* from 'Upon the Dull Earth' to *VALIS*." in *Philip K. Dick: Contemporary Critical Interpretations*, edited by Samuel J. Umland, 81–100. Westport, CT: Greenwood Press, 1995.

Varnedoe, Kirk, and Adam Gopnik. *High and Low: Modern Art/Popular Culture*. New York: Museum of Modern Art, 1990.

Varnum, Robin, and Christina T. Gibbons, eds. *The Language of Comics: Word and Image*. Jackson: University Press of Mississippi, 2001.

Versluis, Arthur. *American Gurus: From Transcendentalism to New Age Religion*. New York: Oxford University Press, 2014.

Versluis, Arthur. *Gnosis and Literature*. Saint Paul, MN: Grail Publishing, 1996.

Walker, Brian. *The Comics since 1945*. New York: Harry N. Abrams, 2002.

Ware, Chris. *Jimmy Corrigan: The Smartest Kid on Earth*. New York: Pantheon, 2000.

Warshow, Robert. *The Immediate Experience: Movies, Comics, Theatre and Other Aspects of Popular Culture*. Cambridge, MA: Harvard University Press, 2001.

Weber, Max. "Science as a Vocation." In *From Max Weber: Essays in Sociology*. Edited by Hans Heinrich Gerth and Charles Wright Mills, 129–56. Oxford: Oxford University Press, 1958.

Weisstein, Ulrich, ed. *Expressionism as an International Literary Phenomenon*. Paris: Didier; Budapest: Akadémiai Kiadó, 1973.

Wertham, Fredric. *The Seduction of the Innocent*. New York: Rinehart, 1954.

Westgeest, Helen. *Zen in the Fifties: Interaction in Art between East and West*. Amstelveen, Netherlands: Waanders Publishers, 1997.

Whitlock, Gillian. "Autographics: The Seeing 'I' of the Comics." *Modern Fiction Studies* 52, no. 4 (Winter 2006): 965–79.

Widmer, Ted. "R. Crumb: The Art of Comics no. 1." *Paris Review*, no. 193 (Summer 2010): 19–57.

Wiley, Peter Booth. "Where Did All the Flowers Go? The View from a Street in Bernal Heights." In *Ten Years That Shook the City: San Francisco 1968–1978*, edited by Chris Carlsson with Lisa Ruth Elliott, 95–107. San Francisco: City Lights, 2011.

Wilhelm, Richard, trans. *The I Ching or Book of Changes: The Richard Wilhelm Translation*. Princeton, NJ: Princeton University Press, 1971.

Wilson, Edmund. *The Wound and the Bow: Seven Studies in Literature*. Athens: Ohio University Press, 1997.

Wilson, S. Clay. *The Mythology of S. Clay Wilson*. Vol. 1, *Pirates in the Heartland*. Edited by Patrick Rosencranz. Seattle: Fantagraphics, 2014.

Wilson, S. Clay. *The Mythology of S. Clay Wilson*. Vol. 2, *Demons and Angels*. Edited by Patrick Rosencranz. Seattle: Fantagraphics, 2015.

Witek, Joseph, ed. *Art Spiegelman: Conversations*. Jackson: University Press of Mississippi, 2007.

Witek, Joseph. *Comic Books as History: The Narrative Art of Jack Jackson, Art Spiegelman, and Harvey Pekar*. Jackson: University Press of Mississippi, 1989.

Witek, Joseph. "Comic Modes: Caricature and Illustration in the Crumb Family's *Dirty Laundry*." In *Critical Approaches to Comics: Theories and Methods*, edited by Matthew J. Smith and Randy Duncan, 27–42. New York: Routledge, 2012.

Witek, Joseph. "Justin Green: Autobiography Meets the Comics." In *Graphic Subjects: Critical Essays on Autobiography and Graphic Novels*, edited by Michael A. Chaney, 227–30. Madison: University of Wisconsin Press, 2011.

Wolk, Douglas. *Reading Comics: How Graphic Novels Work and What They Mean*. New York: Da Capo Press, 2007.

Wong, Hertha D. Sweet. *Picturing Identity: Contemporary American Autobiography in Image and Text*. Chapel Hill: University of North Carolina Press, 2018.

Worcester, Kent, ed. *Peter Kuper: Conversations*. Jackson: University Press of Mississippi, 2016.

Wright, Bradford W. *Comic Book Nation: The Transformation of Youth Culture in America*. Baltimore: Johns Hopkins University Press, 2001.

Wuthnow, Robert. *After Heaven: Spirituality in America since the 1950s*. Berkeley: University of California Press, 1998.

Wuthnow, Robert. *Experimentation in American Religion: The New Mysticisms and Their Implications for the Churches*. Berkeley: University of California Press, 1978.

Yutang, Lin. *The Wisdom of China and India*. New York: Modern Library, 1955.

Zaehner, R. C. *Mysticism Sacred and Profane: An Inquiry into Some Varieties of Praeternatural Experience*. Oxford: Clarendon Press, 1957.

Zaehner, R. C. *Zen, Drugs and Mysticism*. New York: Pantheon Books, 1972.

Zimmerman, Nadya. *Counterculture Kaleidoscope: Musical and Cultural Perspectives on Late Sixties San Francisco*. Ann Arbor: University of Michigan Press, 2008.

INDEX

272

202; childhood, 4, 5, 10–11, 69–70, 91–93, 119, 177, 181, 183; Christian iconography in work, 12, 26, 90, 91, 110–11, 118, 122–23, 125–26; on comics, 7–8, 144–45; on drawing, 164, 204, 214–15; dreams, 79, 92, 99, 154, 184, 203, 210; ecological awareness, 19, 45, 58; erotic content, 213; family, 78–79, 146, 155, 161, 188; fetishes, 48; on free will, 150–51; on God, 186, 187–88; hippie culture, 23–24; on LSD, 14–15, 16, 90, 104, 172; on meditation, 96, 206–8; on mysticism, 13, 35, 104–5; nostalgia for America, 37, 61; panel composition, 52–53, 57–58, 61, 66, 73, 76–77, 79–81, 82, 83–84, 87, 90, 91–93, 98–99, 106, 108–10, 111–13, 114, 115, 117, 120, 121, 123, 130, 132, 134–41, 146, 148, 150, 158, 167, 169, 189, 193, 194, 205; ocular imagery, 35–37, 106; on relationship between drawing and text, 206; relationship with women, 155, 200; satire, 62, 214; selfhood, 3–4, 6, 18–19, 105, 141, 119–20, 128–29, 205, 213; on sex, 91–93, 146, 204; on socialism, 128; stereotypes, use of, 94; on Taoism, 145; themes, 6, 31, 42, 45, 48–49, 82–83, 104, 119, 155, 174, 181, 184; transgressive sexuality, 63–65; on truth, 206; as writer, 145, 154

Influences: African American culture, 10, 49, 70, 73, 89–90, 91, 93–94, 96, 195; Assyrian art, 191–93; Buddhism, 6, 33–34, 38, 40–42, 47–48, 49, 51–55; Eastern thought, 210–11; Eskimos, 164–65; esoteric, 208–9; expressionist artists, 163; France, 203–4; German expressionism, 10, 12; Gnosticism, 4, 7, 12, 17, 26, 38, 59, 93, 100, 102, 104, 110, 120, 124, 125–26, 128–29, 189, 190; Hinduism, 15, 33–34, 43–45; hoodoo, 7, 77–78; Jewish, 156, 157, 172–73; literary, 3, 6; musical, 69, 70, 71–72, 82; mythical, 42–43, 86, 98, 110, 200; Native American, 195; popular culture, 10, 11, 19, 20, 21, 37, 119, 129, 131, 155, 165, 183; surrealism, 87–88, 89–90, 91; voodoo, 7

Works: album covers, 15, 22, 102; "Bo Bo Bolinsky: He's the Number One Human Zero," 53; *Book of Genesis Illustrated by R. Crumb, The,* 26, 82, 114, 178–202, 203; "Can You Stand Alone and Face Up to the Universe?," 16, 41–42, 90–91, 99, 120, 123–24; "A Cowardly Cartoonist," 214; "A Day in the Life," 203; "The Dharma Bhums," 45–47, 153; "Dirty Dog," 72–73, 158, 161; "Ducks Yas Yas," 45; "Eleanor Rigby," 148; *Fritz the Cat,* vii, 21, 22; "Hey Boparee Bop," 89–90; "Hypnagogic Hoodoo," 79–81; "I Remember the Sixties: R. Crumb Looks Back," 15, 172; "I'm a Ding Dong Daddy," 53–54; "I'm Grateful! I'm Grateful!," 69; *Introducing Kafka,* 154, 156; "Jelly Roll Morton's Voodoo Curse," 17, 73–75, 76–77, 79, 81, 83, 86, 94, 105; *Keep on Truckin',* vii, 70, 121; "Klassic Komics," 64, 130; "Let's Be Honest," 51; "Life Certainly Is 'Existential'!," 148–50; "The Many Faces of R. Crumb," 172; *Maxon's Poe: Seven Stories and Poems by Edgar Allan Poe,* 5; "Meatball," 47; "Mr. Natural: Zen Master," 51; *Mystic Funnies,* 13–14, 37, 41, 42, 158–60; "No Rest for the Wicked," 71; "Patton," 73–74, 76, 81, 82, 84–85, 94; "People ...Ya Gotta Love 'Em!," 60; portraits, 32–33, 37–38, 59, 65, 73; *The R. Crumb Handbook,* 191; "R. Crumb Presents R. Crumb," 54; *R. Crumb's Dream Diary,* 13, 59, 60, 79, 99, 154, 174, 204, 208, 213; *R. Crumb's Yum Yum Book,* 29, 98; "The Religious Experiences of Philip K. Dick," 17, 78, 103; "Rough Women of the Dark Ages," 98; "Self Portrait with Novelty Specs from a Photo," 208–9; "A Short

ABOUT THE AUTHOR

David Stephen Calonne is the author of *William Saroyan: My Real Work Is Being*; *The Colossus of Armenia: G. I. Gurdjieff and Henry Miller*; *Bebop Buddhist Ecstasy: Saroyan's Influence on Kerouac and the Beats* with an introduction by Lawrence Ferlinghetti; and biographies of Henry Miller and Charles Bukowski (in the Critical Lives series of Reaktion Books, London). Most recently he has published *Conversations with Gary Snyder* (Jackson: University Press of Mississippi, 2017); *The Spiritual Imagination of the Beats* (Cambridge: Cambridge University Press, 2017); and *Diane di Prima: Visionary Poetics and the Hidden Religions* (New York: Bloomsbury, 2019). He has edited several volumes of the fiction and prose of Charles Bukowski for City Lights and has lectured in Paris and many universities including the University of Chicago, Columbia University, the University of California, Berkeley, the European University Institute in Florence, the University of London, Harvard University, and Oxford University. He has taught at the University of Texas at Austin, the University of Michigan, the University of Chicago, and presently teaches at Eastern Michigan University.

www.ingramcontent.com/pod-product-compliance
Lightning Source LLC
Chambersburg PA
CBHW051955270326
41929CB00015B/2660